Semper Fi!

Bestselling author Tom Clancy teams up with one of the most knowledgeable and outspoken Marine generals of our time in a book that propels you into the politics and passions of war . . .

"A BOOK THAT DEMANDS OUR ATTENTION." —*Booklist*

Marine General Tony Zinni was known as the "Warrior Diplomat" during his nearly forty years of service. As a soldier, his credentials were impeccable, whether leading troops in Vietnam, commanding hair-raising rescue operations in Somalia, or—as Commander in Chief of CENTCOM—directing strikes against Iraq and Al Qaeda. But it was as a peacemaker that he made just as great a mark—conducting dangerous troubleshooting missions all over Africa, Asia, and Europe; and then serving as Secretary of State Colin Powell's special envoy to the Middle East, before disagreements over the 2003 Iraq War and its probable aftermath caused him to resign.

Battle Ready follows the evolution of both General Zinni and the Marine Corps, from the cauldron of Vietnam through the operational revolution of the seventies and eighties, to the new realities of the post–Cold War, post-9/11 military—a military with a radically different job and radically different tools for accomplishing it. It is an eye-opening book—a front-row seat to a man, an institution, and a way of both war and peace that together make this an instant classic of military history.

"We must salute Clancy for profiling Zinni . . . You come away thinking that you would have trusted your kid to Zinni's command . . . Down at the Army's infantry school at Fort Benning, the instructors have a saying: 'Managers do things right, while leaders do the right thing.' Zinni did the right thing."

—*St. Louis Post-Dispatch*

"Fascinating . . . Clancy supplies lucid contexts for the general's recollections that are the book's meat . . . Zinni's passion for 'his' Marines infuses *Battle Ready* . . . Zinni's achievements and discontents make *Battle Ready* important . . . deserves to be widely read because of its timeliness and clarity."

—*Houston Chronicle*

"It is Zinni's twenty-four-page closing statement, 'The Calling,' that will sell the book to nonbuff civilians, summing up his service and the ways in which he feels his generation's legacy is in jeopardy."

—*Publishers Weekly*

A BOOK-OF-THE-MONTH® CLUB MAIN SELECTION
A MILITARY BOOK CLUB MAIN SELECTION

BATTLE READY

TOM CLANCY

WITH
GENERAL TONY ZINNI (RET.)
AND TONY KOLTZ

BERKLEY BOOKS

NEW YORK

THE BERKLEY PUBLISHING GROUP
Published by the Penguin Group
Penguin Group (USA) Inc.
375 Hudson Street, New York, New York 10014, USA
Penguin Group (Canada), 10 Alcorn Avenue, Toronto, Ontario M4V 3B2, Canada
(a division of Pearson Penguin Canada Inc.)
Penguin Books Ltd., 80 Strand, London WC2R 0RL, England
Penguin Group Ireland, 25 St. Stephen's Green, Dublin 2, Ireland (a division of Penguin Books Ltd.)
Penguin Group (Australia), 250 Camberwell Road, Camberwell, Victoria 3124, Australia
(a division of Pearson Australia Group Pty. Ltd.)
Penguin Books India Pvt. Ltd., 11 Community Centre, Panchsheel Park, New Delhi—110 017, India
Penguin Group (NZ), Cnr. Airborne and Rosedale Roads, Albany, Auckland 1310, New Zealand
(a division of Pearson New Zealand Ltd.)
Penguin Books (South Africa) (Pty.) Ltd., 24 Sturdee Avenue, Rosebank, Johannesburg 2196,
South Africa

Penguin Books Ltd., Registered Offices: 80 Strand, London WC2R 0RL, England

Copyright © 2004 by C. P. Commanders, Inc.
Text design by Lovedog Studio.

Excerpts in chapter 8, "The Calling," reprinted from addresses given by General Zinni at the U.S. Naval
Institute's conference at Cantigny, March 2000 (for more information, visit www.navalinstitute.org);
at the U.S. Naval Institute/Marine Corps Association's "Forum" conference, September 2003 (for more
information, visit www.mcausniforum2003.org); and at the National Defense University, reprinted in
Strategic Forum, July 2001. All reprinted by permission.

PRINTING HISTORY
G. P. Putnam's Sons hardcover edition / May 2004
Berkley trade paperback edition / May 2005

Berkley trade paperback ISBN: 0-425-19892-8

The Library of Congress has catalogued the G. P. Putnam's Sons hardcover edition as follows:

Clancy, Tom, date.
Battle ready / Tom Clancy ; with Tony Zinni and Tony Koltz.
p.   cm.
Includes index.
ISBN 0-399-15176-1
1. Zinni, Anthony C.   2. Generals—United States—Biography.   3. United States.
Marine Corps—Biography.   4. United States—History, Military—20th century.
5. United States—History, Military—21st century.   I. Zinni, Anthony C.
II. Koltz, Tony.   III. Title.
VE25.Z56C47   2004   2004044581
359.9'6'092—dc22
[B]

Most Berkley Books are available at special quantity discounts for bulk purchases for sales promotions,
premiums, fund-raising, or educational use. Special books, or book excerpts, can also be created to fit
specific needs.

For details, write: Special Markets, The Berkley Publishing Group, 375 Hudson Street, New York,
New York 10014.

TO THE ENLISTED MEN AND WOMEN
OF
AMERICA'S ARMED FORCES

They are our children.

They are our nation's greatest treasure.

They are our True Heroes.

They made four decades of service worth every second.

They granted me the greatest honor of my life—
the privilege of leading them.

—TONY ZINNI

Contents

BATTLE READY

CHAPTER ONE

☆ ☆ ☆ ☆

DESERT FOX

THE TOMAHAWKS WERE SPINNING up in their tubes.

It was November 12, 1998. U.S. Marine General Tony Zinni, the commander in chief of United States Central Command (CENTCOM), was standing in his command room overlooking the command center at CENTCOM's Tampa, Florida, headquarters, leading the preparations for what promised to be the most devastating attack on Iraq since the 1991 Gulf War.

The spacious command center was fitted out with desks, phones, computers, maps, and large and small screens showing updates and the positions of aircraft and ships. In addition to the usual office-type furnishings, the windowed room had secure phones and video communications with Zinni's superiors and his commanders in the field. It was Zinni's battle position—the bridge of his ship.

At the end of the First Gulf War, Iraq had agreed to the UN-supervised destruction of its weapons of mass destruction (WMD) and the programs to develop and build them. That agreement had been a lie. The Saddam Hussein regime had never intended to give up its WMD program, and for the next seven years it had conducted a running battle with UNSCOM, the UN inspection operation in Iraq, to protect its programs in any way possible . . . by hiding them, moving them around, lying, stonewalling, delay, and noncooperation.

The two essential issues covered by the UN mandate were compliance and accountability. That is, the inspectors had to ask and get satisfactory answers to these questions: "Are the Iraqis in compliance with the UN requirement to destroy their WMD and completely dismantle their WMD programs? And are they satisfactorily accounting for the programs and WMD they claim to have destroyed?" The absence of Iraqi cooperation on both of these issues led UNSCOM to make the obvious assumption that the Iraqis were hiding something—either that the weapons still existed or that the Iraqis at least wanted to maintain their capability to make them. UNSCOM had to look hard at the worst case.*

When UNSCOM had persisted in carrying out the UN mandate, the Iraqis had raised the stakes—by making it ever harder for UNSCOM to do its job. There had been greater and greater threats and intimidation, lies, obstruction, and hostility . . . allied with a diplomatic assault aimed at splitting off powerful states friendly to Iraq (principally France, Russia, and China) from the rest of the Security Council and using their support to sabotage the disarmament effort.

With each Iraqi escalation came a counterthreat from the United States: "If UNSCOM is forced to leave Iraq with their work unfinished, the U.S. will hit Iraq and hit it hard." The threat caught the Iraqis' attention. As each escalation neared its climax, and the inspectors started to pull out of the country, the Saddam Hussein regime blinked, backed down, and let them return—though each time with fewer teeth.

But now it looked like the Iraqis were not going to blink. The day before, November 11, the UN inspection teams had left once again, apparently for good. As they left, President Clinton had given Zinni the signal to go. The twenty-four-hour launch clock had started.

Zinni knew the moment was approaching for the cruise missile

---

* In 2003, during and after the U.S. invasion of Iraq, it became clear that at that time the Iraqis actually possessed few, if any, WMD. The point of all their many games during the years of inspection now seems to have been to hide their ability to restart their WMD programs.

launch—the moment of truth. These weren't airplanes. Once the Toma-hawks were in the air, they could not be recalled.

Before him was an open line to the White House, where the Joint Chiefs of Staff (JCS) vice-chairman, Air Force General Joe Ralston, was sitting. Before him, too, was another line to his Navy component com-mander, Vice Admiral Willy Moore, in Bahrain. Moore was in constant communications with the eight ships that would launch the initial cruise missile salvo. The clock ticked on.

The twenty-four hours passed. Zinni had told the President that the strike could be stopped at any moment up to six hours before the bombs were scheduled to hit. That was the drop-dead time for a no-go decision. As it happened, he had built in fifteen minutes of fudge time as a safety margin.

But the no-go deadline had passed. And so had Zinni's fifteen minutes of fudge time.

He took a deep breath—and then the line from the White House lit up: Saddam was backing down again. He'd agreed to UNSCOM's demands.

General Ralston's voice came down the wire: "It's a no-go. Don't shoot," he told Zinni. "Do we have any time left? Is it okay?"

Zinni honestly didn't know. All he could do was grab the phone and call Willy Moore. . . .

FOR ZINNI, this story had begun fifteen months before, on August 13, 1997, when he'd been appointed the sixth CINC (commander in chief) of CENTCOM.*

As commander, Zinni watched over a vast region including most of the Middle East, East Africa, and Southwest and Central Asia. His challenges

---

* His predecessors included Army General Norman Schwarzkopf, the Coalition com-mander during the First Gulf War; Marine General Joe Hoar, one of Zinni's oldest friends; and Army General Binnie Peay. He was succeeded in 2000 by Army General Tommy Franks, the CENTCOM commander for the 2001 war in Afghanistan and the 2003 war in Iraq . . . distinguished company.

were legion: the delicate, complex relationships with his regional allies; the rising threat of terrorism, led by the not yet world-famous Osama bin Laden; the growing proliferation of weapons of mass destruction; the chronic problems of failed or incapable states, civil wars, border disputes, and criminal activities such as drug trafficking and smuggling; and the difficult task of containing the two regional hegemons, Iran and Iraq.

Though he would have preferred a balanced approach to all the regional issues rather than having to concentrate his energies and CENTCOM's capabilities on America's obsession with Saddam Hussein, by far Zinni's biggest challenge proved to be enforcing the UN-imposed post–Gulf War sanctions on Saddam's regime. In his view, Saddam could be contained and marginalized; making him *the* issue only gave him more clout and distracted the U.S. from more important regional issues, such as the Israeli-Palestinian peace process, Iran, terrorism, and the building of security relationships.

Not long after he became CINC, he proposed a six-point strategic program to William Cohen, President Clinton's Secretary of Defense, aimed at this more balanced approach. After a polite hearing with Cohen and a session with the Senate Majority and Minority Leaders and the Speaker of the House, Zinni was told to stay out of policy and to stick to execution. "Yes, sir," he said—always a good Marine.

Meanwhile, the magnitude of the Iraq problem was once again brought home only five days after he took command, at an extended meeting at CENTCOM headquarters with Ambassador Richard Butler, the new head of UNSCOM. CENTCOM provided support for UNSCOM with UN-supervised U-2 flights over Iraq.

Zinni was already familiar with these missions. Before his appointment as commander, he had, as General Peay's deputy, coordinated the CENTCOM support missions with Butler's predecessor, Rolf Ekeus.

On the face of it, UNSCOM's mandate was straightforward. UN Resolution 687, which set up UNSCOM (and which Iraq had accepted and agreed to support), had directed Iraq to "destroy, remove, or render harmless" its WMD and any missiles with a range greater than 150 kilometers. This process was to have three stages: Iraq would declare its WMD and missiles, UNSCOM would verify the declaration as accurate, and then together UNSCOM and the Iraqis would destroy them.

The Iraqis had given Ekeus a hard time; but his problems were nothing compared with the obstacles they were already putting in the way of his successor. Iraqi efforts to conceal their WMD programs—their "hideous charade," in Butler's words—were to have dramatic consequences for Tony Zinni.

THOUGH TONY ZINNI did not look like a recruiting poster, he was instantly recognizable as a Marine. He was slightly under medium height, solidly built, barrel-chested, with dark hair cut in the jarhead Marine fashion—very short with shaved back and sides. His look was normally intent, thoughtful, direct, and friendly; laughter came easily to him; and he had the social openness, warmth, and common touch that came from long exposure to all kinds and varieties of people. Hardened by a lifetime of military service—and most especially by Vietnam, which had radically changed him—tough decisions didn't faze him.

Before becoming the head of UNSCOM, Richard Butler had been the Australian ambassador to the UN, with considerable expertise in arms control and WMD issues. Like Zinni, he came out of a working-class urban Catholic background (Zinni grew up in Philadelphia, Butler in Sydney); and, like Zinni, he was a burly, physically imposing man, friendly, direct, outspoken, and tough.

Not surprisingly, the two men connected easily. Both men listened well and were not reluctant to express their views.

Butler's first words to Zinni made it clear that he would not play favorites. He'd call the pitches as he saw them. But a successful outcome to the inspections was all up to the Iraqis. If they opened up and came clean with their missiles and WMD, he would give them a clean bill of health, and they'd get their reward—the lifting of the draconian sanctions imposed as a consequence of their invasion of Kuwait in 1990.

So far they had shown zero inclination to come clean—anything but— while crying crocodile tears over their fellow Iraqis, who were enduring the terrible sanctions imposed by the American Satan. (Saddam's henchmen, meanwhile, lived royally in palaces.)

When it came down to the naked truth, Saddam's regime was far more interested in keeping their WMD and missile programs than in lifting the sanctions. Yet if they could get the sanctions removed while keeping their WMD, all the better.

Butler had no illusions about the other players in this high-stakes game, either: he was well aware that the Americans had their own agenda—not to mention the UN bureaucracy, the French, the Russians, the Chinese, and everyone else with a stake in what went on inside the nation with the world's second-largest proven oil reserves . . . a nation whose government was arguably the most repressive since Stalin's USSR.

The Iraqis, well aware of these agendas, played everyone off against each other, trying various gambits aimed at ending or at least weakening UNSCOM—from conning Butler, to putting a wedge in the Security Council, to appealing to the Secretary-General for a diplomatic solution (meaning a diplomatic surrender to Iraq). The Iraqis rightly believed that the French, Russians, and Chinese would stand to gain if the sanctions were removed; but their backing had conditions. It had to be covered over by a mask of support for the previous resolutions calling for disarmament. The Iraqis also rightly believed that the Secretary-General and his staff were hopeful of attaining a "diplomatic solution," even if that meant sacrificing the Security Council's goal of achieving Iraqi disarmament.

The U.S. agenda was even more subtle and complex. The Americans were increasingly coming to understand that disarmament would never happen with Saddam in power. It was therefore not in their interest for the Iraqis *to be seen* to comply with UN directives and thus to have the sanctions lifted. In the American view, if Saddam *appeared* to comply with the inspectors, *seemed* to meet the conditions set by the UN resolution, and was given a clean bill of health, then he would no doubt restart the WMD programs he had not successfully protected from inspection.

As time passed, the Americans' goal for Iraq shifted from the WMD-sanctions equation to regime change—a goal they could not openly advocate because of the UN resolutions they had backed. Yet it was clear they had no intention of dropping the sanctions as long as Saddam Hussein's regime ran Iraq.

The American policy shift did not make Richard Butler's job any easier. It obviously meant there was no motivation for Saddam to comply with the UN conditions. If the regime and not the WMD was the issue, then there was no reason for them not to keep the WMD programs. . . . Of course, that was an excuse and not a reason. Saddam intended to keep his programs no matter what.

OVER THE next months, the Iraqis did their best to scam Butler. The scam didn't work. As they realized he was not a pushover—and was becoming increasingly exasperated by their lies and tricks—they ratcheted up the stakes with attempts at intimidation. By the end of October 1997, they were putting more and more obstacles in the way of the UNSCOM inspectors, and making serious and quite naked threats. At this point, they had two immediate goals: to protect several key sites they had designated "presidential"; and to remove anything "American" from the inspection process, including the U-2 flights. (Of the approximately one thousand UNSCOM inspection staff, about a quarter were American.)

Meanwhile, the Iraqi failure to cooperate had provoked CENTCOM contingency plans for retaliatory air strikes. Though there had been U.S. strikes against the Iraqis before Zinni became CINC, they had been relatively limited. Zinni's strikes were intended to hurt.

The crisis came to a head in early November, when the Iraqis ordered all the American inspectors to leave Iraq and threatened to shoot down the U-2. Although hitting the high-flying aircraft would have taken a very lucky shot, it was possible.

The question: How to respond to the threat? A U-2 mission was scheduled for November 10. Obviously, an attempt to knock it out would be followed by American bombs. But was the threat alone reason enough to hit Saddam?

That was Zinni's position. He did not favor flying the mission, preferring instead to strike Iraq immediately (based on the threat), or else to punish them in other ways, such as increasing the airspace in the no-fly zone/no-drive zone enforcement area.*

---

* Large zones of northern and southern Iraq were interdicted by the UN after the First Gulf War. The Iraqi military (with some exceptions) were not allowed to fly military aircraft or drive military vehicles in these zones.

But Washington thought otherwise. Their decision was to fly the U-2; and Zinni was ordered to be prepared to conduct immediate air and missile attacks on Iraq if the plane was fired upon. In preparation for the strike, he flew out to the friendly countries in the Gulf to secure agreements to use their airspace, bases, and territorial waters for the strike—a round of visits he would make several times as head of CENTCOM.

On the way, he visited the U-2 pilots at their base in Saudi Arabia. There he learned that the squadron commander had decided to fly the flight himself, an act that impressed Zinni, who later awarded him an air medal for flying into the engagement zones of hostile Iraqi surface-to-air missiles.

Getting agreement from the friendly leaders in the region was not automatic. They were nervous about the strike. Though none had any illusions about the Iraqi leader, they all had a great deal of sympathy for the long-suffering Iraqi people—Arabs, just as they were. A solution that did nothing for the Iraqi people made no sense to them. Thus they all backed an attack that would remove Saddam, but in their minds, yet another round of "pinprick" bombings only made him stronger.

In the end, however, they agreed to a strike if the U-2 was fired upon. Despite their serious questions about the benefits of the U.S. air strikes, they always came through with their support (contrary to U.S. media reports), but preferred to keep the extent of their support private.

The U-2 flew as scheduled on November 10. During the flight, Zinni sat with senior Saudi leaders in the Saudi Ministry of Defense in Riyadh, but in direct communication with CENTCOM's air operations center, ready to give the order to strike at the first indication that the plane was threatened.

As had often happened before, Saddam's threat turned out to be hollow. The flight was uneventful.

On November 14, in the face of the Iraqi demand to remove the Americans, Butler evacuated the entire contingent of inspectors; but after several days of intense diplomatic activity, they were all able to return—though, once again, with less freedom to operate than before. Every "diplomatic solution" lessened UNSCOM's ability to get the disarmament job done.

Meanwhile, the Iraqi lies and threats did not stop; and over the next months, Saddam raised the stakes again and again—always probing for weaknesses, always trying to limit UNSCOM's effectiveness.

In response, CENTCOM built up forces in the region to be ready to strike if the inspectors were no longer able to do their business. This operation became known as "Desert Thunder."

In February, Secretary of Defense Cohen and Zinni conducted a four-day trip to eleven countries to gain support for a major air strike if Butler's inspectors were unable to carry out their mission. By February 17, when a confrontation with Saddam seemed imminent, President Clinton announced in a televised speech that the U.S. would act if he did not cooperate with the inspectors. Zinni briefed the President and key cabinet members on the planned strike and defense of American allies in the region.

But once again Saddam made a last-minute retreat. A February 20 visit to Baghdad by UN Secretary-General Kofi Annan got an agreement from Saddam to resume cooperation with Butler; yet it was clearly only a matter of time before this cooperation would collapse.

Meanwhile, the U.S. forces that had been added to the units already in the region remained in the Gulf, poised to strike.

DURING THE target selection process for Desert Thunder, the President had injected a new and unprecedented element into the planning—he had clearly begun seriously to face the question raised by the likelihood that Saddam would finally block UNSCOM's work. "Can we militarily eliminate Saddam's weapons of mass destruction program?" the President asked Zinni. Previous air strikes had simply punished the Iraqis in the hope of forcing their cooperation. Now he was asking whether bombing could accomplish militarily what the inspectors seemed no longer able to do on the ground.

Zinni's answer at that point was negative. "We don't know enough about the WMD program," he said, "much less where the components of the program are. That's why the inspectors are in there."

But Clinton persisted. "What can be done militarily about the WMD?" he kept asking. "To what level can we take them out?"

As time went on, Zinni began to come up with answers.

Once they are built, WMD are relatively easy to hide. But the facilities and processes that are used to build them are much harder to conceal. Zinni's people knew quite a lot about these. The delivery systems and the fuels that powered them were vulnerable, as were the security systems and personnel that protected the programs; the various documents, information, materials, and the research-and-development operations; and the special and difficult-to-acquire machinery required to fabricate high-tolerance parts (such as centrifuges needed to separate fissile uranium from its more stable forms).

Whenever an air strike was imminent (normally tipped off by a buildup of CENTCOM forces in the region as tensions mounted), the Iraqis would move the more vulnerable elements of their WMD programs out of harm's way. These were the elements that could be taken out . . . if they could be hit before they'd been moved to safety.

"The Iraqis are allowed to have certain missiles," Zinni reported to the President. "But within that capability, they can research and develop an expanded capability, which at some point can be turned into a delivery system. We can eliminate that. We can bomb their missile facility.

"They also have experimental, developmental programs on fuel for missiles and rockets. We can take these out.

"We know the security forces charged with protecting WMD program information, documents, materials, and R & D studies. The Special Republican Guard is charged with these missions. We can hit them.

"We know the facilities where they keep high-tolerance machinery that is necessary for a nuclear program. We can hit those facilities.

"And we can add targets vital to the regime, like their intelligence headquarters and the Ba'ath party headquarters. Taking out such targets will do serious damage to their command and control capabilities.

"Taking out all these things will not end forever their WMD program," Zinni said in conclusion. "If the strike goes well, if we are really lucky, the best we can do is set back their programs for two years. It will take about that much time to reconstitute and replace what we've destroyed."

With the President's approval, Zinni was given the go-ahead to plan for striking these targets.

DESERT VIPER

Butler and his UNSCOM inspectors soldiered on, but with ever-increasing difficulties. From May 1998 to the end of that year was a time of almost constant crisis.

Though UNSCOM was intended to be a verifying and not an investigative body, the Iraqi obstacles to its proper functioning had required the creation of an investigative and forensic unit. In June 1998, the UNSCOM investigations discovered long-sought smoking guns—stores of Scud-specific propellants and incontrovertible evidence of VX production (one of the most vicious of the nerve agents*).

Because the propellants could be used only for Scuds, there was no reason for the Iraqis to have kept the stuff around—*if,* as they had long claimed, they had destroyed all their Scuds.

The Iraqis were later proved to have produced close to four thousand liters of VX long ago—after claiming far lower estimates. "But of course," they told UNSCOM, "we've destroyed all that we made during the years they had actually made the stuff."

The UN resolution demanded UNSCOM verification, but the Iraqis always blocked UNSCOM from verifying anything significant.

Naturally, UNSCOM successes did not sit well with the Iraqis.

On August 5, the battle entered its final phase, when the Iraqis officially suspended UNSCOM's disarmament work. Though Kofi Annan and others shuttled to all the usual capitals in an effort to attain another "diplomatic solution," by October 31 no one serious doubted that the work of UNSCOM was finished. No one knew how the end would come—whether the Iraqis would throw the inspectors out, or the inspectors would give up and walk out—but one way or another it was certain that the UNSCOM operation in Iraq was untenable.

When that happened, the heavy air strike would inevitably follow.

As that moment approached, Secretary of Defense Cohen, communicating through General Hugh Shelton, the chairman of the Joint Chiefs

* A single droplet on the skin is lethal. And enough could be loaded into a missile warhead to kill most of the population of Tel Aviv.

of Staff, directed Zinni to prepare two attack plans—a heavy option, and a lighter one. The heavy option would attack many targets over several days. The lighter option would be shorter, and hit fewer targets.

Though he could have lived with either option, Zinni preferred the heavier. "If you're going to hit him, hit him," he told the Joint Chiefs.

ON THE SEVENTH of November, he flew up to Washington to brief the plan.

If he thought the briefings would be easy, and followed by an automatic approval of his plan, he was wrong.

A briefing with the Joint Chiefs was held in the small Pentagon conference room called "the Tank." When Zinni had finished, the chairman called for a vote on the options.

To say that the vote surprised Zinni was an understatement; the vote itself made no sense. Not only was there no serious discussion beforehand, nor to his knowledge had there been earlier sessions to discuss the options, but, most important, the Joint Chiefs were not in Zinni's chain of command (which went directly through the Secretary of Defense to the President). The CINCs are operationally independent of the Joint Chiefs, whose primary job, in their Service Chief role, was to provide the CINCs with the personnel and equipment they needed to do *their* job. In other words, to Zinni the vote was meaningless (though no CINC casually ignores the recommendations that the JCS gives on employment of U.S. forces). He was even more shocked when the JCS voted 4 to 2 for the lighter option, after he had recommended the heavier one. Since there had been little discussion before the vote, the reasons for their choice were unclear. Whatever the reason, Zinni could sense their nervousness: Going against the CINC's recommendation made them all uneasy. None of them liked to second-guess a field commander.

Though Zinni repeated that he could live with either option, his difference with the Chiefs remained. Since the place to resolve their difference was higher up, General Shelton recommended to Secretary Cohen that Zinni attend a meeting of the principal cabinet members and the President at Camp David in order to discuss the options.

The next day, November 8, he flew out to Camp David.

The meeting was held in the wood-paneled conference room of the main cabin. Bill Clinton, seated at the head of the table, was flanked by the Director of Central Intelligence, George Tenet; the Secretary of State, Madeleine Albright; the Secretary of Defense, Bill Cohen; the National Security Adviser, Sandy Berger; and the JCS chairman and vice-chairman, Generals Shelton and Ralston. Though the Vice President was not present, he was on a speakerphone.

As the group discussed the choices, Zinni sensed that the cabinet was as divided as the Joint Chiefs; and when it came time for a vote, there was again no consensus. The Secretary of State leaned toward the heavier strike, the Secretary of Defense the lighter, George Tenet the heavier, and so on around the table. The cabinet members were all over the map.

It was left to Sandy Berger to square this circle.

"Are these two options mutually exclusive?" he asked reasonably. "Why couldn't we start with the lighter one and see how it goes, but hold open the option of going heavy?"

"That's fine with me," Zinni answered. This was neither the time nor the place for drawing a line in the sand. At this stage, he just wanted to get on with it. "I'm not trying to make this hard. If that's what you want, we'll work it that way."

The President approved the compromise.

THE TRIGGER for Desert Viper was to be the end of the inspections. As soon as Richard Butler announced, "We've had it; we're out of here; we can't do business," the clock would start ticking. The bombs would start dropping within hours.

Preparing for this takes time. Bringing bombs to their targets is an enormously complex process, involving land-based aircraft, carrier aircraft, and cruise missiles fired from both ships and B-52s. The various strike aircraft have to be in the air—along with tankers, the Airborne Warning and Control System (AWACS), and all the other support aircraft; the ships and carriers have to be in position for launch; the crews must all have their required rest; and much, much more. Zinni's people needed about twenty-four hours before the actual strike in order to make all that happen.

At some moment after the inspectors climbed into their white UN SUVs, drove out to Habbaniyah Air Base* eighty-five miles northwest of Baghdad, and took a plane to Bahrain—or some other friendly place—the President had to give the "go" decision for Desert Viper. Twenty-four hours later, the bombs would fall.

Once the twenty-four hours started, the strike could be stopped at any time up to six hours before the scheduled impact. But six hours was the drop-dead moment. That was when the first cruise missiles were launched.

This fact had caused some controversy—Clinton's advisers didn't want to tell the President what he couldn't do.

"You don't understand," Zinni told them. "When you get beyond six hours, the launch is a done deal. Nobody can stop it."

"But you can't tell the President that," they replied. "He has to be able to call back his decision up to the last moment."

"I've got no problem with that," Zinni persisted. "What I'm telling you is that the last moment is six hours before the bombs drop. And you need to tell him he can't."

The controversy came to a head at a Pentagon session, attended by the President. Zinni had with him what was called "the Master Air Attack Plan"—an enormous and labyrinthine time/event matrix that came rolled, like a scroll.

When the advisers began to sense that Zinni intended to show the plan to their boss, they were horrified: "You can't do that! It's too complex!"

But when the opportunity came, Zinni unrolled the plan on the conference table. "Mr. President," he said, "you need to see all the moving parts that have to be in position and all the timelines and limits we're working from. You need to see when you have to make the decision to start.

---

* Even though the UN resolution stated that UNSCOM would have unrestricted access to any facility they needed, the Iraqis had insisted on granting air access to only a single Iraqi site, the very inconvenient base at Habbaniyah. There had been protests, but it was a battle nobody wanted to fight.

And you need to see exactly what's happening with the cruise missiles. They spin up and launch six hours before the strike. Once launched, that's it. They're going to go until they hit what they're aimed at.

"This is the absolute drop-dead time. If you want to send us a no-go, you have to do it before that."

The advisers' fears were of course groundless. Zinni knew from previous briefings that Clinton was a very quick study; he instantly caught what Zinni was trying to show him.

"Right," he said. "Fine, you'll get the decisions you need in time."

As November wound on, Zinni's people kept tabs on the inspectors . . . watched their progress—or lack of it—waiting for the launch trigger. It came in mid-November. The inspectors had continued to demand access and cooperation, which the Iraqis continued to refuse to give.

As this drama unfolded, CENTCOM built up air and naval forces in the Gulf in preparation for the strike.

Finally, on November 11, the inspectors gave up on the fiction of Iraqi cooperation. They'd had enough. Butler ordered the evacuation of his team; and the President ordered the execution of Desert Viper on the heels of their departure. . . .

. . . **AND ON** November 12, Tony Zinni, in his command room in Tampa, with his fudge time completely gone, grabbed a phone and called Willy Moore, hoping against hope that Admiral Moore could stop the Tomahawks anyway.

The admiral said: "You may be in luck, sir. I built in fifteen minutes of fudge time myself. But we're already into it." Moore scrambled. He had to get word out to all eight ships to shut down the missiles—by then their gyros were already spinning, the last step before they are launched.

And with exactly eight minutes left until the launch—he succeeded. Meanwhile, Zinni got the planes in the air recalled. Desert Viper was averted. But it achieved its aims: Saddam had blinked once again. Richard Butler's inspectors flew back into Habbaniyah and attempted to resume their work.

DESERT FOX

One aspect of their (temporary) success troubled Zinni and other senior American leaders, though. A few days after Desert Viper was aborted, General Shelton called Zinni to talk about this frustration. "You know," he said, "every time we deploy forces out there, Saddam sees them coming and moves his sensitive equipment and files out of targeted facilities."

"You're right," Zinni answered, "and because he knows about our precision bombing and concern for collateral damage, he doesn't have to move it very far."

"What we need to do," Shelton continued, "is catch him with these things in place. If we can hit him without any warning, we can do a lot more damage."

Zinni agreed.

"We need to do something that outsmarts him," Shelton went on, "something that outfoxes him." He laughed: "We ought to call the next strike 'Desert Fox.'"

"Yeah," Zinni laughed with him. But both generals were deadly serious.

"Really," Shelton continued, "what that amounts to is this: We've got to set up the next strike with forces already in the theater, so he doesn't see any buildup. Or if we have to build up, we do it quietly, or trickle it in bit by bit.

"So here's my question: Can we do a strike with forces we have in theater, and with maximum operational security and limited numbers of people in on the planning?"

"Let me look at it," Zinni said. "I'll see what we can do, and I'll get back to you."

The answer Zinni came up with was "Yes"; and General Shelton's suggestion was put in place in the next CENTCOM strike plan—Desert Fox.

The name proved to be controversial after somebody pointed out that it was also the epithet given to German Field Marshal Erwin Rommel—the bane of the British and Americans in North Africa in the early 1940s. "How can you name an air strike after a famous Nazi?" they asked . . . a thought that had not occurred to Shelton or Zinni. To them, it was simply a sly joke: They were going to outfox the fox.

In spite of the doubts, the name stuck.*

THE THREAT posed by Desert Viper had not ended the Iraqi games. During the rest of November and the first two weeks of December, they continued to jerk Butler and his UNSCOM inspectors around.

Finally, in mid-December, Richard Butler pulled them out once and for all. As the inspectors prepared to leave, the twenty-four-hour clock started yet again, and Zinni once more took up position in his Tampa command center to lead the attack.

This time, there was no last-minute reprieve. Four hours after the inspectors landed at Bahrain, the surprise Desert Fox attack began. It lasted from the seventeenth to the twentieth of December, with an option to continue on if it seemed desirable, either to restrike targets or to go heavier.

The attack was perfectly executed. Over six hundred Air Force, Marine, and Navy sorties were conducted (including over three hundred night strikes), over four hundred missiles fired, over six hundred bombs and precision-guided munitions dropped, using more than two hundred aircraft and twenty ships. Surprise was total. None of the equipment or facilities targeted had been prepared for it. None had been moved (no shell game). All the targets had been hit—and hard.

The attack was so successful that Zinni decided not to move on into the hard option—especially since Ramadan began that year on December 21, the day after the fourth day of bombing.

"There's no point in bombing for three or four days into Ramadan," he told General Shelton. "We've done about as much damage to the WMD program as we're going to do. Any more would just be bombing for bombing's sake."

Following the departure of the UNSCOM inspectors and the Desert Fox strike, Saddam became much more aggressive toward the planes still

---

* The system naming military operations always uses two terms, with the first term indicating the theater. Thus, "Desert———" indicates a CENTCOM operation.

enforcing the no-fly zones. Nearly every other day, his air defense units would fire on coalition aircraft, or his Air Force would attempt to lure the planes into missile range. In response, the U.S. unleashed attacks on the entire Iraqi air defense system, resulting in significant losses in Iraqi Air Defense Command weapons, radars, and command and control assets. This attack-counterattack routine lasted from the end of Desert Fox (December 1998) until the beginning of Operation Iraqi Freedom (March 2003). Coalition forces never lost an aircraft and Saddam's air defense forces suffered greatly for his folly.

DESERT CROSSING

Tony Zinni continues:

Desert Fox accomplished everything militarily that we wanted it to accomplish. But it also brought political consequences that none of us expected. These totally surprised me.

Soon after we turned off Desert Fox, we started to get really interesting reports from inside Iraq—from diplomatic missions and other people friendly to us—indicating that the attack had badly shaken the regime. They actually seemed shocked into paralysis.

Although they'd had suspicions that we would hit them when the inspectors walked out, it turns out that the absence of visible preparations for the strike and the approach of Ramadan seem to have lulled them into a lackadaisical approach to their own preparations. Somebody put out the word to move the equipment and documents, the way they normally did; but nobody was in a hurry to do it; so they got caught with their pants down. And they totally didn't expect us to take out the Ba'ath party headquarters and the intelligence headquarters—the "House of Pain," as Iraqis called it, because of all the torturing that went on in there.

For a time, they were so dazed and rattled they were virtually headless.

After an attack, we could usually expect defiant rhetoric and all kinds of public posturing and bluster. But there was none of that. And there were reports that people had cheered when the "House of Pain" was hit.

Some of us even began to wonder about the stability of the regime; and I began to hear stories (told to my Arab friends by senior officers in the Republican Guard) that there may have been a move against it if the bombing had lasted a little while longer.

That we had really hurt them was confirmed again in January 1999, in Saddam's yearly Army Day speech, when he viciously lashed out at all the other Arabs—blaming them for all the harm they had sanctioned, threatening reprisals, calling regional monarchs "throne dwarfs." These were all people he hoped would feel sorry for him—or at least for his people. Showing such fury toward them was unheard of; it meant we'd hurt him really bad.

ALL THIS got me thinking: What if we had actually tipped the scale here? What if we'd hit Saddam or his sons, and that had somehow spurred the people to rise up? What if the country imploded and we had to deal with the aftermath?

Before Desert Fox, we'd looked at the possibility that we would have to execute the takedown of Saddam; but we always thought that would come after he attacked a neighbor or Israel, used WMD again on his own people, or committed some other atrocity so outrageous we'd have no choice but to go in there and turn over the regime.

"But what if it just collapsed?" I began to ask myself.

It didn't take me long to figure out the answer to that: Somebody'd have to go in there to rebuild the country.

"Who?" I asked myself.

"As the CINC, I have a plan for militarily defeating Saddam. Doing that isn't going to be hard. But after we defeat him, who takes care of reconstruction and all the attendant problems?"

It was clear that we had to start looking hard at this possibility. It didn't take a rocket scientist to see that if we didn't, we could find ourselves in deep trouble.

"What we need to do," I realized, "is come together and work out a comprehensive and joint plan. We need to get the other agencies of government—not only CENTCOM and the DOD [Department of Defense], but the CIA, the State Department, and their Office of Foreign Disaster Assistance and USAID, and everyone else with something to contribute. And we'd also have to plan to bring in the UN, various NGOs, and Coalition members for this phase of the operation."

"Who's doing this?" I asked myself.

When I probed around Washington, I quickly learned that nobody was doing it; nor was there much interest in doing it.

"Then we have to create interest," I told myself. "We need to organize a conference, a seminar, or a war game that will spark people to generate an interagency plan for dealing with this issue. Out of this I can also develop a specifically CENTCOM plan, which would cover some of the more immediately practical issues."

I decided to organize a "war game" that presented several post-Saddam Iraq scenarios. The game—called "Desert Crossing"—was conducted in the Washington, D.C., area late in 1999 at Booz Allen, the contractor (who run secure games for the government); experts from all the relevant branches of government took part.

The scenarios looked closely at humanitarian, security, political, economic, and other reconstruction issues. We looked at food, clean water, electricity, refugees, Shia versus Sunnis, Kurds versus the other Iraqis, Turks versus Kurds, and the power vacuum that would surely follow the collapse of the regime (since Saddam had pretty successfully eliminated any local opposition). We looked at all the problems the United States faces in 2003 trying to rebuild Iraq. And when it was over, I was starting to get a good sense of their enormous scope and to recognize how massive the reconstruction job would be.

Desert Crossing gave us the ammunition we needed to define the post-Saddam problem, but that was only a start.

"Well, who's going to take the next step?" I asked.

The answer: Nobody. There was no interest in Washington in pursuing it. Most of the participants in the game were sympathetic; but none had any charter to develop a plan. They were more than willing to help us define the problem, maybe learn a little bit about what needed to be done; but nobody was in a position to sign up to anything. Post-Saddam Iraq was simply too far down the priority list of any agency with a reason to be interested in the problem.

You can't really blame them for this. Nobody saw Iraq as a really pressing threat. Saddam's military was down. Our policy was containment, the policy was succeeding, and we were whacking Saddam when he got out of line. At this stage of the game, there was a near zero likelihood that he could attack Kuwait, Iran, or Israel again. And there was no way he was going to initiate a serious attack against us, nor were we going to initiate anything major against him.

Besides, we had other, more pressing crises to manage. We were working the Kosovo problem, the Bosnia problem, the Israeli-Palestinian problem, the drug problem in Colombia . . . India-Pakistan, Korea . . . and much of Africa was going to hell.

So if you look at my inability to drum up interest in a post-Saddam Iraq in the light of what's going on right now, you have to ask how they could have passed it up. But back then, it just didn't seem high priority to anybody in Washington.

You also have to keep in mind the structural barrier to getting anything like that done in Washington. In Washington, there is no one place, agency, or force that directs interagency cooperation. The only such cooperation is on an ad hoc *person-to-person or group-to-group basis. So if you have a problem like putting Iraq back together after Saddam, that requires the joint work of many government agencies (not to mention international agencies— NGOs and the UN), there's nowhere to start.*

I could go to DOD. But where does DOD go? Possibly to the President's National Security Adviser. He or she might then interest the President. Or possibly someone will take the issue to a cabinet meeting and interest the President that way.

Failing that, you're in limbo. There's no way you can move the bureaucracy without action from the top.

OF COURSE *the problem did not go away. I knew then there was a very good chance it would come back to haunt us. Which meant that if Saddam's regime did collapse, "somebody" was going to get stuck with putting Humpty back together again.*

I knew who that "somebody" was likely to be. It was "us"—the military. I knew that all the king's horses and all the king's men were far from the best solution, but we would have to do until we came up with something better.

So I said to my guys, "We need to start planning on this." And they did. But by then we were well into 2000 and I was coming to the end of my tour. And when I left CENTCOM (in mid-2000), the plan was nowhere near materializing.

I'm not sure where it went after I left.

As far as I can tell, the plan was pigeonholed. And by the time Iraqi Freedom rolled around, nobody in CENTCOM had ever heard of it. There's no longer any corporate memory of it.

Meanwhile, we're living through the fall of Saddam Hussein, and my concerns have come true. Since nobody in Washington had seriously planned for the consequences of the fall, the military—by default—got stuck with the nation building that followed it.

On February 11, 2003, a month before the start of Operation Iraqi Freedom, Tony Zinni was called to testify before the Senate Foreign Relations Committee on the subject of post-Saddam reconstruction planning. He followed a panel of Defense and State Department officials who'd just been heavily criticized by the committee for their obvious lack of serious attention to that critical phase.

In his own testimony, Zinni recounted the lessons learned from Desert Crossing, and continued by relating from his own numerous past experiences that defeating hostile forces militarily does not necessarily mean victory. In Zinni's view, victory only comes when the defeated people see that they have a livable future and that they have some say in it.

He first learned this lesson as a young lieutenant in Vietnam.

CHAPTER TWO

12,000 MILES FROM PHILADELPHIA

TONY ZINNI NEVER FORGOT the first time somebody shot at him.

It was at the end of April, in 1967. He was a green U.S. Marine first lieutenant, barely a month in Vietnam, where he was assigned as an adviser to the elite South Vietnamese Marines, that nation's most effective fighting force.

The advisers' job was not to give the Vietnamese Marines tactical advice (they had more fighting experience than most Americans, and it was their country). Rather, the obligation of the advisers was to apply American air and artillery firepower when that became necessary (which was frequently), and to provide American logistics, coordination with American units, and American intelligence. The Vietnamese were weakest in these areas. The job of the advisers, in other words, was to make the Vietnamese system work.

As the most junior adviser, Zinni was not assigned to one unit, the usual practice, but sent wherever he was needed. In his words, he was "the utility infielder." He bounced around from unit to unit.

In his eyes, this was not at all a bad thing. He got a chance to see all kinds of different people and places, and soak up a wealth of varied experiences.

In his first advisory assignment, he'd spent a couple of weeks in the tidal swamps of the Rung Sat—"the Forest of Death"—near the Mekong Delta. Now he had been ordered to Binh Dinh Province in the northern part of the II CTZ (Corps Tactical Zone), where he was to take up duties with the Vietnamese Marines 5th Battalion, replacing an adviser returning home on emergency leave.

The 5th Battalion had long been heavily involved in an operation the Americans were calling "Pershing." Its aim was to use the U.S. 1st Cavalry and the VNMC (Vietnamese Marine Corps) to root out and destroy the communist infrastructure: to clear and pacify, to interdict infiltration routes, and to reeducate the people ("win hearts and minds"). Pershing took up the better part of 1967.

It took Zinni three days to travel from the Rung Sat to Binh Dinh. The last leg was by helicopter. He arrived at the battalion position at sunset.

The helo landed in a dry rice paddy next to a tree line, where he was met by Jim Laney, the 5th Battalion junior adviser, now filling in for his boss on emergency leave. Laney was a mustang, a onetime enlisted man who had received a meritorious commission as an officer.

He led Zinni through the tree line and into the battalion command post, a half-destroyed hut (it was roofless, and the wall facing the line of troops and paddy area had been completely blown away). As they walked past the Marine positions, Zinni noticed that they were digging in at the edge of the paddies just a few meters from the hut, obviously getting ready for serious action. The battalion had been conducting a parallel sweep on both sides of a vast east-west open rice paddy complex.

"We've been in continuous contact since we began the sweep," Laney explained, "and they've attacked us every night. They consider this area to be theirs. They've owned it for a long time. We're intruders."

"You'll move across the paddy area tomorrow morning," he continued, "to join the battalion executive officer who has two companies on the other side."

"Why can't I just cross the paddy now?" Zinni asked.

Laney laughed. "You won't get ten yards before they pick you off. In the morning, the Marines will clear the area just to our west. Then you can cross."

Zinni stepped into the roofless, three-sided hut and met the battalion commander, a tough but friendly and wise old Marine major named Nha, and a combat legend. He gave Zinni a warm welcome, insisting that he join him for chow.

Later, as they ate, a full moon left an eerie glow across the paddies. After dinner, as Zinni was settling into a corner of the hut for the night, Laney reminded him that they surely would be hit; he should be ready.

That got young Zinni's attention. Excited to be getting into a close-quarters firefight for the first time, he carefully laid out his M-16 and harness, figuring out how he would roll out of his poncho liner, grab his rifle and gear, and come up ready to shoot.

Sure enough, around midnight, the whole area erupted with fire.

Zinni bolted out of a deep sleep and spun into action, surprising himself with how quickly he rolled, grabbed the gear, and was down in a shooting position ready for action. There was one problem. It was dark as a coalpit in hell. What happened to the full moon? He heard the others on the radio and the return fire, but he couldn't see a thing, not even tracers.

He shouted to Laney: "Can you see anything? I can't."

"You're facing the wrong way," Laney yelled back over the firing.

Zinni then realized that his planned "roll" into action had been in the wrong direction and he was facing the back wall of the hut. Red-faced, he crawled around. Major Nha was laughing sympathetically; he felt for the new guy.

Anyhow, Zinni's embarrassment passed quickly when it hit him that rounds were whizzing overhead and slamming into the back walls. He could clearly see the enemy muzzle flashes and the outgoing tracer fire of the Marines.

In time, he would develop into an experienced veteran who could remain focused in the madness of a firefight. The sounds and flashes from the weapons would tell him what types were firing, at what distances, and how many there were. But at this point, all he heard was a cacophony of noises, flashes, and blasts.

After about twenty minutes, the firing trailed off and eventually ceased. The others crawled back under their poncho liners, but Zinni was still too excited to sleep. This was his first experience with a close exchange of fire.

He was standing at the front of the hut, gazing out across the moonlit paddies and thinking about the attack, when a single round cracked, zinged
right between his legs, and slammed into the hardened mud base on the
hut floor. "Oh, shit!" he realized. "I shouldn't be standing up!"

He dove back into the hut and slipped under his poncho liner. The next
morning at first light his Vietnamese cowboy,* who had witnessed this adventure, handed him a cup of steaming coffee and the spent round he'd
dug out of the floor. "Keep it as a reminder not to be stupid," he said.

"Thanks," Zinni replied, meaning it.

MEANWHILE, the scouts and lead units had already started forward,
and Major Nha determined it was clear enough for Zinni, his cowboy, and
his radio operator to cross over to join the other half of the battalion on
the south side of the paddies.

After the linkup, the battalion executive officer provided Zinni with a
running description in fluent English of the area and the operation.

"The Vietnamese Marines have operated in Binh Dinh Province on
and off for the last three years," the executive officer (XO) explained as
they moved out. "Our area of operations is on the Bong Son Plain, which
starts at the coast of the South China Sea and spreads west into the
foothills and mountains of the Central Highlands. It's a critical area, with
major seacoast cities, airfields, and ports; it's a major rice-producing area,
with many lakes and waterways; the principal north-south highway of
Vietnam, Highway 1, runs through it; and it's also the major food-
producing area of the central region.

"In 1965, the U.S. Army's 1st Cavalry Division (Airmobile) moved into
the area and remains the primary American unit operating here.

"This is a hard-core VC region; stay-behind cadres were left by Ho Chi
Minh after the French Indochina War," in violation of the peace treaty that

---

* The advisers were assisted by a small team of Vietnamese Marines, a "cowboy," a radio
operator, and at times a driver: The cowboy looked out for the adviser's security and basic
needs. He cooked for him and took care of laundry and sleeping arrangements. The radio
operator carried the radio, which was the adviser's link to his own headquarters. Without it, he couldn't do the job. It was his lifeline.

divided Vietnam; "there are heavy concentrations of VC [Vietcong] sympathizers; and many homes and classrooms still have pictures of Ho Chi Minh. The dense forests and mountains in the western part of the province give sanctuary to the enemy and easy access from the Central Highlands near the Cambodian border to the populated areas on the coastal plain. You can expect almost continuous enemy sniping or hit-and-run attacks."

Not long after Zinni moved out with the battalion XO and the two companies, they made contact with the VC again. They were at a crossing point between rice paddies and a line of trees when their point squads came under fire. The lead company quickly moved up on line and got into a heavy exchange of fire with dug-in VC. With only three to four hundred meters of paddies separating the VC from the Marines, the rounds were zinging all over.

In order to get a better sense of the fight, Zinni and the XO moved forward. The XO stood at the edge of the tree line and examined the enemy positions, then looked around for Zinni, signaling for him to join him. Zinni was soon standing beside him, anxious not to screw up.

"I'd like to put some artillery on the enemy positions," the XO told Zinni, pointing at the area he had in mind, about five hundred meters away. At that moment, rounds hit a tree nearby and Zinni hit the deck. "Don't worry," the XO said, with a smile, "the VC fire is high. It's okay to stand up."

Zinni stood, then started his radio call for fire procedure. Though he had never before called in a fire mission, even in training, he knew basically how it was done, and he'd been tested on it. He carefully went through the remembered procedure. A few minutes later, artillery rounds smacked into the VC positions a few hundred meters away. While trees exploded all around from flying shrapnel, he stood, observing and adjusting the fire . . . without noticing that the VC were also adjusting their fire, bringing it down. VC rounds were starting to hit all around him; but this did not faze Zinni, focused as he was on the artillery.

After a time, the VC fire slacked off and he could tell they were breaking contact.

But when he turned toward the XO to get his take on that, he noticed that everybody was on the ground covering their heads. "Get down!" the XO was yelling. "Now they're shooting low!"

Moments later, the Marines began moving across the paddies and pursuing the enemy. As they went by, they smiled and gave him a thumbs-up.

Later, the XO told him how impressed they'd been that he'd stood up under the enemy fire and called in the artillery rounds "danger close" on his first mission. Zinni didn't know what he was talking about (the term was new to him), but since he seemed pleased, Zinni didn't ask questions.

He realized later what had happened: In his unfamiliarity with the whole process of targeting artillery, he had called the fire mission directly onto the enemy positions rather than creeping it in from behind, the usual procedure when the target was within six hundred meters—"danger close."

Meanwhile, the Marines treated him like a fearless hero. God protects the innocent and the ignorant.

The rest of the sweep was a continuing series of hit-and-run gun battles:

At one point, VC burst up from camouflaged holes just as the head-quarters element came by, but they were taken out by the security platoon almost before Zinni realized what was happening. The platoon leader, a big guy and half French, carried a Thompson submachine gun without a stock and was deadly with it.

After another firefight, they found several VC bodies, including—to Zinni's amazement—two young women, obviously twins and beautiful. "This isn't unusual," a lieutenant told him. "The VC have a number of women in their ranks."

"Strange war," Zinni thought.

TONY ZINNI had arrived in Vietnam a month earlier, on March 26, 1967, leaving behind a large and loving blue-collar Italian family in Philadelphia and a bride of only a few weeks, who stayed with her own family in Atlanta in Tony's absence.

He had come to be a Marine by way of Villanova University in Philadel-phia, where as an undergraduate he'd joined a Marine equivalent of

ROTC, called the PLC—"Platoon Leaders Class." He had received additional basic and officers training at Quantico, and graduated from Villanova as a Marine second lieutenant.

After additional training at Quantico, he had been sent to the 2nd Marine Division based at Camp Lejeune, North Carolina, where he spent a little over a year as a rifle platoon commander, infantry company commander, and commander of an infantry training company.

After his stint at the Infantry Training Regiment, he returned to his parent unit, the 1st Battalion, 6th Marines, where he expected to be a platoon commander. But because they were short of officers, he became a company commander . . . incredibly good luck, since it was a captain's job, and he was still only a second lieutenant.

Meanwhile, the lieutenants in his battalion were getting orders to Vietnam. Soon, two-thirds of the Marine Corps were in that country fighting the first big battles. They were short of officers.

But there remained one lieutenant without orders to Nam—Tony Zinni. All of his contemporaries—his buddies—were going to be combat vets and he was going to remain a virgin. He wanted to go to Nam.

He got his wish after his wedding and brief honeymoon in Williamsburg, Virginia. When he returned to his battalion, his orders to Vietnam were waiting for him. They were strange orders. His buddies had all gone to U.S. Marine units, mostly to one of the two Marine divisions then in Vietnam. Zinni was to report to the Marine Advisory Unit, of the Naval Advisory Group, of the Military Assistance Command, Vietnam (MACV). He had no clue what this meant. He would only find that out in Vietnam.

But first, he was sent to attend the Army Special Warfare School at Fort Bragg and go through the school's Military Assistance, Training, and Advisory (MATA) course at Fort Bragg, where, among other things, he would learn to speak and write basic Vietnamese.

AFTER A WEEK of orientation in Saigon, Zinni was taken to the headquarters of the Vietnamese Marine Corps on Le Thanh Ton Street, a collection of old colonial buildings that had once been the headquarters of the legendary French Foreign Legion.

After the inevitable processing and issuing of uniforms (he thought the Vietnamese Marine tiger-striped camouflage uniforms and green berets* were very macho), he was taken to an assigned hotel room. Advisers were provided with rooms either in Saigon or in Cholon, the Chinese section of Saigon. Zinni's, in the Five Oceans Hotel in Cholon, became his "home" when he was in town from the field, and was a welcome oasis where he could clean up and get a decent night's sleep.

The first days at Le Thanh Ton were devoted to briefings on the unit and its mission.

These were condensed, technical, and very fundamental: the number of VNMC battalions, their structure, their locations, their weapons, their day-to-day operations, what the advisers were doing . . . but not much history, background, or military culture. Though Zinni was eager to pick up much more information about this fascinating unit, that had to come later—on the fly or in bars.

Here are a few basics:

The Vietnamese Marine Corps—the Thuy Quan Luc Chien (TQLC) in Vietnamese—was formed in 1954 and had its origins in the French *Dinassault*, the river assault units of the Indochina War. From small postwar detachments, the TQLC grew to become the premier fighting force of the South Vietnamese military. It saw combat during its whole twenty-one-year existence and won numerous battle honors. Along with the Vietnamese Airborne, the TQLC comprised the National Strike Force—"fire brigades" that were only committed to action where there was a critical threat or military emergency. The Marine battalions consequently saw action in all the Corps Tactical Zones in South Vietnam during the war (as well as in Cambodia and Laos), building a reputation as tough, courageous fighters and superb light infantry. They also had a reputation as a powerful political force whose support was necessary for any Vietnamese leader who aspired to seize or hold power.

In 1963, they were the force that engineered the coup that captured

---

* In every other military except ours, the green beret is a symbol of Marine commandoes. The British Royal Marines wear green berets, for instance. Only in our system does the Special Forces wear that particular headgear (though berets in other shades have spread to other branches of service). The Marine Corps doesn't have any of that.

and later executed President Diem. They continued to play kingmaker in subsequent coups and what were called "elections"—including the one in 1967, which Zinni observed at close hand.

During 1967, the Vietnamese Marine Corps had five infantry battalions in the field (another, then forming, entered service that year). When the war ended in 1975, the TQLC had reached division size.

They were not desk warriors. Better than eighty percent of a Vietnamese Marine's time was spent deployed in the field conducting combat operations. The remaining time was spent at the National Training Center or back at their battalion base camps where their families usually lived. These were all located near Saigon, except for the 4th Battalion whose camp was in Vung Tau, a beautiful seaside resort on the South China Sea.

Though they occasionally conducted amphibious operations with the U.S. Marines and more extensive riverine operations in the southern part of the country, most of their operations had them fighting as light infantry task forces comprised of one to three battalions plus support elements.

The heart of the TQLC was its infantry battalions, each with its own proud identity and colorful unit name—such as "Crazy Buffalo," "Sea Wolf," "Black Dragon," "Monster Bird," and "Killer Whale."

They were much respected and admired by the Vietnamese people (anyone wearing their uniform—including Americans—was customarily honored in cities, towns, and villages throughout the country). And they traditionally marched at the head of the military formation in Vietnam's annual National Day Parade, a place of honor that had to be earned each year from combat performance. A very different reaction came from areas controlled by the Vietcong—further confirmation of the respect they commanded.

Enlisted Marines were wiry, tough volunteers who'd earned the right to be Marines by going through a challenging boot camp. It did not take most of them long to develop the ability to accept hardships and pain and soldier on under extreme conditions that would break most men. Most of them had mottoes like "Cop Bien" ("Tigers of the Sea") or "Sat Cong" ("Kill Communists") tattooed on their forearms, thus ensuring their fate if captured and encouraging them to fight harder and never surrender. Many had been wounded, and most suffered from bouts of malaria. All had seen friends and comrades die in battle. Yet they were by no means grim; they looked for every opportunity to let loose their lively spirits and sense of humor. They were irrepressible practical jokers, never losing a chance to pull somebody else's chain—yet never cruelly or meanly. It was always to share a laugh and not to cause pain.

The Vietnamese officers were no less tough, and no less lively. But they had also received serious professional training at the Vietnamese equivalents of our military academies, all graduating near the top of their class. Like the enlisted men, they spent more time in action in the field than at home bases. This experience had honed most of them into tactically competent leaders whose small unit skills and technical proficiency were exceptional; they all tended to lead from the front. Many older officers were highly decorated with both Vietnamese and American awards for heroism.

Discipline in the TQLC was predictably harsh.

The second-floor offices of the advisory unit at Le Thanh Ton overlooked the Vietnamese Marine brig where inmates were made to run in circles carrying huge rocks during the hottest part of the day. They were constantly harassed or struck if they faltered or failed to instantly meet a guard's barked instructions.

They handled security with similar severity.

During a break one day, Zinni was standing out on the second-story balcony over the headquarters main entrance watching the traffic on the one-way street. A young man on a motor scooter was coming down the wrong way. The Vietnamese Marine sentry shouted for him to stop; but he just laughed and sped on. The sentry then aimed his rifle and shot him dead.

The incident shocked young Zinni, but gave him a quick insight into the Vietnamese Marines: They did not fool around.

THE ADVISERS

The Marine Advisory Unit traced its beginnings back to a U.S. Marine colonel named Victor J. Croizat. A fluent French speaker and World War

Two veteran, Croizat had experience with the French forces in Algeria and in the Indochina War; served an initial tour in MACV as it formed after the Indochina War; and was directly involved in the forming of the Vietnamese Marines. He modeled the advisory effort to support the Vietnamese Marines after the French approach: Instead of American advisory "teams," as was the usual American practice with Vietnamese units, there would be only two U.S. Marine advisers per infantry battalion, and specialty advisers for artillery, communications, medical, motor transport, and senior staff positions. The advisers completely immersed themselves in the units. They and the Vietnamese troops were essential parts of the same team; the Americans couldn't isolate themselves. They wore Vietnamese Marine uniforms, ate their food, spoke their language, and shared their hardships. This forced total integration and dependence, and built mutual trust.

In 1967, there were thirty-five advisers total in the Marine Advisory Unit. The number would grow in later years as the VNMC grew toward division size.

Between two and three hundred U.S. Marines served in the Marine Advisory Unit during the war. Since they were generally among the top U.S. Marine officers, they were respected and valued by the Vietnamese (and called "covan," a term of respect). Overall, the personal relationships between Americans and Vietnamese were superb, though now and again an adviser would suffer severe "culture shock" or experience a serious problem adjusting to the Vietnamese way of doing things and have to be moved from the unit.

The role of the adviser was not specifically defined. Zinni never received a briefing or written description of the duties he was to perform. He was expected to immerse himself in the job and figure out what he had to do.

This did not surprise him. It is the U.S. Marine way: You are given what you need and then the job is your responsibility; the assumption is that you can do it. Such an approach to life suited Zinni.

Though he didn't receive much initial guidance, the specific military responsibilities of the advisers quickly became obvious to him: They coordinated all operational activities with U.S. units and with the support provided by U.S. units, such as airlift, logistics, and fire support. They controlled and directed all artillery, naval gunfire, and air support. Beyond this, each adviser contributed whatever else he could add, based on his own experience and the desires of the Vietnamese commanders.

VIETNAM IS a vastly diverse land. It has steep mountains, broad coastal plains, thick mangrove swamps, tangled jungles, and a vast flooded delta. Because the Vietnamese Marines moved all over the country, they had to adapt to a great variety of terrain, enemy, and operational characteristics that shaped the unique nature of the local conflict. The advisers saw it all.

Because they moved from unit to unit or could be called back to their headquarters at any time, they saw more of Vietnam than any other group of U.S. military personnel. (They were given blanket travel orders that authorized them to travel anywhere in Vietnam at any time.) As the junior adviser, Zinni moved from unit to unit all over the country wherever a hole had to be plugged, scrounging rides from all sorts of military and nonmilitary means of transportation.

Each area presented a unique set of challenges for conducting military operations and for surviving from day to day. As an example, unlike with U.S. units, the Vietnamese Marines had to come up with their own food. Where they couldn't buy it, they had to catch it. Food was plentiful in the delta region, where fat white grubs could be cut out of the mangrove trees and large iguana-like lizards were easy delicacies to come by. In the jungle, food was more difficult to acquire unless you knew what to look for and were patient enough to forage or hunt for such delights as monkeys, snakes, bamboo shoots, or breadfruit. In the northern mountains, food could be scarce, especially in the dry season, and bitter greens, dried fish, and a little rice could be all you ate in a day.

There were two seasons in Vietnam: wet, and dry. Each was extreme. During monsoon season everything was drenched by afternoon deluges and the constant damp made it hard to dry out. In the dry season, the heat was intense and unrelenting, even at night. The killer heat made field operations difficult. For Americans like Zinni, it took a while to acclimatize and learn how to survive.

South Vietnam was divided for the war into four Corps Tactical Zones (CTZS), the Rung Sat Special Zone (RSSZ), and the Capital Military District (CMD).

During his tour of duty in 1967, Zinni experienced what amounted to five very different wars. He served with the Vietnamese Marines in the mangrove swamps and river complexes of the RSSZ; the water world of endless rice paddies, canals, and rivers of the Mekong Delta (IV CTZ); the dense, steamy jungles near the Cambodian border (III CTZ); the broad coastal plain and high mountains of the central region (II CTZ); and the complex of villages and colonial plantations that surrounded Saigon (CMD).

In his second tour of duty in 1970, he completed the circuit by serving in the northernmost zone (I CTZ—better known as I Corps).*

The enemy in each of these regions could range from first-rate North Vietnamese Army (NVA) regulars to competent mainline, or full-time, Vietcong units, to guerrilla forces of varying fighting skill. They cleverly adapted their style of fighting to the environment and local conditions to add to the uniqueness of operating in each area. The style of VNMC operations differed greatly, depending on the type units assigned to the region and their own adaptations to the area.

Zinni learned very quickly that this was a war without consistency. There was no way to reliably characterize it. In the First World War or the Korean War, there had been battle lines and fronts—one side here, the other side there. In Castro's revolution, the war had been won by guerrillas and insurgents, embedded in the people; they could be anywhere. In Vietnam, many different kinds of wars were fought.

Tony Zinni's travels allowed him to experience most of them. The experience affected him deeply.

He has thoughts on the subject:

---

* The NVA and VC also had versions of regional and district divisions that were to some extent aligned with those of the U.S. and South Vietnam.

Back in the United States, those who considered themselves knowledgeable about the war tended to call it an insurgency, with all the usual props and trappings: clandestine rather than overt operations, political actions to win hearts and minds, acts of terror and intimidation, guerrillas—workers or farmers by day, fighters by night—no fixed battle lines, skirmishes and raids rather than pitched battles.

In Vietnam, there were times when we ran into guerrilla-type actions. But there were also times when we'd find ourselves in pitched battles with regular North Vietnamese forces. In fact, in the northern parts of South Vietnam, that was more often the case than not. In the south, the reverse was more usually the case. There we were more likely to encounter guerrilla action; but even there we ran up against different kinds of war. At times, we would be dealing with farmer by day, guerrilla by night, a very different kind of situation than dealing with mainline VC units, who were full-time guerrillas. But these were very different, again, from NVA soldiers, as was the nature of the combat with them.

And then to add to the complications, each environment had its own special requirements. If you were in the Mekong Delta in the Rung Sat Special Zone, you had a much different style of fighting than you might encounter patrolling in the jungle or in the large unit engagements we had in the north, along the coast, or on the open plains. And combat was different again up in the mountains.

The geography, the nature of the enemy, the style of fighting, and even the nature of some of the units all added their own particular character to what we might encounter. All tended to create different types of wars, if you will, or a different type of the same war.

Because I experienced so many different aspects of the war, I came back with a real understanding that this war was multifaceted; everything was all over the place. There was no clear and simple way to look at it. But most Americans who served in Vietnam had perhaps a year tour and saw only one geographical area. For them it was like the blind man and the elephant. The war they saw was real, but partial.

I remember talking to Marine friends who might have been up north in I Corps, where most Marines fought. They all thought their vision of the war *was the true war. Yet I had to think, "Jeez, you saw only a small part of it." I'd have the same experience talking with an army officer who'd served in the Mekong Delta or the Parrot's Beak. Each man's definition of the war would turn out to be completely different.*

So my experience was almost unique. I didn't see every possible way the war was fought, but I saw most of it.

What all this teaches is not how to deal with every possible situation. Fighting in delta swamps teaches you how to fight in delta swamps. Fighting in triple-canopy rain forest teaches you how to fight in triple-canopy rain forests. Fighting in mountains teaches you how to fight in mountains. Fighting in flat, coastal country where there are lots of rice paddies and villages teaches you how to do that. And you learn a lot simply shooting and getting shot at a lot, and working closely with others on a combat team. But there isn't a great deal of carryover from any of that one to the other. The biggest lesson, in fact, is learning how to be open to surprising new experiences and then turning that openness into resourceful and creative ways of dealing with the challenges you face.

I was to rediscover these truths later in life when I began to be engaged in peacekeeping, humanitarian operations. After I'd gone through my first, I thought I'd learned everything there was to know about them. "These lessons apply everywhere," I told myself.

But on the second one, it hit me that few of these lessons actually apply anywhere else. The previous experience helped, sure; it put me in the right frame of mind; but it didn't tell me how to solve particular problems.

You have to be open to each new and very different reality. It's wrong to use models and to think stereotypically about problems and issues.

Tony Zinni had come a long, long way from Philadelphia. He was to travel much farther.

THE FOREST OF DEATH

After Zinni completed his orientations in Saigon, Colonel Nels Andersen, the commanding officer of the advisory unit, decided that he should not wait for a hole to open up in one of the units, but immediately go out into the field to learn the ropes with experienced advisers. It was to be Zinni's first taste of combat.

He was ordered to report to the Vietnamese Marines 4th Battalion, then conducting riverine operations in the Rung Sat Special Zone.

Rung Sat was a four-hundred-square-mile, strategically vital area southeast of Saigon—massive mangrove swamps and labyrinthine tangles of waterways. The shipping channels out of the South China Sea up to Saigon came through the Rung Sat Zone; and the Vietcong tried to interdict the shipping. They would pick people off the decks with snipers, shoot rockets or recoilless rifles at the ships, or mine the waterways—often attaching mines to ropes stretched from bank to bank. They kept it slack to let acceptable traffic pass and pulled the mines up when they spotted a target they wanted to strike.

Operating in the Rung Sat was tremendously difficult, with its tangled swamps and water levels at high tide so elevated that everything, including the villages, was under water. No place down there was dry all the time.

ADVISERS HAD "blanket" travel orders authorizing them to use any means of military transportation to get anywhere in South Vietnam if they weren't moving with a unit. Usually this involved going to a nearby air base, such as Tan Son Nhut near Saigon, where you scrounged a ride to the region closest to your unit's position. This could take days and involve a series of plane, helicopter, boat, and/or motor vehicle rides.

Even this basic knowledge didn't much help Zinni. He had no idea how to get to the Rung Sat; he'd simply been told to go there, but was so green he had no idea about the best way to go.

He eventually found himself on a Vietnamese civilian bus overloaded with men, women, kids, grandmas, chickens, and bundles of possessions. The men, women, and kids all found this lone American in a Vietnamese Marine uniform, with all his combat gear, a puzzling curiosity. Americans in Vietnam didn't travel on civilian buses.

He ended up at the gate of a small U.S./Vietnamese naval base at a place called Nha Be, not far from his destination. When he asked how to get to the 4th Battalion in the Rung Sat, he was led to the operations center, where he met the U.S. Navy operations officer.

"How did you get here?" the Navy officer asked, staring hard at Zinni, as though he had dropped out of the sky.

"I took the bus from Saigon."

"You took the bus from Saigon?" he snapped. "You want to get yourself killed? You've got to be totally nuts! That's offering yourself to the VC on a platter!" He then proceeded to chew the young lieutenant out for putting himself into such a risk.

Zinni tried to explain that he hadn't realized taking the bus was dangerous, and besides it had been a pleasant ride and he'd met some nice people.

The Navy officer shook his head in amazed disbelief; and then cracked a tolerant smile. "Fools and children . . ."

"A resupply helo makes daily runs out to the 4th Battalion," he said. "I'll get you on tomorrow's run. You're welcome to spend the night here with the other officers in their hooch."

The rest of the day Zinni met with other officers and NCOs learning about operations in the Rung Sat. They provided him with a wealth of knowledge about the local region, riverine operations, and the enemy.

Nha Be was home to U.S. and Vietnamese river patrol boat, helicopter, minesweeper, and River Assault Group (RAG) units (South Vietnamese units with U.S. advisers; the U.S. equivalent in the Mekong Delta was known as the Mobile Riverine Force). The RAGs used specially configured landing craft that were modified to move troops, control operations, and provide fire support on the complex of waterways in the southern regions of Vietnam. "Mother Ships"—really, barges—provided floating bases for these units. The Vietnamese Marines operated as the assault troops with the RAGs and had their own small boat units for these kinds of missions—high-speed fiberglass boats, called Dong Nai boats, with powerful outboard engines.

These operations were sometimes supplemented by air strikes using Vietnamese AD Skyraider aircraft. The ancient, prop-driven American planes were godsends to the guys on the ground. They carried huge loads of ordnance, remained on station for long periods, and flew slowly over targets to pinpoint their locations. Jets were sexier, but they couldn't provide anything like the long-term satisfaction.

Spotter planes were also often used to cover waterborne movements and observe the areas in front and to the flanks of the Marine movements. The natural tendency was to run these parallel to the route, but the VC watched out for this. It tipped them off to which waterway the Marines were on and to their direction of movement. The best technique was to vary the route of the planes and to run them back and forth across the waterway.

The resupply helo the next morning touched down at a small village called Tan Hiep in the middle of the mangrove swamps and river mazes that made up the Rung Sat. The village's thatched houses were perched on high stilts, with rickety ladders leading up to the doorways. Debris on the ground indicated it was low tide. Zinni couldn't imagine what high tide would bring.

The two battalion advisers, Captains Joe Hoar and Bob Hamilton, greeted him as he scrambled off the helo. Soon they were explaining that Colonel Andersen had radioed instructions to "snap Zinni in" for a few weeks; but their skeptical looks told him they were wondering what a junior lieutenant was doing here.

They took Zinni to meet the battalion commander, Major Tri, and some of his officers, including the battalion operations officer, Lieutenant Hoa Dang Nguyen. Hoa was a slender young officer, about Zinni's height (5 feet 9 inches), and a Military Academy grad. He spoke English well— as did many of the Marine officers—was very friendly, open, and outgoing . . . and very Westernized. He and Zinni hit it off instantly, and later became close friends.

Tri was just as Westernized as Hoa, but also very polished and smooth (having graduated from American military schools), and obviously intelligent. He was considered by his community to be one of their most brilliant and innovative commanders, with a more intellectual approach to less operations than some of the more instinctive, seat-of-the-pants types who'd gotten most of their experience in the field. By 1967, he had considerable combat experience and was highly decorated, including a couple of American Silver Stars. Tri was expected someday to be the commandant of the Marines.

Bob Hamilton then showed Zinni to the stilted house where he would sleep. It belonged to a hamlet chief, and the battalion doctor was also quartered there. Though Zinni could not believe this was not an imposition, the head of the house seemed genuinely happy to host him.

After he settled in, Hamilton gave him a rundown of their operations in the Rung Sat:

The mission of the Marines, he explained, was to root out the VC and keep the water routes open. The terrain was miserable, with slimy mudflats at low tide and extremely high tides that flooded virtually the entire region. Because the tangled mangroves were almost impossible to move through, travel was difficult and slow, with snakes, huge saltwater crocodiles,* and swarms of mosquitoes adding to the dangers and misery.

The tactics used by the Vietnamese Marines involved patrolling the rivers and streams, launching surprise operations from the RAG boats against suspected VC bases, interdicting and inspecting waterborne traffic, and laying in ambushes on the waterways at night. Zinni was to start going on these missions the next day.

"What do the Vietnamese expect me to do?" Zinni asked.

"Look," Hamilton replied, "you're not going to give them any tactical advice. They won't need it. But this is where you are of value to them, this is what their expectations are." He went on to explain technical matters Zinni needed to know in order to help the Vietnamese Marines in the Rung Sat—things like operating with the river assault groups, calling in artillery, calling in air support, calling in medevacs, and how all that worked.

After Hamilton left, Zinni had a hard time containing his excitement at finally seeing action.

---

* Whenever the Marines saw a croc, they'd open up fire at them. At first, Zinni thought they were killing them because they feared them. Later, he learned the skins were worth sixty dollars in Saigon. Bagging a croc was almost as good as bagging a VC.

. . .

THE NEXT MORNING brought reports that a rifle company had made contact with the VC. During the brief firefight that followed, the Marines took casualties, and the company was requesting a medical evacuation— "medevac," a U.S. medevac helo. The rule was that U.S. helos had to be under a U.S. adviser's control going into the landing zone (LZ). Though none of the advisers had gone out with the company, the pilots agreed to pick up an adviser and take care of the LZ coordinates from the air. Since none of the Vietnamese Marines on the ground spoke English, the entire affair would be managed by the adviser flying in with the medevac helos.

Hamilton and Hoar decided this was a good time for Zinni to get his feet wet.

Zinni was nervous and excited as the helos touched down and he climbed aboard. As they took off, he briefed the pilots, trying his best to act professional.

Minutes later, they were over the LZ—a muddy clearing.

The radio was crackling with excited Vietnamese chatter. Zinni did his best to respond, yelling in his best Vietnamese, trying to translate quickly, and then giving instructions in English to the pilots.

The Vietnamese popped a smoke grenade, Zinni confirmed the color,* and they headed down toward a small opening in the tangled mangrove masses below. A little closer, he saw three or four Vietcong bodies in black pajamas strewn about the LZ and the poncho-covered bodies that were dead Marines. The wounded Marines were waiting for the helo at the edge of the zone.

As they touched down, the rotor wash from the helo's blades sent debris flying. The Marines rushed to get the friendly casualties into the chopper and out of there before drawing enemy fire. The wounded were quickly loaded aboard, then the poncho-covered bodies were pushed in behind them. One landed in Zinni's lap (he was sitting on the deck in the back, by the door). As he grabbed him so he wouldn't tumble back out,

---

* Since the VC often popped smoke when they heard or saw helos, it was important to confirm color to ensure you didn't land in the wrong place.

the poncho flew open to reveal the pale gray-green corpse. They rapidly lifted off and headed for the evacuation hospital, with Zinni still holding the body, his eyes locked on the dead and wounded Marines. Halfway back he realized that his hand was still clutching the radio handset. He replaced it in its holder.

Cradling a dead body on the deck of the helo and staring at the bandaged and bleeding troops brought the war home for the first time. The high adventure he had imagined had a nasty side.

During the following days, Zinni went on several night missions with the Dong Nai boats and the River Assault Group craft, setting up ambushes. Some of these were successful; and in one instance they nailed a pair of VC sniper teams carrying Russian sniper rifles, scopes, and special ammunition in brand-new leather cases.

ZINNI WAS in the Rung Sat from April 3 to April 21. He then received orders to report to the 5th Battalion in Binh Dinh Province (II CTZ) and Operation Pershing—the most fiercely contested of Vietnamese Marine combat operations. He was there three times: April 24 to May 13; June 20 to August 10; and November 8 to December 13.

By the midpoint of his second assignment to Binh Dinh Province— sometime toward the end of June—Tony Zinni had become technically proficient in the arts of combat.

These skills came from several sources: from the day in, day out experience of the firefights themselves—calling in medevacs, calling in artillery and air, coordinating with U.S. units, and doing it over and over again under great stress; learning from the more seasoned and experienced advisers (like Joe Hoar and Bob Hamilton); learning from the Vietnamese Marines, especially in those tactical operations they performed well; and finally, from his own passion for mastering the arts of war. He *really* wanted to figure out what went on in combat. When he got into firefights—especially firefights with North Vietnamese or hard-core Vietcong units—he was fighting an enemy who possessed tremendous fighting skills. They were a tough enemy (not ragtag, like the Iraqi Army). Trying to take this war apart, figuring out what worked and what gave his guys the advantage, meant imagining how somebody on the other side—a North Vietnamese captain or other commander—was deciding how *he* could get the advantage. It was a contest of wills, intellects, and experience. "What is he thinking? What is he trying to do? What do I need to do to outguess him, to outplay him on this field?"

By the end of his tours in Vietnam, Zinni had become a master of the combat arts.

OPERATION PERSHING

Though several factors made operations in Binh Dinh Province more difficult than in other areas, the worst of these were the deadly booby traps found virtually everywhere in the province. The VC were masters of every kind of booby trap, from the sophisticated to the makeshift; and for reasons that remain mysterious to Zinni, the Vietnamese Marines were especially vulnerable to them. Despite their well-demonstrated field skills and understanding of their enemy, the majority of Vietnamese Marine casualties suffered on Operation Pershing came from booby traps. In one instance, twenty-two Marines, including an adviser, were killed or wounded at a stream crossing where the VC had put in a "daisy chain" string of explosives under remote control.

The VC especially liked to rig booby traps along trails, paths, streams, and other likely movement lines. Sometimes small signs would warn other VC or civilians friendly to their cause. Zinni and his companions learned to watch for these—rocks or twigs arranged on a path or bent trees near a stream crossing, or the like. And they tried to avoid trails and obvious lines of communication. Since booby traps and the kill zones of ambushes tended to be oriented along these lines of movement, the best tactic was not to travel parallel to them but to zigzag across, always approaching from right angles. Zigzagging permitted the Marines to come in behind these positions.

Trails and streams were always crossed as danger areas, following a predetermined and rehearsed drill: The point signaled the trail ahead; a machine gun or automatic rifle was positioned to cover the crossing; the far side was checked; and when there was a "clear to go" signal, the

Marines crossed in teams. The drill could be more elaborate for larger danger areas, such as clearings or paddies.

At one trench, hedgerow,* and trail complex in an area loaded with booby traps, it was decided to go one at a time. When Zinni's turn came, he ran and jumped the trench, but as he landed, he felt his boot drag across a wire. He immediately went limp, hit the ground, and flattened out as a muffled explosion detonated behind him. He wasn't hit, he realized, to his immense relief. But when he looked back into the dust-filled trench, he noticed movement at the bottom. A Marine was lying there, one of the company cooks, in obvious pain, his face mangled. Since they were crossing one at a time, he should not have been there; but he had rushed across right on Zinni's heels, contrary to instructions.

Though he had taken a blast in his upper body, remarkably he was still alive. He'd been carrying a small cage with two doves in it, no doubt dinner. The doves were unharmed.

Zinni and other nearby Marines jumped into the trench to help him. Zinni then called in a medevac, but did not hold out much hope, since the man was bleeding badly from both eyes.

Several months later, Zinni learned that he had survived, though with the loss of his eyes.

At another path crossing one day, Zinni stepped into a shallow, camouflaged pit. He tensed, expecting sharp bamboo stakes to pierce his foot; but nothing happened. Puzzled but relieved, he climbed out, and the camouflage was cleared away, revealing the real nature of this booby trap—though fortunately, its shelf life had expired. At the bottom of the pit was a small dead snake, a krait, one of the most poisonous of all the vipers. (There had been no food in the pit, and it could not climb the pit's sheer walls.)

The VC also placed booby traps in likely helicopter landing zones, making heliborne assaults sporty and medevacs dangerous. Since the American adviser ran the medevacs, Zinni had to check out the zones to ensure they were safe for the helicopters. He always performed this task with great care, concentration, and gingerly placed steps.

---

* The Vietcong often dug trench lines behind the hedgerows that frequently bordered trails, leaving them there as ready-made ambush spots.

In placing booby traps, the VC did not distinguish combatants from noncombatants. Any kind of cooperation was punished. Civilians who assisted Vietnamese forces less often came home to bombs set to go off at their arrival. Even civilians required to gather in designated areas for processing of identification paperwork or for government information programs might find explosive devices in their homes or villages. Since the processing was compulsory, the ordinary people were once again caught between a rock and a hard place.

THEIR SUSCEPTIBILITY to booby traps aside, the Vietnamese Marines were masters of fieldcraft.

The Vietnamese Marines traveled light. They lived off the land, partly out of necessity and partly out of the importance they placed on being light and mobile like the enemy. This points out the most significant difference between the Vietnamese Marines and their American allies.

Americans always took it for granted that the full might of America was behind them. Not only did they expect to get three squares a day, but American units always operated under the conviction that, no matter what, they would somehow get bailed out and that American firepower would prevail. Sure, there might be an occasion where you got stranded for a while before help came, but eventually help was going to get to you—rescue, firepower, or logistics.

The Vietnamese Marines did not have that certainty. They never knew if they were going to eat on any particular day. When they got in a firefight, there was no guarantee that the cavalry was going to come and save them. They knew they had to fight with what they had.

Thus they had no use for the heavy loads American soldiers carried, and their carelessness with weapons and supplies; and they were happy to do without the daily helo resupply lifts that gave away positions.

The Vietnamese Marines were masters of make-dos and work-arounds. They ingeniously prepared fighting positions, living facilities, early warning alarms, and many other needs from what was available in the bush. A premium was placed on quick reaction and agility on enemy contact. They were well aware of these qualities in the enemy they faced.

Their gear was not only light but practical. They slept in nylon hammocks tied with nylon cord, compact enough to fit into the cargo pocket of their tiger-striped field uniform. The U.S. jungle hammock, by contrast, was heavy and bulky and totally unsuitable for the field. Cooking stoves were small and made of lightweight aluminum, as were their food containers. Their packs were the original rucksacks that made stowing and carrying gear easy for infantry units on the move. They rarely wore flak jackets and preferred camouflaged soft hats rather than helmets, especially on patrols. Light, loose-fitting nylon rain gear was often purchased by the Marines to replace the heavy rubberized U.S. ponchos they were issued. They did, however, cherish the soft American poncho liner, which, along with the jungle boot, was probably the best piece of gear to come out of the Vietnam War.

Their weapons were a hodgepodge of World War Two American small arms, mortars, machine guns, recoilless rifles, and artillery pieces. These included M-1 rifles, carbines, submachine guns, and other vintage weapons.

During Zinni's tour in 1967, the VNMC received the M-16 rifle and M-60 machine gun, but the process was closely controlled by the U.S. The policy was that no Vietnamese units could get them until every American unit had them, and then the Marines and airborne units would be the first to receive them. In reality, the Vietnamese already had a few M-60 machine guns before they were officially supposed to get them. They'd either been captured from the enemy or scrounged from U.S. units by the advisers.

Reports of the M-16's unreliability preceded its arrival. The plan was to pull the VNMC battalions back, one at a time, to the national training center for two weeks to switch weapons and go through a training program on the new rifle.

U.S. Marines brought the weapons to the center and oversaw the delivery and training. But just as the first units to receive the new rifles began their training, an emergency developed in the Mekong Delta area. The units were pulled out and sent to engage a large enemy force there, even before they had actually fired their new weapons (they'd barely gotten the first classes on care and cleaning). They performed brilliantly, defeating a tough force in fierce fighting. The fact that no weapons jammed or malfunctioned drew considerable attention from the U.S.

military command; and an investigation was launched. But the explanation was simple: The Vietnamese Marines cleaned their weapons. They were meticulous—almost obsessed—with weapons care, often complaining to Zinni about American carelessness with weapons and equipment.

They were just as meticulous about fire discipline. They were, for example, masters at hiding their crew-served weapons and not opening up in response to probes by North Vietnamese or mainline VC units (the idea was to get them to fire so they could pick out the key weapons they needed to take out).

The emphasis on care and conservation carried over to most other areas.

Like all Vietnamese, the Vietnamese Marines enjoyed the midday break. Unless operational necessity demanded otherwise, they would stop to string up their hammocks for a couple of hours during the hottest part of the day for a noon siesta. But they also took care to rest at any other time that offered itself. Whenever possible, they conserved resources, strength, and the energy of the unit.

Their endurance was remarkable. They could walk all day, day after day. But they were not especially strong. Rather, they tried to pace themselves and conserve energy.

American commanders were all in a hurry. They wanted to end the war on their one-year tour of duty. Vietnamese commanders realized they would be in it for the duration. Though they never backed down or failed to fight bravely, they did weigh risks carefully and approach battle methodically. Plunging headlong into battle, as Americans liked to do, was not an option for the Vietnamese.

Zinni had this truth pressed home on an operation in II CTZ. Here is how he remembers it:

It was summer, and our VNMC battalion had been operating for weeks in an area astride Highway 1 when we pulled back for a much-needed day of rest in a village along the highway. The battalion commander, the senior adviser, and most of the officers and troops went to a nearby city for an R & R break, while I stayed behind with the units that were the designated security element. The battalion operations officer, a lieutenant, was the officer in charge. He was a bright young officer and we had become instant friends.

On one hot summer day, with the stay-behind troops resting, cleaning equipment, or manning the small security guard, an excited, very animated woman came running up to our location.

"The VC are holding a meeting with local communist bigwigs in a nearby hamlet west of the highway," she cried.

"We have to go get them," I told the ops officer.

He was not so sure. All the commanders were gone and this was a big decision for him, especially since he only had bits and pieces of units available for the mission.

But he was an aggressive officer, and I knew I could get him to go. And that's what happened. We quickly grabbed a group of Marines, saddled them up, and charged off.

As luck would have it, we caught the VC as they were leaving the hamlet after their meeting broke up. A running, chaotic gun battle followed, as we chased them into the countryside. The chase went on for several hours, and we moved farther and farther into the brushy foothills west of the highway.

During the pursuit, we managed to capture one VC and could tell from the blood trails that we had hit others. But in our excitement and enthusiasm we failed to realize how far we were moving from our base of operations. Enemy fire was also picking up, and the terrain was becoming more rugged. Though I didn't realize it then, it was becoming distinctly possible that we would be drawn into a trap.

Eventually, we received a radio call from the obviously angry battalion commander, ordering us to break off contact and return to the base area.

On the way back, I realized I had put my Vietnamese lieutenant buddy in a bad position. He was not looking forward to seeing the battalion CO.

And sure enough, the commander had harsh words for him, and likewise my senior adviser had harsh words for me. Though I was upset that we'd had to break contact, I kept quiet about that. Instead, I tried to take the fall for the action, and explained that I had convinced my friend to go.

Later, the battalion commander asked to speak to me privately. He was a highly decorated officer, tactically brilliant and courageous; and I had great respect for him.

"Look," he explained to me, "my unit is not a U.S. Marine unit. It's smaller and less capable, we don't have a steady stream of replacements flowing into it, and I can't rely on the formidable arsenal of firepower that U.S. units have at their disposal.*

"My troops," he continued, "have fought for years; they'll fight for many more; and the enemy will still be there tomorrow. All of this means I have to carefully choose where and when I take risks that might bring me a disadvantage on the battlefield.†

"This is not," he explained, "a matter of courage, aggressiveness, or fighting spirit; and I hope you've seen enough of those qualities in my Marines to know that wasn't the issue."

In this, I totally agreed with him. And I also fully understood all of his very valid points. Yet privately the U.S. Marine in me still found it difficult to pass up an opportunity to mix it up with the enemy, regardless of the circumstances.

"Do you have any idea why the VC didn't break contact and fade into the countryside?" he then asked me. "After all, they're masters of that sort of tactic."

It was a good question. As I thought back on the firefight and chase, I realized how easy it would have been for them to break off the fight. Instead, they stayed engaged. They'd take a few shots, and then withdraw, leaving easy signs to follow.

That was when it dawned on me that we'd been in danger of getting lured out into the hinterland, far from our base and support, where they had forces positioned to ambush us.

"You're right," I admitted. "We were brash to chase them. But please be aware that doing it was my fault. Don't take it out on your operations officer."

---

* U.S. assets went to U.S. units as the first priority.
† The same was true of the enemy. Something like eighty-five percent of contacts were initiated by the VC or NVA. They always tried to fight on their own terms and to refuse battle whenever it wasn't to their advantage to engage.

"Don't worry," he said with a smile. "I'm satisfied that two young lieu-tenants learned something . . . without serious consequences, for a change."

In time, Zinni became an expert in firefights and had a wealth of other experience about how to move in a fight, how to conduct a patrol, how to cross a road, how to deal with snipers in trees, how to build alert systems with bamboo and vine (the bamboo would clap). He became a collector of these techniques.

He quickly discovered that many of the techniques he had been taught were wrong—lessons learned from old wars. He had a passion to get such things right. The best fighting techniques bring an obvious advantage; they can keep you alive. But Zinni was also a committed professional. The best military leaders will play their units as the best conductors play an orchestra, blending and focusing disparate elements into a single, splen-did "sound." However this was done, Zinni wanted to practice and per-fect it.

He has further thoughts on this:

Right from the beginning of my Marine Corps career, what most fascinated me as we would engage in tactical problems during field exercises is that it was all about facing an enemy, trying as hard as he could to do to us what we wanted to do to him. . . . You didn't just go into a patch of woods and that's it, like a hiker. There's an enemy somewhere in there, and here you are try-ing to use everything you know, have learned, and have trained for, in order to reach your aims . . . and stop him from reaching his.

You don't get much more real than that.

I've always had a theoretical understanding of sports—offense and de-fense, how you organize plays, and what you're trying to do. But, of course, the theory is one thing, and playing is another.

And in a firefight, you're experiencing much higher levels of complication and risk—all the bullets flying, the rounds, the explosions, the confusion—and you're trying to figure it out, trying to move quickly on a course of ac-tion that makes sense, and keeps you and your buddies alive.

What's really going on? How do you organize yourself? How do you apply

*the fires? How do you move against your enemy? What are the techniques
you need to use?*

*For example, if you're out in the woods, and you're trying to find your
enemy, you don't want him to find you. What techniques will best bring that
outcome? What do you need to know?*

*I was always really interested in learning everything I could about that.
I've always been a collector of small-unit fighting techniques. It's always fascinated me . . . consumed me. I'm a Catholic. In my faith, we think of the
priesthood as a calling—a "vocation," requiring total dedication. I looked at
the "call to arms" the same way. The warrior profession is a calling, and requires the same kind of dedication the priesthood does. That meant that I read
books about it—history books about small unit warfare, books about Burma,
Malaya, and Vietnam before our war (places where the fighting was similar
to what we were experiencing).*

*Some of what I picked up from books, or from my instructors, turned out
to be bogus. Even before I went to Vietnam, it didn't make sense to me; it
didn't seem natural; it didn't jive with what was really likely to happen. I don't
know where the people came up with it.*

*And then when I got out there in, say, the II CTZ, we were doing it for
real; and a lot of what I'd been taught made even less sense.*

*But there I couldn't have had better teachers. I would watch the Viet-
namese, who of course had incredible battlefield experience, and I was able
to see how they did things and really analyze their technique.*

*One great thing about being an adviser: You're not commanding the troops.
Sure, you're busy; you have to be ready to apply fires and all the other responsibilities advisers had. But you also have a lot of opportunity just to observe, from a semidetached point of view. You could watch how the fighters
moved, you could listen to what they were saying. And since you weren't directly caught up in the action, you could think through it and analyze it.*

*Later, I'd ask the seasoned veterans about it: "Why did you do this?" and
"What do you think about this?" And they would talk to me about their experiences.*

*It was from this seed in low-level tactics that my career started to grow,
eventually leading to the construction of multinational strategies at CENT-*

COM and elsewhere where I'd be dealing with a part of the world where we were trying to develop a military relationship and a military policy.

One especially vital type of tactical knowledge is what we might call the "sense of a firefight." That is, the sense from sound and visual cues of what is actually happening when the bullets are flying. Closely allied to that is a sense of what you have to do to respond and act. These can only be learned from experience. Tony Zinni also has further thoughts on this:

Though I had a lot of operational experiences from the beginning of my time with the Vietnamese Marines, it took about three months into my tour before I was at a level of competency where I had a real "sense of a firefight."

At first, when there was shooting, it was a cacophony of sounds to me. I didn't know what was going on. I had no idea whether I was in World War Three or a small firefight. At the beginning, I wasn't even sure which direction the firing was coming from.

But by the end of three months, I could tell which kinds of weapons were firing, where they were firing from, and about how far away they were. I could also get a pretty good sense of what was happening by the way the firing was taking place: Was somebody just taking potshots? Or was the firing building up to a larger engagement? Was the enemy going to stand and hold in place (and all the implications of that)? Or were they simply going to engage us and then try to move away?

By three months, I could quickly process situations like these with just a few sensings.

Something similar goes on with really good athletes when the play is really intense.

I remember going to a playoff football game in which the Miami Dolphins were playing San Diego. I had a really great seat right down near the field, which gave me the best possible visibility; and I was able to observe Dan Marino, one of the greatest quarterbacks ever, at the very height of his powers. The San Diego quarterback (I forget his name) was a good, solid player, but he was several rungs down from Dan Marino.

Very often, Marino would come out of the huddle, go up to the line, and call an audible. You'd expect he would take a panning scan over the entire defense before he did that. But he didn't work that way. He'd look at one guy in the defense and then make his call—and it was almost always the best call he could have made.

The other quarterback, though, would come up to look over the defense the way you'd expect. He'd have to look all over the place before he could make his decision. And I thought, "Dan Marino has reached a level of expertise that allows him to key on only one thing, and from that picks up what he needs to know. He has a much greater 'sensing' ability than the other quarterback."

This has analogies with combat: The more experience you've got, the larger is your inventory of pattern analysis that allows you to pick up on what you need to know; and like Marino, you can make a solid decision based on a very few key indicators, rather than having to try to mentally process a complex or even chaotic set of inputs. So after I'd had sufficient experiences of firefights, I was able to process one or two indicators fairly quickly and come up with a satisfactory course of action.

I have to add that the kind of sensing I'm talking about is not just a matter of experience. It also involves understanding what you were sensing. There's a strong analytical component, involving reading, research, and applied intelligence. If you don't have a background of knowledge and understanding that allows you to appreciate these "sensings," you might undergo these experiences and miss everything they're trying to offer you. For example: Now that I know I'm hearing an AK-47 and not an M-16, I need to judge from the pattern of firing whether this is somebody who's just taking a couple of random shots and moving away or somebody who's hanging in there in a fixed position and plans to stay.

How is it that I can judge that the firing is coming from five hundred and not two hundred yards (in the beginning I couldn't tell you if it was twenty or two thousand)? The answer: You estimate by means of the flash-bang method (as we called it): There's a delay between the flash of a firing weapon and the bang. As soon as you see the flash, you begin counting seconds— 1001, 1002, 1003. You then use a formula you've learned that lets you determine the distance of the weapon.

Why do sounds seem much closer at night? The answer: Because of at-

mospheric conditions and because activity levels are lower, creating less interference from white noise.

I gathered in information like this wherever I could find it—from reading, from Vietnamese Marines, from other advisers, from training.

There were times of course when what I'd learned did not compute with my own experience, and I had to come up with a different solution.

One example: In training, we were always told when you see a flare pop at night, you freeze. You don't move. When they pop the flare, they're looking for motion. When they detect it, they have your location.

This didn't make sense to me. Your natural instinct is to go to ground and take cover. "Follow your instincts, go to ground," I told myself. "Better they detect a motion but I end up under cover than me sitting there sweating and thinking, 'Hope he didn't see me.' "

You also have to understand that there are different kinds of flares, each sending a different kind of message: A hand flare or a grenade flare tells you something different from an artillery flare—though they all illuminate. An illumination grenade or a hand flare tells you your enemy is fairly close to you and he's shooting it because he expects something, he heard something, or thought he heard something, so his senses are up. What do you do? Get your butt down.

My own processing of this information led me to a different conclusion from the one I received in training.

Later, I became directly involved in improving Marine Corps training—challenging much of what I had learned. I made several videotapes that are still used at basic school. Some validated what I'd been taught and some didn't.

Zinni's plunge into Vietnam was not confined to military operations. Along with his Vietnamese Marine companions he lived much of the time with ordinary Vietnamese in their villages and hamlets. Vietnam had a quartering law that required the people to allow troops operating in their area to move into their houses. This was not the burden on the people that it might seem. The Marines didn't take a place over and throw people out of their houses. They treated the local people with respect, paying for their food and helping with the village chores. (The country-bred troops especially enjoyed helping out with the familiar tasks that reminded them of their own home villages.)

But for Zinni, moving into somebody else's home was initially hard to get used to; he thought of it as an imposition and an intrusion. But after he saw that the villagers seemed to accept it, and in most cases welcome it, he began to overcome his own discomfort and realize that the kid from Philadelphia was onto a very positive thing. In time, he came to a further realization that all the hardships and extremes he and his companions had to endure were worth his interactions with the Vietnamese people.

HERE ARE some memories of life in the villages—and of related encounters with the enemy:

Rarely did my contemporaries serving with U.S. units ever get to really know the Vietnamese; and then they viewed them with suspicion and even contempt. But living among the people gave me long-lasting insights into a very rich and wonderful culture . . . and into the impact of so many terrible decades of war and suffering.

When I'd talk with families at meals or during their daily chores, I always found them warm and friendly, yet shy, polite, and reserved. But once I took time to get to know them, they opened up. Making friends was harder, since they didn't make friends easily. In their eyes, friendship was a serious long-term commitment—not lightly undertaken. But once you made a Vietnamese friend, you had a friend for life.

Where the war touched them, they were enigmatic and stoic. I never encountered self-pity; and this was hard to get used to. Where did they find the resources to stoically accept the pain and anguish I often saw them endure? Why did they so rarely show emotion even after the most traumatic experiences?

Though American units passed through the villages in large numbers, there was little contact. Neither the Americans nor the Vietnamese wanted it. So a lone American taking up residence in a Vietnamese village was a novelty—a curiosity to be checked out. In fact, the local kids were often initially unsure if I was real. They liked to give me a poke, to test if I was.

Though I always had a wonderful time with the Vietnamese, and was al-

ways treated with respect, it was hard to know what they thought of Americans in general or of our part in their conflict.

One memorable insight into that came during a warm, friendly conversation with the family of a village chief (I was sharing his house). It was a welcome cool evening in a picturesque hamlet, and we were sitting outside the house after an enjoyable meal.

"Show me pictures of your family and of your house in the USA," the chief's wife, an elderly lady, asked. "Do you have any?"

All I had was a picture of my wife and me taken in front of her parents' home. I pulled it out, the old lady stared at it for a while, and then she looked up at me with a deeply penetrating expression.

"Why are you here in Vietnam?" she asked me.

I gave her the standard answer about stopping communism and protecting democracy and our Vietnamese allies.

She shook her head. "It's sad that you have to leave your family and get involved in this tragic mess," she said.

I continued to offer the party line.

"But what are you going to do to protect us from 'them'?" she asked, her hand pointing toward the south.

At first I thought she had made a mistake—the enemy was to the north, after all. But then I realized she was saying exactly what she meant to say. She was talking about the corrupt South Vietnamese government. As far as she was concerned, the enemy was both to the north and to the south.

These people, I was just coming to understand, were trapped between two options, both bad. And that was when I began to realize that the "center of gravity"* was the people . . . and that winning hearts and minds was not just a slogan; it was the only route to winning the war.

Meanwhile, they had to do whatever they could to survive.

EVENTUALLY, the winning of hearts and minds was thought to be important enough to engage the Vietnamese Marines in it—engaged specifically in running pacification programs in the II CTZ. The mission involved going into

---

* Clausewitz's term for the key capability of a combatant. Without it, he loses.

villages to ID, interrogate, and win over the population with civic action projects; and the Marines did not initially warm to it. They thought of themselves as fighters and not civic action wimps.

Usually the operation entailed setting up a "county fair." They'd put up a series of tents, booths, and stations where the questioning and identification processes were mixed in with medical treatment, food distribution, and entertainment. Some political propaganda was also added in order to win "hearts and minds."

It turned out that the people actually enjoyed these events, and the Marines soon learned the benefits of these efforts, became more receptive to them, and actually enjoyed running the fairs. Most of the Marines were kids from the country and villages. They liked connecting with folks who were very like themselves. And as time went on, the Marines developed a positive relationship with most of the population in II CTZ.

This did not please the VC, who began to threaten villagers who participated in the fairs.

But despite the intimidation, more and more villagers began to come forward and provide intelligence on enemy activity.

In one incident, a mother in a remote village brought her baby—its face hugely swollen—to a medical station we'd set up. When it turned out that the Marines' medical personnel weren't equipped to handle the baby's infected abscess, she was brought to me.

I called the U.S. Army unit nearby, and they agreed to arrange a medevac and treatment at a hospital in the city of Qui Nhon. The anxious and frightened mother and baby, together with an aunt, were then assembled in the landing zone to wait for the chopper. By the time the helo was actually touching down, they were on the edge of panic. The mother immediately squatted down and peed right there, with the shocked helo crew looking on. But then she somehow mustered up the courage to scramble onto the helicopter. And off they went. Though I wished them well, they quickly slipped out of my mind.

Several months later, I was again in this village, but now with a company from another battalion.

The company commander told me a lady from the village wanted to see me. And I said, "Sure," though I had forgotten all about the incident.

But when the lady approached us, proudly showing off her now chubby, healthy baby, I immediately recognized her, and I was of course pleased and happy for her as she thanked us for saving her baby. She then chatted with me about the care she'd received and her trip back to this remote village. Later, as she got ready to leave and was about to say good-bye, she turned to me: "There are VC hiding in tunnels nearby," she whispered, "and I'll show you where."

We immediately mustered the troops and went to the location she pointed out to us, just outside the village. There we found the camouflaged entrance to a large underground complex.

As we began to clear the complex, we realized there were people inside. Our troops talked them out by threatening to blow up the holes.

Soon—to my amazement—a group of VC emerged, clad in pinkish uniforms. They turned out to be a regimental medical unit whose aid station was located in the tunnel complex. And then by some kind of wild coincidence that was not really surprising, once you thought about it, our battalion doctor recognized the VC doctor. They'd both attended medical school in France together and had once been friends. A friendly lunch and chat followed (strange but interesting to me), with the old friends bringing each other up to date about their lives and careers since they'd last seen each other. At the end of the meal, friendly good-byes and handshakes were exchanged; and the VC were handcuffed and moved out as POWs.

As they moved off, I recalled that similar events had occurred in our own Civil War.

THE VC and NVA were masters at constructing well-hidden underground tunnel systems. We discovered elaborate networks connecting large, furnished subterranean rooms, fully equipped with handmade cloth gas masks with charcoal filters, and carefully booby-trapped dead-end wings.

When the deep rice paddies dried up in summer, the entrances to some of these complexes, submerged during the rainy season, would often be exposed.

We once stopped for a noon break and meal by one of the deep paddies where a tunnel entrance was visible near one of its corners, big enough to walk into standing up. Since it was the dry season and the entrance was ex-

posed, we assumed the tunnel was empty. But while we rested, some of the Marines began poking around the entrance, and then suddenly became alerted when they detected noises from inside. We quickly surrounded the opening and ordered whoever was inside to come out. After some coaxing and threatening, we got an agreement to surrender; and out of the entrance came two young men dressed in sharply pressed khaki uniforms, with close-cropped haircuts. One was a NVA lieutenant and the other an NCO [noncommissioned officer]. When the lieutenant spotted me, he called the NCO to attention and snapped me a very sharp salute. And to the delight of the Marines, I returned it. The two were then taken off as POWs.

Other captures were much tougher. In the following, the VC tried to hide among fishermen on a lake, using them as human shields:

The area along the coast of Binh Dinh Province was filled with lakes, tidal inlets, and swamps, with fishing villages all around them. (Many of the villages in the area had been abandoned because of the resettlement program.) Since the availability of food and the population concentration made the area a favored objective of the VC, we never had any problems making contact with the enemy. We ran any number of sweeps in the region and never failed to end up in a firefight.

One day we had a big one on the Dam Tra O, the region's major lake.

During a major sweep two of our battalions were conducting with the 1st Cav, we got into a running gun battle as we pushed eastward toward the lake with the lead element of our battalion. The other battalion was moving toward the lake from the south.

As we closed on the lake, rapidly forcing the VC toward the water, we could clearly see that we'd trapped them in one of the swamps. There was no way they could slip out to our flanks. Their only way out was into the lake.

When we made our initial contact, the Cav sent us an observer helicopter and a gunship (called a "a Silver Team"). They came on scene as we reached the villages near the water. I directed them over to the swamp where we'd last seen the VC, and they spotted several of them lying in the shallow water breathing through hollow reeds. The gunship fired into the water and killed a number of VC; and the others there surrendered to us. But the ma-

jority of the VC had reached the lakeshore, grabbed boats, and moved to the center of the huge lake, mingling with the civilian fishing boats.

We then gathered on the shore to decide what to do. As we were talking, I could hear on our radio net the senior adviser from the battalion to our south calling in an artillery fire mission—a VT (variable time fuse) mission, meaning the rounds would explode overhead and rain deadly shrapnel on the boats. I immediately jumped on the radio and called a check fire. "Wait a minute," I shouted into the mike, "you can't call in artillery. These are innocent people out there. The VC have gone in among fishermen. If they try to get away, the VC will shoot them." While I was doing this, the VNMC company commander with me was pleading with his own chain of command not to fire.

This brought on a heated argument with the other adviser, a captain, who kept insisting that the boats were all VC. Since I was a lieutenant, it was a touchy moment. Soon a task force adviser, a major, came on the net to sort it out.

Meanwhile, dozens of panicked civilians had crowded along the shore, all anxious about their relatives out on the boats. "These are our fathers, our brothers, out there fishing," they kept pleading. "They're not Vietcong."

Even when I pointed that out to the major, he seemed to be leaning toward the captain's version. At that point, since I was sort of a wiseass anyhow, I let it all hang out. "I've got to tell you, sir, if we shoot this mission, in my mind we're killing a lot of innocents, and I'm on record for that."

"So do you have any other ideas?"

When I threw this question at the VNMC company commander, he knew what had to be done: "My men will go out in boats and get the VC," he answered.

This was dangerous, but he and his troops did not want to see innocents killed. When I passed on the proposal, the adviser from the other battalion broke in to say that he and his Vietnamese counterpart didn't think much of it.

"Stay out of it," I told him. "It's not your ass on the line."

I knew I would pay for that comment, but I didn't care.

Though I knew that a lieutenant can never be sure he is doing the right thing when he's challenged by seniors, I'd already run into a number of situations like this, when my only recourse was to stand up for what my gut told me was right and take the flak for it. After seeing the results of doubting myself and backing down, I'd sworn I would never cave in once I'd reached down inside and determined that what I needed to do felt right.

Though this position did not endear me to the others on the radio, no one was ready to challenge me.

As the Marines began to climb into the boats, my mind fixed on the likelihood that many of them would be killed or wounded in this risky attack. Even though the Marines assured me we were doing the right thing, and I certainly agreed with them, I knew that any deaths would be on my conscience.

What unfolded next was just amazing—a scene right out of a pirate movie.

The Marines sailed onto the lake. Soon they'd chased down the VC boats, started firing, and then boarded them. Moments later, they'd taken down every enemy boat and killed or captured every single VC . . . all without a single Marine or civilian casualty.

Afterward, a few prisoners suddenly fell "very ill" with a high mortality rate disease. Our Marines were not happy they had used civilians as human shields.

By then I'd experienced dozens of incidents that made me proud of these courageous fighters, but this one definitely made the top of the list.

BECAUSE OF the demonstrated competence and fighting ability of VNMC units, American commanders gave them ever tougher jobs. In July, U.S. units in II CTZ began moving their operations out toward the Western Highlands, where there was especially heavy fighting, leaving the coastal plain more exposed. This move was feasible only because the VNMC were available to pick up much of the action.

II CTZ headquarters specifically proposed that the Marines begin more aggressive night operations (promising full support, to include helicopter lift and fire support—a big plus in the eyes of the Marines). The Vietnamese were game for that.

The proposed operations involved a series of night helo raids, to be triggered by hot intelligence . . . a challenging but exciting mission for the VNMC (we had no night vision goggles then). It also excited me. By then I *was confident I had my act together where fighting was concerned. I had be-come good at it.*

We ended up conducting four of these raids. I was the adviser on three of them, but only one resulted in enemy contact.

That raid began on the twenty-fifth of July with an urgent call from U.S. Army command: A hot intelligence tip claimed that a squad-sized VC unit was moving a U.S. Army POW through the villages, using him for propaganda and recruiting. Army command thought a well-conducted raid might successfully rescue him. Since we were the only unit able to react quickly enough, we were tapped to conduct it.

The Army immediately sent an intel team to brief us: The tip had come from a local villager who had additionally reported that the VC squad was heading for a deserted village along the coast to spend the night. The intel team were not certain about the accuracy of the tip, but it seemed worth a serious follow-up. They then provided a description of the prisoner and his suspected identity.

We quickly began planning.

Raid planning had to be very precise and exacting, taking deception into account (we knew the VC were watching), and intel had to be very good. We worked hard on all this.

We decided on a raid force of eighty Marines. In order to deceive watch-ers, this force would move as part of a larger unit headed out that day for a routine relief of one of our mountain village outposts. The raid force would peel off from the larger unit in a remote area of the bush on the approach to the mountain villages and wait at a prearranged landing zone for night pickup by U.S. choppers. We coordinated all this with the pilots to minimize their time on the ground in the remote landing zone.

In those days we didn't yet have M-16s, so we took Thompson submachine guns, grease guns, carbines—all automatic weapons—with extra ammo mag-azines, to ensure plenty of firepower for this relatively small force operating in very hostile territory. We wanted to make the raid as violent as possible. Our idea was to really shock them, hit them fast when they were sleeping (or so we hoped), and just open up. Machine guns would cover our flanks.

We knew the deserted village that was our objective from previous sweeps in the area. It was on the coast of the South China Sea and had a several-

hundred-foot-high rocky ridge projecting out into the water to its north. We decided to land the helos up on the rocks; small, cleared areas there could take one helo at a time; and landing on the side of the ridge away from the village would mask the noise. We could then climb down the rocks and attack the village from the sea side—an unexpected route. (We were assuming that the enemy would be orienting their defenses inland.) There was one potential problem: Though we could cut off the north-south routes out of the village (the routes along the coast), we could not do much to cover escape routes to the west, which went out into vast, open rice paddies that led to more villages and wooded areas. Since our assault was going in from east to west, we didn't want to put teams out west of the town into our potential fire zones. Instead, we hoped to put teams quickly into the western side of the village. This was another reason for instant violence. Without that, the VC might be able to melt away into the paddies.

The move out and helo lift went perfectly. The pilots flew well out to sea (thus promoting surprise) and came into the ridge area from the north as planned. We did have problems when some of the LZs proved too small for a helo landing, requiring troops to jump out of the helos from four or five feet up. A few of the guys got a little banged up with twisted ankles and the like, but not enough to take them out of action.

Our climb down the jagged rocks was tricky and painfully slow, but everyone got down with only a few bruises and cuts and moved quickly to our objective rallying point at the base of the rocks. From there we dispatched the four-man security teams that would cut off the village from the north and south. To avoid premature discovery, we tried to synchronize our movements to place the security teams and the assault force in position at the same time.

I moved with the attack force down the beach toward a long, north-south-running sand dune we were using as our line of deployment. This was an ideal place for launching the assault. It was about a hundred meters from the edge of the village and allowed us to come up on line for the attack from a covered and concealed position, with the crashing surf providing noise cover.

Things went well as we moved to our release points and began coming on line at the base of the dune. I hoped both of our main assumptions were correct—that the enemy's defense would be oriented inland and that we were facing only a squad-sized unit.

Both assumptions were wrong.

We weren't facing a squad but a reinforced company; and their defense was either oriented toward the sea or out over a full 360 degrees.

We crossed the crest of the sand dune and slowly started down, waiting for the signal to start the assault—the firing of the machine guns on our flanks. This was to lead us by fire to the edge of the village, then the machine guns would displace forward to join the attack and protect our flanks.

But before that happened, the enemy spotted us and opened up with machine guns and everything else they had. We immediately responded and went into the assault.

As we raced down the dune firing away, I saw the enemy tracers streaming over our heads, flying everywhere. Too many for just a squad, I realized. I also realized that their defense was facing the sea . . . and us. I could tell it was a well-organized defense, with the fires interlocking—a wall of flame, not something you want to move into—but, fortunately, all the fire was high. This can happen when a defense is oriented on a piece of terrain, like the dune, that slopes upward. In those seconds it took us to close on their lines, I said a quick prayer of thanks for that. Another prayer of thanks came a couple of seconds later, when it became clear that our fire, unlike the enemy's, was effective, and their line was breaking.

As they retreated back into the village huts, we began a house-to-house fight, trying to stay on line so no enemy would get behind us. This meant we had to scrap our plan to race some troops through the village to the western end to cover the paddies, but there were too many bad guys and too many places to hide to take a chance with fire from our rear.

Meanwhile, I could also hear firing from our security teams covering the north-south trails.

The systematic clearing of the village took the remainder of the night (we fired flares to illuminate the area).

We were scheduled for a helo pickup at first light, and I hoped we wouldn't be hit by VC reinforcements before then (though we had a plan to bring in a reaction force of Vietnamese Marines if we ran into a tough spot).

By sunrise, we had cleared the village, consolidated our position, and secured the landing zone for the helos.

The Vietnamese Marine captain who was our raid force commander then received the reports: We had taken a considerable number of wounded, but remarkably none had been killed, and none of the wounded had life-threatening injuries. We counted nineteen enemy killed and thirty-two captured. From these we learned that the American POW had indeed been with them, but he had been moved out across the paddies when the shooting started.

I immediately requested that air observers try to pick up any fleeing VC, but they saw nothing, and when our reaction force came in to search the area later that morning they also had no luck. A disappointing end to an extremely well-executed raid.

THE KEY to the Vietnamese Marines' success was their superb set of battalion and company commanders. At one time or other, I operated with most of the infantry companies, so I had a good sense of their strengths and weaknesses.

Only one commander failed to reach the high operational standards I'd learned to expect. His leadership ability was poor and his tactical skills were marginal. He was also unusually vain and prissy for a Marine (he always had much more "stuff" with him than the normally lean-traveling Marines); he seemed to have the "privileged" attitude that you more usually found in ARVN (Army of the Republic of Vietnam) officers. But his major problem was his inability to handle more than one thing at a time—a critical requirement for a combat leader. A combat commander in a fight has to do twenty things at once. This almost cost me and his men our lives.

At that time, we were operating among the deserted villages near the coast, continuously moving a company through them to keep the VC from establishing a base of operations—and to keep the former inhabitants from sneaking back home. Though we rotated companies every couple of weeks to give them a break, junior advisers were scarce, and I stayed out to join each company returning to the area.* After a while, some company commander must have noticed that I was looking haggard and mentioned to the battalion com-

---

* The senior adviser stayed with the battalion commander, but the junior adviser had to be out in the field where the fighting was.

mander that I should get a break. I didn't like that idea. A lot was going on out there that only an adviser could take care of.

But on the next turnover the commander ordered me to come back to base. "You come in with the company coming in," he told me, "and we'll just put a company out there without an adviser."

"No way," I said. "I'm staying. We can't have a company out there with no adviser."

"Well, look," he said, "come in with a company. Get cleaned up. Take a break. We've got mail back here for you. Just take a day, at least, and then you can go back out. We'll hold a platoon commander and a squad back from the company going out to accompany you back to the unit."

"Okay, I'll come in and take a day," I said. I had to admit that a break was tempting; it didn't seem like there was a hell of a lot going on; and a day was not a long time.

I had one major concern, however. The company going out was the one commanded by the weak officer. It was actually a good company with good platoon commanders, but the short time I'd already spent with them had given me worries about his competence in a tough situation on his own.

At any rate, I came in and cleaned up, got my gear squared away, ate a decent meal, got caught up on my mail, and had a few hours of uninterrupted sleep.

About midday, I got together with the lieutenant platoon leader to go over the patrol route and review the procedures for our move. This was bad guy land, and we took no chances. I was impressed with this savvy young man; he was mature and proficient beyond his years.

We met early the next morning at the agreed time and departed friendly lines.

As we got closer to the company's position, we heard firing. That was a surprise. There had been no reports of their contact with the enemy; and when I called back to battalion to check, they didn't have any reports, either. Since it was obvious we had to find out what was going on, we stopped the patrol close to their lines and got hold of the company commander on the radio.

"I have VC on three sides and am under heavy fire," he told us. The volume of fire we could hear seemed to confirm this.

A lot of questions instantly ran through my head: The VC and the NVA were a very sophisticated enemy. They almost always initiated contact—always probing and testing to see how good you were. If you responded and you nailed them hard, they'd break off quickly and fade away. But if they saw they weren't getting hit hard, they'd press the attack and bring in reinforcements, hoping for an easy kill. My experience was that if we burned them right at the start, they'd break off. No way were they going to get into a pitched battle with somebody who seemed have their stuff together and could get on them quickly with fires. For that reason, I always tried to get artillery and air on them as soon as they hit.

But that was clearly not happening here. "Why?" I asked myself.

The bad guys could certainly see that they were facing a good company that was well dug in. But they were not getting pounded. There were no helicopters, observer aircraft, or jet fighters up there, and no artillery slamming in. And when they realized that, they said, "These guys don't have it together, or else maybe they don't have access to their heavy stuff. And we have enough forces in position to take them on. Let's do it."

The company had dug in at a deserted hamlet. Because they were surrounded on three sides, the only clear route in was from the west. So we had to carefully work our way around to that side and then slowly close on the company position. The young lieutenant platoon commander handled this tricky move extremely well. We could have easily run into the VC or (just as bad) been mistaken for them and drawn friendly fire, but his coordination and deft handling of our patrol were superb.

When we finally entered the company lines, the scene was intense. Marines were firing from cover at the attacking and ever-probing enemy. The fighting was at close quarters; the enemy were everywhere. (What I didn't realize then was that the fighting had also been going on for quite some time. This fact came back to bite me.)

As I made my way through the mud huts to the company command post, the lieutenant broke off to join his platoon. They could use him . . . and I had a sudden wish that he was the company commander.

At the command group, several Marines were chattering away on radios propped up against the mud walls of the huts. From what I could tell, the company commander was talking to his platoon commanders and seemed to have the defense under control. Yet I still couldn't figure out why he hadn't reported the contact or requested fire support. The fighting was heavy and the VC were obviously working to encircle him.

About the time I was approaching the command group, the company commander decided to call in artillery. But typically for him, it was an afterthought. He hadn't given any specific direction to the forward artillery observer, who was—as it happened—confused about our coordinates. As it also happened, I had just checked the coordinates of our position, and when I heard the Vietnamese artillery forward observer calling in the fire mission, it dawned on me that he was giving our location and not the enemy's.

I grabbed my radio handset and called a "check fire" back to our U.S. artillery adviser, but was too late. The "shot out" return call indicated rounds were on the way. "Get down!" I yelled, as two rounds whistled in and exploded behind us. Remarkably, they hit in the open to our rear, and the Marines, under cover, were not hurt.

At this point, the U.S. Marine artillery adviser, our battalion senior adviser, and the task force senior adviser were all screaming on my radio, trying to find out what was going on; and from the activity on their radios, the Vietnamese chain of command was equally energized. I tried giving my command a quick explanation, asking them for time to sort this mess out, but they were not having it. Since they were hearing about the problem from me, I had to be the problem. But at least they trusted me enough to listen to my requests for help, and I managed to get control of things enough to have them bring in an Air Force spotter plane over our position and cancel the artillery mission until I was ready for it.

Since the company seemed well organized in their defense, I was confident there wasn't an immediate problem with the maneuver units.

I then grabbed the company commander and asked him for a heads-up.

"We've been hit three or four times," he said. "Each time has been harder and from more directions than the last." Though he had, as I had thought, concentrated on the fight and maneuvering of his units without also reporting his situation or calling in fire support or air observers, I felt I could get these last under control when he hit me with an "Oh, by the way": "My men are very low on ammunition."

At first I wondered when he intended to do something about this (that should have been done long before I showed up), but it was quickly obvious he was dumping the problem on me.

"How low?" I asked.

"A few rounds per man," he answered.

"Great!" I thought.

Fortunately, the VC fire was dying off just then. They seemed to be regrouping.

I immediately put in an emergency request for ammo, which drew more yelling from the rear echelon, who were still on my ass for what was happening.

"What kind of ammo do you need and how much?" They asked after they'd calmed down a little. But they were still thinking that this should be a "by the book" request. I didn't have time for that.

"Thirty caliber, forty-five . . . just get anything you can out here." The Marines of course had a grab bag of old weapons, and no M-16s. "I can't give you an ammo request. This is an emergency. We're down to three or four rounds per man and we're getting hit hard."

This was just minutes after they'd become aware of our fight. So it didn't sound right to them. You don't normally get in so much trouble so fast. "Where the hell's this coming from?" they were asking. It was clear that the seriousness of our situation was not sinking in back there and they thought they had an overly excited lieutenant on their hands. The fact was none of the guys in the rear had enough true combat time to understand the situation; I had more trigger time by then than any of them.

Meanwhile, I told the company commander to get on his radio and give his battalion a full situation report, and to be accurate and detailed on his ammo status.

Just then the U.S. Air Force 0-1 Birddog light observation plane came on scene. They were called "Herbies" after their call sign, and we loved these guys. I can't praise them enough.

"Thank God for the Herbies," I thought. I gave him our position and the direction the last enemy contacts had come from, and asked him to check those areas.

A few minutes later, he came back up on the net: "You have enemy mass-ing on three sides of you," he said. "You've also got VC on foot, bicycle, and motorbikes all heading your way. I'll work up an air strike, but you need to get ready for a big hit soon. They may get to you before I can bring in our air."

He was right. The VC hit us before the air strike hit them. When they saw the Birddog, I'm sure they knew they had to attack before fire was rained on them.

When they closed in, the fighting was fierce, but the Marines were careful with their shots. They had to be. During the close-quarters fighting, a few VC broke through. A red hand flare signaled that we had an enemy penetration of our lines.

At that moment I was concentrating on the Herbie, who was feeding me coordinates for an artillery mission on the enemy positions. My head was pressed against a wall of one of the huts, with a finger plugging one ear and the radio headset over the other. The firing and yelling made hearing difficult. But before I could complete the fire mission, I was spun around by my radio operator, trying to warn me down.

As I turned, I saw an old man in khaki shirt and shorts with a Thompson submachine gun firing directly at me from about twenty yards away. Fortunately, his rounds were smacking into the mud wall just above my head. But then when I reached for my .45 caliber pistol, my holster was empty. My radio operator already had it and was firing at the old man. So was my cowboy. Everybody was "spraying and praying"; but no one was hit.

A moment later, the old man's magazine was empty, and as he tried to put in a new one from the magazine belt around his shoulder, my radio operator and cowboy bolted over and tackled him. They whacked him around a bit, then dragged him over to the wall.

"Great!" I thought. "Now we have a POW to deal with along with all the problems I'm trying to sort out."

As my guys were tying up our prisoner, I noticed the fire dying away. We had beaten back another attack—the fourth. That was the good news.

The bad news: The company commander came over to tell me that the troops had only one or two rounds apiece remaining. He then gave the order to fix bayonets.

"Great!" The effect of his order on everybody in the company was chilling.

At that moment, I got a radio call from a U.S. Army helicopter inbound with our ammo resupply. I gave the pilot a quick brief on the situation: "Come in from the west," I told him. "Quickly kick out the ammo, and get out the way you came in."

Meanwhile, the Herbie spotted the VC regrouping. They were getting ready to hit us again.

It was looking like a very close call coming up. If we could bring the helo in and get some ammo out to the troops, we might buy time for the air and arty missions to hit.

The helo came in low and pushed out the crates of ammo. The Marines were on the crates quickly, and runners raced the ammo out to the troops on the line. So far so good.

But then the helo pilot came up on the net to say he was about to go out to the east to "take a look around."

I screamed into the radio: "The east is full of bad guys! Go out west!" But he blew me off and started east. He instantly took heavy fire as he cleared our lines, barely missing him. He then went into a steep climb out of there, with the Herbie pilot cursing him as he flew out.

The helo pilot then reported to our task force headquarters that I'd led him east and almost got him shot down, which brought the task force advisers down on me like a ton of shit. By then the arty and air strikes were coming in, so I told them I didn't have time to deal with all that. (They still hadn't caught on about how bad the situation was.*)

These hit just as the VC hit us.

For a tense moment, I wondered if the ammo had made it to the troops, but that worry quickly disappeared: the heavy volume of outgoing fire was music to my ears. By this stage of my tour, I could distinguish the types of weapons firing, whether the firing was incoming or outgoing, even at these close quarters, and which side had the advantage in a firefight. It was clear that we were beating them back and that the air and arty were breaking the VC attack. This was the VC's fifth and final attack.

The enemy was fleeing in all directions on every mode of transportation they had, the Herbie reported excitedly. He chased some of them as they tried to scatter away from the air and helo gunship strikes he was calling in.

---

* Later, I got chewed out again for "letting him go out toward the east," but I explained again that I'd told him not to go out that way. Nothing more came of the incident.

Not long after that, we were able to evacuate our casualties and regroup for what we hoped would be a quiet night. Fortunately, it was; and I was able to settle the company commander down and make sure we had a solid night defensive plan. I also spent a lot of time that night trying to explain what had happened to higher headquarters. They were still confused and angry. I was the guy they were talking to, so I was the guy who got yelled at. That's just the way things are.

Later that night, I told my radio operator and cowboy that I was proud of how well they had performed under fire. "But we're going to be getting some shooting practice very soon," I told them, "and no one is ever to take my weapon!"

Several months later, the company commander was relieved, arrested for corruption, and jailed. I never got the details, but his departure was no loss to the VNMC.

IT'S OFTEN hard to think of the enemy as human beings. But sometimes I'd run into a situation that powerfully demonstrated that that is what they are.

One morning, I went out with another company into the hills west of Highway 1 to block for a 1st Cav sweeping operation. We moved over the crest of some low hills to set up positions above a few small hamlets. As our lead elements began working down the hill toward the villages, they suddenly stopped and gave the hand signal for "enemy ahead." The Marines quickly and quietly came on line toward the direction indicated by the point men.

As I came up with the company commander, I could see about seventy-five meters below us a small gathering around a cooking fire among the village huts—probably a family eating the morning meal. At the same time, I noticed two AK-47 assault rifles on the ground next to two young men.

Just as this registered with me, the people around the fire noticed us. The young men grabbed the weapons and made their way toward a shed or barn, firing as they went. They never made it. The Marines cut them down in a hail of fire. One was hit so many times his body literally skipped along the ground.

Meanwhile, the rest of the family—women, kids, and old folks—had scattered in the opposite direction.

We quickly moved down the hill, rounded up the family, and put them in a covered animal pen for safekeeping, while our troops continued searching the area. They discovered uniforms, equipment, and papers belonging to the two young men—including a diary, the work of the senior of the two, a lieutenant in the NVA . . . the one we'd hit so many times by our fire. The other was his assistant.

Later we learned from the family that the lieutenant was a platoon commander home on leave, and this was his family—his mother, father, wife, and kids. He'd traveled from the west near the Cambodian border back to his home village.

During our noon meal on the stoop of the family's house, the company commander and I read selections from the diary and other papers. Soon rain started coming down, so we moved back under the palm frond overhang of the roof.

The diary was a fascinating and incredibly meticulous account of the young lieutenant's life as a platoon commander. He seemed to leave out nothing—from personal details about his wife and family, to the money spent on food for his troops, to the money he'd allotted for his troops to hire prostitutes. There were photos of his graduation from the military academy in North Vietnam and photos of his wife and children. He was an idealistic young man, caught up in his cause—as committed to his "faith" as we were to ours . . . a sobering realization.

As I read, I had a disturbing sense that I was being watched. When I looked up, the family was standing in a shocked, emotionless cluster, like zombies, just staring at me through the rain pouring off the thatched roof of the animal pen where they were confined. Though they were stoic, like all Vietnamese, their gaze was a powerful judgment.

There were many dizzying and disturbing moments in this seemingly senseless and confusing war that shook my certitudes. This was one of the most disturbing.

Zinni was promoted to captain in July. The war had shortened the old time-in-grade requirements.

UTILITY INFIELDER

As the advisers' utility infielder, Zinni never stayed long in one place. Here is how all that traveling broke down chronologically:

★ April 3 to April 21: Rung Sat Special Zone
★ April 24 to May 13, June 20 to August 10, and November 8 to December 13: II CTZ—Operation Pershing
★ May 15 to 19, September 2 to 9, and October 19 to November 15: Capital Military District (CMD)
★ May 24 to May 31: Mekong Delta
★ June 7 to 17, August 11 to September 2, and September 9 to October 10: III CTZ—Jungle
★ October 24 to 30: R & R in Hong Kong
★ December 13: Evacuated to Qui Non

Zinni saw constant action during his times in II CTZ, but his times in the jungle—III CTZ—were every bit as memorable.

He operated there for three periods during his tour: for ten days in June (when he was still comparatively green), and for most of August and September. The specific area of operations was called the Ong Dong Forest, a classic triple-canopy rain forest, thinly populated, but containing immense varieties of exotic flora and fauna—elephants, tigers, all kinds of biting insects, poisonous snakes, and other nasties. Operations in the jungle were exercises in survival as well as military operations to find the enemy. Zinni loved it. His most fascinating times in Vietnam were in the jungle.

He takes up the story:

Truly, when you're out there in the jungle, you're in a strange, new world—a world that feels untouched by humans . . . totally alien. Nothing seems familiar. You have a real sense of uncertainty about what might confront you. There were constant surprises. And even though I went in with savvy, experienced companions, I always felt as though I was on my own. The jungle does that to you . . . it makes you feel solitary.

Our operations in the jungle were known as Operation Billings by the

Americans, and Operations Song Than and Dong Nai by the Vietnamese. The U.S. unit in the area was the 1st U.S. Infantry Division, "the Big Red One." Though we conducted a few coordinated operations with the U.S. forces, the jungle was too dense for large operations. You had to literally hack your way through vines and thick foliage, moving very slowly, mostly in small units—squad-sized, platoon-sized, maybe company-sized patrols. I learned a great deal about jungle craft, patrolling, tactics, and survival from the skilled Vietnamese Marines on these patrols.

The aim of Billings was to interdict the enemy coming down the Ho Chi Minh Trail through Laos and Cambodia and infiltrating through the mountains and rugged terrain of the jungles into the populated regions near the coast. We didn't actually encounter large numbers of the enemy in the jungle, but we knew they were there. Our job was to search for indications of them, their infiltration routes, or base camps or other places they might be using as sanctuaries; and we frequently found unoccupied VC positions— often clever bunkers tunneled under thick bamboo clumps, providing them with a natural cover.

Because of the difficult terrain, the Vietnamese command wanted top troops there, and that meant the Marines.

We operated out of a small village on the edge of the jungle called Tan Uyen, where the Marines had a base. From there we'd send a company into the jungle for six or seven days at a time to look for enemy moving eastward from the Cambodian border.

Under the thick jungle canopy, we were on our own; we could not expect reinforcement or resupply, and we carried little food. We had no field rations, for example (such as American C rations). With the exception of a few balls of precooked rice packed in small aluminum cans, a chicken or two bound and gagged over our packs (to be killed and eaten the first or second day out), and some nouc mam, Vietnamese fish sauce, everything we ate had to be foraged (like breadfruit or bamboo shoots) or killed (like monkeys and snakes) in the field.

Once in the jungle, the Marines knew how to use materials found there to enhance their living conditions and improve their security.

I learned how to quickly build bamboo platforms for my gear, how to set up alarms and booby traps around our night base, and how to read tracks and signs in the jungle from our expert scouts. The most important lesson I learned was how to travel light. Before each patrol, I found a new way to lighten my load and leave behind another previously "indispensable" piece of gear.

On my first patrol, I carried a heavy U.S. jungle hammock and a "rubber lady"—an inflatable mattress. As I settled in for the night, the Marines warned me not to sleep on the ground. "Set up your hammock in a tree," they told me.

I thought that was a bad idea. "We shouldn't sleep in the trees," I answered. "We have to be ready in case the enemy attacks."

They shook their heads knowingly and slept in the trees.

Just in case, I tied my hammock up in a tree, but went to sleep on my rubber lady.

In the middle of the night, my mattress suddenly deflated like a tire blowing out, and I was stabbed by hundreds of burning hot stings. Slapping wildly at them, I jumped into the hammock. I didn't need further persuasion. In time, the pain subsided and I was able to sleep.

The next morning, my skin was a red mass of bites. And when I poked my head over my hammock, I could see my mattress—or what was left of it— being devoured by thousands of ants. Only a two-foot square remained.

The Marines gave me an "I told you so" look. Then advised me to get rid of my heavy hammock and grab one of their light nylon ones (they folded up small enough to be stowed in a pocket). I did.

THE FIELDCRAFT *of the Vietnamese was impressive.*

Every activity on the patrols was a preset drill. Before we set out, we rehearsed everything—occupation of a patrol base; getting water; acquiring food; setting up our night defenses; crossing danger areas such as streams and clearings; setting up ambushes; and even using the field sanitation pits. Nothing was left to chance or improvisation. No one did anything alone (some Marines' only function was to maintain security while others fetched water or gathered food). And no one did anything until the order was given. Anyone attempting otherwise did so at his peril.

On one patrol, we lost a new recruit who went off to get water from a nearby stream before the order came to go. All we found after a search was his helmet by a stream.

In the jungle, it wasn't only the enemy you had to worry about; other dangers could easily strike. I awoke one morning to hear an obviously upset company commander chewing out his men for some nighttime security breach. This was strange, since the Vietnamese Marines were reliably vigilant, especially at night. When I asked him about it, he showed me a huge steaming pile of dung in the middle of the patrol base. It was tiger shit.

The Marines swore that they'd been alert; and I believed them. The tiger had come in without tripping any of our bamboo clapper alarms or claymore mines and had been undetected by our security. I didn't sleep too soundly after that.

On another morning, I was awakened by a group of Marines around my hammock, chattering excitedly and pointing above the poncho I had rigged over it. Pulling back the poncho revealed a gigantic snake curled on a branch a few feet above my head—a twelve-foot python with a big bulge in his middle. He had recently eaten.

To the Vietnamese this was gold. They quickly cut down the snake, twisted the lethargic reptile around a makeshift pole cut from a branch, and sewed up the snake's mouth with a rawhide-like chord. Though the snake seemed half-dead, I assumed that condition had been brought on by his recent meal.

The Marines decided we should take the snake back to the village, since killing and eating it in the field would be a waste (food spoiled fast and had to be consumed shortly after killing it). We had three days left on our patrol.

Toward the end of the patrol, the snake grew increasingly active, but we made it back with him and enjoyed a grand meal.

THE MARINES were as careful in their departures as they were in their preparations. They tried never to leave any trace of their presence behind. When we pulled out of our bases, we meticulously cleaned them. The aim was to leave behind as little evidence of our presence as possible and to prevent the VC from getting their hands on anything they could use . . . a discarded C ration can and a grenade could quickly be turned into a booby trap.

Several times we came across positions once used by U.S. or South Vietnamese units. Since these were always booby-trapped by the enemy, I was glad *our policy was never to occupy a position used before. The Vietnamese were always angered by the carelessness of U.S. forces. Abandoned U.S. bases or night positions normally had claymore mines still in place and discarded or forgotten equipment strewn about.*

THOUGH ENEMY *contact on jungle patrols was rare, it was not never:*

On one patrol our base was hit for several nights in a row by indirect fire. Fortunately, the heavy canopy and ground cover kept us from suffering casualties, but we knew it was only a matter of time before our luck ran out.

Since it was small-caliber fire and always right on us, somebody nearby had to be calling it in. That meant somebody was following us. We decided to set in a stay behind ambush the next day to try to nail them.

The plan was to find a clearing (an ideal killing zone) and set up the ambush with our lead elements on the far side, as the rest of the patrol crossed it (we always crossed clearings carefully, as danger areas). Once they had passed through the ambush area, they'd set up as a reinforcing element behind it.

The plan worked. A four-man VC team came into the killing zone a few minutes after our patrol had supposedly left. The Marines killed three of them, and wounded and captured the other. Though the prisoner was in bad shape and not in the best of health to start with, we were able to learn from him that the four VC were a forward observer team who tracked and called in fires on units patrolling the jungle.

Since enemy prisoners in this region were hard to come by, III Corps headquarters wanted this guy right away. We were ordered to secure a landing zone and I was told to bring him and the equipment the VC had with them back to a rear location.

When the U.S. helo came in, I loaded him and the equipment aboard and we took off for wherever they wanted him. We landed on an LZ near some buildings, where a group of officers and troops in starched uniforms and spit-shined boots were standing around. When the helo touched down, I picked up the VC with the equipment, carried him to where the group was standing, and dumped the load at their feet. I was sure this was the closest they would ever get to the enemy. I looked at their startled faces and walked back to the helo and asked the pilot to get me back to my unit right away. On the flight back, I wondered how many of them would get combat decorations for their rear echelon jobs. I was glad I was not one of them.

MY TWENTY-FOURTH birthday came in September, during one of my times in the jungle. It wasn't exactly a lead item on my mind. But during the day a helo dropped off resupplies and some welcome mail that I knew would have to be quickly read and destroyed.

In the mail packet was an envelope with my name on it and nothing else. Inside was Miss September, the Playboy Playmate of the Month, naked and lying in a hammock. Written in the margins of the foldout were birthday greetings from the advisers back at the task force headquarters and a list entitled, "9 Things Wrong With This Tactical Picture":

1. No Overhead Cover
2. Flanks Exposed
3. No One on High Ground
4. No Probing Patrols
5. Not Tied In with Friendlies
6. No One on Duty
7. Not Expecting Immediate Attack
8. Reserve Committed
9. Susceptible to Penetration

I shared the centerfold with the delighted Vietnamese Marines as we set up our hammocks in the patrol base that evening. I still have it to remind me of the little things we did to pump each other up.

THE BATTLE OF THE BONG SON PLAIN

The battle that became known as the Battle of the Bong Son Plain in II CTZ is regarded by some as the first battle of the Tet Offensive. Although it was fought a month before the January attacks of Tet, it signaled a change in the enemy's strategy.

Tony Zinni continues:

It began in a strange way. By the later months of 1967, things had become very quiet, and fighting seemed to be limited to the border areas of South Vietnam in places like Khe Sanh and the Ia Drang Valley. Many of us thought the VC and NVA were now incapable of large-scale attacks outside of areas along the Cambodian and Laotian borders near their bases and supply routes.

We were, of course, mistaken. The series of attacks that became famous as the Tet Offensive was forming up. The targets of Tet were the cities of South Vietnam. The North Vietnamese command under General Giap believed that if the attacks battered the allies enough to make them seem to lose control, the people would rise up and the war would end, as it did with the French decades before.

One of the target cities was Qui Nhon, a coastal city in II CTZ.

One morning an aerial observer on a routine flight over the area north of the city spotted what looked like a field expedient radio antenna. A local ARVN division dispatched a patrol to check it out. The patrol was never heard from again. A company sent to the area ran into a large VC force and was wiped out.

These events launched a major U.S.–South Vietnamese military operation. The ensuing fighting was fierce, with the friendly units taking severe casualties. Our two-battalion task force of Vietnamese Marines was alerted and designated the II CTZ reserve for the battle that was raging.

At this time I was again with the 4th Battalion. The old battalion commander, Major Tri, had gone to the U.S. to attend a military course, and the executive officer, Major Voung, was now the commander. Captain Kinh, a colorful and much revered old warrior (he had many wounds and many wives), was now the executive officer. Bob Hamilton was now the senior adviser, and I was filling the junior adviser position. As the battle raged, we did what we could to monitor it, but had no way of knowing how serious the fighting had become until a call came that we (the reserve) would be committed.

As the battalion got ready to go, the task force advisers and some officers from the Corps headquarters showed up at our position to brief us. "The situation's bad," they told us. "The ARVN division is in desperate shape and the U.S. unit from the 1st Cav has also taken serious casualties. It's urgent that you reinforce these units as soon as possible."

The plan was for our battalion to conduct a helicopter lift in two waves directly onto the ARVN position. I would go with Captain Kinh and two companies as the lead. Then the helos would lift the remainder of the battalion to join us. The other battalion and our task force headquarters would move by trucks up Highway 1 to join our battalion. The task force was put under the operational control of the 22nd ARVN Division, the unit fighting the battle.

What we were to do once we landed was unclear, which left all of us uneasy. The fighting was heavy and our mission was hazy. Because no one seemed to have a good handle on what was happening, it was left to us to make contact with the units on the ground and work out the scheme.

From the briefing and the maps, I could tell the VC held a group of villages, while the ARVN and U.S. forces were on high ground overlooking them. The battle had gone on for days with lots of air and artillery fire and several unsuccessful ground attacks launched by the forces we were to join.

I knew the villages well from previous operations—beautiful places with postcard scenes of thatched houses, palm trees, and rice paddies . . . and prosperous (they made rice wine); so life was good. I'd enjoyed my times there and truly liked the people. I was anxious to see what the fighting had done to them.

I met Captain Kinh in the pickup landing zone as we waited for the helos to come in. I would coordinate with the pilots and wanted to be sure we were ready for a "hot" zone in case the situation had worsened. I was not confident that our briefs had given us a clear picture of the conditions on the ground.

I was glad to see my best Vietnamese friend, Captain Hoa, and his company would be one of the two companies going in our lead helo lift. The other company was also a good unit, and I felt reassured with this team of experienced fighters. Everyone seemed somber; we all shared the uneasy feeling about this mission.

The helos landed, we went through our briefs, and then lifted off toward the north and whatever awaited us.

As our helos started their descent into the landing zone, I looked out to get a quick sense of the situation on the ground.

"There's no sign of hostile fire," the pilots told me. But I could see the devastating aftermath of truly fierce fighting. The once lovely villages were totally destroyed, and the terrain where the ARVN were located looked like a moonscape, pockmarked by shell craters and scoured of trees and brush. I had a quick flashback to the beauty and serenity of the area not long ago.

As the helicopters slowed close to the ground, we got another disturbing sight. Panicking ARVN soldiers were running for the birds, many discarding their weapons and equipment in their dash for the helos. Though a few officers made halfhearted attempts to stop them, they couldn't check the stampede. Our pilots, meanwhile, were very unhappy about the safety problems this mad dash was causing.

Our Marines glared at the ARVN soldiers in disgust as we debarked from the helos and rapidly took up defensive positions around the LZ. My immediate concern—as well as Captain Kinh's—was that the VC might be aware of the apparent mayhem and see it as an opportunity to attack.

The helos lifted off with ARVN troops clinging to the skids and frustrated helo crew chiefs giving up on trying to push off the frightened soldiers. It was clear that this ARVN unit was beaten and useless in any action that might follow.

Kinh, Hoa, and I looked around in disbelief, our grim expression mirrored on the faces of the other Marines.

Kinh instructed the company commanders to quickly get their positions prepared to protect the zone for the follow-on lifts and not to depend on the units already there for security. He then told me to join him. "Let's try to find someone in charge," he said.

It seemed strange that no officer had approached us by now.

We moved from position to position, until we came to a very deep hole with radio antennas sticking out of it. To my surprise, an ARVN brigadier general was inside. When he realized we were there, he jumped out and started screaming at Kinh. He was so frightened and panicked it was difficult to understand what he was saying. He was clearly over the edge. But the gist of it was orders to Kinh to launch into the attack.

Kinh yelled back at him. "We will attack," he said, "but given the size of the enemy, we should wait for the rest of the battalion, and preferably wait for both battalions of Marines to get on the ground."

The general kept screaming, "No, you have to attack now! You have to attack now!"

Kinh glared at the general with such total disdain that I feared he'd hit him on the spot.

At this point, I decided to walk away from the confrontation. I didn't think it was my place to be there as these two Vietnamese commanders were screaming and yelling at each other. My job was to do what I could to help Kinh and the Marines. I knew another American unit was in the area. I wanted to get a fix on them to see if we could link up with them. I also wanted to check to see when the rest of the battalion was going to arrive.

But the first thing I did was hook up with Hoa, who told me that the flank of his company was reporting U.S. armored personnel carriers a short distance away (the American unit I'd wanted to link up with). He and I walked over to take a look. As we got there, U.S. soldiers were making their way toward us, led by an Army captain whose company had shared a security position some weeks back with one of our Vietnamese Marine units. He was a good officer and I was glad to finally see something positive in this mess.

After we greeted each other, he told me that his mechanized infantry company was supporting the ARVN regiment, but had suffered some casualties, including losing a couple of their M-113 armored personnel carriers in futile attacks that were poorly conducted by the ARVN. The ARVN infantry had held back in the attacks and then fled, leaving his tracks exposed to VC "spider traps"—camouflaged holes from which the VC would spring up and hit units after they'd passed by. In this case, the VC had fired rifle-propelled grenades (RPGs) into the rear of the M-113s.

Just then, the Marines behind us began to pick up their equipment, preparing to move out. After checking in on his radio, Hoa confirmed that.

This seemed crazy. The VC were dug in below in strong positions at the *edge of the village. There were a lot of them, and they were in good shape (we thought), while we were not yet up to full strength. The three of us hurried toward Kinh's location to find out what was happening.*

Kinh was furious: The ARVN general had persisted in his order to attack the dug-in VC.

"This is insane," I told Kinh. All the air and artillery strikes and ground attacks had so far failed to break the VC. Two light infantry companies would be slaughtered.

"You're right," he shrugged angrily. There was nothing he could do. He then gave me a bitter look. "I don't want you to go in this attack," he said.

I looked at this man whose warrior spirit I greatly admired. "There's nothing on this hill worth staying for," I told him. "I want to be with our Marines."

He smiled.

Then the U.S. Army captain added his two cents. "If you attack," he said, "my company is going with you. I agree. Nothing on the hill is worth staying for."

Kinh smiled again.

We quickly coordinated plans and made preparations for the attack.

As we walked away, the Army captain asked me to make sure the Vietnamese Marines stayed in front of his tracks this time.

Hoa had overheard him. Before I could answer, he'd shoved himself inches from the captain's face. "We are Marines," he said. "We will always be in front of you."

The captain smiled at me. "I like this guy," he said.*

After issuing orders and coordinating our attack, we formed up and moved out.

It would have been nice to lay down air strikes before we hit the VC, but we were out of luck this time. Though we had some air on station, we did not have any discernible targets for them. We knew the VC lines were at the base of our hill and on the edge of the village complex beyond it, but I could not see any indications of the enemy. Since they were masters of camouflage, this was not significant.

It turned out that our worries were groundless.

---

* This fine U.S. Army captain was later killed in action.

As we moved closer to the base of the hill, I expected heavy fire; but we were met only by light, sporadic shots. Our lead troops returned them.

Moments later we were on top of the VC defensive positions, and there was still no serious fire. They were withdrawing. They did not intend to fight. The light fire had obviously come from their rear units trying to delay us and protect their retreat.

At that point, we made three quick assumptions: that they had not observed the ARVN chaos, that the sight of the helos landing had convinced them that reinforcements had arrived, and that they were in no condition to handle another attack from fresh troops.

A short time later, these assumptions proved to be true. They'd taken far more casualties than we'd thought: Our Marines had uncovered mass graves behind the enemy fighting positions—large pits containing piles of bodies hastily covered with palm fronds. We estimated there were as many as eighty bodies in one, and the others contained perhaps ten or twenty apiece. (I learned later that a total of 650 VC had been killed before the Marines arrived. This had been a major battle.)

By then I was up on the radio reporting our situation to our task force headquarters. Though Kinh did not want to be careless with such a potentially large force in front of us, he was an aggressive commander and eager to move out fast to catch the retreating VC.

In the light of this chance to grab more enemies, the reply from the task force was incredible. "The Corps command wants you to count the bodies in the pits," they told me. Americans had a fixation on body counts. It was some mad managerial types' way to "statistically" measure battlefield success. And it was senseless. Counting dead bodies was always nuts, but in this case it was triple nuts: Many of these corpses been in the pits for days; the intense heat had made the stench unbearable. But far more important, our troops were ready to move on. There was enemy out there that was reeling and vulnerable.

When I told Kinh what Corps command had ordered, he quietly said, "We don't count bodies," and gave the order to move out. That was good enough for me; and I happily told higher headquarters we weren't going to do it. I took a lot of grief for that; but I'd been in Vietnam for ten months by then, and telling the rear to go pound sand no longer bothered me.

Soon we were moving into the remains of the village I remembered so well—an eerie scene that will always haunt me. The once-beautiful village was now rubble, the houses blown apart, the palm trunks snapped and twisted. There was a strong stench of dead bodies and animals; and a gray fog-like mist hanging over the place at treetop level made it difficult to see beyond a few dozen meters. (I guessed it had been caused by dust stirred up by the bombs and shells that had impacted in the area.)

The ghastly scene spooked the Marines. The VC didn't scare them; but their highly superstitious nature was clearly convincing them this was a bad place.

We slowly moved on line across the destroyed village, staring intently into the mist. At one point we noticed a large portion of an animal hanging in a tree—a section of a water buffalo that had been blown apart. A little later, we came upon a man's body, his face pale gray and the top of his head blown off. As we stared at him, we were startled by a sudden movement—a snake crawling out of his open skull.

To the Vietnamese troops, this was definitely a bad omen.

We nervously pressed on.

A little later, I dimly made out a motionless figure in the haze. The Marines, seeing it too, began to ready their weapons. The figure remained motionless. As we got closer, we began to realize it was a small boy. He was frozen, just staring straight ahead, totally unaware of us. When we reached him, a Vietnamese Marine took his hand and brought him along with us. He trotted along, still mute.

We continued on for several days* through many more equally horrific scenes.

Though we made occasional contact with the enemy, the VC was not interested in a fight. They'd just throw out a few shots to slow us down. We took some wounded from these small contacts, but nothing serious.

An officer lying next to me during one exchange of fire was hit by a round that penetrated only about an inch deep into his thigh—evidence that the enemy was shooting at us from a great distance, desperately hoping to keep us off their back. He easily popped it out.

---

* The rest of the Marine battalion caught up with us later the first day.

After a time, intelligence reports from prisoner interrogations and accounts of villagers who had made their way out of the battle area began to filter down to us. The enemy unit we were chasing was identified as the 22nd NVA Regiment, augmented with some local VC elements. Badly mauled, the remnants were cut off by other U.S. and South Vietnamese units and further hammered as they fled for the hills to the west.

Some reports claimed the NVA commander was a woman, but that was never verified. We often got similarly crazy reports: A commander was seen riding a white horse or was a Chinese officer or a Russian. I put this report in the same category.

Our mission ended when we reached Highway 1, the western boundary of our assigned zone of action—now cleared. The enemy escaping to the west were now in zones of other units. We'd suffered a few wounded and bagged a number of the enemy; but, overall, the fighting was a lot lighter than we'd anticipated. Our troops were drained from several days of continuous movement and running firefights, but even more from the horrible sights they'd witnessed. The small boy, though, was still with us, cared for by the Marines. He never spoke a word. Later, we turned him over to civilians on Highway 1 who knew him.

Much of Highway 1—as the main thoroughfare of South Vietnam—was a commercial strip, with small shops, cafes, market stalls, and restaurants all along it. Normally there was heavy traffic on the highway; but this had been swelled by crowds of refugees who had fled the fighting, many of them injured.

As we started heading south along the highway, we came upon an ARVN mechanized unit at a semidestroyed railroad station who didn't look like they'd done any fighting. When our Marines spotted the unit, I sensed some bad blood; but didn't think much about it.

Meanwhile, we learned that trucks were on the way to take us back to our original bases to the south. Since no one knew exactly when they would arrive, the commanders decided to let the troops take advantage of the cafes and soup stalls along the road for a rare time-out from more serious business. Hoa invited me to join him for noodle soup and a beer in one of the shops. It sounded great.

Hoa and I were enjoying our bowls and beers when we noticed Marines in combat gear moving past the shop's open entrance, stealthily creeping forward as though to an enemy target. Curious, we went to the doorway to see what was going on. Kinh was directing the Marines, getting them in position for an attack.

"Kinh," I called to him, "what's going on?" But he ignored me.

Suddenly the street erupted in fire.

Hoa and I ducked down inside the shop, and I grabbed my radio to find out what was going on. The shopkeeper repeatedly motioned for us to get into the family protection bunker he had built into the floor. "No, no, you go in," we told him. We had to try to sort out what was happening.

When I contacted Bob Hamilton, he told me that the Marines seemed to be deliberately attacking another South Vietnamese unit. I could see from the doorway that the Marines were firing at the ARVN mechanized unit we'd seen earlier. By now the firing was heavy and rounds were zinging all over. We were at the point of contact between the two units.

The task force senior adviser came up on the radio, really energized. "I've got the U.S. Army adviser of the ARVN unit on the radio net," he told me. I acknowledged that. "What we've got to do is get our units to stop this intramural firefight," he continued.

"I'll go out into the street to try," I said. I thought that if I went out and both sides saw my uniform, they might stop this thing.

"I'll go with you," Hoa said. I passed that on to the senior adviser.

I also linked up with the Army adviser to the ARVN unit. But when he chimed in that he didn't get paid to stop friendly firefights and refused to leave his bunker, I decided I wouldn't get anywhere arguing with him. I had better things to do.

When Hoa and I looked out into the street again, we realized that many of the rounds whizzing past were .50 caliber rounds from the ARVN armored personnel carriers. And the Marines were firing recoilless rifles. Really heavy stuff was whizzing back and forth through the space we intended to occupy. We looked at each other, shrugged, then went slowly out into the street yelling in Vietnamese: "Cease fire!"

As we moved farther out into the street, and the guys on both side saw who we were, they all sobered up, and the fire began to drop off a little . . . though not before some .50 caliber slugs had zinged by my ear. At that moment, a figure came running toward us from the ARVN unit and met us midway. It was a black U.S. Army staff sergeant, one of the advisers.

"I was cleaning up," he said, "when I heard the firing. I rushed out as soon as I could."

When I told him what his officer had said, he rolled his eyes. "It figures," he said.

The three of us then huddled between the forces, yelling to our respective sides to stop firing. After a few minutes, thankfully, the shooting stopped.

The situation remained tense until Major Voung and the other Vietnamese commanders (as well as Bob Hamilton) came screaming up the road in jeeps and drove into the railroad station. Moments later, a helicopter landed. A Vietnamese major general climbed out and joined them—obviously sent there to sort out the mess and get the units separated. When Major Voung passed us on the way in, he looked angrier than I had ever seen him.

We waited to hear what was being decided inside. The discussion was obviously heated; and there was a lot of yelling.

While this was going on, Hoa had a few moments free to explain what was going on. "We've hated these guys for a long time," he told me. "Years ago, the ARVN unit bugged out in a firefight and abandoned us. Seeing them spurred the old hatred; and some of the troops got into a brawl that boiled over into this mess."

A little later, I began to sense something was coming to a head. Kinh was moving troops around, positioning our battalion to surround the train station. When he completed this movement, he went inside and whispered something to Major Voung. The major immediately stopped the discussions. "The station is surrounded," he announced. "The Marines will attack unless the commander and executive officer of the ARVN unit are turned over to the Marines for execution."

The major general couldn't allow that. But the situation was almost out of his control; and Kinh wanted to attack in the worst way. Voung remained open to reason, though, and, after a lot of jawboning, he was persuaded to back off.

The arrival of our trucks helped the situation. The troops were anxious to *get back to our bases. And so we boarded the trucks—to my enormous relief—and got out of there. We arrived back home late that night; and I slept until midmorning.*

After breakfast, when I joined Bob Hamilton in his bunker, he told me he was putting me in for a Navy and Marine Corps Medal (given for heroism in noncombat situations, normally for saving lives).

"Thanks," I told him, "I appreciate it. But the Army staff sergeant should also be nominated for the Soldier's Medal [the Army equivalent]."

"I'll take care of it," he said, after I'd described what happened.

Though I never received the medal, I did get a letter some months after I left Vietnam from a U.S. Army colonel, the senior adviser of the 22nd ARVN Division. "Your timely intervention during this confrontation," the last paragraph said, "prevented a situation which could have been extremely embarrassing to the Vietnamese government."

It was obvious the brass wanted to bury the incident without the publicity of awarding medals. That was fine with me.

MEDEVAC ONE

In the tenth month of his one-year tour, Zinni was with the 4th Battalion, operating in a remote and heavily vegetated area of the hills near the Central Highlands in II CTZ. It had been a good ten months; he was thinking about extending for another six.

He was caught up in this conflict. It had become his life. He knew this was where he belonged. He knew exactly why he was there and what he was doing . . . and felt absolutely confident about that. He knew he could handle himself in a firefight, or in any other tactical situation he might encounter. He had a very close relationship with the Vietnamese Marines. They were his buddies and friends; he'd seen a lot of them die. "My purpose for being was right there," he explains now.

The bad news: He felt terrible. The rigors of constant field operations had taken its toll. Though other advisers were commenting on his weight loss—about forty pounds (and he was small to start with)—that didn't bother him much. They had all lost weight. He was sick with something he couldn't shake. All the advisers had bouts of dysentery, but his latest round didn't go away. His urine had turned black as coffee, his skin was turning yellow, sleeping was difficult, he was having trouble eating (everything he tried made him nauseous), and he was growing weaker by the day. Something had to be done. But what? He wanted to hang on until he got back to a rear area, but he knew he needed to see an American doctor (the Vietnamese doctor had given him shots that had no effect). He thought an American doctor would have medicine that would work better and get him back to full strength faster.

One day the patrol he was with passed close to an American Army forward logistic base set up on a mountaintop (making it easy to defend and to support troops in the field by helo).

"I'd like to go up to the base and pick up some medicine," he told the patrol leader.

"Let's go," he agreed.

As they approached the hilltop position, the soldiers providing security challenged them. "I'm an American Marine," Zinni announced. That did not compute with them. He was accompanied by Vietnamese troops; he was wearing a Vietnamese Marine uniform, tiger stripes, and a green beret; and he was carrying a grease gun. Since the Army troops didn't know that Marines were in their Corps area and were unfamiliar with advisers, they decided not to take any chances. They didn't ask for the Marines' weapons, which remained slung, but they weren't about to welcome them like friends.

"I need to see a doctor," Zinni told them.

They contacted their officer, who told them it was okay to take him to the medical aid station—but under guard. They did that.

As they approached the field hospital, a voice yelled out to Zinni. "Stop. Hold it where you are."

A captain with medical insignia came out of a tent with a bottle and handed it to Zinni. "Piss into this."

As black urine filled the vial, he said, "I don't know who or what you are; but if you're an American, your tour is over and I'm medevacing you."

"I can't go now," Zinni answered. "Just give me some pills, and I'll be okay."

He gave Zinni a quick visual once-over. "Listen," he said, "if you don't get to a hospital soon, you could die."

That got Zinni's attention.

As the doctor went about arranging a helicopter evacuation to the U.S. Army hospital at Qui Nhon, Zinni called the task force headquarters to tell them what was happening, then turned his gear over to the Vietnamese Marine captain who was the patrol leader.

"I'll be back," Zinni told him, and as the helo came into the landing zone near the aid station, he and the captain said good-bye.

When he arrived at the hospital at Qui Nhon, he was immediately put through a series of tests. At that point, force of will failed him, and his body gave out completely. He could no longer eat. Simply looking at food sickened him. The little strength keeping him going in the field was now gone. He didn't have energy enough even to get out of bed.

A doctor brought in his test results. "You now weigh 123 pounds," the doctor told him. "You have a severe case of hepatitis, dysentery, mononucleosis, and probably malaria. The good news," he continued, "is that all of them require the same treatment—lots of rest and food, even if you have to force it down."

He was put on intravenous hookups to increase his strength and fed six meals a day. The medics brought tempting cheeseburgers, fries, and milk shakes at all hours, but stomaching more than a few bites of anything proved nearly impossible.

Tony Zinni was a very unhappy young Marine. He wanted in the worst way to get back to the advisory unit; and lying in a hospital bed was not his idea of how he wanted to spend his time.

His mood was not much improved when he started feeling a little better. "Well, let's see what I can do," he said to himself and tried some push-ups near his bed. He collapsed after three.

The biggest blow came a few days after that. "You're going to be evacuated to the Naval Hospital on Guam," the doctor told him, "and then back to the States." That was when he realized that return to the Marine Advisory Unit was not in the cards.

An Air Force evacuation plane carried Zinni and a number of other evacuees to Clark Air Force Base in the Philippines, where they spent

Christmas Day. Another plane carried him to Guam, where he spent several weeks regaining enough strength for his return to the United States.

The stay at Guam was even more difficult than at Qui Nhon. Though the staff was caring and supportive, Zinni felt isolated—the only patient on an officers' ward. His morale plummeted further as the Tet Offensive unfolded in all its gut-wrenching fury. The VC and NVA were mounting coordinated attacks against the major cities of Vietnam. And all Zinni could do was lie in his bed and impotently watch the TV.

The Vietnamese Marines, always at the heart of the action, were fighting in Cholon, the Chinese section of Saigon.

On one occasion, Zinni watched his Marines bring a captured VC before the Saigon police chief, where he was summarily executed. Zinni had accompanied one of the Marines he saw there, a platoon commander from the 4th Battalion, on many operations.

Other Marines went on to fight in the desperate battle for Hue City, distinguishing themselves in the hard fighting to take the city and its citadel.

EVENTUALLY, he was brought home to a hospital near Philadelphia, and was soon well enough to be made an outpatient—meaning that he only had to report in every day; otherwise, he could stay at home with his parents (where Debbie, his wife, joined him).

It took a while to decompress. On the drive home, on his first night out of the hospital, he gave his brother a scare. "Why are we going down a road at night unarmed and with no security?" he asked him.

IN FEBRUARY 1968, he received orders to Quantico as an instructor at the Basic School, where the Marine Corps trains its new officers. He spent the next two years teaching scouting, patrolling, and counterinsurgency tactics at the Basic School, then attended the career-level school for captains, graduating in the summer of 1970. During that time, he also worked hard (running, lifting weights) to recover the strength he had lost. By 1970, he had fully recovered, and was ready to return to Vietnam.

He received orders for the 1st Marine Division based in Danang, and once again prepared to go to war, assigned to the 1st Battalion, 5th Marines, known as "the Pacifiers."

THE PACIFIERS

During the process of Vietnamization, it was expected that the NVA would try to press the withdrawing American forces and cause serious harm. To counter that threat, the division wanted a quick reaction force—a powerful unit that could act as a "fire brigade," troubleshooter (something like the Vietnamese Marines, but with a far more localized area of operations), and rescue unit (that could bail out anybody who needed rescuing).

That job went to "the Pacifiers" (the code name for their special mission). The Pacifiers, as their official description put it, provided "a swift striking, highly mobile heliborne task force which is able to react to any situation on short notice."

The battalion was under direct control of the 1st Marine Division and had a dedicated air package that consisted of command and control helos, troop transports, helo gunships, observer aircraft, and attack aircraft. Its four companies rotated through four levels of alert. The highest was Pacifier 1—requiring a company to be ready to lift out on ten minutes' notice. The second level was one hour, the third twelve hours, and the fourth twenty-four hours.

A company usually stayed on Pacifier 1 for a couple of weeks, and it was tough. Pacifier 2 was tough, too. Pacifier 3 was a little easier, and you provided security for the division headquarters. And if you were on Pacifier 4, you provided security for the base camp.

The battalion's rifle companies were very large and specially organized. Unlike most other units, they were kept at Table of Organization strength, with the full complement of officers and NCOs—over 260 Marines and sailors. This was probably two to three times the size of other rifle companies during the Vietnam War.

In addition, they had extra machine-gun and mortar squads, as well as some experimental weapons, such as an automatic grenade launcher (the

XM-174, called "the Super-Blooper" by the troops) and a flamethrower (the XM-202).* And each company had its own engineer unit, scouts, Kit Carson Scouts,† and scout dog units.

Pacifier units were only committed on hot intelligence of enemy contact, or to rescue crews from downed aircraft, with the mobility of the helos being the key to their movements. They did not pursue the enemy on foot unless in direct contact. And in order to facilitate identification from the air, each platoon had their own color patches sewn on their helmets.

Tony Zinni continues:

The battalion's commanding officer was Lieutenant Colonel Bernard E. "Mick" Trainor (later a lieutenant general and noted journalist), one of the smartest officers the Corps has ever produced. Trainor would demonstrate his tactical skill and genius many times while I was with the battalion.

When we met, he jumped on the fact that I had been to school and had a previous tour as an adviser. He wanted me to be his assistant operations officer. I begged and pleaded for a company; I did not want a staff job. I wanted to be out in the field doing real work. He agreed to think about it.

After I went through the check-in procedure, I moved into the captains' tent where the battalion staff officers lived—a great bunch who quickly brought me up to speed; the battalion operations officer, a big, smart, calm major named W. M. Anderson, really knew his stuff. We quickly hit it off.

When I blurted out how badly I wanted a company, he told me not to worry about it. "I'll see what I can do. Relax for a couple days and get your feet on

---

* Normally, a grenade can be lobbed about forty meters. Earlier during the Vietnam War, units had been equipped with the M-79 grenade launcher, which the troops called "the Blooper," which lobbed a grenade about 150 meters. The Super-Blooper had an even greater range and a drum full of grenades that could be cranked out in a stream. This gave units the capability of covering with bursts of grenades an area between that covered by the 60-millimeter mortar and the M-79. It jammed often and was experimental when the Pacifiers got it. The flamethrower was a multishot—four cylinders in a boxlike frame.
† Kit Carson Scouts were former VC who'd come over to our side. After an indoctrination program, they were assigned to units operating in areas where they had operated as VC.

the ground. I think you'll be more valuable to the battalion in a company. And I'm sure I can convince the CO of this."

I loved the guy.

After two days of anxious waiting, I was called to Lieutenant Colonel Trainor's hut, where I was informed I would be the commanding officer of Company A, 1st battalion, 5th Marines.

I was ecstatic.

When I took command, the company was on Pacifier 3 on Division Ridge, providing security for the division base area. If we were alerted and moved, other non-Pacifier units took over its security mission. The mission was relatively easy and allowed the troops to get a break after their stretches on the more demanding Pacifiers 1 and 2.

Danang is on the seacoast, with a massive mountainous ridge area just to its west. Since the division headquarters was on the eastern side of the ridge, protecting that—as well as the division rear, the logistics area, and the air base—meant occupying Division Ridge.

That job was given to the Pacifiers on lowest levels of alert, and it was pretty good duty. During the day, we only had to keep a platoon up there, which allowed us to get our troops down into some of the base areas for rest and cleanup—impossible to do when they were out in the field.

The change of command took place on the ridgeline on September 8 (we remained on Pacifier 3 status until the twenty-first). It was a bright sunny day, and my first act after walking through the ranks to shake hands with every Marine and sailor was to meritoriously promote several deserving Marines.

"What a day!" I thought.

I SPENT the two weeks we had left on the security mission getting the company in good shape. Because there'd been no enemy contact for months at that position, the permanent support units and the South Vietnamese militia units on the flanks had gotten sloppy. We dealt with that problem.

On September 21, we moved to Pacifier 4. And from October 1 to November 3, we were on Pacifier 1—ten-minute alerts: A siren went off, and the Marines grabbed their gear and formed up, double-timed past the ammo bunkers in a predetermined order to get their prestaged and sorted ammo load, ran in formation to the pickup zone, and embarked into the helos in the preplanned order. Securing of the landing zone at the other end also went according to a drill, as did the actions in a "hot" zone.

Life in the base camp during Pacifier 1 was relaxed when we weren't training or on alert. Each squad had its own SEA hut; the lieutenants' hut, called "the Silver Bar," was where we officers spent most of our time planning . . . but also playing cards. I wanted the company to fight and train hard and well, but I also wanted them to know there was a right time to take a break. We tried to find one day during the week to barbecue the noon meal and play team sports between units. Though these days were rare, they were appreciated.

Since the Pacifier alert could come out of the blue, we had to be constantly prepared. Though it could begin with an immediate launch (as in the case of a downed aircraft), more often I'd get a call to come to the battalion combat operations center for a brief. I liked the op center briefs; they gave us time to plan. If I was to be the guy going in, I wanted to know what I was facing, and what I had to do. I never wanted to have to wondered what the hell it was like out there or whether I could do it. That meant, for instance, that I tried to stay abreast of ongoing operations nearby, since they were the most likely triggers for our commitment. The morning ops and intel briefs were also obviously important for us.

THOUGH I didn't know it then, my last and most dramatic operation in Vietnam had already started. Over a month earlier, one of the companies on Pacifier 1 had reacted to an intelligence report of a VC cadre meeting in a small village. Soon after landing nearby, the company had engaged fleeing enemy. During the short firefight, one of the Marines took matters in his own hands and ran out to tackle one of the VC. He ended up capturing Nguyen Dac Loi, the VC intelligence chief for the Quang Da Special Zone, and reputedly the highest-ranking enemy intelligence officer captured during the war.

The significance of our catch was not evident to anybody in our battalion until the first days in November, when we were notified to prepare for a very special mission. Loi had agreed to lead us to his headquarters in the Que Son Mountains.

While I was at the op center for a brief on the mission, my company got ready to move. According to the briefer, Loi had offered our intel guys a wealth of information, much of it implicating senior South Vietnamese government officials in the region as VC collaborators.* This made things difficult: Though the South Vietnamese had gotten wind of a major capture, they didn't yet know who we had or how important he was. The U.S. command wanted to keep them in the dark as long as they could, so we could fully take advantage of Loi's cooperation before the South Vietnamese became involved. Once that happened, they'd almost certainly compromise any further operations.

The plan was for Loi (escorted by a Marine Interrogator-Translator Team— ITT) to lead my company to his headquarters—a massive cave complex in a deep draw. Because he was unclear about its exact location, Marine Recon teams would cordon the general area, while Company B, along with our battalion command post, took and occupied a dominating piece of high ground.

When all this was briefed, the number of "heavies" there was a pretty good indication of the importance they were giving to this operation.

I met Loi in the landing zone before the birds arrived. He was studying a map. He was obviously intelligent and educated, but also nervous. "Can you point out your headquarters on it?" I asked him.

"I can't be sure," he told me, pointing to a general location. "Our maps differ from yours. But I'm sure I can spot it if I fly around the area."

I didn't like flying around without a definite, preplanned landing zone; but it was obvious we had to go along with Loi.

When all units for the assault were ready, we took off. Loi, sitting next to me, tried to orient the map to the ground below; but got even more confused and uncertain when we reached the area he identified. We circled—a bad idea; it gave away surprise.

I kept pressing him, but that didn't do much good.

---

* The enemy didn't have a code of conduct as Americans do; there was no "name, rank, serial number" kind of thing. It was simply assumed that everything they knew was compromised. Some VC and NVA proved to be open; others were harder to crack. Though Loi gave us a lot of information, we could tell that he was having a hard time deciding where his actual loyalties lay; and there were times when his wavering proved to be tense-making.

"I've never been in a helicopter," he said. "It's hard to pick out landmarks from above."

At last, he seemed to recognize something. "There," he pointed down. "I know that place."

We radioed the other helos and set up for an assault into the zone he'd indicated. The landing was uneventful. We set down into a large muddy, grassy area. Though Loi assured us that he could pick up the trail into his headquarters from there, the terrain didn't look right to me: We were some distance from any deep draws.

As Loi and his ITT went off to look for his trail, I directed my platoons to spread out and search the area.

A short while later, a platoon commander called me to his position. When I got there, he showed me a wide muddy patch of ground covered with fresh boot prints—lots of sneaker-tread NVA boots. A big NVA unit had recently moved through.

I immediately reported our discovery to the battalion and then called my other platoon commanders and organized the company into a hasty defense. It was a good but unnecessary precaution; there was no enemy contact.

Meanwhile, another platoon had found a dud five-hundred-pound bomb. After my engineer officer, Lieutenant Bill Ward, looked at it, we debated what to do with it. After some discussion, we figured we had already lost any tactical surprise; and no one wanted to leave this potential booby trap behind. So Bill's engineers rigged up the explosive charges and we blew the bomb.

Loi returned during this diversion—empty-handed. He hadn't found anything recognizable. All we could do was bring in the helos and start the search again.

After a few minutes in the air, he gave a shout and pointed toward trails at the base of a large hill. "Those trails lead to my headquarters," he announced.

This was more like it. The trails led up a huge mountain combed with deep draws. One draw in particular looked capable of holding the vast cave complexes Loi had described.

When we set down, the zone was again quiet; but the trail network nearby looked well used. "There haven't been U.S. or South Vietnamese troops in this area for years," Loi told us. "The VC and NVA use it freely."

"That's great," I thought, remembering my experience with the Vietnamese Marines. "That means they'll be ready for us." I badly wanted to attack Loi's headquarters, but I didn't want to try to get there on those trails.

I then formed the company in a column, with the first platoon in the lead, and my scouts and our Kit Carson Scouts moving out ahead. I had Loi with me at the head of the first platoon. Because of the possibility of booby traps, I told my scouts to take it slow and careful.

Loi still could not make up his mind where he was. He'd start us up one trail, back up, and off we'd go on another. This tended to make my company bunch up like an accordion; it was hard to keep the troops properly spaced. My scouts were meanwhile reporting hasty booby traps strung across the trails, as well as recently abandoned outposts in the rocks, with cooking fires still burning. After I'd gone forward to check them out, I made an appeal to get off the trails; but I knew the answer before I asked: Loi's confusion had already wasted half a day; and the VC were well aware of our presence by now. We needed to get on them before they could destroy what we were after and slip out. Moving off the trail would be safer, but take more time. We stayed on the track. I knew that was a difficult call for my boss; but I had to agree that it was correct.

In order to keep a handle on Loi's direction changes, I moved him up to the head of the company, with only the scouts and the point team in front of us. I was determined to get on his ass and stop his confusion. And, in fact, things started to move more smoothly as soon as I started pressing him hard.

My scouts (led by Corporal James, a black Marine from Washington, D.C., with an uncanny ability to read tracks and detect booby traps) were doing a magnificent job. This was very rough terrain—high mountains with flanking ridges.

In time, we approached a prominent ridge. On its other side, I was certain, lay the draw containing Loi's headquarters. It was clear we were pushing against security forces for something important. We could see little cuts down in the rocks, which were obviously listening posts and sentinel posts. In one case, we found a little cup of rice, still warm, left there when they ran out ahead of us. My scouts were also coming across hastily strung booby traps—wires with grenades and the like.

I wanted to get to that high ground as quickly as possible, since it was only a matter of time before we made contact with the enemy. I expected first contact would come from some security outpost firing at us to hold us up or perhaps from one we'd overrun before the enemy troops could fall back.

I was wrong. About two hundred meters from the top of the ridge, Loi stopped and looked at me, "They won't let you go any farther," he said, then shifted his gaze again toward the trail to the top.

"What are you talking about?" I asked him.

"A VC and an NVA company are defending this ridge," he said. "They will not let you get within 150 meters of the crest."

That was information we had to check out. I called up a pair of scout Cobra helos we had up above the ridge to get their view. I was talking to them when the enemy opened up.

I had turned sideways to give the handset back to my radio operator, Lance Corporal Franky, when I was hit. Three AK-47 rounds at fairly close range, close enough to easily pass through my flak jacket. It felt like I'd been whipped across the side and back with a burning hot, wet towel. I went down. As I rolled into a shallow erosion ditch, I tried to get a sense of what was happening. Moments later, Lieutenant Bob Myers, my 1st Platoon commander, and Lieutenant Pete Metzger, our battalion intelligence officer, who was with our company, both rushed over to me.

I was still conscious. . . . I never actually lost consciousness until I was medevaced out. Neither did I feel overwhelming pain. But I could feel the energy draining out of me, and I could tell I'd been badly hurt.

This couldn't have come at a worse time. My company was under heavy fire. I knew they'd need me as long as I could stay lucid.

"Get the platoon spread out and return fire," I told Bob Myers. The enemy was well hidden; the Marines were having a hard time picking out targets, but I just wanted to get the enemy's heads down as we moved troops around. A Marine with a multishot flamethrower was nearby. When I told him to fire, he asked, "At what?"

"I don't give a damn," I told him. "Just fire."

He did, and it slowed down the enemy's shooting.

Bob then helped me get my flak jacket off. I hated these heavy things; but it was the policy to wear them. The Vietnamese Marines never wore them, nor did our advisers with them; and I was convinced the added weight and discomfort worked to wear down the troops and make them less alert.

"Great," I thought, "now that I'm shot." The flak jacket had been useless in stopping the rounds.

As he peeled off the jacket, a bloody piece of flesh fell out. Not encouraging. Bob then started to apply a battle dressing; the look on his face told me the wound was bad. While he was doing that, I called Colonel Trainor to give him a situation report. By then, one of our corpsmen, Doc Miller, was working on me. I was now feeling so weak I was afraid I would pass out.

"You'll have to take over the company if I lose consciousness," I told Bob. "Or worse," I added. Bob was a good man, and capable. The officer who would normally have taken over for me, my company XO, Dan Hughes, was at the battalion command post on some coordination task. He'd try to get out to us as soon as he could, but I knew that until he came, it would be up to Bob to run the company.

All the while, I still had a company to run. I'd been on my stomach while they had dressed my wound. Now I raised myself up a little so I could see what was going on. I noticed a rise of high ground off to our left, and sensed the enemy was trying to get up to it. From there, they could fire down our flank with devastating effect. At the same moment, it dawned on me that we could do the same to him if we got there first.

"Get a squad with a machine gun on the hill," I told Bob. He immediately tasked one of his squad leaders, Sergeant Bamber, to take the rise. The squad rapidly moved out and took it in a quick fight.

Meanwhile, calls of "Corpsman up!" were coming from the point team in front of us. They were taking hits.

At that point, Doc Miller gave me a rundown of what was wrong with me. "Your back is a mess," he told me, "I can see your spine. I don't know whether or not that's been injured. If it was, then we've got to be worried about paralysis. Keep pinching your legs to be sure you have feeling. You've also lost a lot of blood, so there's a good chance you won't stay conscious." And finally: "I don't know how bad your pain is. I can give you morphine, but you're better off without it unless you absolutely need it."

The pain wasn't actually excruciating. And besides, I really didn't want to use the morphine, because once I did I knew I was no good to Bob Myers or anybody else.

The calls for a corpsman were growing more insistent. I looked into Doc's eyes and said, "Doc, they need you." The area between us and the point team was being raked with fire.

He looked up from me, stood up, and yelled "Fuck!," then charged off toward the wounded.

"We have to get the point team and the wounded back," I told Bob. "Send a squad to get them." Corporal Rocky Slawinski, the squad leader whose team was on point, had heard me. He came over to us. "I'll get them. They're my Marines," he said. He and the remainder of his squad then ran up under fire and carried back the wounded.

It looked like we had several wounded, including my Kit Carson Scout, who was shot in the shoulder.

During the excitement, Loi had somehow grabbed a rifle (which really pissed me off), worked his way forward toward the enemy, and then crouched down in no-man's-land, looking desperate. His former comrades had obviously seen and recognized him, and this had brought on a crisis of conscience. "They are calling my name," he kept saying, over and over. It looked to me like he was about to make a crucial decision about which team he was going to play for.

"Take the rifle from him," I told the ITT and Bob's platoon sergeant, Staff Sergeant Lambert. Though he was initially reluctant to give up the weapon, his hesitation died when Staff Sergeant Lambert jacked a round into his shotgun. His "crisis of conscience" over, he gave up the rifle and moved back in our direction.

We had another serious problem.

There was no way we could get medevac helos in. There were no landing zones, and the enemy was tightly mixed in with us in the thick brush.

Just as this was sinking in, two Marine CH-46 helos came up and identified themselves as our medevac birds.

"We didn't call for you," I told them, "and we can't take you now."

The pilot said, "I know. I just want you guys to know we're here, and we'll come in whenever or wherever you ask."

By then, a couple of hours had passed since I'd been hit, and I was feeling weaker than ever, and cold from the loss of blood.

Bob, who had done a great job of consolidating our position, had also found a possible LZ for the medevac helos farther down the slope. There was a rocky outcrop butting out over a cliff (the drop was several hundred feet). The pilots thought they could back up the helos against it and lower the helos' end ramps. The wounded could be loaded while they hovered. It might be a sphincter tightener for some guys, but it should work.

I was determined to walk down to the helos in front of my Marines; I didn't want to be carried. Though I knew I wasn't going to last much longer, I managed to march/stagger, with help, down the trail to where the other wounded were gathered. Before I moved up the ramp, I gazed out at my troops. The looks of comfort, reassurance, and concern for what lay ahead from those grim faces will always stay with me.

As the helos hovered next to the cliff, a VC raised up to take a shot at them with his RPG (rifle-propelled grenade) launcher, but a Marine spotted him and opened fire, and the VC had to duck down before he could take the shot.

The helo crew chief strapping us into the stretchers noticed that I was shivering on the bare canvas. He took off his white, fleece-lined flight jacket to wrap around me.

"Don't do that," I told him. "It looks new. The blood will ruin it."

"I don't give a shit about that," he said, and laid it over me.

Before I got on the chopper, the excitement and my adrenaline kept the pain manageable. But by the time it lifted out, it was coming on full force. I felt worse than I ever had in my life—in body, mind, and spirit.

SEVERAL WEEKS LATER, I received a letter in the hospital from Colonel Trainor. It read:

"I don't know if Lt. Hughes [Dan Hughes, my XO] or any of the others have written you about the events subsequent to your evac. At any rate let me fill you in. Dan and I went down to Red's pos [my first platoon's position] and Dan took command of the company. We shifted Becket [my second platoon] to the low ground. You trained your team well, Tony, they performed mag-

nificently. We stayed on the operation for two weeks and had a real war going. Alpha [my company] had most of the action. The VC tried to prevent us from penetrating, but when Bravo [Company B] came down on them from above, they skied [ran]. After that they kept firing at us from outside the cordon. Obviously they were trying to draw us away from the area. In this they failed. It was a grand war for a while."

He went on to add that we had suffered three killed and nine wounded during the operation, and we had killed forty-one VC of the enemy's C-111 Company.

The day after I was hit, my company found Loi's cave complex and eighteen thousand pages of documents: dossiers, pay rosters for agents, and agent lists with names and photos of senior South Vietnamese officials. Weapons and food caches were also discovered. The intel find was the largest and most important of the war.

"It was a pleasure having you in my command," Trainor added. "I have put you in for the Bronze Star."

Though Trainor liked to give medals to the troops, he didn't easily give them to officers. This endeared him to all of us, and made a medal he'd recommended a special privilege. It was a great honor to receive it.

MEDEVAC II

The medevac helo took the wounded to the 85th Evacuation Hospital, a U.S. Army field hospital south of Danang.

Zinni's wounds were serious enough for an immediate operation. After the pre-op X ray (rounds were still in his back), he was cleaned up and prepped, and IVs were inserted. As he lay there on his stomach after the prep, he noticed an unexpected flurry of whispers and huddling among the doctors and nurses. Something was up.

After a time, the huddles broke up, and a nurse pulled a chair up to his gurney, turned it around, and sat down backward, with her face almost touching Zinni's.

"I'm the senior nurse," she said. "Can you clearly understand me?"

"Yeah," Zinni said.

"We have recently received an experimental drug called ketamine," she continued, "and we'd like to use it on you. An officer like you can give us good feedback on its effectiveness."

Zinni gave her a tentative nod. These were medical people. He trusted them to know what they were doing.

"The drug is experimental," she added. "We'll need your permission before we can use it. You should know that you'll remain conscious throughout the operation and won't have tubes jammed down your throat, the way you normally might in an operation of this kind."

"That sounds good," Zinni said. "But how can I be conscious?"

"It's a hallucinogen," she said, "but it's an effective anesthetic without the ill effects of normal anesthesia."

"I guess that's okay," Zinni answered, "and not having tubes jammed down my throat is appealing. So let's do it."

"That's a good decision," she said. "I'm sure you won't regret it. And you'll be helping us."

THE KETAMINE turned out to be living hell. Though there was no physical pain, he had nightmares so vivid that he actually felt he was living through them: One was like an out-of-body experience—floating above his body as the surgeons were cutting into it. In another, he horribly re-lived the chaos, carnage, and deaths of the battle where he had taken his wounds. In another, he was dead and in a box, returning to his wife and family back in the States. The nightmares were so present, powerful, and *fierce* that he started thrashing around wildly during the operation, and had to be tied down and heavily sedated.

He woke up in a sweat, strapped to a bed in the intensive care unit.

With him was his first sergeant, Alls, with tears in his eyes, grasping Zinni's hand. He'd been holding Zinni's hand since he'd arrived in inten-sive care (Zinni had been vaguely aware of the squeeze; it had been a small and welcome comfort). After giving Zinni a heads-up about his company—who had been hit and evaced—he left.

"You went through a really rough trip," the nurse told him after he had gone.

"I know," Zinni told her. "I still remember it."

At that moment, he tried to move. And that was when he began to realize something was wrong. Not much above his waist worked right—like his arms.

Later, the surgeon explained why. "As we removed the rounds from your back," he said, "we couldn't just clean the wound and put you back together. The injury had wrecked too much. What we had to do, in order to prevent infection, was to debride the wound. That is, cut away about a third of the muscle tissue on your back and side. You've got a pretty big crater back there," he added sympathetically.

"What's going to happen," the surgeon went on, "is we'll keep you here for about a week, then we'll send you to Guam for extensive physical therapy. There they'll also take skin grafts taken from your legs and butt to cover the hole in your back.

"I have to be honest with you," he concluded. "I doubt if you'll regain full use of your arms and back."

This was a shock. "What will this mean for my family and my future?" Zinni asked himself.

On his way out, the surgeon gave Zinni one of the rounds he'd dug out of his back.

The next week was tough. Twice a day the medics literally ripped the bandages off the wound, with the most excruciating pain he'd ever known. Before this ritual, any troops on the ward who could move left the area. It was too painful to witness.

"Sir, you're really fucked up," a wounded lance corporal told him. "You should see your back."

"No, thanks," Zinni thought.

AFTER A few days, he was able to get up and walk a little. It wasn't easy, but he was able to get himself upright and to shuffle around the ward. The troops on the ward did everything to help.

One day, a nurse came in with disturbing news. Zinni's Kit Carson Scout (wounded in the same engagement and now in another ward of the hospital) was in bad shape.

"He has a shoulder wound," she said. "It's not serious. So there's no reason he should be doing so badly. But we don't think he's going to make it. It's as if he's lost his will to live."

This did not surprise Zinni. He'd experienced the fatalism of the Vietnamese many times before when he was an adviser. But that experience also gave him an idea how he might help his scout. "Can you move him into the bed next to me?" he asked.

"We really shouldn't," she said. "Our policy is to keep the Vietnamese patients separate. But," she added, "in this case we can make an exception."

Zinni spent the next several days keeping his scout going. His family on their visits also helped.

After days of touch and go, he came out of his funk.

One day, Zinni felt strong enough to try to find the troops from his company who'd been medevaced when he was; but after a search of the wards he only found one still confined to the hospital—Lance Corporal Maui, a big strapping Hawaiian kid from the point team. He'd been hit in the ankle and had a badly screwed-up leg. He and Zinni had a good talk, but it was clear he was depressed; he didn't know if he would fully recover.

But that wasn't the only thing bothering him. Something larger was on his mind; and after the two men had talked for a while, he blurted it out. "Sir, why are we here?" he asked.

Zinni gave him an answer, but it was the "party line" response; and by then he realized that was "piss-poor," as he thinks of it now: "I knew we were fighting a war that neither the South Vietnamese nor the American people were backing, and we were doing it with a lousy strategy, the wrong policies, and terrible tactics. After I walked away from Corporal Maui, I swore that from then on no troops of mine would ever again get such a shitty answer from me. They'd know from me why we were fighting. And if I felt something was wrong that put the lives of our troops in needless risk, I swore I would speak out, never hesitating to put my own career on the line for doing what was right by my men."

AFTER A WEEK, Zinni's time in Vietnam came to an end. His stretcher was loaded on another medevac plane headed for Guam.

Several hours later, lying on his bed in the ward of the Guam hospital, he began thinking about the dressing on his back. It had been there for two days. Removing it was going to be agonizing.

Later, a corpsman came in to discuss his injury. "You're lucky," he said. "The finest surgeon in the Navy will be handling your case."

At that moment, a doctor appeared at the side of Zinni's bed. "Let's take a look at this guy's wound," he said gruffly.

Zinni began his ritual of rolling slowly over on his stomach and putting a death grip on the bed rails.

"What the hell are you doing?" the doctor said.

Zinni explained the procedure back at the hospital in Vietnam.

"You're shittin' me," he said. And then he said to the corpsman, "Make him happy."

Zinni got a shot in each shoulder that made him very happy. Then the corpsman soaked the dressing in a solution that loosened the adhesive. A few minutes later, he simply lifted off the bandage.

"I wanted to kill the other medics who'd ripped it off twice a day," Zinni says now.

After examining the wound, the surgeon explained what would be done. "In a couple of days, I'll close the wound," he said. "I'm going to reattach muscles in your back." In other words, he saw no need to take muscle tissue from elsewhere in Zinni's body. "If you're willing to do serious physical therapy afterward, you can be back to normal. But it's going to take a lot of work . . . not to mention good luck in avoiding infection."

That was very good news. Zinni's morale was instantly raised higher than it had been since he was wounded; and he began to give serious thought to recovering and getting back to his company.

Two days later, he was wheeled into the operating room. The operation was a total success, and the physical therapy soon started paying off—though he knew he had a very long way to go. His body was doing strange things; muscles and nerves were all mixed up; when something touched his back, he felt it on his chest. He had to get used to all kinds of new muscle "hookups." But they worked!

During the next month, Zinni endured a few localized infections, re-

quiring massive doses of penicillin, but at the end of the month he'd recovered enough to leave the hospital.

Zinni begged to go back to Vietnam. He knew that was where he belonged. His time in the hospital had convinced him more than ever of that.
Though the doctor was very reluctant, he liked Zinni's drive and his ea-
gerness to get back with his guys. He gave in and released him to full duty,
but with a promise to continue to work out.

Zinni promised.

His orders sent him to Okinawa . . . "a stop off on the way back to
Nam," he thought.

IN THE SPRING of 1975, Vietnam collapsed, abandoned by the U.S.
whose people could no longer support the war.

The Vietnamese Marines were badly mauled in the final battles. The
remnants fought on in the hills for a time, and then the Marines ceased
to exist.*

---

*Any who survived were put in reeducation camps and not released for many years.
When Zinni's friend Hoa and his old battalion commander Tri were finally released, they
were allowed to come to the States with their families.

CHAPTER THREE

THE POINT OF THE SPEAR

THROUGHOUT HIS CONVALESCENCE, Zinni remained unaware that the Vietnam War had ended for him when he was evacuated from the Que Son Mountains.

By late December 1970, he had recovered enough to be transferred to Camp Hauge on Okinawa, where every Marine posted in the Western Pacific (including Vietnam) had to go for processing. When he arrived, Zinni expected a short stay, swiftly followed by return to duty to his unit in Vietnam. But new regulations, reflecting the growing reduction in U.S. forces, ended that hope: Since he'd been wounded and evacuated for more than thirty days, he was not allowed to return to combat. Neither could he go back to the States, since he had convinced the doctors, despite their strong concerns, to release him to full duty. Nor, finally, could he be assigned to an infantry unit based in Okinawa, such as the 3rd Marine Division, recently returned from Vietnam, since they were potentially redeployable to Vietnam, and Zinni could not be deployed there, by virtue of the rule previously stated. He had learned firsthand about catch-22s.

Zinni spent the remaining eight months of his yearlong Vietnam tour in the 3rd Force Service Regiment (3rd FSR), a logistics unit based at Camp Foster, Okinawa.

He expected to be bored. He was wrong.

Camp Foster was not boring. In fact, if his wish had been for combat, then his wish was granted. Camp Foster proved to be not all that different from a "real" combat zone . . . in many ways tougher than Vietnam.

After a few days of administrative processing, he set out to report in to 3rd FSR. His total possessions included a Red Cross–donated shaving kit and civilian clothes purchased out of his meager pay advance from the tiny post exchange at Camp Hauge.

Late one night, he walked out of the main gate and hailed an Okinawan taxicab to drive him to Camp Foster to report in. As the little car headed up the island road, his mood could not have been darker, thinking about his Marines in Vietnam and his family back in the States. He had managed to miss going back to either of them.

OKINAWA — barely sixty-six miles long and perhaps nineteen miles at its widest—runs roughly north to south. In the north, the country is rugged, much of it jungle. The more populated areas are in the south. Its people are of mixed race—partly Chinese, partly South Pacific islander, and partly Japanese—with a complicated history. Before World War Two, the island had been occupied by Japan, but before that it had had an even longer history of independence. Okinawans have never considered themselves Japanese, and the Japanese in turn have always treated them like a poor sister. Most wanted a return to independence.

In those days, the island was still U.S.-occupied territory, governed by an Army three-star general—a situation much resented by Okinawans. (When the occupation ended, the U.S. returned Okinawa to Japan.) It was also crawling with U.S. military facilities—another cause of friction. Infantry units were located in the more remote areas in the north. Farther south were the base- and logistics-type units. Among these was Camp Foster, located in the southern third of the island near Kadena (the U.S. Air Force base) and the major city of Koza, one of the island's two largest cities. The other, Naha, is the capital.

By 1970, this once-tranquil and beautiful island had become one large camp town for the American military. The devastation of World War Two had been followed by a huge influx of American military forces, and that in turn had been followed by seedy commercial strips, complete with bars, girly clubs, and pawnshops set up to service the troops. Women, booze, and drugs were readily available outside the gates.

As the cab entered Koza, Zinni noticed flames ahead; sirens were screaming. By the time they'd reached the main road in the city center, the driver had grown visibly anxious. For very good reason. A large, angry, chanting mob was roaming up ahead, many wearing red, communist headbands. Overturned cars were ablaze.

Some rioters, spotting the cab and the American inside, started running toward it. Without waiting for instructions, the driver threw the car in reverse, turned down a side street, and then raced through a maze of backstreets, his passenger bouncing around in the seat behind him. The driver was explaining all the while in broken English that the rioters were Okinawan communists, demonstrating against the occupation. Though he kept trying to reassure Zinni that they'd be okay, the whole city was in turmoil. They seemed to run into angry crowds at every turn, requiring yet another close-call getaway.

At last, with visible relief, the driver had them on the street leading to Camp Foster's main gate.

His relief quickly evaporated. Massive numbers of Okinawans with red headbands and long bamboo poles were charging a line of Marine guards in riot control gear, using the poles like jousting lances to knock over the guards. The taxi again raced away, as the driver sought a safe way into the camp.

They eventually discovered a gate that wasn't under attack, and the cab finally pulled up to its destination. Zinni rewarded his driver with a generous tip in gratitude for his courage and driving skills.

"Don't judge all Okinawans by what you've seen," the driver said in his broken English as he pulled away.*

---

* Zinni learned later that eighty-five American cars, mainly military police cars, were burned that night during the communist attacks on U.S. posts around Koza.

.   .   .

ZINNI CHECKED in the next day. Since his evacuation had left him nothing from his last command, he had to get new uniforms and set up new records. Going about this business, he picked up interesting and disturbing information about his new assignment:

Though the previous night's riot had been exceptionally bad, it was not uncommon. The race and drug crisis then coming to a head back in the States had reached Okinawa. Racial tensions were high. The threat of serious, large-scale violence was real. Between the communist demonstrations outside and the frequent race riots inside, the nights at Camp Foster tended to be exciting.

The race problems extended into the city. One Koza district, called "the Bush," was dominated by the "Bushmasters" and the "Mau Maus," gangs of black military men wearing distinctive gang garb. No white military man dared enter.

Inside the base, the gangs, in their gang uniforms, had taken to demonstrations—against real or perceived injustice, to let out rage, or sometimes just for the hell of it. Racially motivated incidents occurred daily. Some were minor, just knuckle-rapping displays and jive talk, but others were serious—like knifings. There was a white backlash as well—a Ku Klux Klan cell and cross burnings. And the racial divide was not simply black versus white. The Hispanics also had complaints, as did other minorities in the ranks.

Among the demonstrators were groups that were simply violent: gangsters and—literally—murderers. Other groups (largely out of the inner cities) felt oppressed, objecting not just to the Marine Corps but to society in general and its long-standing treatment of African Americans. Others saw everything white as an enemy, and still others had specific, military gripes of all shapes and sizes. One big one: Though the Corps was taking in ever-increasing numbers of young black officers, the senior officer ranks were still lily-white. The minority troops had reason to resent this.

Meanwhile, the Camp Foster guard force was unable to cope with the increasingly bloody racial incidents. Not only did other 3rd FSR units have to provide untrained, and therefore also ineffective, augmentation to reinforce it, but the 3rd Marine Division, located in camps at the northern end of the island, had to keep rifle companies on alert as reaction forces.

AS HE wandered around on his check-in rounds, Zinni noticed units practicing riot control formations and use of special riot control equipment. He knew that racial tensions were high throughout the military, made worse by growing opposition to the war and feelings of intergenerational betrayal; he was also aware of violent incidents in Vietnam and back home; and he'd himself handled a small riot as the officer of the day on duty in his battalion back at Camp Lejeune a few years earlier; but he'd never actually experienced significant racial problems in the units he'd commanded.

"This is a camp under siege," he told himself. "We're sitting on a powder keg."

As the weeks passed, and as he came to personally face the problems of this command, Zinni grew to appreciate the depth of the issues he was then encountering for the first time.

The emerging Vietnam War legacy was evident.

During Vietnam, the need for bodies had been so great that recruiters were sending people into the military who never should have been there. The draft was in place (even the Marine Corps accepted draftees); the initial training was reduced; and, later, promotions came too fast—ignoring the normal leadership development. People were suddenly wearing grades they were too inexperienced to wear; they did not have the education and training needed to perform complex jobs. Many sergeants weren't real sergeants; and many lieutenants, captains, and even higher should not have held those ranks.

There were also misguided attempts to turn the military into a big Head Start program for dropouts and other low achievers. Chief among these was Project 100,000—a Robert McNamara brainchild—which dumped a hundred thousand young failures into the military in hopes this would lead to a better society. Things didn't work out that way. Project 100,000 simply unloaded the problems of society on the military. As if that weren't bad enough, judges were using the military as an alternative to jails or rehabilitation.

The result of all this: The military were forced to accept below-standard troops, who were incapable of coping with the demands of service.

On top of all that, the growing drug culture had impacted heavily on the military. At Camp Foster—and at every other military facility—the number of troops caught, treated, and discharged for drug use was on the rise. This turned out to be Zinni's first experience with it on a large scale. Like other leaders of his generation, drug use was alien to him. He was scrambling to understand it. "What makes so many people want to do this to themselves?" he would ask himself time and again. "Doesn't beer do the job?"

Back home, wearing a uniform was not popular. Nobody was coming home a war hero; there weren't a lot of ticker-tape parades. It was even hard to find Americans who'd actually chosen to fight in Vietnam. Most who served there had been forced to go.

AFTER WORKING through the administrative requirements and meeting the commanders, Zinni was assigned to command the Headquarters and Service Company of the regiment's supply battalion—his fourth company command. Since command of a company was what being a Marine captain was all about, he felt grateful for that at least.

The H & S Company was a collection of troops with a variety of occupational specialties* and technical skills, who worked in numerous units throughout the battalion. The computer data processors, the cooks, the motor pool, the maintenance and housekeeping people, and so on were all placed in the H & S Company for administrative and command structure and for military training and proficiency (since they were Marines, they were still expected to be able to shoot), but otherwise they'd all go off every day to their own various offices or workplaces.

It was clear to Zinni that this was going to be a difficult company to command and in which to instill a sense of unit cohesion. Though it was a challenge he was willing to take on, his attitude was improved by some good advice from senior officers. "This is a difficult assignment for an

---

* Called MOSs—Military Occupation Specialties.

eager young infantry officer," they told him, "but like every other Marine, these men respond to good leadership. It's important for you to provide that without showing how dissatisfied you are to be in a unit outside your specialty. And," they added, "the experience will give you a unique opportunity to learn something about the various logistics functions the unit performs. It won't hurt you at all later to know something about that."

Zinni did his best to take this advice, and to put aside his disappointment and immerse himself in the job.

Unlike an infantry company, where unit cohesion and unit pride tend to come fairly naturally, the H & S Company was a grab bag. Nobody felt like he belonged in it. The data processors thought of themselves as data processors, the motor pool guys went off to the motor pool, the cooks went off to the mess hall, and none of them thought of the company, H & S, as anything but an administrative element.

Coming from an infantry unit, however, Zinni wanted to try to build unit cohesion and unit pride. He knew this was going to be hard. Not only did everybody go off to their very different jobs every day, but there was a lot of friction between the company and the workplace.

For example: Every Marine has to fulfill specific military skill requirements. They've got to shoot their rifle. They've got to be in good physical condition. They've got to be capable of actually fighting. Zinni, a captain, was responsible for making sure they were proficient in such things—which was all well and good until the head of the data processing center, a lieutenant colonel, found that such training interfered with his guys' data processing job.

Zinni did his best to minimize this friction and work out some kind of mutual understanding; but there was really no way to eliminate it totally. There was only so much time in a week. It was a zero-sum game.

In order to build unit cohesion and pride, he engaged with his guys as much as he could, to let them know who he was and to find out what made them tick. He organized more group events with the company— cookouts and sports and the like. He did what he could to look after their welfare, showing that there was command interest and proving that he was not just the administrative guy in charge but their company commander.

He was blessed in his support team—a feisty, hard-charging first sergeant who'd come out of Vietnam; an excellent gunnery sergeant who came from the Physical Fitness Academy and had been a drill instructor and on the Marine Corps shooting team; and a fine executive officer, a young lieutenant.

Over the weeks and months Zinni had the company, the unit began to come together in a satisfying way.

There were still worries. He wasn't so naive as to believe that none of his troops belonged to gangs or took part in demonstrations or riots. Some troops were bad actors, and some had serious drug problems. By and large, however, they were mostly just regular Marines looking for leadership and direction and somebody to care about them; and everybody tried to work with that. Eventually, everybody's hard work began to enhance the morale, the discipline, and the sense of a unit identity within the company.

IN THE SPRING of 1971, the rising racial tensions exploded. All during the winter, confrontations had increased; and the guard unit was increasingly incapable of handling them. A major eruption was inevitable.

Zinni was in his room at the Bachelor Officers' Quarters (BOQ) after a hard day when a call came: A riot had broken out near his company area. He rushed back to his company. On the way, he passed the scene of the riot. The guard was clashing with blacks wearing gang-logo jackets. It was a mess.

As soon as he reached the company quarters, he ordered the doors secured and a personnel head count. By good luck, few of his troops were away. After those on liberty returned, he stopped all further liberty for the evening. He didn't want any of his guys anywhere near the riot. He knew some might join the confrontation; but he also did not want to add curious bystanders to the mess.

It was a tense night, made more tense as the confrontation grew worse and the camp guards lost control. Some of their own minority troops joined the rioters, or just walked away.

Inside the barracks, Zinni and his guys talked about nothing else, and listened as events got out of hand—the shouts and the physical clashes— all confirmed by phone reports. Rioters tried to enter the barracks and coax some of Zinni's Marines to join them. They got sent away.

In the end, military police units and reaction forces had to be called in to bring back order.

The next morning revealed a scene of destruction and a sick bay full of injured people.

THE FOLLOWING night at the officers' club bar, some of the younger officers were talking about the riot, when Zinni—his brain lubricated by a few beers—made the mistake of offering an opinion about the breakdown of the guard. "I can build a guard unit that can handle the problems we've got here," he boasted.

His remarks got back to the regimental commander, and he was ordered to report to him.

A most embarrassed young captain stood before the colonel's desk the next morning. "So," the colonel said, gazing up at him, "I heard you think you can get the guard to handle the situation."

"I did say that, sir," Zinni admitted.

As he started to make his apologies, the colonel interrupted: "Good, you're now the new guard company commander."

"Oh, shit," Zinni told himself, cursing himself for mouthing off at the club.

"You've got a free rein," the colonel continued. "You can set up the guard any way you want. Take a day to decide what you want and get back to me with what you propose."

That got Zinni's attention. That just might make an impossible job possible.

He spent the rest of the day thinking through what might work.

The next day he laid out his request: He wanted a hundred-man guard force—all racially mixed volunteers. Each would be over six feet tall and weigh more than two hundred pounds (Zinni would be the shorter, lighter exception); and he wanted permission to interview anyone in the command he felt would make a good guard member.

That particular number was not chosen for any special reason. Zinni wanted a larger guard force than currently existed, and one that could handle any conceivable incident without having to be augmented by poorly trained troops, but he also had practicalities that had to be dealt with, such as the number of watches, posts, and hours he had to cover.

The colonel had doubts that Zinni could get a hundred volunteers, much less a hundred who were racially mixed; and so did Zinni, but he wanted to try. "Go ahead," the colonel told him. "See what you can do."

The response proved overwhelming—with an especially gratifying number of African American, Hispanic, and other minority volunteers. Nobody thought that so many guys would be so fed up with the bad situation. Within two days Zinni easily had his hundred men, all good Marines.

Among those he convinced to come on board as one of his two guard chiefs was the company gunnery sergeant from H & S Company, Gunnery Sergeant Bobby Jackson, an African American and a model Marine. Gunny Jackson had spent tours of duty as a drill instructor, competitive shooter, and instructor at the Marine Corps's Physical Fitness Academy, and would go on to achieve the grade of sergeant major. Zinni knew his outstanding leadership abilities firsthand, and felt an African American enlisted leader was critical for the guard.

For the other guard chief, he recruited Gunnery Sergeant Dick De-Costa, a big, 250-pound Marine who had been made a temporary officer during the Vietnam War but had recently reverted to his enlisted grade as the war wound down. DeCosta had spent most of his career in the Orient, had married a Chinese woman, and was an expert in Oriental martial arts. He was a third-degree black belt in judo and the Marine Corps heavyweight judo champion.*

For his two lieutenants, he chose an impressively bright and dynamic black officer and a Jewish American from New York City.

Zinni's plan was not to create just a reaction force, but to make the guard a very visible model for unit cohesion and spirit. He wanted every-

---

* DeCosta later took Zinni under his wing. "While you're on this island," he told Zinni, "you can be like all the other Marines and just go out to town and see it as one big bar. Or else you can begin to take in a whole other culture. I'd be glad to take you around and be your guide." DeCosta took Zinni to places few other Americans ever knew—to geisha houses . . . real geisha houses, not houses of prostitution. He took him to historical sites. He introduced him to Okinawan families and his many Okinawan friends—many of them martial arts experts, who introduced Zinni to the nonphysical side to martial arts . . . its mental and "spiritual" aspects. Zinni of course found all this fascinating.

one to see that a diverse team could work together and play together. But he also wanted all to see that they were capable of knocking heads if they had to. He wanted to show everyone the new guard's capabilities—psyops aimed at troublemakers:

The new guard did their physical training (PT) very visibly at times when the entire camp would see them, making sure nobody lost sight of the fact that these were big, tough guys who lifted serious weights and took martial arts training. They always made their PT runs through the barracks areas at double time, chanting and making a lot of noise. They worked out their riot control formations on the camp's big parade deck in an area that everybody could see. They'd set up barrels to stand in for rioters; then bring out the water cannon truck and hose down the barrels. Zinni would leave the barrels where they'd fallen, and afterward people would go up and stare at it. He wanted them to think: "This could be me." And that's what they thought.

He would also bring individual units in for "riot control training." The guard would take a unit—say, the supply company—and explain to them that they might be called in to augment the guard and had to go through training classes to show what the guard did to rioters and how they did it.

Zinni had no real intent to use them; he wanted to let them know what the guard could do to anybody who joined a riot.

Though all this psyops worked as intended, Zinni knew that wouldn't keep his guard from being tested.

The first weeks of the new guard were filled with demonstrations and confrontations, requiring a response by the entire guard roughly every third day. Sometimes a demonstration turned violent. During one incident, a guard trooper was stabbed; many others suffered cuts and bruises. None of these setbacks, however, prevented the guard from containing, controlling, and ending every incident quickly.

Predictably, the minority members of the guard received threats from the gangs. They didn't waiver, even though they sometimes actually sympathized with some of the demonstrators' complaints.

When one obviously intelligent black NCO volunteered for the guard, Zinni asked him why.

"Look," he said, "somebody's going to have to enforce discipline and maybe even crack their heads. That's got to happen. What they're doing is wrong. Still," he continued, "even though they're going about it the wrong way, I sympathize with a lot of their issues. I see their point. They're my brothers, but they're going to be dealt with. And I would like to be on the other end to ensure it isn't excessive and that it's handled the right way, and to try to be a force for reason."

"You're exactly the kind of guy I want," Zinni told him.

Integrating the guard did not come naturally; it took a lot of work. In those days, it was the natural thing for young men coming into the Marine Corps to separate by race. After Zinni integrated the guard, the threats continued, and not just to minority members. It was partly for purposes of security and partly to show that this was the right way to go that Zinni's guard had their own after-hours bars and liberty spots, the only integrated group on Okinawa hanging together on liberty. This turned a lot of heads, including some native ones. Several Okinawans commented that these were the only places where they saw whites and blacks and Hispanics and Samoans mixing together and socializing as friends.

Zinni's policy from the start was, in his words:

To respond to every incident with one of every kind. That is, I had the guard organized so that no matter what happened, we would get a black Marine, a white Marine, an Hispanic Marine, and a Samoan Marine—a rainbow detail—going out to handle it.

When we failed to do that, we always regretted it:

One day, we had an incident at the sick bay. The Navy doctors called to say that a Marine in there was going berserk, rampaging around, breaking things, and making wild threats. It turned out that the kid who had lost it had mental problems and had gone through some really bad times. It also turned out that he was black.

On that particular day, my duty sergeant sent four white Marines out to handle the problem.

When the four guards got to the sick bay, they found the crazy Marine in a recreation area, with a pool table and some soda machines, brandishing a pool cue and threatening to beat everybody up.

The four Marines did what they would normally do to take care of him.

They grabbed him, cuffed him, and wrestled him down—with him kicking and fighting all the while. Then they manhandled him out to their jeep in order to take him to a holding cell until they could get him to a hospital for treatment.

As it happened, it was noontime—chow break—so everybody was coming out of the supply areas and warehouses. When the black Marines saw the four white Marines roughing up this guy, throwing him into the jeep, and bringing him back to the guard offices, it sparked a riot.

When I came back to the guard offices after my own lunch, I found a large number of black Marines surrounding the place. I was instantly up to my neck trying to figure out what had happened and calm it down.

The black Marines had a leader—a lance corporal and a hard worker they called "Superman," because he was built like Arnold Schwarzenegger. This guy who looked like Hercules came up and confronted me, all fired up that we had been beating up on one of the brothers. (And of course I was still in the dark about what was going on.)

He and I talked it over for a while, and I was starting to think I could maybe calm this thing down when in walked Gunny DeCosta, who instantly decided he didn't like the way this guy was talking. He launched into him and had him blasted in short order. This shocked everybody and brought the situation under control. We learned from incidents like these how to handle things firmly and how to quickly defuse tense situations.

Zinni studied and used riot control techniques the way he had previously studied combat. Inspired by Gunny DeCosta, he and his guards trained in kendo, stick fighting (using their batons), and other martial arts with the riot police from the city of Naha, at their dojo.

Zinni encouraged innovation and experimentation in the unit, and his guards developed creative new ways to handle rioters. One big problem: How do you identify the bad guys after a riot? When a riot is raging, the idea is to shut it down. When that starts to happen, the rioters melt away, and then the next day they show up at their jobs looking like everybody else.

The eventual solution was to fill a fuel bladder on a truck with a solution containing the indelible blue dye that's stamped on meats (the medical supply guys provided it). During a riot, the guard would hose down everybody there with this solution. The next day they'd check the barracks and pick up anybody who was purple.

AS WEEKS PASSED, other lessons were learned.

For starters, there were too many weak commanders:

Though no units at Camp Foster escaped its problems, Zinni learned to predict where he'd find the biggest problems by identifying the weakest commanders. Not surprisingly, the worst incidents involved troops from units with the weakest leadership . . . a failure obviously stemming from the personnel imbalances resulting from the war, but amplified when officers in the more technical MOSs were suddenly confronted with major leadership crises they just weren't equipped to handle.

ANOTHER, far more important lesson: The value of openly thrashing out the issues with the troops.

In those days, the Marine Corps was only just starting to require human relations training—trying to get the message across that just because a person's skin was different, or he wore his clothes differently, or liked different music, he was not radically different from you or anybody else. You still shared the same basic values. The Corps tried to teach all Marines to understand and respect these differences, even as they had them looking inside for prejudices they didn't realize they had . . . the unconscious automatic stereotyping with which they'd grown up.

This training got off to a rocky—and sometimes hokey—start (for instance, they tried Soul Food Nights at the mess hall, with fried chicken, hominy grits, and chitterlings . . . everybody thought these were a joke) and was more often than not poorly conducted; yet it did encourage dialogue and frank discussion of problems. When these discussions were well led and troops were able to talk constructively about their concerns, they paid dividends that overcame the poor initial construct of the program.

For all of its rocky beginnings, the Corps' human relationship training had the right idea; the organization was doing its best to get at the real roots of its troubles; and it didn't give up. The Marine Corps kept at the effort for as long as it took to make it work.

It took many years.

Needless to say, there was a lot of resistance to this process. The old tough Marines didn't like it: "This is all touchy-feely shit we don't need," they said. "Forget all that race crap. There's no black or white Marines; they're all green. Every Marine's green. Just put Marine discipline in the unit, that'll solve any problems we got." Fortunately, the leadership of the Corps combined a strict adherence and maintenance of its standards with a more open means for communications.

As a result, the quality of the training picked up, and it came to be more and more accepted. Not always, but every once in a while, troops would really let loose, air out what really bothered them, and begin to connect.

Eventually, as the good changes became the norm, the need for the training went away. For many, it got to be seen as a pain in the butt.

That was not a sign of failure but of success.

THE OTHER SIDE to the process involved weeding out real trouble-makers—the thugs, the radicalized, the violent. The best place for such people was the brig, followed by an aircraft back to the states and jail. But the Corps also found ways to get rid of lesser troublemakers without having to go through a long legal process, by issuing what were called "expeditious discharges." That is, people were given the opportunity to choose to leave with general discharges, and so avoid legal procedures and a worse discharge. It was easier for everybody.

Throughout the 1970s, as the size of the post-Vietnam Corps came down, the Corps was increasingly successful at weeding out those who'd come in under Project 100,000 and others who didn't fit or had chronic qualification problems.

Meanwhile, a few weeks of firm and effective guard work stopped riots and demonstrations at Camp Foster, and Zinni's guard became very popular. Many in the command now wanted to join it. It was *the* elite unit, the best place to be at the camp.

• • •

ZINNI'S EIGHT months in 3rd FSR, he later realized, were the most difficult of his Marine career. He'd never imagined he'd face Marine-on-Marine confrontations; at Camp Foster, he had to deal with them almost daily . . . not to mention levels of violence that made a logistics base feel like a combat tour. These were hard realities for an eager and dedicated young Marine to accept. On the other hand, he was able to leave Camp Foster with some confidence. He had encountered the worst of the problems facing the Corps, and the rest of the military, and knew that they could be handled.

He left 3rd FSR in August 1971 and one month later reported in to the 2nd Marine Division at Camp Lejeune, North Carolina. He was back in his original command.

BACK TO THE INFANTRY

When Zinni checked in to the 2nd Marine Division, he fought off the personnel officer's kindly attempt to give him a break after his two tough Vietnam tours and life-threatening wounds. He didn't want an undemanding staff job; he wanted to go to a rifle company, where the action was—the heart of the Marine Corps. You don't get more central to Marine identity.

"Okay, then, you got it," the personnel officer told him, "if that's what you want." And he sent Zinni down to the 1st Battalion, 8th Marines. There the battalion commander offered him command of Company D, which was in cadre status* at that time. It was to be remanned in the coming weeks.

Zinni was delighted. He was to get command of his sixth company; and it was a rifle company.

A Marine rifle company is usually made up of three infantry platoons—

---

* Because of the post-Vietnam shortage of manpower, many units had been stood down in what was called "cadre status," with no troops and just a few caretaker administrators to maintain unit records and equipment. As the months went by, the Marine Corps refilled their ranks.

called "rifle platoons"—and a weapons platoon, which has the company's crew-served weapons: in those days, 60-millimeter mortars, M-60 machine guns, and perhaps an antitank capability. The number of men in a company varied based on a number of organizational changes at that time and the fluctuations in manning levels. Zinni found himself with a 120-man company, a far cry from the 250 he had in Vietnam, and a sign of the times.

He now had an opportunity to gain further command experience with a rifle company as well as to put into practice the many new training ideas that had come out of his time in Vietnam and his constant reading in matters military, from technical manuals to history and biography. Like most company commanders, he wanted to produce the best, most tactically proficient company in the division, but he also enjoyed actually teaching the skills he'd come by through trial and error, study, and observation.

Training a company takes many forms: There's weapons and tactics, obviously, but also more specialized training for cold weather,* desert, or mountain operations; for working with tanks and armor; for amphibious operations (especially before a deployment). Some kinds of training were standardized, some were unique to whatever specialized mission or deployment was on the schedule.

Zinni's company did it all—below-zero training in sixty inches of snow in upstate New York, training for jungle operations in Panama, and for amphibious operations in the Caribbean. The latter was Zinni's first serious experience with the Marine Corps' bread-and-butter mission, which was also the most complex of all military operations: the transfer of elements from a ship onto some form of transport (surface or air), and then moving them in a closely timed and synchronized way to a landing under fire on a hostile beach, followed by a continued buildup ashore. The entire process—from coming out of the ships through what's called "the ship-to-shore movement" and into combat operations—must be accomplished in one smooth, continuous flow. Using air strikes and naval gunfire to support the units going ashore, passing control of the operation ashore from

---

* The Marine Corps had a Cold War commitment to deploy to Norway, above the Arctic Circle, in the event that the Cold War turned hot.

the ships, getting in the logistics and supplies, and matching it all up is an undertaking of tremendous complexity, requiring equally complex planning (landing sequence tables, assault schedules, helicopter deployment schedules), very close coordination, and a great degree of communication . . . while facing an enemy doing its best to disrupt and destroy it all.

As his career developed, Zinni made many sea deployments and amphibious ops—missions he came to love. He enjoyed life at sea, and the traditional image of the Marine Corps storming ashore and rushing up the beaches always excited him. In time, he became fascinated by these operations *because* of their enormous complexity—putting all the myriad pieces together in a synchronous yet dynamic way. The mission grew to be one of his passions. Later, he taught courses in amphibious ops at Marine Corps schools; and in Somalia, he was to command a force in an actual amphibious operation—the largest since the Inchon Landing during the Korean War.

ZINNI COMMANDED Company D for a little over a year, by which time he was sure they could handle any combat mission that came their way—an opinion he would soon have to prove when D Company took the division-directed company tactical test.

The test contained a series of tough challenges: The company might, for example, be asked to make an amphibious landing and then go into an armor-mechanized attack, or a night heliborne assault. The idea was to stretch the commander's capabilities by whipping a number of missions on him and putting him under a lot of stress. He got no sleep, he had to keep moving; and all the while, the judges were looking at his ability to give orders and to successfully execute his tasks. At the same time, the judges were examining his troops' performance, endurance, and tactical skills, and the NCOs and officers and their tactical skills.

So far, every company in the division had failed it.

Zinni and his company passed.

It was a big moment for Zinni, and (justifiably) swelled his ego. Soon came letters of congratulations and glowing calls from the regimental and the division commanders. Since the company was also excelling in its discipline statistics, reenlistment rates, and other nonoperational measures, there were further occasions for pride. Although Zinni reveled in his success, it came with a price.

He loved being a company commander; he couldn't think of anything else he wanted to do except possibly to get back to the advisory unit in Vietnam.

The successes of his company ended that bliss.

TONY ZINNI continues:

Not long before the end of one of our Caribbean deployments, my battalion commander called me to his office at our camp on Vieques Island (near Puerto Rico) and handed me a message from the division commander, Major General Fred Haynes. Haynes was asking for nominees from each battalion to be his aide-de-camp. The last line of the message directed that our battalion's nominee be me.

"Do you know anything about this?" my battalion commanding officer asked. "Why are we the only battalion with a directed nomination?"

"I'm as much in the dark about this as you are, sir," I told him. "I definitely do not want the job." It was a staff job, and I never wanted staff jobs.

"Okay, then. I'll tell him that," the CO said, and sent a message back to the commanding general stating that I declined the nomination.

I forgot all about this thing and went back to the field with my company.

Two weeks later, as our ship docked at Morehead City, North Carolina, to off-load our battalion landing team, I was greeted by an officer from the division staff who told me I was to immediately get in the staff car waiting at the bottom of the brow and proceed to the division commander's office to report to General Haynes.

"I can't do that," I said to him. "I have to get my company back to Camp Lejeune and settled back into our barracks."

"That's an order," he laughed.

So I let my battalion commander know where I was headed, took off for the division headquarters, and nervously entered the general's office. Haynes was a tall, distinguished-looking Texan, an Iwo Jima veteran, who was con-

sidered one of the most brilliant men in the Marine Corps. At his invitation, I took a seat.

After asking me about the deployment and how things were going, he explained what he was looking for in the job. "I want my senior aide to be my 'operational aide,' " he explained. "I'll have the junior aide, a lieutenant, to handle all the social requirements, the proper uniforms, and all that kind of business. For my 'operational aide' I want an adviser, somebody who's been in the pits whom I can trust. I want a guy that knows what the hell goes on in a division, knows about training and operations, and who's been in combat. I want someone who the junior officers and NCOs of the division will honestly talk to, who'll be my point of contact with them, and who can tell me what they're thinking and their perspective on what we need to improve.

"When we go out in the field and see what's out there, I want a guy savvy enough to say, 'What you're seeing there, General, is not good,' because he knows it's not. . . . I'm removed from that. That's years ago, in my past. Now I get screened and filtered. If I talk to colonels and other generals, I get good information, but it doesn't come from the ranks. I want my operational aide to give me that sense.

"I've already interviewed all the nominees," he went on, "but waited to make my decision until you returned and I could interview you." He then read to me the list of other nominees.

"Sir, I know most of them, and you couldn't pick a finer group of captains. I'm sure you'd be satisfied with one of those guys."

Then he looked at me. "You know, Captain, the message from your CO is very interesting. It seems that you're the only nominee who does not want the job."

"I don't feel that I'm really aide material," I told him; and I meant it. You always think of an aide as a tall, bullet-headed, poster Marine. And here I was, a short, squat Italian guy, rough around the edges, and he's a better than six-foot-tall Texan—a golf-playing gentleman. (A little later, when I told him I didn't play golf, I thought I'd put the final nail in the coffin.)

By then he was smiling at me . . . just playing with me. "I take it that's just because you want to stay on as a rifle company commander," he said. "This I can understand. You don't have anything against being my aide, do you?"

"Certainly not," I said, thinking, "Shit, I hope I haven't insulted him"—the last thing on my mind.

"Well, I understand you don't want the job. I've had some tremendously talented captains who are interested and who've interviewed for it; and I appreciate your coming by. I didn't want to make the decision until I interviewed all the candidates."

This kind of confused me because I didn't think I was a candidate. I thought the message from my CO had killed that. But because I thought there might have been a misunderstanding, I said, "Well, I appreciate your interest, sir. But, no, I really don't want the job, and you have some fine officers there."

"I do; and I also understand your position; and we'll go ahead and make the decision."

"Thank you, sir, for the understanding," I said, and left.

When I got back to the battalion area, I went to my CO's office and told him everything was okay. It all seemed to be just a formality the general needed to go through so he could say he had interviewed all the nominees. But when I arrived back at my company area, there was a call waiting as I walked in. It was my CO. He'd just received a call from General Haynes. I was selected as the aide and was ordered to report for duty the next day.

It was obvious that Major General Haynes had made up his mind before he met me. Later, I found out why:

He had prepared a list of eight or nine criteria—most of them fairly obvious, like commanding a company in Vietnam in combat, attendance at the career-level school for captains, and commanding a company in the 2nd Marine Division. As luck would have it, I came out as the only guy in the division who met every one of the criteria.

Meanwhile, his current aide (I didn't know him well) had talked to other people who had mentioned my name; and when they matched these recommendations up with the other thing, he seems to have fixed on me.

I SPENT a year as the aide to two generals—first to General Haynes; and after he got orders to Korea, I became the aide to Brigadier General Jake Poillion, who'd been Haynes's assistant division commander. When Haynes left,

Poillion was fleeted up as the CG and told it was just an interim; a major general would be coming down the track very shortly. In fact, the interim turned out to be six or seven months. Later, when the major general did finally come down, he started making noises like he was going to keep me in place, too. So I had to really fight to get out of the job.

Though in many ways my tour as aide was a valuable experience, I never really enjoyed it; my original reasons for not wanting it remained valid. Still, I was fortunate to work for generals who were interested in my views and were highly respected leaders. And the experience exposed me to a different level of perception than I was used to. Problems I'd been sure I had absolute answers to when I commanded a company got a lot less simple. I came to realize that there was a great deal I didn't know and had to learn.

When you're down at the company level, you see things in black and white; you don't have a broader view. I'd see all kinds of things wrong in the weapons ranges, for instance, and it seemed obvious to me: "These ranges should be better. They're shabby. They need serious maintenance and renovation. This is what we're all about, and we're letting it go to hell."

Well, all of a sudden I was seeing things from a general's point of view, looking at the budget he has to work with, looking at all the alternatives, realizing he has to give some things up. Now, suddenly, I was forced to realize that my "absolute answers" were not as absolute as I'd thought. And I came to appreciate that a lot of the choices generals had to make did not come out of a lack of interest or a failure to care. It was a matter of priorities. It was a matter of other realities you don't have a sense of when you're down at company level.

ONE THING really bothered me while I was an aide, however: The captains were more interested in war fighting than the senior officers.

The captains loved talking about operational issues—working them through, worrying over them, coming up with new ideas. We were the Vietnam guys. We'd suffered through all the lousy tactics, the poor policies, and the shitty things that went on in the field. So we had a burning desire to make sure we had the skills we hadn't seen there. We went into the crucible right out of the blocks.

But the senior officers were another thing; and this really shocked me. I expected to learn a lot about war fighting from the horse's mouth; but it didn't happen that way. They certainly knew war intimately; they had all experienced it in World War Two, Korea, and Vietnam. But war fighting was pretty far down on their agenda. Operational competence was simply not valued or demanded as much as administrative competence. In those days, they were judged on their management and not their tactical skills.

It was rare, in fact, to find anyone above the rank of captain who talked tactics and war fighting.

I understood that Vietnam was ending and the big concerns presented by the war's aftermath—race and drug problems, the critical shortage of personnel, the severe budget cuts, reorganizations, and many other issues—consumed their time and attention. Yet I expected there would be far more focus on the core of our profession—how to fight. This was my passion; I thought it would be the passion of every Marine. It wasn't.

One day I was chatting with General Poillion.

"My God," I said to him, "there's something badly wrong with us. We're losing our operational edge. We don't hold people to task. I see senior officers—battalion or regimental commanders—that either don't know anything about war fighting, or else they've forgotten it. They were in Vietnam and all, but they've lost it. There's no way we hold them accountable. We run TAC tests on the company commanders and the tests are tough. But after that there's nothing. What happens to test the others?"

He thought a moment, then he looked at me. "Have you ever heard of anybody being relieved for poor, shitty tactics?" he asked.

"No," I said.

"Have you ever heard of anybody being relieved for poor administration or logistics?"

"Yes."

That happened all the time—for badly managing money and personnel and the like.

"Well, there it is," he said. "Officers are held accountable for poor leadership or poor administration, but not for poor operational skills. That's the problem."

There was one notable exception to this pattern.

Back when I commanded D Company, a fellow captain and company commander, my friend Jack Sheehan (I'd known him since my early days at Quantico; he eventually became a four-star general), had bragged a lot about his great battalion commander. Jack's commander really knew the stuff the gung ho younger officers were living and breathing and spending every spare moment talking about—landing plans, tactics, small units, patrol formations, weapons employment, all of that stuff. He'd had a long stretch in Vietnam, five or six years, and his operational skills were legendary; and like all the best leaders, he'd read everything. Not only that, he was one of the few senior officers who actually liked to sit down and talk tactics and hold forth on his own with the junior guys. His name was Al Gray.

"Hey, how about coming to dinner?" Jack said to me. "You and I can hook up with Colonel Gray—sort of like a guys' night at the club."

"Sure," I said.

I knew something about Gray; it was hard not to at Lejeune. He was a legend. The troops loved him, and he was truly great with the enlisted Marines. He himself had come up through the ranks and never lost that connection. Later, as the aide, I learned that he was held in equally high regard by the generals.

So I met Al Gray at the officers' club at Camp Lejeune with Jack Sheehan. When he walked in, the first thing that impressed me was how down to earth he was. He talked to us, not down to us (he was not patronizing). But what really impressed me was how much he was really into the operational stuff. "He knew his shit," as the troops would put it. He had the same sort of fire that I had. No matter what came up for discussion, he had an informed and pointed opinion about it. I had seen this kind of fascination for tactics and war fighting in only a very few senior officers. I was really impressed.

Of course, I hoped I'd have a chance to see him again and take our discussions further; but being realistic, I figured it was unlikely. Not only was I in another battalion, I was in another regiment, and probably just another captain to him. Well, it turned out that he must have seen something worth cultivating in me; and he stayed in contact—took me under his wing.

By the time I became the general's aide, he had moved up to become regimental commander of the 2nd Marines, and I saw him frequently . . . he al-

ways had a lot of business with the general; and we grew increasingly friendly. Later, as we both rose up the ranks, the friendship continued to develop and mature—the classic mentor relationship. I've always considered him as my strongest mentor (and I've had several, starting with General Mick Trainor). It was a relationship that has stood for thirty years. Gray went on to become the commandant of the Marine Corps and significantly change the way the Corps thought and conducted combat operations.

WHEN MY *tour as aide ended, I had an offer to command another company (it would have been my seventh). I jumped at the chance, but General Poillion snuffed out that idea. I'd already had six companies; it would not be well received if the general's aide got a seventh.*

I was assigned to the G-3, the operations section of the division—a disappointment. But the good news was that Al Gray, now a colonel, had just given up command of his regiment and was to be the new G-3. If I couldn't be in an infantry unit, then the next best assignment, in my view, was in an operations or training assignment. I knew I would learn a lot from Colonel Gray.

When I checked into the section, Colonel Gray surprised me. "What do you want to do?" he asked.

"Something in training will be great," I said, thinking the best I could get as a captain was to be some sort of training assistant—an administrator who kept the statistics or arranged schedules. It was a boring job, but it would at least allow me to observe training. Such was the fate of junior officers on a division staff.

"No, Captain, you didn't hear me," Colonel Gray said. "I didn't ask you what job you expected to get stuck with. I asked you what you really want to do. I want you to take a few days to think about your answer.

"You and I have talked a lot about improving the infantry skills of the units in the division," he continued. "We both think that our units lack tactical skills they should have and that company commanders have not been given the assets and help they need to train their units. Since you feel so strongly about that, why don't you think about something you can do to help that situation."

I came back a few days later with a wild idea—a center of excellence for infantry operations and weapons skills that provided training and training support for the infantry companies and battalions, a facility that could put units and their leaders through training courses and programs, and offer training "packages" containing references, support materials, suggested schedules, ranges and training area recommendations, specialized instructor support, and unit training evaluations.

Colonel Gray liked the idea; and we drew up detailed plans. We'd get around the limited assets, personnel, and funds available in the postwar drawdown by converting an old training facility scheduled for demolition and running it with a minimum staff. It was in the most remote part of the base, and deep into the woods and swamps. Access was only through dirt roads, and many of the old firing ranges from the now-defunct Infantry Training Regiment were close by. It was perfect for what I had in mind.

After reviewing the final plans, Colonel Gray took them to the new commanding general, Major General Sam Jaskilka, a hard-as-steel old fighter whose heroism in Korea at the Chosin Reservoir under massive Chinese attack was legendary.

The general liked the idea and gave the go-ahead, with directions that the center should be austere and the training tough and realistic, with lots of live fire and fieldwork. "I'm going to spend a lot of time out there checking up on Zinni," he told Colonel Gray. "I better not see rugs on the floor, or troops living in anything but tents." He was a man after my own heart—a warrior general and not a business manager.

The center proved to be a great success, for several reasons.

First, the assessments were only given to the commanders' training there and never to their superiors. So they could test their limits and work on their weaknesses without fear of report cards. (I fought off attempts to use the center to make reportable evaluations on the units training there.) This allowed me to be brutally honest about their shortfalls; and it allowed them to fail and improve.

Second, though my instructors were not always the very best available (and this was deliberate; taking the best guys would have gone down very badly with everybody else), all of them were competent enough to do the job, and I sent them to the best leadership and tactical courses to increase their knowledge and skills. The work for my instructors was hard and demanding and the hours were long, but they loved it.

We also did a great deal of instructor training at the center. I revised the Special Operations* courses and further trained my instructors in these specialized skills. To spice up the training for the troops we added courses on survival and adventure training, but we never lost sight of our primary mission, to develop advanced infantry skills in the division units.

As time passed, the shooting qualification scores of troops and units that went through our training skyrocketed upward, and the positive feedback from the division was overwhelming. We even trained the division's Competition Squads for the annual Marine Corps competition at Quantico, Virginia. The 2nd Division squads were traditionally the doormats in this competition, but the squads we trained that year took the top two honors.

I ran the Infantry Training Center for well over a year—loving every minute of it, learning a great deal, and experimenting with ideas I had wanted to try ever since Vietnam. Some worked and some didn't; but the chance to concentrate on small-unit tactics, weapons, environmental operations, and combat leadership training was invaluable.

Later on, the Marines addressed the problem of tactical evaluation of units beyond the company level. Their eventual solution came from an Army program.

After Vietnam, all the services faced serious problems, but, of all the services, the Army had the longest way to go; they needed the most radical reforms. To their credit, they did what they had to do and did it superbly.

One of their biggest and most enduring reforms was to create the Battle Command Training Program (BCTP), which allows them to tactically evaluate unit and command performance all the way up to the corps level. The idea is to train people by letting them see how and where they make wrong decisions or wrong moves, and to see how they can more reliably make the right choices. The program is not used as a measure for promotion, or as a hammer to beat people with. But it is tough. A three-star Army general at the

* In those days, Marine Special Operations meant something different from what it has come to mean today. These were operations in harsh environments like mountains, deserts, or the Arctic.

corps level goes through a battle test and an evaluation; and it's cold and pointed, and the evaluators don't want to hear any gripes, bitches, or excuses. That's it.

The first time I observed a BCTP exercise, a three-star general screwed up somehow, and admitted it without excuses. "Yeah, I screwed up," he said. "I should have made a different choice."

This was a sign of a remarkable transformation.

When the Marine Corps saw how well the BCTPs worked, we grabbed onto the idea and developed a similar program, now called "the Marine Air Ground Task Force Staff Training Program" (MSTP). We found a site for large-scale combined arms field exercises at Twentynine Palms in California where battalion units and larger get tested and evaluated. (The Army does the same thing not far from there at the NTC—National Training Center.) And we developed a Marine Corps Combat Readiness Evaluation System (MCRES) that provided unit and individual standards and a test for our units preparing to deploy.

STAFF DUTY AND SCHOOL

As 1974 rolled around, Tony Zinni had been a captain for eight years and a company-grade officer for over nine. Early that year, he was selected for major, but the actual promotion was a long time coming, since he was very junior on the list. Since majors generally got staff jobs, he knew that his wonderful and exciting times "in the field" and "with the troops" were coming to an end. Since Marine advisers were still operating in Vietnam, he had dreams of still getting back to the advisory unit . . . yet he knew that possibility was becoming ever more remote.

Barring that, he hoped to teach tactics again at Quantico. But that did not happen. Toward the end of the year, he was ordered to Marine Corps Headquarters in Washington, D.C., to the Manpower Department, where he became the retention and release officer and later the plans officer of the Officer Assignment Branch. He couldn't imagine a worse fate.

Zinni doesn't like Washington—doesn't like the high concentration of brass and paper pushing. His first job in the Manpower Department (think "Personnel Department") was to be a plans officer, running the program that assigned occupational specialties to officers at the Basic School and that determined augmentation.*

In his words, "It was really boring . . . really boring."

ANY AVAILABLE free time was spent moonlighting at Quantico (which is only a few miles southeast of Washington), helping with field exercises and teaching tactics. And the young officers continued their informal seminars in tactics and operations.

In those days, the feeling was growing among his peers that the Corps needed to revamp and reassess its operational thinking; officers at the schools at Quantico began meeting after hours to talk about these issues and discuss the future of the Corps. Much of their thinking was far outside of the conventional box, which some of the senior leadership and even some of Zinni's peers perceived as a danger. But not Zinni. He was excited by this quiet revolution in the ranks.

With Vietnam winding down, the services were turning their focus back to the Cold War requirements of defending Europe. Because this was also a time of tough budgets, military value was being measured primarily by the capability of the services to meet that commitment and only that commitment. Since the battle with the Warsaw Pact was going to be fought by the heaviest mechanized forces, many questioned the existence of the Corps—at least in its current form as an expeditionary light infantry. Many defense experts were recommending everything from disbanding the Marines to radically altering it.

There was a battle over the soul of the Marine Corps.

TONY ZINNI continues:

The first thing Marines have to realize is that our service is not vital to the existence of the nation. The second thing we have to realize, however, is that

---

* The augmentation program made regular officers out of young reserve officers deciding to make the Marines a career. This was a very tough competition, given the few slots that were available.

we offer to the nation a service that has unique qualities—qualities and values that the nation admires, respects, and can ill afford to lose. These include:

One: Our first identity as Marines is to be a Marine. We are not primarily fighter pilots, scuba divers, tank gunners, computer operators, cooks, or whatever. The proper designation for each Marine from privates to generals is "Marine."

Two: Every Marine has to be qualified as a rifleman. Every Marine is a fighter. We have no rear area types. All of us are warriors.

Three: We feel stronger about our traditions than any other service. We salute the past. This is not merely ritual or pageantry. It is part of the essence of the Marine Corps. One of the essential subjects every Marine has to know is his Corps' history; he has to take that in and make it an essential part of himself.

Four: We carry a sense of responsibility for those who went before us, which ends up meaning a lot to Marines who are in combat. We don't want to let our predecessors down or taint our magnificent heritage.

Five: We make the most detailed and specifically significant demands on our people in terms of iron discipline and precise standards. Yet of all the services, we probably have the greatest tolerance for mavericks and outside-the-box thinkers. In other military services, if you don't fit the usual pattern, you rarely succeed. You punch all the right tickets, and you move up. In the Marines, you're much more likely to find people who succeed who don't fit the usual pattern.

This means also that we are encouraged to speak out . . . to let it all hang out, no matter whose ox gets gored. Outside the Marine Corps, I have a reputation for being outspoken. This has always sort of surprised me, because within the Corps being outspoken is the expectation.

This also means that we are an institution where people are judged on their performance and not their opinions.

Six: We have a reputation for innovation. After the Battle of Gallipoli in World War One, a badly blundered amphibious attack, the instant wisdom became: "You can't accomplish an amphibious operation under hostile fire against a hostile beach." But the Marine Corps decided, "We don't agree with that," and we created the nation's invaluable World War Two amphibious capability.

Later, we looked at the traditional separation of air, ground, and naval power, and we came up with the idea of integrating all three capabilities at a much lower level. So today, we don't need much artillery; we rely on our own close air support, closely integrated with ground actions into a single focused force.

We were the first to recognize the value of helicopters and used them effectively as early as the Korean War. Now we have the tilt rotor MV-22. Though it has been controversial, it will end up adding greatly to our mobility.

We've always gone after innovations like these.

Seven: Unlike other services, we aren't tied down to fixed techniques and doctrines. We have never been hidebound doctrinaires. We are more flexible and adaptable; concepts based rather than doctrine based. That is, we really believe in the individual. We don't like big proscriptive structures. We really believe that if we educate and train our leaders and our officers to take charge, and give them broad conceptual guidelines, but don't bind them to these as a strict "doctrinal" necessity, they'll do a better job.

Eight: We are by our nature "expeditionary." This means several things. It means a high state of readiness; we can go at a moment's notice. It means our organization, our equipment, our structure are designed to allow us to deploy very efficiently. We don't take anything we don't need. We're lean, we're slim, we're streamlined. We don't need a lot of "stuff"—whether it's equipment or comforts. We can make do with what we have, or else live off the land. We are the taxpayers' friend.

It's a mind-set, too, about being ready to go, about being ready to be deployed, and about flexibility. We can easily and quickly move from fighting to humanitarian operations.

There are also systems we have to know, either to board ship or get into airplanes or get our gear ready to go; and there are computer programs that tell us what we need and how we can load it rapidly. The Marine Corps has perfected all these systems.

Finally, it is how we organize, prepare, and train.

ALL OF this came home to me most powerfully back when I was lying in the hospital after I'd been wounded in Vietnam. It wasn't a conceptual thing *then, but an overwhelming feeling. It just sort of hit me: This is my home. These are my guys.*

In the hospital, I was seeing how my Marines were dealing with their own wounds. And on TV I was watching images of my Marines fighting for other Marines. I was watching how we all care for each other, and how they cared for me.

The moment took my breath away. Suddenly, all of what the Marine Corps means in itself and as an institution came home to me. These were my Marines. That's the only way I can put it. These were the guys I wanted to lead and to care for. I loved my Marines. They're the greatest treasure America has.

There were times later on when I was tempted to get out. But, ultimately, that's why I stayed in.

MEANWHILE, *in 1974, '75, and '76, those of us within the Marine Corps recognized that we had to change. The battle was over how.*

Some defense thinkers began talking about the Marine Corps as an institution that had passed its prime. In today's world, they believed, light forces were fading into extinction. The future was with heavy forces.* In their minds, we could neither adapt nor contribute to the kind of fighting we could expect in the Fulda Gap (the plain in Germany where it was expected the battle for Europe would be decided). Their solution was for the Marines to make itself over into a very different kind of organization . . . to "heavy up"—"mech up"—with many more tanks, armored personnel carriers, and heavy artillery pieces.

Others felt: "No, that's the wrong way to go. It's going after what's trendy and not what's necessary and right. It's not our mission to duplicate the Army's heavy units. They do that job just fine. Yes, we've got to change; and yes, we've got to find ways to make ourselves more relevant in Europe; but we shouldn't dump our expeditionary nature doing it. The nation still needs a highly expeditionary and ready crisis response force, and that's what the Marine Corps does best."

---

* Interestingly, even the Army is now starting to abandon their heavy forces. Smart ordnance is making tanks obsolete.

This was another area that really fascinated me: How the Corps could mech up and fight tanks and infantry in this new environment but not lose its expeditionary character. And I got caught up in these debates and injected myself into them wherever I could.*

Meanwhile, a number of thinkers inside and outside the Marine Corps were beginning to look at ways to fight that differed from the traditional force-upon-force, attrition-type models. Though these people came to be called "maneuverists," the term was not used in its normal technical military sense—the movement of forces to gain position. Rather, it was a mind-set, where you weren't necessarily looking to apply brute force and then grind your enemy into submission. The idea was to find innovative—and unexpected— ways to checkmate the other guy. The concept became known as "Maneuver Warfare."

In history, there have been many cases where small forces have defeated much larger ones after creating a situation that convinced the opposing commander that he had lost, or that made the larger force's situation untenable, by outpositioning it, or by disrupting, dislodging, or destroying what Clausewitz called "a center of gravity"—anything essential to a force's ability to operate. There are many centers of gravity: It can be a person, like an indispensable leader; a place, like a national capital or other strategic location; command and control; transportation; fuel supplies; and much else.

The Maneuver Warfare advocates looked to discover an enemy's centers of gravity, pick one that would cause the enemy's eventual unraveling, and focus on it.

The primary objective was to get inside the enemy commander's decision cycle and mess him up—gaining both a psychological and a physical advantage by gaining control of the tempo of operations, conducting relevant actions faster and more flexibly than the other guy can.

Accomplishing these aims became quite complex, sophisticated, and subtle. It was not easy to correctly blend the components of maneuver, fires, control and protection of information; and then to sustain and secure the force and put it into action. We had always been too rigid about the standard or-

---

* During the next years, the Marines demonstrated in several major European exercises that they could indeed successfully "mech up" and hold their own in a highly mechanized battle space.

ganization of units, thinking it had to fight that way and only that way. Instead, the maneuverists began to realize that we might have to break units down and modify them in the field in a more flexible and adaptive manner.

I took to these revolutionary ideas like a duck to a pond.

Naturally, the old thinking was very hard to change. Not only did senior officers feel challenged because these ideas were new and different, but these same ideas challenged an entire operational culture which didn't take easily to its subtlety and intellectual sophistication. There was a lot of controversy and many camps; and all kinds of people misunderstood the new ideas; but the Marine Corps eventually grasped them and adopted them—though it took several years for that to happen.

When General Gray was named commandant, he came in as a strong proponent for Maneuver Warfare. We had someone at the top advocating change in operational thinking, the way we fight, and the way we train and educate our leaders. This generated a tremendous upheaval as we transitioned over into the 1990s; but acceptance did come (though with holdouts).

Years earlier, in the spring of 1975, Tony Zinni had been hit by a double blow. Shocked and sickened as South Vietnam crumbled, he'd followed the remnants of his Vietnamese Marines as they fought on in the hills north of Saigon until all radio transmissions ceased.

The day Saigon fell, he took off from work, and then for several hours immersed himself in what you could call "a warrior's meditation" . . . thinking about all the troops—and the many friends—that had been lost, and about the fate of the many Vietnamese he had known.

As these thoughts pressed down on him, he had a sudden flash: He had been a Marine for ten years, halfway through a normal career, and he had never made a conscious decision to stay in . . . or even given staying or leaving much thought. It was always just a matter of not leaving because he couldn't do that while there was a war to be fought. It was always the war—and his connection with the guys on the ground fighting it—that had given his life in the Marine Corps meaning. And now that meaning was gone. His whole purpose for being was ripped away.

Fortunately, it was not a lasting depression, and as it faded, he came to realize that an era had ended for himself, for his nation, and for the Corps. It was time to move on.

With that came a deeper realization: He was going to stay in for as long as the Corps wanted him. He could think of nothing else he could ever do.

AS THE years passed, Zinni's career followed a more or less traditional pattern, considering his antipathy to staff jobs: a year at the Marine Corps Command and Staff College at Quantico; operations officer for the 3rd Battalion, 2nd Marines, at Camp Lejeune (beginning in August 1978); battalion executive officer, 1st Battalion, 8th Marines; regimental executive officer (1979–80); and in April 1980, he took command of the 2nd Battalion, 8th Marines (initially as a major, which was *very* rare; he was selected for lieutenant colonel during his time commanding the battalion). Battalion command was, in Zinni's mind, a perfect completion to his third tour in the 2nd Marine Division. He had deployed several times to significant NATO exercises and Mediterranean commitments with the Sixth Fleet and was proud of the superior achievements of his battalion by virtually every administrative and, more important, operational measure.

Zinni's promotions and command experiences were great sources of pride; but his high spirits were deflated when his father passed away in 1980. He was able to see his father one last time before he lost him.

In 1981, he went back to Quantico as an instructor at the Marine Corps Command and Staff College to teach operations and tactics (and to earn a master's degree in management and supervision). And during the 1983–84 school year, he attended the National War College.

In October 1983, while he was at the War College, the Marine barracks in Beirut was suicide-bombed by Hezbollah terrorists—a horrific event that impacted heavily on everyone in the Corps. The growing threat of terrorism not only in the Middle East, but also in Europe and Latin America, began to increasingly occupy Zinni's interest and attention.

The disaster in Beirut put a lot of scrutiny on the Marine Corps (many asked if they were to blame for the security failures that allowed the tragedy to happen), but it also pointed up how little understood was the terrorist threat to U.S. forces abroad. Terrorist groups were becoming more active and deadly throughout the world, and U.S. military personnel were an attractive target.

In the spring of 1984, a few months before graduation, Zinni got a call from his old Vietnam battalion commander and mentor, Mick Trainor, now a lieutenant general and the deputy chief of staff for Plans, Policies, and Operations at Marine headquarters. After the War College, Zinni had been told he would be a plans officer in the Marine Corps Headquarters dealing with European and NATO issues. "That's not going to happen," Trainor explained. "We have other plans for you."

"After the Beirut bombing, there's been enormous pressure to get our act together on the terrorist threat," he continued. "I need you to follow through on an effort we've started to develop a program aimed at dealing with that threat. We want to beef up our counterterrorism and security efforts and to educate the Corps into a far greater awareness of the threat we are facing; and we also want you to work on the emerging programs and issues regarding special operations." (By this time, the Marine Corps had begun to use the term in the now commonly understood sense—as referring to all forms of unconventional warfare.)

"So you can forget about the plans officer assignment. We're going to make you the Special Operations and Terrorism Counteraction officer at headquarters." This sounded like exciting and interesting business to Zinni. He knew the Marine Corps had been hit hard in Beirut and was serious about dealing with this new threat of terrorism.

"Yes, sir," Zinni replied, his brain churning. He knew how hard it was going to be to get himself up to speed on both terrorism and special operations.

Since he had not taken any of the elective courses on terrorism offered by the War College, opting instead to study Europe and NATO (since that was the area of expertise he had expected to use next), he had to scramble to pick up anything he could on the subject from literature and faculty experts. Thus armed, he reported for duty to Marine headquarters immediately after graduation.

Soon his five-man section had built a program that aimed to make every Marine aware of the new threat. It provided realistic training and education on countering it; developed the concepts, tactics, and special equipment needed to fight terrorists; improved the Corps' intelligence capability in this area; and improved security at Marine installations.

Meanwhile, as the Marine Corps' special operations officer at headquarters, Zinni represented the Corps in the joint arena on all matters dealing with that ever-more-important area.

A Marine sailing into these seas knew they were infested with dragons, for the Corps had long rejected special operations forces and capabilities. The aversion to special units comes from a belief that the entire Corps is "special"; it does not need elites within elites.

Ever since the disaster at Desert One (the tragically failed special operations attempt to rescue the American hostages held in revolutionary Tehran), developing a credible joint special operations capability was a top priority. In a 1983 memo from the Deputy Secretary of Defense, all the services were directed to designate special operations forces for this capability. When Zinni put on the Marine special operations hat, the Army, Navy, and Air Force had already designated their own "special" units, and the controversial issue of organizing them into a joint force was being dealt with in Washington. This action would eventually lead to the creation of the Special Operations Command, a separate unified command with its own budget authority (making it *not quite* a separate service). This ensured the services would evenly support their force contributions to this command.

The Marine Corps chose to ignore the directive, and, true to its long-standing policy, refused to create or designate any "special" units or capabilities.

This policy went back to the Second World War, when the Corps had created Raider Battalions at the insistence of President Roosevelt, but had quickly disbanded them and other special units.

Later, when President Kennedy attempted to persuade the Marine Corps to form special capabilities to deal with counterinsurgency missions, General David Shoup, the commandant, countered that the Marines could handle these missions as they were currently structured; they didn't need special units. Kennedy, not impressed with Shoup's answer, turned to the Army and supported the development of Army Special Forces.

By 1984, it was clear that the Marine Corps could no longer avoid taking on a special operations capability . . . in some form. The question was: How? In what form?

When at one point a powerful congressman actually proposed putting all the special operations forces under the Marine Corps, the Marines had to scramble desperately to make a reply. A Marine study came to the (unsurprising) conclusion that there were obvious benefits to having all the special capabilities under one service, and the Marine Corps was the ideal service for that; but taking that course would be prohibitively disruptive and create animosities and disadvantages that would outweigh the benefits.

The Marine Corps efforts to dig in their heels ended there. The growing pressure for a special capability caused the then commandant, General P. X. Kelley, and Lieutenant General Trainor to relook at developing a special capability.

As the Corps' action officer on special operations, Zinni attended all meetings, briefings, and joint sessions on the subject; observed all training; and visited all service units with these capabilities. He soon knew special operations as well as any other Marine.

He was charged with developing the initial study, which concluded that the Marines needed some "special" capabilities, and proposed several options, including the formation of special units. Some of the "special" missions the study looked at were the Corps' amphibious raid and amphibious reconnaissance capabilities (missions the Marines were already very good at), as well as counterterrorism operations and direct action missions like oil platform takedowns, noncombatant evacuation operations, raids, and other highly specialized missions.

Generals Kelley and Trainor then decided to take these findings to Fleet Marine Forces Atlantic, now under the command of Lieutenant General Al Gray, for further study (Zinni participated as the headquarters representative). This led to Gray's development of the Marine Expeditionary Unit (Special Operations Capable) program, which took forward deployed Marine Expeditionary Units (MEUs) and drastically changed their training, organization, equipping, taskings, and certification so that they could better meet the new crises. Since the "new" units remained designated as conventional forces, the change didn't violate the Corps' long-standing special operations policy. The units were just made far more capable.

Though the program was controversial both in and out of the Marine Corps, the MEU (SOC)s proved to be one of the Marines' greatest innovations—often called the "jewel in their crown" . . . and an ongoing demonstration that the Corps has maintained its expeditionary heritage.

Late in 1984, Zinni was selected to become a colonel, and then made head of the Concepts and Capabilities Branch, a recent creation of his immediate boss, Major General Jack Godfrey, the director of the Operations Division at headquarters. The Concepts and Capabilities Branch was charged with conceptually integrating all the exciting new Marine programs with existing capabilities and operating concepts. It was another job that allowed Zinni to work where he loved to be—on the cutting edge of operational issues and thinking. His branch worked on several major emerging capabilities such as the Maritime Prepositioning Squadrons, Norway Prepositioning Program, and Tilt Rotor Aircraft development (which turned into the Osprey). It became the central source for providing the "how to fight" basis for all new capabilities.

In the summer of 1986, Zinni was assigned as a fellow of the chief of Naval Operations Strategic Studies Group (SSG)—six Navy captains and three Marine colonels selected to spend a year working a strategically significant special project under the direction of a retired senior diplomat. The group was based in Newport, Rhode Island, but traveled extensively to interview both U.S. and international military leaders. The 1986 project reexamined the American maritime strategy in a war with the Warsaw Pact. The current strategy, which had been in place for several years, had already been very well discussed and practiced in many exercises. The CNO, Admiral Trost, and the Secretary of the Navy, John Lehman, wanted the SSG to examine Soviet reaction to the strategy and to propose improvements.

To that end, they were given access to Soviet defectors, and highly classified U.S. intelligence material and programs. They also structured war games to test out their recommendations. For Zinni, this was a heady time, something like going through another year at a war college; the depth of understanding he gained on strategic issues and on the ways the war with the Soviet Empire was actually expected to go down was invaluable.

Since he also had free time (his family had remained at their home at Quantico), he decided to enter a second master's program in international relations at a university in Newport.

While Zinni was at the SSG, the Marine Corps gained a new commandant, General Al Gray.

During a visit to the group, Gray offered Zinni a chance to return to Camp Lejeune to command a new MEU (SOC). Naturally, returning to the operational forces greatly pleased—and excited—Tony Zinni. But a few weeks later, he received a call from Lieutenant General Jack Godfrey, his old boss at headquarters and now the commanding general of the Marine Expeditionary Force in the Western Pacific (III MEF), offering command of one of his infantry regiments, the 9th Marines—"the Striking Ninth."

The choice was tough, but Zinni decided to ask for the regiment.

As an infantry officer it was difficult to pass up a regimental command. But he had several other reasons as well: He already had three tours of duty at Camp Lejeune and in the 2nd Marine Division, and he had deployed twice to the Mediterranean and was familiar with Europe and the Caribbean, while his tours in the Pacific were limited to Vietnam and Okinawa. The only division he had not served in was the Third, and this would also allow him to experience more of the Western Pacific . . . and ensure he would not be seen as one of General Gray's "pets." Since many officers did not want to serve overseas in accompanied tours (that is, with their families), and particularly on Okinawa, it was hard to find officers who'd accept assignments there. This was a chance for Zinni to show he wasn't getting special consideration. Though his family was truly happy living at Camp Lejeune, they were willing to try something new.

The decision to take the regiment proved to be one of the best he had ever made.

THE STRIKING NINTH

I began the '70s on Okinawa, and ended the '80s there.

The "Striking Ninth" Marines, a legendary regiment that had seen tough combat on Iwo Jima and in Vietnam, was now based at Camp Hansen in the northern part of Okinawa. The regiment's three battalions were rotational units that deployed to Okinawa for six-month periods from parent commands on the West Coast and Hawaii. This meant that the regiment always had full-up, highly trained units.

Along with command of the regiment came command of Camp Hansen, which was the largest Marine Corps camp in the Western Pacific, with over fifty units and agencies based there. A total of seven thousand Marines and sailors and over one thousand civilians worked at the camp, and many of the troops were housed there.

The demands on running a base like Camp Hansen was a new experience for me and presented a lot of challenges—from the day-to-day business of keeping things running, to planning for future growth, to securing our facilities during severe typhoons.

The camp consisted of 421 buildings spread over 605 acres; and during my tour, it underwent tremendous construction and reconstruction, requiring a great deal of planning and supervision.

THESE TWO commands came with a third responsibility—maintaining relationships with the local Okinawan community. The district included a number of small towns and villages and the major town, Kin, adjoining the camp.

Operational command of the camp gave me the fascinating and new experience of running what was in effect a small city, while my connection with the local community added to the diverse cultural experiences I've always enjoyed and taught me a great deal about the art of negotiations and cross-cultural communications. This would come in handy many times in the future.

In Oriental cultures, form and politeness can be more important than our preferred in-your-face direct responses. Orientals see these as insulting.

My Civil Affairs officer, a local Okinawan, taught me a great deal about the customs and procedures necessary to be effective in that community. I also tried to pick up a little of the language—not just Japanese but the local Okinawan. I rehearsed speeches in front of the "mama-sans" who worked at the camp as laundry workers and housekeepers.

As time went on, I made a number of Okinawan friends, frequently attending family dinners, weddings, and funerals. I also participated in festivals and social events, and met regularly with the mayors, the assembly, the chamber of commerce, police chief, and other civic leaders and groups. Civic action programs that we set up allowed volunteer troops to do good works for their Okinawan neighbors: We fixed up orphanages and schools for special children and helped with local celebrations. Days of recognition and appreciation for the local community on the base encouraged understanding.

At times we had tensions, but the strong personal relationships we built allowed us to work through them. Fortunately, our troops did not cause any significant problems during my tour. According to my local friends, this was the longest period without a serious incident between our troops and Okinawans. (All the work to cure the myriad problems from the aftermath of Vietnam was now paying off.)

LATER TWO *other commands were added to my original three responsibilities:*

The 9th Marines was designated to provide the core unit for Regimental Landing Team-9, the Ground Combat Element of the 9th Marine Expeditionary Brigade (MEB), our amphibious force in the Western Pacific. And during a visit to Okinawa, General Gray directed the commanding general of III MEF to develop and establish a MEU (SOC), the first in this command. I was ordered to organize, train, and command this unit.

The MEU has a battalion landing team as a ground component, a reinforced helicopter squadron as an air component, and a logistics component. We did extensive training in the highly specialized equipment, tactics, techniques, and procedures for the unit's unique missions. This involved intense and demanding certification evaluations conducted in difficult locations like the Philippines.

In one night helicopter training event, we had a helo crash at sea and lost a number of Marines. This was not the first time I'd seen a fatal training accident, and it wasn't the last. Despite all of our best efforts, shit happens. Yet, each time I've been torn by the loss of some great Marines. Peacetime training deaths in your unit are, in many ways, far more difficult to deal with than combat deaths. After a memorial service the next day and an extensive air and sea search, we resumed the training. Though I knew this was difficult for young men to understand (and it was hard for me as well!), I felt I had to send a message that we had to immediately get our minds back into our training. I knew the demands of combat don't give us the luxury of grieving for long.

For over two years, 1987–89, I was blessed with these five grand responsibilities. The icing on the cake was the enjoyment my family got out of this tour of duty. They loved Okinawa. They had never been happier.

MEANWHILE, like any commander, I wanted to have the best-trained and operationally capable regiment in the Marine Corps. We immersed ourselves in rigorous training and education programs.

Okinawa is small, which meant there were serious live fire and range restrictions. These problems had given the island a reputation as a difficult place for training, and impossible for large unit training. But I refused to accept this. To prove it could be done, I took the entire regiment to the field on exercises. This meant we had to look for innovative approaches and to ignore imagined limitations, but we got the job done. Of course, the island did have training limitations; and I scraped or volunteered for every opportunity to get my units off the island for training and exercises. They went to Korea, the Philippines, Thailand, Guam, Iwo Jima, and many other locations in the region. In my two-plus years in command of the regiment, the RLT, and the MEU, I took these units to over twenty large-scale exercises, and sent smaller units to many more.

I have always enjoyed teaching operations and tactics. This experience had led me to conclude that most commanders neglect the operational education of their subordinate leaders. As a result, I established an extensive officer, Staff NCO, and NCO education program in the command. All the twice-weekly officer school sessions—classes, map exercises, and field sessions—were focused solely on war fighting, and were taught or supervised by me. We made every attempt to make them fun and challenging.

I tasked my sergeant major to run the Staff NCO sessions, and (together with the battalion sergeants major) to supervise the NCO program. But I taught many of these sessions as well.

Since the contingency requirement to respond to a crisis in Korea was our most demanding potential mission, the regiment and RLT spent a great deal of time engaged in enormous exercises there, involving thousands of U.S. and Republic of Korea (ROK) troops. Conducting operations in the Korean countryside among the small villages and towns made the exercises realistic and interesting for our troops. The training was tough, often done during the winter or early spring months when the weather was extremely harsh.

TWICE MY MEU was called out to handle crises in the Philippines, when assassins from the NPA, a Philippine terrorist group, murdered U.S. military personnel.

In the first incident, U.S. airmen from Clark Air Force Base were killed in the town near their base. In the second, the U.S. military attaché to the Philippines, Colonel Nick Rowe, was shot while driving in Manila (Rowe was a hero, having escaped from Vietnam after surviving years of captivity there).

Our mission following both incidents was to provide immediate security to the naval base at Subic Bay and the nearby naval air base at Cubi Point. Our units patrolled the jungle around the bases and provided security for forces required for missions outside the bases.

I knew this jungle well, since we had done extensive training there. The Negrito scouts, from one of the many Philippine ethnic groups, had conducted the jungle training, and they were superb—teaching us about jungle plants that stopped infections and bleeding and helped wounds heal quicker, about other plants that were ordinarily poisonous but which could be bleached (to remove the poison) and eaten, and much else . . . a tremendous wealth of field skills. Though I had taken a number of jungle training courses and had firsthand experience in Vietnam, these scouts taught me more about jungle craft than I had ever learned before.

The most significant event during these deployments came when the admiral in charge of our forces in the Philippines decided we should conduct a humanitarian mission after a fierce typhoon had hit a remote area of southeastern Luzon. When U.S. troops were locked down on the bases the resulting tensions from the loss of revenue to locals had started to cause problems. The admiral saw the opportunity to help the ravaged coastal villages as a way of easing some of these tensions and improving relations.

The humanitarian mission he laid on us required my aircraft, C-130s and CH-53s, to move relief supplies. The C-130s flew the supplies to a dirt airstrip in the region, while the big CH-53 helos took the supplies from the dirt strip staging area into the villages.

Though I certainly appreciated the humanitarian and public relations benefits at a sensitive time, I was not comfortable with the mission. The area we were operating in was over three hundred miles from our base, and no one was paying much attention to security requirements and potential threats from the NPA and other terrorists and local insurrections.

Our aircraft ran the first missions with no problems and were into the second day of operations when I received a call that one of our CH-53s had made an emergency landing in a village and suffered minor damage. No big deal, my squadron asserted. They'd make a quick inspection and minor repairs, and the helo would be out in a few hours.

That estimate turned out to be wildly optimistic. . . . The fallen helo was about to become the bane of my existence.

The next day, the news from the helo was not so positive. Damage was now seen to have been somewhat worse than originally reported, but the CH-53 could still be easily fixed.

"Okay," I said to myself, but when I asked the Philippine Marines about local security and threats from bad guys I was shocked to learn that this particular area was heavily threatened and influenced by the NPA. The situation there was so bad that the Philippine military sent in only their most elite forces, Marines and Rangers. Though I was aware that these forces were operating in the region, I had not connected that with the threat information. My upset got worse.

I immediately ordered my battalion to rush a satellite communications—equipped platoon to the village to provide security for the one more day of work needed to get the helo functioning.

When the platoon arrived, its commander reported that the village chief was worried that all of this American military activity would attract NPA guerrillas. The platoon commander had accordingly set up security for the helo and the village. That was the good news. The bad news was that the helo was actually in much worse condition than previously reported.

I decided to get down to the village for a firsthand look. After putting my executive officer in charge of the security mission at the naval bases, I scheduled a C-130 to take me and additional security personnel to reinforce our platoon down to the dirt strip near the village. From there, we'd move on to the village by helo. We were to leave the following morning.

That night I was awakened by an urgent report from the platoon commander at the village. The NPA had killed a villager and left his body near our positions; an attached note threatened our troops. I immediately ordered more troops added to the security force on the C-130.

Before we landed the C-130 at the dirt strip, I had the pilot fly over the village so I could get a sense of the area.

The downed helo was an incredible sight. "Minor damage? No big deal?" Forget about it. It was stuck in the mire of a coastal tidal stream; its blades snapped off. This was no minor, easily repaired problem.

After flying into the village via chopper, I made a quick inspection of our position with my battalion commander, then turned the security situation over to him and turned my attention to the helo. I came down on the squadron like a ton of bricks. This, I learned, was how the crash came about:

The lieutenant flying the CH-53 had overloaded it with heavy sacks of food. As he was coming into the tiny landing zone in the center of the village, it hit him at the last moment that the zone was too small for his big bird. He pulled up sharply, but the weight onboard did not let him get the lift he needed, and he settled into the nearby tidal stream, just missing the straw huts crowded between the LZ and the water.

Time then became a critical factor. The tide was coming in within a few hours. When the helo could not be repaired as quickly as everyone had hoped, the rising saltwater tide set it drifting into the trees bordering the stream, which further damaged the bird, making it impossible to get it out on its own power. It was now stuck in the mud.

I was furious. I understood the squadron's focus on repairing the helo and appreciated their round-the-clock efforts to work on the bird under difficult conditions, but the squadron's failure to accurately report the status of the helo was inexcusable. Their failure had caused me to put them in a very dangerous situation for more than a day.

That wasn't the only source of my fury. Those who had tasked us with this mission had failed to properly analyze the intelligence and security situation, and I expressed my feelings to those up the chain of command who needed to pay more attention to what was going on. Fortunately, we had Philippine Marines in the area to help.

We eventually arranged for a powerful CH-53E to pull the helo out of the muck. From there it was to take the damaged helo to a recovery tug offshore. The operation started out all right. The CH-53E successfully raised the busted bird; but on the way to the tug, the CH-53E dropped it into the Philippine Sea.

The tug skipper said, "Not to worry. I can easily recover it from the seafloor."

He actually made good on his promise, and the tug recovered the helo, then brought it to the naval base and dumped it on the shore near our own base camp . . . now a total write-off.

The story does not end there.

On a later deployment, we were ordered to clean up the helo and put it aboard a ship bound for Okinawa. Since it had been sitting on the edge of the jungle for almost a year, the cleanup was a tough job. In the helicopter's current condition, the Navy was not eager to have it aboard their ship, and this caused heated discussions.

The helo was again making my life miserable.

When we got the helo back to Okinawa, it was placed at Camp Hansen, for use in training on helicopter embark and debark drills (old helo hulks are often used for this purpose). And there it sat, in clear view, every day for the remainder of my tour, as a reminder of all the griefs it had dragged me through.

DURING MY tour of duty with the Striking Ninth, General Gray called me back to Washington several times to participate in studies aimed at tackling the many problems arising from the inevitable shrinking of the military. He wanted the Corps to be able to reduce personnel and forces with minimal disruption and without losing capabilities. These were hard efforts to sell. Though the commandant's study group had a highly select membership from all over the Marine Corps, several commanders fought our recommendations. Nobody wanted to give up anything. Nobody wanted to face the reality of impending reductions and change.

Meanwhile, it became increasingly difficult for me to handle these time-consuming studies while running my other duties on Okinawa—a conflict that General Gray did not fail to notice. "I doubt that you'll finish a regular three-year tour of duty on Okinawa," he told me.

He was right. After two years and a couple months, I received orders back to Quantico, where I was to become the chief of staff of the Training and Education Center, an organization recently established by General Gray to implement the changes he had directed. My experience in this area made it inevitable that I'd be returned early to help.

CHAPTER FOUR

THE NEW WORLD DISORDER

QUANTICO'S TRAINING AND EDUCATION Center was a General Al Gray innovation—part of his overall effort to revitalize the Marine Corps' education system. The aim of the center was to improve Marine training by providing realistic and demanding standards (which would define a Marine, the duties of his occupational specialty, the responsibilities of his grade—i.e., rank—and the duties of his billet—e.g., squad leader); and by providing methods for testing and evaluating whether these aims were being achieved in individuals and units.

These innovations were significant and far-reaching; and given the realities of a change-resistant military culture, their implementation was not a sure thing. Gray wanted a ramrod who shared his vision and had the credibility and capability to make it all happen. Zinni got the call to be chief of staff at the center.

Just before Christmas 1989, less than six months after arriving at the center, Zinni received a congratulatory phone call from Gray; he had been selected to the grade of brigadier general.*

---

* The actual choice is made by a selection board, but the procedure is for the commandant to personally notify all the selected colonels.

The Marine Corps is a very lean organization . . . the opposite of top-heavy. Meaning, there are very few generals, and selection for the promotion is a true honor. Every year, perhaps one in ten Marine colonels make the leap to general officer. Of these only three or four come from the ranks of infantry colonels, such as Zinni.

Though Gray wanted Zinni to be assigned within the Marine Corps after the promotion, Zinni's friend Jack Sheehan had other ideas. Sheehan, now a major general (he would later go on to be the commander in chief of the Atlantic Command), headed the personnel assignment division at Corps headquarters. If Zinni was going to have a shot at rising higher, Sheehan knew he would need what is called "a joint tour"—a position at a command staff manned by all the services.* Sheehan had just the place for him—a onetime near backwater that the fall of the Soviet Empire was just about to make one of the busiest spots on the planet.

After the holidays, Sheehan informed Zinni that the following summer he would become the deputy director of Operations at the U.S. European Command (EUCOM) in Stuttgart, Germany.

"This is the very best joint tour we have," Sheehan told him. "It's hands down the best billet for Marine Corps brigadiers."

"Sure, sure," Zinni was thinking. "But, Jeez, what I'd really like is to be an assistant division commander or something like that in the Marine Corps, and forget the joint crap. What I'm getting is maybe okay for a staff job, but it's still a staff job and goddamned painful."

On the other hand, Zinni was excited about being a general. "So you've just gotta go over there two years and gut it out," he told himself, "and hope you get something real when you come back."

Later, after he was in Europe actually witnessing the landslide of transformations following the end of the Soviet Union, he began to have a very different take on his new job. "This place is changing," he told himself then. "It's getting exciting over here. We're seeing something entirely significant taking place."

---

* Regulation required new general officers to have a joint tour of duty as a first assignment if they did not have a previous joint tour.

Before going to EUCOM, Zinni attended the Capstone course for new one-stars at the National Defense University in Washington.

THE COLLAPSE of the Soviet Empire came with a whimper. The bangs came later—almost always in unexpected places . . . as unexpected as the actual end of the empire. No one had predicted it. It happened so fast that even the most savvy foreign policy and intelligence professionals failed to get a handle on the specific events, much less to grasp their bigger picture implications. The disintegration started in '89 when Gorbachev's perestroika first let the demons out of the bottle. Later, Boris Yeltsin tried to pick up the pieces, but with limited success. What had once been the huge, proud, and powerful USSR had within a year fractured into separate republics, including Russia, Ukraine, Belarus, Georgia, the Baltics, and the Stans.

The Soviet rapid free-fall collapse caused a series of quick reactions from the Western powers. Since the collapse was unforeseen, the reactions were unplanned—and inadequate. It was astonishing that the collapse came as such a surprise . . . or that none of the Western leaders had thought through what to do if containment actually worked and the Soviet Union imploded. "But here we were," says Tony Zinni, "scrambling to stay ahead of remarkable events that surprised us virtually every day."

This was not the hoped-for replacement of a worn-out and discredited communist structure with a new, better democratic and free-market one. The fall was far messier than that. True, the old structures had mostly vanished; but their replacements are even now nearly fifteen years later only still emerging. Nobody in or out of the former Soviet Union (FSU) had any idea about what had to be done next. So not very much was done.

When the Soviet Empire slouched off the world's stage, there was a certain amount of euphoria (many wrongly imagined, for example, that its departure would remove the nuclear threat) and even more relief. "Thank God," Americans sighed, "the Cold War is over. The Big World will take care of itself. We no longer need the vast, powerful military presence that kept the Evil Empire checked. Peace will bring incredible material dividends. Now we can go about our smaller, private business and get on with our personal lives. Everybody's going to be secure . . . and happy."

President Bush announced the emergence of a New World Order . . . without defining it.

It's hard to find anybody then who realized that the fifty-year-old bipolar world structure—for all the risks and dangers it represented—had kept the lid on myriad and terrible demons . . . demons that made the ones Gorbachev had let loose almost seem harmless as spaniels.

Since conflict in the first and second world heartlands had been unacceptable, the superpower competition had mostly played out in the third world peripheries, where the norm among governing regimes was illegitimacy, instability, and corruption. No problem, these regimes could be propped up, bought off, or provided with military backing by one or the other superpower, in exchange for their support. Thus the world's balance was maintained . . . though at the price of denying better lives to third world peoples. No matter. They didn't have much to live for anyway.

But the long-suppressed demons of ethnic and national competitions and ancient seething hatreds and blood feuds remained alive. Once the lid was removed and the demons released, nobody was prepared to deal with them.

The Balkans exploded. The Horn of Africa. The Middle East. Iraq. West Africa. Rwanda. Zaire-Congo. Afghanistan. The Philippines. Colombia . . . And this is only a partial list.

THE CAPSTONE course is designed to give new brigadier generals and admirals* a heads-up on major strategic and national security policy. It lasts a relatively short six weeks. Part of the time is spent in study and seminars. Part of the time is spent with very senior leadership in Washington. And part of the time is spent in travel, talking with CINCs and other combatant commanders.

Zinni's Capstone class trip, in March, took him and a handful of his

---

* Later expanded to include new "flag-level" State Department and intelligence professionals.

Capstone colleagues to Europe—to Naples, where there's a NATO and U.S. naval command; to Brussels and NATO headquarters in Belgium; to Germany and to EUCOM headquarters in Stuttgart; to Army headquarters in Heidelberg; to Air Force headquarters at Ramstein; and to Berlin. Their briefings at these commands all indicated that the impending collapse of the Soviet Union was about to unleash tremendous changes—changes that U.S. forces in Europe were having difficulty understanding or accepting. The rapidly unfolding events in Eastern Europe and the Soviet Union were occurring so fast that U.S. and NATO leaders could neither grasp their implications nor make studied adjustments to them.

During their visit to Berlin, the Capstone team's escort, a feisty second lieutenant from the U.S. Berlin Brigade, suggested an excursion through the recently abandoned Checkpoint Charlie into East Berlin. At that time, this was a bold idea. The famous security barrier that controlled access between East and West Berlin had ceased operation, there no longer being a reason for it. But its absence had left a rules vacuum. Nobody knew what regulations—if any—governed travel between the two parts of the no-longer-divided city. The new flag officers' only guidance: They had to wear their uniforms.

"Is it okay to go across?" the Capstone team asked.

"I don't know," the lieutenant said, "but everything's so confusing now that I doubt anyone will stop us. What's to lose? Let's give it a try."

Though most of the new one-stars were a little concerned about getting stopped or even detained by East German or Russian guards—and about getting chewed out for putting themselves at risk without a good reason—they were unable to resist such a dare from a hard-charging young officer. So they piled into a van and headed for Checkpoint Charlie, where, to their astonishment, they found no guards. It was like the ghost of an old Cold War movie set.

On the other side, the main streets of East Berlin—Unter den Linden and Karl-Marx-Allee—offered a façade of modernity, an East German communist Potemkin village. But turning off the showplace avenues revealed the real differences between East and West—pockmarked walls still bearing bullet scars from the war—while more recent buildings were cheap and ugly Soviet-style cinder block and concrete, run-down and shabby. Instead of the new BMWs, Mercedes, and Audis of the West, they saw small cheap East German Traubis.

The most striking aspect of East Berlin was its quiet. Few people were about; there was no vibrant, urban bustle, as in West Berlin. In fact, there was little evidence of commerce . . . or activity of any kind.

East Berlin was a far cry from a great, modern world city like New York, London, or Paris . . . or its sister to the west. It was a poor, depressed, patched-together relic from the 1950s.

As they were taking all this in, the lieutenant came up with another bright idea. "Let's go find a Russian military compound," he said.

"Sure," the one-stars agreed. "A terrific idea." They were really game by then to push their luck. This was an opportunity they could have only dreamed about before this moment.

They drove around until they found a Russian military facility (they never figured out its function); drove inside; and out of the van stepped a group of American flag officers in uniform, who must have had the same impact on the stunned Russian military personnel and their dependents as squid-people out of a starship. The Americans wandered around the compound for most of the afternoon. During that time, no one spoke to them; there were no greetings, no questions, no challenges, no ideas about what to do with the American "invaders"—shoot them, kiss them, or say hello. There was no decision; nothing was done. The Russians and their families went about their business; the wives pushed their baby carriages or dealt with their children; in the commissary, people pushed their grocery carts and grabbed cans and boxes off the shelves; and without a "by-your-leave," the American officers checked out everything that caught their interest. The only response they got from anybody was a shocked, deer-in-the-headlights look. When the Americans left the compound, the shocked looks followed them out the gate.

On the way back to Checkpoint Charlie, they stopped at a Soviet museum celebrating the fall of Berlin (the surrender had been signed in the building that housed it), and then at the Berlin Wall. "Do you want a piece?" the lieutenant asked, producing a small hammer. The others then chipped souvenir shards from the most powerful symbol of the Cold War.

Zinni had never before felt so close to living history. "It's over," he said to himself, truly realizing it for the first time. "There is no more Soviet Union. It's gone. There is no more Soviet enemy."

He wondered what new shape the world was taking.

IN JUNE 1990, Zinni arrived at EUCOM headquarters, located in Stuttgart at a place called "Patch Barracks," an old Second World War German Army casern taken over by U.S. forces at the end of the war. These had emerged from Hitler's policies during the military buildup that preceded the war: Since he wanted both to hide the buildup and to connect the army closely to the people, he'd built small regimental caserns in towns all across Germany, rather than large, centralized military installations such as those in the U.S. Patch Barracks had originally housed the 7th Panzer Regiment, a moderately sized armored unit. When U.S. Forces took Stuttgart, the casern became known as Patch Barracks, after U.S. General Patch, the commander of the troops who liberated that part of Germany.

It became EUCOM headquarters when the command was established. The original 1930s vintage stucco-clad barracks were turned into offices. In the '50s and '60s, apartment-type housing and a few individual houses were built on the post, but the majority of the people stationed there lived—as the military puts it—out on the economy (off the base).

EUCOM is the U.S. Unified Command that runs military operations and relations in an area that includes Europe, most of Africa (CENTCOM had the rest), and part of the Middle East (Turkey, Lebanon, Syria, Israel). During the Cold War, its primary focus was NATO support; and the CINC of EUCOM was also the Supreme Allied Commander Europe (SACEUR), the NATO military commander. Except for the occasional African or Middle Eastern crisis, planning and logistics support for the NATO commitment were the priority efforts.

Traditionally, EUCOM has been an Army and Air Force–dominated theater of operations; and up until very recently, this dominance has been reflected in the service affiliation of the top officers.

When Zinni first arrived there, it struck him as odd that the Operations Directorate (J-3) was so heavily dominated by Navy and Marine officers;

but he soon realized why: The emphasis in this command had not been on operations (this is not the case in other unified commands, where operations normally are the center of the staff). The difference lay in EUCOM's NATO mission. NATO went to war, and EUCOM was primarily the U.S. base providing NATO with the American wherewithal for that. In consequence, it was not operations but plans (J-5) and logistics (J-4) that were traditionally the key elements in EUCOM. This was reflected in their personnel—primarily Army and Air Force—while the Operations Directorate had come to be predominantly manned by the Navy and Marines.

The operations shop mostly worked out on the edges—perhaps dealing with some minor crisis in Africa or the Mediterranean. It had the standing operating procedures for forming a Crisis Action Team (CAT) and could, in theory, gear up for a battle staff, but they'd never actually been called on for such a large-scale commitment; they'd never had to work twenty-four-hour operations over a long period of time. Suddenly, all that was changing. The NATO confrontation with the Soviet Union and the Warsaw Pact was gone, and the plethora of crises emerging from that were changing both EUCOM and NATO priorities. The Operations Directorate was no longer a sleepy hollow. During Zinni's tour, the J-3 shop was on twenty-four-hour operations virtually the whole time he was there. It became the EUCOM centerpiece.

TONY ZINNI takes up the story:

Since this was my first joint tour, getting used to serving in an environment and culture that wasn't solely Marine Corps required adjustments; but I quickly found that the command was blessed with superb officers from all services. I could not have had better mentors—men who over the next two years entrusted me with the carrying out of several challenging and important missions.

I was particularly impressed with our CINC, General Jack Galvin, USA—probably the finest soldier-statesman I've known . . . the best we've had since George Marshall. Though his talents and accomplishments never got the recognition they deserved (they were probably lost in the rush of events like the Gulf War), if those events had not turned out as they did, he would have had the kind of recognition and stature Marshall enjoys. His vision, his depth of strategic understanding, his insightfulness, his statesmanship, his military competence, and his exceptional intellect were unsurpassed among CINCs I've known. Just as with Marshall, when you were around him, you sensed you were in the presence of somebody who's really great.

Galvin was a soldier's soldier, older than his peers. An enlisted medic in the Second World War, he had worked his way up through the ranks. When I got to Europe, he had been the CINCEUR for nine years, a long time.

Our deputy CINC was General Jim McCarthy, USAF. McCarthy's a brilliant, high-energy guy, with exceptional organizational skills—qualities I've always admired. But I especially admired his openness . . . he was never set in his ways. He never met a new idea he didn't like; they were all worth pursuing . . . even the wildest schemes would bring an open response: "Well, let's think about that," he'd say. "Let's talk about it."

The other reason he impressed me: He was the first true joint officer I met. The DCINC is a full general, a four-star, the same rank as the CINC. Since CINCEUR is a full-time, all-consuming job, the DCINC runs EUCOM. This puts a lot of distance between him and a lowly Marine brigadier general. But Jim McCarthy never paid the slightest notice to that distance. He looked at you and not the uniform you wore or the badge of rank on your collar. Air Force officers can be parochial (so can Marines and officers of all the other services), or, worse, hung up on "Air Power Doctrine" (bombing is the war-winning strategy par excellence), but McCarthy was never caught up in that kind of stuff. He was always totally open to all the possibilities and capabilities all the services could contribute. He took what you had to offer, regardless of your service. I learned a lot about being a general officer from him.

Our chief of staff was Lieutenant General Bob Chelberg, a very personable Army artillery officer, who, like McCarthy, had superior organizational skills.

The EUCOM staff was overflowing with strong personalities. They were like bumper cars, slamming into each other . . . challenging each other. Chelberg kept all these big egos working smoothly; he held the staff together.

He also had a gift for picking talent, and for encouraging everybody. He made you eager to work for him on his team; and he paid attention to morale, to the troops. He knew we were working long hours; he and McCarthy glued us together socially and created a strong sense of unit camaraderie that was remarkable in a joint environment.

My immediate boss, the director of operations, was Rear Admiral Leighton Smith, USN—better known as "Snuffy." Snuffy Smith was the embodiment of the positive spirit that kept us going. He brimmed over with energy and was intellectually brilliant, yet nobody was quicker to laugh; he kept us smiling with his humor and animation. At the same time, he demanded the highest degree of professionalism and commitment, and he set the example by demanding no less from himself. He would go on to earn four stars and become a CINC in NATO.

These four officers provided me with an incredible learning experience.

On the EUCOM staff, I was operating at a totally new level. I was no longer dealing with just Marine Corps operations. Almost from the moment I arrived, we were doing joint planning, executing joint missions, forming joint task forces; and we were kluging together Air Force, Navy, Army, Marine, and Special Operations units to do these missions.

These were the consummate pros in these areas. They knew everything there was to know about them. . . . And in some cases we were plowing ground nobody had been into before.

Just watching them operate, watching them explore options and poke into new and untried ways, watching them encourage and apply innovative thinking and refuse to get bound up by old paradigms . . . all of these things really left a deep mark in me.

One example sticks hard in my memory: In the 1990–91 Gulf War, EUCOM was behind the opening of a second, air front, attacking Iraq out of Turkey. We would never have opened up that front if it hadn't been for General McCarthy.

Some young USAFE majors had come up with the idea and put together the basic work. But CENTCOM didn't seem that interested in it. And I thought for sure it would be pooh-poohed away. But McCarthy said, "No, let's pursue this. Let's see what these guys can do." And he kept pressing until Schwarzkopf came around. The second front made a difference.

. . .

THE OPERATIONS shop is normally the part of a military staff that's responsible for training, for exercises, for oversight on exercises, and for contingency planning. They also run the Op Center—the command center—and all its associated communications. We also had some unique duties. We ran the EUCOM flight detachment, for example—a few C-21 and C-12 VIP aircraft and helicopters.

When I arrived, the J-3 command center had just been renovated. It was in a big room, with computers and data centers, screens for videoconferencing, CNN, and such, and spaces for charts and maps from the areas and regions where ops were taking place. There we'd get updates and briefs and would then process the information. It was an information center, intelligence center, and reaction center all in one. And this was where we would fuse all the information together and plan our response when a CAT was stood up in times of crises. (The function of a Crisis Action Team—CAT—was to handle a short-term event. You'd stand it up, deal with the event, and then it would go down.)

In normal times, when not much was happening, we kept a simple watch in the command center, with a duty officer and a few people. But in time of crisis, when we stood up a CAT, the number could rise to ten or fifteen or more, and we'd man it full-time (in eight-hour watches) with people from different sections, like logistics, plans, and intelligence—keeping tabs, keeping things updated, communicating with the people operating in the field, processing information, developing briefs and options, issuing orders . . . all the things that planners and operators do. This put a great demand on the staff, as they had to do their regular jobs and man the CAT as well. The numbers also depended on the kind of team we needed for a particular mission. For example, some events—like humanitarian relief—required the participation of Civil Affairs elements.

If the crisis grew big enough, or if we had multiple crises, the numbers would be higher still. And if the crisis got really serious—like the Gulf War—the CAT would transform into a Battle Staff, and we'd man it with as many as fifty or sixty people. Before 1990, the EUCOM J-3 shop had never done this; but 1990 brought a state of constant crisis, and we had to dust off and *set up all these procedures. That responsibility fell on me. As deputy J-3, one of my jobs was to be the director of the Crisis Action Team and the Battle Staff. The CAT was in being for the entire two years of my tour of duty. (The more elaborately manned Battle Staff was up for a significant part of that time.)*

WHEN I *checked in, the Operations Directorate was already bustling with activity. We had just started what is called a NEO (Non-combatant Evacuation Operation) of our embassy in Liberia—Operation Sharp Edge. Ships were off the coast, and a CAT had been formed. Meanwhile, the embassy had decided to call off the evacuation and hold out, so we now had to support and protect them in that mess.*

Liberia wasn't an isolated case. All sorts of challenges were starting to show themselves on the other margins (meaning outside the NATO area).

But the NATO area also brought its share of headaches: The end of the Cold War brought with it a "peace dividend" drawdown of forces—not an easy transition to plan and implement. Some Cold War armaments, like chemical munitions, were no longer needed. That meant moving them out of Europe on to destruction sites on Johnston Island in the Pacific—a dangerous and delicate operation (which was called "Operation Steel Box"). Arms reduction agreements with the former Soviet Union required inspections and verification of the destruction of weapons of mass destruction. We were involved. We were running the "Beirut Air Bridge" (security, supplies, and transport for our newly reestablished embassy in Lebanon had to be airlifted by Army helicopters from Cyprus). And General Galvin was beginning to push visionary ideas about starting military-to-military connections with the Russians and Eastern Europeans. The operations shop had a big part in managing all of these.

Very soon after I came to EUCOM, listening to the daily intelligence briefings, I began to get the sense that all this wasn't going to be an aberration but a sign of the way things were going to be happening for a while. For instance, some of the really sharp intelligence analysts had begun to suggest that the Balkans might start coming apart. Though this tragedy was still months away, we would have been stupid not to start thinking about the pos-

sible consequences. As this and other impending crises began to show up on our radar screens, we came to realize that what we were getting into with, say, Operation Sharp Edge might not be all that unusual. The unusual might become the usual.

All this manifested itself in increased day-to-day tasks. The Crisis Action Team that had been put together for Operation Sharp Edge was left in place to deal with all of these ongoing crises and operational missions.

ONE OF *my first orders from Snuffy Smith was to get out and visit our components—the four service and the special operations subordinate commands. "Spend most of your time with the Army, Air Force, and Special Operations people," he said. "You already know the Navy and the Marine Corps."*

I didn't know it then, but Snuffy's "get out and get acquainted" directive was the start of something, launching me on a series of trips that took me pretty regularly out of the nest: I spent most of my time at EUCOM away from our home base. It turned out that there was always some exercise, conference, or crisis area where they needed to send somebody on the staff, and only a general would do. I always volunteered for these. Since I always wanted to get the whole experience, I was willing to travel wherever I could get it; so I was constantly on the road. And I enjoyed the hell out of it. I just loved it.

I used to kid my wife Debbie. "You're a bachelorette," I told her. She took it well, though. She's a resourceful, independent woman.

Since we had our own airplanes and helicopters and could travel easily, during my first weeks on the job I would take a day or two here and a day or two there to visit our components. I didn't have a lot of time because the crises started hitting fast and hard, but I had enough to get out and get a sense of who we were working with—how they functioned, how they were organized, what they were like, and what were their capabilities.

As I traveled about, I got to see the vestiges of the Cold War—the massive prepositioned stocks in storage sites throughout Europe (including caves in northern Norway); the vast complex of bases and caserns around the continent; and the total orientation toward fighting a major land and air war in the center of Europe. This Cold War construct had served us well for half a century, but it was a difficult paradigm to restructure. Time and events were passing it by.

I wasn't sure we could adjust fast enough.

Probably the high point of these visits was my first encounters with two splendid officers, Brigadier General Dick Potter and Major General Jim Jamerson. Potter ran the Special Operations Command at EUCOM—SOCEUR. Jamerson was the director of operations at the U.S. Air Force Europe (USAFE) headquarters. During the coming months he went on to command several joint task forces on EUCOM missions. (He later became a four-star general and the DCINC of EUCOM.)

Potter was a tough and colorful old Special Forces (SF) soldier, a consummate pro with more operational experience than anyone I knew, including major combat experience in Vietnam. His wealth of knowledge and experience had made him one of the premier people in Special Forces circles.

He was very operationally oriented and combat savvy in a straightforward, no-nonsense way (he didn't tolerate fools). He got difficult things done efficiently, effectively, and thoroughly; and he'd put together an extremely competent staff; his people accomplished their missions extremely well. (Snuffy and I had tremendous respect for him.)

I liked Dick instantly. We were kindred souls, both of us brigadiers, sharing nearly identical views on operational issues. And since it happened that we were neighbors, our families got to know each other. So we hit it off right away and became close friends.

Jim Jamerson was the Air Force guy we dealt with day to day, and was one of the best joint officers. The first time I met him I could see that he really had his stuff together; he was sharp and perceptive, yet cooperative, responsive, and very easy to deal with.

I got to know him a lot better later on, working with him when he commanded Operation Proven Force—the joint task force air strikes and Special Operations missions we launched into Iraq out of Turkey during the First Gulf War. I worked under him as his deputy when he commanded Provide Comfort—the humanitarian relief effort that saved the lives of tens of thousands of Kurdish refugees after the Gulf War. Both experiences convinced me of his skills and brilliance. Like Potter, he was a great operator, with tremendous strength of character, a great leader, and always willing to accept new ideas and innovate.

We also became close friends.

I experienced many strange adventures with these two warriors over the next two years.

BIG CHANGES continued to pile up faster than anyone could handle them—German reunification, troop reductions, peace dividends, opportunities and problems rising from the opening to the east, a restructuring of NATO, a restructuring of Europe . . . and of course the New World Order (whatever that meant). It was all very heady.

So heady that very few noticed the fundamental conflict between what was called the "peace dividend" and the actual work it would take to reorder the world.

By late summer of 1990, what I was hearing from our leaders made it clear that the peace dividend was far more important to them than the reordering. They were looking at the fall of the Soviet Empire as though it was a winning lottery ticket that would let us cut defense spending, cut our troops and bring them home, close down overseas military bases, and use the money saved for all kinds of worthy projects (or tax cuts). The free world had triumphed, nobody ever again would suffer under the threat of communism, and all would be right with the world.

What I didn't see was anybody trying to ensure that this new order would actually come into existence. Order doesn't come out of chance. Somebody has to design it and make it happen.

Before the collapse of the USSR, the twentieth century had passed through two major democratic attempts to reorder the world—President Wilson's after World War One and President Truman's and George Marshall's after World War Two. We were now embarked on the third. But now no one was trying to shape the new order. No one seemed to think we needed a vision. It would all work out on its own.

I could only wonder at that.

It seemed to me that our "victory" in the Cold War over the Soviet Union, or the Communist World, or whatever we might want to call it, had presented *challenges similar to those we took on in Europe and Asia after World War Two. (The failure to address the challenges presented by World War One had led to the continuation of that war twenty years later.) Marshall and other visionaries had recognized the need to reshape the conditions that had given birth to the war, knowing that failure might make us again have to repeat it.*

Now, as then, we were in a postwar situation. But here, the challenge wasn't necessarily to reshape the conditions that had led to the war. The new threats were not going to emerge from out of the Soviet Union. Rather, the challenge was to reshape the world in the absence of the bipolar structure that had held all the other potential competing—or disruptive—forces in check. We had to replace the bipolar world order with a new structure that would create new balance, control, and justice. The alternative—the disorder— would unleash uncontrollable horrors . . . a chaos of failed states armed with WMD and exporting terror.

It was clear that the bipolar environment we had lived under for half a century had suppressed forces few politicians, statesmen, and foreign affairs analysts had paid much attention to. But now that the bipolar containment was off, the threats had broken loose.

During the Cold War, no one ever let a little remote country in the mid-dle of nowhere go wobbly, because every little country was involved in the competition between the Soviets and the Free World. Each side invested whatever it took to keep the little countries in their camp. Though these in-vestments went by names like "foreign aid" and "humanitarian assistance," they were actually payoffs. These ended with the end of the bipolar world structure. There wasn't a lot of support for humanitarian assistance and na-tion building once the Soviet Union had faded away.

The East-West competition had suppressed an underlying conflict (that emerged most visibly toward the latter part of the century): the North-South competition between the first world and the third world. This competition had never appeared serious because the East-West competition kept it sup-pressed. But when that was gone, it was immediately evident that the third world (South) had a serious quarrel with the first world (North).

Every world crisis we face today is a manifestation of that. Whether it's the drugs and the political failures and instability in Latin America, the turmoil of extremism and violence as the Islamic world adapts to modernity, or the chronic health problems, deprivations, and violent anarchy in Africa . . . all of these were brewing as the last century neared its end. They were there; but kept down. They were secondary to the East-West struggle, which effectively suppressed the concerns of those who served the first world; namely, the third world. When the East-West struggle died, the third world came out fighting . . . but in unexpected ways.

It took us a while to see that we were in a conflict, and longer to begin to recognize its nature. The signs weren't instantly obvious, we were feeling very good about ourselves after our great victory in the fifty-year war, and we were starting to enjoy the benefits of the emerging globalization. Globalized businesses, information technologies, borderless nations—all the webs that were increasingly linking everyone and everything in the first world did not inspire the same sense of hope and opportunity in the third world. They didn't see the wonder. They saw inside the palace doors and knew they weren't allowed in.

We took a stab at doing something about that. We began to invite them to our party . . . but without allowing them a place at the head table. (They saw this as patronizing and prejudiced.) We thought we were bringing in people who were seeking democracy, capitalism, freer trade, and a better life. We didn't realize we were at the same time very subtly putting down a third world that already felt alienated, oppressed, and suppressed, and wanted to take on the first world.

The conflict that resulted is not primarily a fight between state and state—third world states versus first world states. . . . Yes, we've seen state-against-state wars (such as those with Iraq); but that's not where the serious action is. Again, we have to understand that this is a different kind of conflict. That is to say, it's not a conflict born out of the ashes of some system that failed; namely, the former Soviet Union (as World War Two was born from the ashes of World War One). It's a conflict with non-state entities.

By non-state entity, I'm not just referring to terrorist groups like Al Qaeda and other violent adversaries but also to globalized corporations and non-governmental organizations (NGOs) that have significant clout and power.

The global information revolution we're now entering enhances the grow-

*ing power and influence of non-state entities. So does the fading away of na-
tional boundaries (we're becoming a borderless society) and the migration of
vast numbers of third world people into first world nations (we're becoming
a transient society). Meanwhile, globalized extremist networks are doing
everything in their power to bring down the structures that hold our societies
together.*

*This whole new world was simmering underneath the Cold War. And
we've had to meet this challenge unprepared. We should have gone full throt-
tle into a visionary program like the Marshall Plan that would have injected
energy, education, money—and hope—into the third world. Nothing like that
happened.*

THE FIRST *changes to affect me as deputy J-3 involved the struggle over
"peace dividend" troop reductions and the reshaping of NATO. These were
soon followed by efforts to create new and productive relationships between
NATO and the militaries of the former Soviet Union and the Warsaw
Pact.*

*In the summer of 1990, when we had perhaps 300,000 troops in Europe,
forces back in Washington were already saying, "It's over. NATO's an anachro-
nism. It's dead. Let's close it down. We've got to bring back troops. We've got
to close military bases. We've got to start getting rid of troops—taking them
off the payroll." Within weeks, these hazy words had gone from thought to
action. No real thought had been given to consequences—what we were losing, what we actually needed militarily, what these troops were actually doing
for us both inside and outside Europe. It was all a matter of numbers: So
many bodies equal so many dollars. The more bodies we can axe, the more
dollars we free up. All for the sake of a vague "dividend."*

*Over the next weeks, I watched the disintegration of the Army in Europe.
It really worried me. All of a sudden all kinds of career officers and NCOs
were simply told to pack up and find other employment.*

*One day, twenty-four lieutenant colonels got RIF (Reduction in Force) or-
ders: "Go home. We don't need you anymore." Great young sergeants, with
careers ahead of them, who wanted to stay in, were given an ultimatum: "Get*

out now and we'll give you fifteen thousand dollars. Stay in and take your chance. You could be riffed, cut, and get nothing."

"What to do?"

The officers were all in the same boat. "I don't know what to tell you," they said to the NCOs when they asked.

By good luck, the thoughts about disbanding NATO remained only thoughts. Though NATO had been born out of the conflict with the communists, it had come to fill many other essential needs. The alliance had to be maintained not just for the defense of the participating countries, but because it had become an organization where competent, responsible nations working closely together could actually get important things done that they could not accomplish on their own. In so doing, they were showing the rest of the world how to do it. NATO had become an irreplaceable model for everyone else.

Disbanding it was exactly the reverse of what had to be done. We needed to enlarge it. Fortunately, we did that. Later events in the Balkans and the NATO expansion to the east proved the continued importance of this vital institution to the stability of Europe.

Thank God for General Galvin. This World War Two enlisted man who'd risen through the ranks had the wisdom, experience, and prestige to keep us ahead of the dynamic challenges. Of all our leaders facing the new, post-Soviet world, he was the one who came closest to the vision George Marshall had given us fifty years before.

General Galvin did what he could to stop the slide in our troop strength: "We're still going to have troop requirements in Europe," he said, in essence. "Let's figure out what they are going to be before we bring everybody home. Let's figure out what new missions we are going to have. Maybe we ought to think about leveling off at 150,000 troops. Wait awhile, think everything through, maybe readjust NATO's structure."

The people back in Washington hit back at him: "Bullshit. 150,000's nothing. That's just a point on the way down. We're cutting a lot deeper than that."

"Wait a minute," he replied. "We can't go down to zero here. We have a position in Europe and NATO that we can't abandon. How many troops do *we need to make that credible? Is it 100,000? Is it a corps? Is it part of a corps? Should these forces be integrated?" (That is, for example, a corps composed of both German and American divisions.) "What's the purpose of NATO? What do we need it for? How do we have to support that?"*

The debate went back and forth, the Washington end of it was real down and dirty (as is the custom too often in Washington) . . . and the effect on our forces in Europe was devastating. With all the disruption and uncertainty, you could forget about morale.

But General Galvin kept plugging away. He was always the gentleman, yet always relentless, in the best Army tradition.

He knew NATO could not remain as it had been. It had to be reshaped. But he had a clear idea what form that should take (and it eventually took that form): He saw that NATO would grow to include the Eastern Europeans, that it would restructure its mission and begin to look at "out of area" operations—operations away from what had been its main objective.* He saw the importance of a continuing American leadership role in the alliance.

Meanwhile, he worried about Russia. The situation there remained troubling. The challenge from Russia was no longer about global hegemony but about the continued uncertainty over what was actually going on there, and what would come out of that. He felt the growing desperation in the former Soviet Union. He was deeply concerned that cutting it off from the West and letting it go adrift to sort itself out could bring serious problems.

His solution: First, to use NATO and the NATO context to connect with the FSU—and particularly with the military (to ensure the process of change was orderly and headed toward democratization). NATO had been their enemy. But that was no longer the case. Now NATO would be their guide on the road to positive change. Second: He realized that we needed a new Marshall Plan for the FSU. This would not have been a gift but an investment in future peace, stability, and prosperity.

Tragically, much of his vision was ignored. Washington was initially blind to his ideas about connecting with the Russians and the Warsaw Pact, the new

---

* NATO has recently taken on a major role in Afghanistan.

*Marshall Plan, and the restructuring of NATO . . . though later, in a differ-
ent environment, many of his ideas were realized. They should have listened.
He had his finger firmly on what had to be done.*

   A remarkable individual.

WEST MEETS EAST

In the fall of 1990, General Galvin realized his goal of connecting NATO
with the military of what was still (just barely) the Soviet Union, by arranging a series of conferences—primarily in Moscow—between NATO
flag officers and their Russian counterparts to discuss the role of the
armed forces and military service in a democracy. The DCINC, General
McCarthy, was tasked to lead the U.S. delegation, and to pick one other
flag or general officer to assist him. Zinni got the call.

General Galvin had both overt and unspoken aims in this:

Because he wanted to communicate to the Russians that the real win-
ners of the Cold War were the Soviet peoples, he did not want the NATO
representatives to approach their counterparts like gloating victors dictating surrender terms. This wasn't a victor-and-vanquished situation. This
was fellow soldiers helping their new friends make the adjustment to
democracy and a better, peaceful existence.

Galvin's unspoken aim was to get a read on the role the Russian military intended to play in the fluid and erratic situation that was emerging
in Moscow.

While the western side of the collapsing Iron Curtain enjoyed a peace
dividend, the eastern side suffered a peace catastrophe. The sudden reductions in overseas deployment and the base closings that seemed such
a windfall on one side were a potential source of political instability to the
other. The Soviets were bankrupt. There was no dividend, because there
was no capital . . . no money for the military, no money even for paychecks.
High-status military officers had become nonpersons.

The Russian troops in Germany could not go home because there was
no place to go. Back in Russia, families of senior officers were living in
boxcars or begging on the streets.

This very unstable situation could easily blow up. There was a real worry that the once-proud Soviet military, fearing they were losing control over a country turning increasingly chaotic, would go into the streets and snatch back power from the obviously shaky Russian democracy, either returning the country to communism or instituting a hard-line military dictatorship.

THE FIRST of the conferences was held in Moscow late in 1990. It opened in the Russian Ministry of Defense (the Russians' Pentagon). The visit—a first for American militaries—was a thrilling moment for Zinni.

The delegation entered the building through the ceremonial entrance, which opened into an enormous marble-walled hall. White marble tablets along the sides displayed the Order of Lenin and all the other awards of the Soviet Union. After a brief wait, tall doors at the far end of the hall swung open and out came an impressive phalanx of uniforms, Russian generals and marshals, led by the Defense Minister, Marshal Shaposhnikov, all large men, all marching in unison, their stomping tread making loud echoes as they approached. They were so formal and official, Zinni wondered for a moment if they hadn't gotten their script wrong and come expecting a surrender ceremony. But the thought passed.

There were formal greetings and Russian-style handshakes (very stiff, very deliberate, and very hearty), and then the NATO officers were ushered into a conference room and seated at a long table.

The initial discussions, led by General McCarthy, focused on General Galvin's message: The NATO delegation had come to celebrate a great victory for the Soviet people and to work hand in hand with the Russian military.

The Russians seemed to accept this gesture of goodwill . . . though without much visible enthusiasm.

Later, McCarthy and the others in his delegation subtly probed to detect if the Russians saw their role as being agents of political change or if they intended to take a more commanding part in the new Russia. It very quickly became apparent that they didn't have much enthusiasm for politics, either.

After the initial, formal presentations, the Russian and NATO officers split up into more specialized groups, and later transferred to a conference center outside Moscow. Zinni was paired off with the Russian director of operations (the counterpart of the J-3 at the Pentagon); they talked cordially about operations issues.*

As the day wore on, Zinni began to pick up strange vibes from this impressive collection of senior Russians. Not the vibes you might expect: He had zero sense that the Russian leaders were dangerous, or posed a threat. Far from it. They were not hostile; they were not unfriendly. Though they recognized that their system was defeated, they did not seem defeated or crushed or resentful. On the contrary, they were welcoming. Marshal Shaposhnikov and his senior staff were cordial and pleasant. But they never probed, never took initiative, never showed the slightest curiosity. If there had ever been fire in this group, the fire was dead.

At first, Zinni wondered why they didn't seem especially enthusiastic about the NATO visit, or get immersed in any way in the discussion, but it soon became clear that they weren't very enthusiastic about anything. Neither did he see any burning resistance . . . or any burning sense of cooperation; yet they proved to be as cooperative as the Americans wanted them to be.

For all their unresponsiveness and lethargy, the Russians were amazingly open . . . and this from some of the most secretive people in the world. Though none of them would take the initiative, they would certainly respond—and with astonishing candor. If asked about the change to democracy, they'd spill their guts. If asked about problems in their military, they'd show their dirty laundry. They didn't blink at talking about the severe hazing in the ranks or the epidemic of alcoholism.† And Zinni was shocked to see the openly permitted dissent and criticism of the senior leadership by junior officers.

---

* The Russian gave Zinni an excellent biography in English of Marshal Zhukov, which Zinni later read with pleasure.
† These problems remain.

And yet—again—the unexpected openness did not carry with it a burning sense that "We have to do something about our problems." There was no sense that these senior leaders expected to do much of anything.*

The truth, Zinni concluded later, was that the Russian military leaders were just there. Events had blown by them, and they were going through the motions. They had no plan. They had no vision—good or bad—about where they fit, what they would do. They were just along for the ride. Their message to the NATO delegation: "This is happening. You're here. Okay. This is what we do today. And fine, you're nice people, we like you. But don't expect us to give a damn."

The organization had resigned itself to being passengers in the car. The car was going wherever it was going, and they were along for the ride. They didn't intend to drive it, steer it, or put the brakes on. They were just in there.

To Zinni, this was simply an astonishing mental state. It was beyond his experience. He couldn't figure it out.

The good news, he realized, was the younger officers. The open dissent and criticism he'd noticed was a sign of hope. Many colonels proved to be fiery, outspoken reformers, railing at the collapse of the military and the corruption of senior officers. The younger officers were far more curious than their elders. They asked questions about America and Europe. They made it clear that they hadn't bought the line they'd been trained to follow, that NATO was the enemy they were supposed to hate. "You guys are not bad guys," they told the delegation. "We need to change things and learn from you."

The most outrageously outspoken of the younger officers turned out to be the aide assigned to Zinni, a cadet from the Propaganda Corps named Vlad. Vlad, who had learned to speak English by watching Arnold Schwarzenegger movies, salted his conversations with Schwarzenegger

---

* Western fears of a military coup in Russia weren't totally misplaced. There were crazy generals running loose on the peripheries of the military. Some of them had gotten elected to the Duma, the parliament. And some took part in the attempt to unseat President Yeltsin in 1991 (giving him his unforgettable photo op on the tank). But there weren't many of these crazies, and they were too ineffective to have become much of a real threat.

clichés—and Schwarzenegger-type attitudes. His irreverence got him in constant trouble with the stern, hard-nosed, never smiling, but extremely beautiful, female captain who supervised the aides. She was always shooting him with killer looks, but he never seemed to notice them. Zinni came to call him "Vlad the Impaler," after his ability to skewer himself.*

In his comic Austro-Russian American accent, Vlad gave Zinni the low-down on life for the troops in the barracks: There was no morale. There was no unit cohesion and unit pride. There was no leadership (the senior leadership spent much of the time drunk). Vlad's pay was so low (he got the equivalent of $4 U.S. every month) that by the end of the month he had no money; if his mother didn't send him food, he was in trouble. He laughed: The old indoctrination had tried to promote the belief that America and the decadent West were on the edge of collapse, where the truth was the reverse. Everything he'd been led to believe about communism had been a lie.

It was hard to believe how far the great Soviet military machine had fallen.

But they were still capable of grand, old-style Russian hospitality, highlighted by lavish banquets for the NATO delegation. For Vlad these were a gift from the gods. He had never seen such meals. He wolfed them down like a starving man (which was not far from the truth), and drank with no less fervor; he never left a banquet sober. "For God's sake," he pleaded with Zinni, "I've gotta eat. Keep your toasts and speeches short. If you make them long, I'll have to translate, and I'll starve."

On a trip one evening to the famous Moscow Circus, Vlad grabbed the tour bus microphone and performed a politically incorrect monologue aimed at the Russian leaders. This did not amuse the senior Russian officers on the bus. When Zinni told him to cool it, he just laughed, "Hey, man, no pain, no gain."

Vlad was always in trouble, but he was also shrewd and a survivor; and it turns out that he had what amounted to an escape clause from the

---

* The first Vlad the Impaler, a Hungarian nobleman who lived centuries ago, is thought to be an inspiration for Count Dracula.

Russian Army. Though his father was Russian, his mother was Latvian. This meant he'd be able to choose his homeland in the emerging breakup of the USSR—Latvia or Russia. Since Latvia was becoming independent and would have its own military, he could, if he chose, join the Latvian Army. . . . This was not an easy decision. The Russian Army was obviously a very bad fit; but did he want to make the big leap to Latvia? (Zinni never learned what happened to his irreverent young aide.)

The Moscow Circus's grand finale was the magical appearance out of nowhere of a man on a white horse, who raced around the ring carrying a Russian flag. The crowd roared with joy. It was the Russian and not the Soviet flag they were cheering. One month later, the Union of Soviet Socialist Republics officially ceased to exist.

SOME THINGS took a long time to change.

On a shopping expedition near the U.S. Embassy, Zinni got interested in a Christmas present for his wife Debbie. Since he was in uniform, he was treated with special attention (he didn't realize how special), but that did not spare him from the incredibly tedious process everyone had to go through to buy anything at a communist store. The idea was to provide as many jobs as possible, which meant that the purchaser had to pass through multiple lines, each presided over by a clerk who had zero interest in serving customers. First, you stood in a line to wait your turn to look at an item. Then, if you wanted it, you were given a chit to pay for it at the end of another line. You then took your chit to another line to wait for your purchase to be wrapped.

Zinni went through this process to buy a Father Frost tea cozy (Debbie collected Santas; Father Frost is the Russian version of Santa).

Back home a few weeks later, as she was getting the Zinni house ready for Christmas, Debbie took Father Frost out of his box, planning to put him on display in the dining room, when she discovered a strange device in his pouch of toys.

The next day, curious, Zinni took the device into the EUCOM security section. They confirmed what he expected: It was a listening device . . . a bug.

Before taking it in, he yelled into it: "The Cold War's over!"
He doubted if anybody heard him.

SHORTLY AFTER the Gulf War, Zinni took part in a Marine Corps delegation that visited several former Eastern bloc nations*—as part of the
growing military-to-military exchange programs developed by EUCOM.
Unlike his trip to Moscow, this proved to be a hopeful experience. Eastern Europe was adapting far more easily to democratization and a free-
market economy than their eastern neighbors in the FSU. Unlike the
Russians, they were ready and eager for the change, having, in their past,
experienced free political and economic systems, while earlier Hungarian,
Czech, and Polish rebellions against their Soviet masters had given their
enthusiasm some bite.

Since this visit came just after the Gulf War, the former Warsaw Pact
militaries were in something like shock over the quick and total defeat of
Iraq's military, trained, organized, and equipped as they were by the Soviets. Since the rout had serious implications for other Soviet-style militaries, Zinni was bombarded by questions about American tactics and
capabilities, as well as considerable curiosity about how Americans had
viewed them as potential adversaries. His answer: "We saw you as formidable enemies; we respected you; and we hoped we wouldn't have to fight
you." His answer—which happened to be the truth—pleased them.

But their chief concern was not about facing the past but about facing
the future. At that time NATO's expansion was beginning to surface; and
all of them badly wanted to bring their military services up to speed to join
it. They were eager to show Zinni the military reforms they had already
implemented, they briefed him on those that were planned . . . and of
course they were quick to tell him that they needed all the help the U.S.
could give.

The most striking change for Zinni was the reorientation of defenses.
For obvious reasons, Warsaw Pact nations had not been permitted forces
facing to the east. Now that had changed; and they had organized all-

* Poland, Hungary, and Romania.

around security, with forces positioned on all of their borders. This must have been demoralizing to the Russians.

YUGOSLAVIA, even then, was already a special and dangerous case. After the death of Tito and the fall of the Soviets, the country had fragmented, and old ethnic hatreds had reemerged. In 1990, the descent into ethnic violence had started in Bosnia, with Serbs, Croats, and Muslims all fighting each other. Of course, the ordinary people who just wanted to live their lives suffered.

That year, EUCOM put together the first of many aid missions to Bosnia, a humanitarian airlift operation called "Provide Promise." Though Provide Promise was actually implemented by the Air Force, the EUCOM J-3, as the Unified Command headquarters, monitored and controlled the operation and supplied intelligence. This new priority caused Zinni to take in the Balkan reports and briefings provided by the command's intelligence experts and analysts—an extremely knowledgeable and insightful collection of young majors and captains.

They were not optimistic about the future of what had been called Yugoslavia. "This place was an artificial nation," they reported. "Tito was strong enough to hold it together by force of personality, but there was never such a thing as Yugoslavia. Its pieces were never meant to be joined together; and it's ready to burst. It's going to come apart like an old suitcase."

Though these insights won't be news to anyone now, better than ten years later, at the time they were prescient. The EUCOM analysts saw the future of the Balkans much earlier than anybody else. Other than Zinni, they got few listeners. And he was in a quandary about how to respond.

"How important are the Balkans?" he asked himself. "Are they vital to American or European security? Can we just let the region go and blow itself up?"

Zinni's answer: "If we want to stop it, we're going to have to get involved in this. Provide Promise does not go far enough. It's a small Band-Aid on a sucking chest wound, and it's only going to get worse. We need to get involved early, when the situation is resolvable. We need to consider an international peacekeeping mission that only the U.S. can put together. It's pay me now or pay me more later."

Meanwhile, everybody in Europe and the West in general was in the euphoric stage of the peace dividend. Nobody was interested in taking on the problem. Though others in EUCOM, like General McCarthy, saw the value of early involvement, they couldn't generate interest in the kind of operation that would have to be mounted.

Eventually, of course, the problems spread throughout the region and forced the UN and NATO to face them.

Flash forward to 1992, near the end of Zinni's EUCOM tour. Zinni was asked to sit in for his boss on a first-time staff brief for the new CINC, General Shalikashvili. During the briefings, General McCarthy asked each person on the staff to give the new CINC their prediction of the single most challenging issue that would dominate his time and attention during his tour.

"That's going to be the Balkans and the former Yugoslavia," Zinni told Shalikashvili, without hesitation, basing this statement not on intuition or inspiration but on hard analysis and the day-to-day involvement he and his colleagues had already been going through in handling the growing problems in the Balkans. These could easily be seen by anyone who was paying attention.

His words, however, did not sit well with everyone at the briefing. The EUCOM director of intelligence, for example, an Air Force major general, jumped all over him. "You're crazy, Zinni," he declared. "Everyone knows that dealing with the former Soviet Union will be the major issue facing us."

What would that general say now?

The other regions in the EUCOM area of responsibility also generated their share of crises.

In Africa, three Non-combatant Evacuation Operations (NEO) were launched during Zinni's time at EUCOM. All of them were run out of the EUCOM Operations Directorate.

The first of these was Zinni's earliest EUCOM crisis.

Operation Sharp Edge in Liberia (mentioned earlier) was conducted by the Sixth Fleet's Amphibious Ready Group, after fighting between various brutal local factions threatened foreigners. It started out as an evacuation mission, but when the ambassador realized he had Marines on hand to protect him he decided he might as well hang in there. And the quick in-and-out evacuation turned into a several-months-long operation to provide security for the embassy. This required a large military presence, because of the chaos and slaughter in the streets of Liberia's capital, Monrovia. And this in turn stirred up a serious debate over whether the mission was worth tying up key Navy-Marine assets of EUCOM's fleet. The embassy was not in fact doing anybody in Liberia much good. Though the battle went upstairs to the State Department and the Department of Defense, months went by before it was finally ended as Liberia calmed after the assassination of the President of the country, Samuel K. Doe.

The other two African NEOs were executed by Dick Potter's Special Operations Command, who conducted flawless operations in Sierra Leone (Operation Silver Anvil) and Zaire.

THE GULF WAR

The Persian Gulf War added tremendous and unexpected demands on top of all the changes and crises EUCOM was facing.

In the Cold War, EUCOM had always been the center of focus—the priority Unified Command. The theater had traditionally been the receiver of forces from elsewhere for NATO employment. Even during a major war (like Vietnam), the command never gave up forces. It was totally geared to take forces in, not to give forces out. That was about to change. EUCOM was now being called on to be a supporting Unified Command and to flow forces out to another theater of operations.

General Galvin immediately saw the significance of this new role for EUCOM: It was ideally suited to become a forward base supporting operations elsewhere from the well-established bases in Europe. The strong relationships among NATO nations, forged over half a century, could be used to build the strategic bridge necessary to reach both the Gulf, and, later, other world trouble spots.

The job ahead was enormous. Creating the strategic bridge meant working out air and sea lines of communications, overflight rights, diplomatic clearances, sea transit permissions. Since most of the troops and supplies for CENTCOM from the States had to flow through EUCOM's area of responsibility, EUCOM was responsible for it all. EUCOM had to worry about getting them down there, protecting them, and coordinating with the countries involved.

It was an entirely new experience for the command, which had to redesign not only their philosophy of getting such things done but the mechanics of doing it. They had to work through all the complexities of the German rail system, barges, road transport, and convoys to the ports. They had to work through the most efficient use of all the ports—using Rotterdam and the ports on the North Sea and the Baltic as well as the more obvious Mediterranean ports.

Galvin's direction to the staffs and commands was simple: "When you get a request for support from CENTCOM, the answer is yes. Then you can ask what the question is."

During Operation Desert Shield, the buildup phase of the war, the EUCOM J-3 formed the Battle Staff to handle the massive transit of air and sea craft moving forces and supplies to the Persian Gulf. Early in this process, they were tasked with sending the U.S. Army Europe's (US-AREUR) largest fighting unit, the heavily armored 7th Corps,* plus other units and material to the U.S. Central Command in the Gulf. This significant accomplishment was superbly handled by General Butch Saint's USAREUR.

Though the EUCOM staffs were working round the clock on the massive logistics effort, they all hoped for a more direct involvement. But it appeared that this would be their only role in the conflict . . . until a much more interesting mission dropped in their lap (and allowed Zinni to "get out in the field" on a series of operations generated by the Desert Storm attack).

Tony Zinni continues:

As Desert Shield was beginning to fall in place, Major General Jim Jamerson, the USAFE† operations officer, called up and said, "Hey, for what it's

---

* For more on this story, see Tom Clancy's *Into the Storm.*
† EUCOM's Air Force component, U.S. Air Forces Europe.

worth, a number of our young, energetic, bright young majors have looked at the upcoming attack on Iraq and come up with a pretty good new idea. This is what they've been saying: 'Look, we have a chance to open up a northern second front in the air. The air defenses at that end of Iraq are not very formidable. If we could base out of Turkey, we could conduct air operations from up there.'"

My first reaction was, "No way. Turkey will never approve this, and neither will CENTCOM. This is CENTCOM's fight; they're not going to like EUCOM coming in and adding their piece."

But the plan caught the interest of Generals Galvin and McCarthy; and the young majors came down to EUCOM headquarters, bearing maps, intel on the Iraqi radar rings and air defenses, info on the bases in Turkey—and all the other elements a good plan requires.

"Well, hell," McCarthy said when he'd given it a look, "let's give it a shot."

After clearing the proposal with Washington and the Central Command, Jim Jamerson, Snuffy Smith, and I went down to Ankara to brief our ambassador, Mort Abramowitz, and (if all went well) to present the plan to the Turkish general staff.

Again, my expectations were not high. I thought we'd get told: "Dumb idea. Go home. Are you kidding?"

But Mort Abramowitz proved to be positive. "It's possible," he said. "Let's do it. I think the Turks will be open to the idea."

He was right. When we briefed the Turks, they approved the plan to conduct the operations from air bases in southeastern Turkey. I was amazed not only that this thing was falling into place, but how quickly.

A joint task force was formed under Jim Jamerson's command, consisting of the air component to conduct attacks in northern Iraq and a Special Operations component, under Dick Potter, tasked to provide Combat Search and Rescue (CSAR) and some psyops. Both the JTF and the operation were called "Proven Force."

During Desert Storm, the JTF attacked numerous targets that would have been difficult or impossible for allied air forces based in the south to hit. The sanctuary of Iraq's northern air bases was taken away and Saddam was forced to send his planes to Iran in order to avoid destruction.

The EUCOM planners kept thinking: "Since the Turks were being so re-

markably cooperative, maybe we could open up a second ground front."
When we talked about the possibility, the Turks seemed game to do it. But
by the time we took the plan to Schwarzkopf, it was fairly late in the air war
(and too close to the launch of the ground attack), and he said no. "I don't
object to the principle," he said, "but it's too late. My plan is in place. Adding
to it now would screw things up too much."

Back to the drawing board: The Army had developed a deception capability that created the appearance of a major headquarters. Now seemed to
be a good time to use it. The idea was to seem to move 5th Corps headquarters down to Turkey as a prelude to a major ground effort from the
north.

But once again, we came in too late. "It's a great idea," CENTCOM said,
"but we just can't accommodate it. We're just too far into our other plans." If
we had come to him earlier, I think Schwarzkopf would have bought into it.

Another disappointment came when they were making the choice for Jim
Jamerson's ground deputy. I would have loved the job, but Snuffy wouldn't
let me go. However, at my suggestion, the job went to Charlie Wilhelm, another Marine. It actually worked out later that I was able to spend a lot of
time down in the AOR; Snuffy and I were down there often. And I also had
a chance to spend time in the field with Dick Potter and his troops doing
CSAR training exercises in the snow-covered hills of southeastern Turkey.

I also had the opportunity to fly on the AWACS over Mosul and Kirkuk
in northern Iraq as B-52s and F-111s bombed airfields there. You can't beat
the view from the cockpit as the bombs explode and the sky is filled with
antiaircraft fire.

These missions were obviously interesting and exciting, but the real learning experience for me came from getting ready for them—going through the
planning and briefs. Because Jamerson and Potter let me spend a great deal
of time both with the planners and the troops who executed these operations,
I was able to get a detailed understanding of how air campaigns and special
operations missions were run. This invaluable joint experience served me
well in the future.

I was especially fascinated with the complexities of air campaigning, a
new experience for me. Though I had run air operations at a much smaller
level in the Marine Corps as a Marine Expeditionary Unit (MEU) com-

mander, this was my first exposure to planning and developing an air mission, generating the air tasking orders, and actually taking part in the operation. . . . And watching the operation unfold with a master like Jim Jamerson was worth a year at War College. I went through all the briefings, the planning, the workups; and during the AWACS mission, I was in back with the guys watching them pull all their thousands of pieces together— the barrier CAPs (Combat Air Patrols—the fighter umbrella), the tankers, and the bombers.

Later on, when I was CENTCOM commander running air attacks against Iraq, my familiarity with master air attack plans came in very handy. Not a bad piece of acquired knowledge for a Marine infantrymen.

DURING THE WAR, *Iraq struck Israel with Scud missiles. Because of their range and their potential lethality (they could carry nuclear, biological, or chemical warheads), Scuds can be delivery systems for weapons of mass destruction. Actually, their uncertain accuracy and Saddam's well-founded fear that using his WMD would provoke even worse retaliation limited the Iraqi Scuds to use as terror weapons. Though they did little damage, the terror they caused was very real; and the Israelis were outraged. It doesn't take much to provoke the Israelis into acts of retaliation. As Saddam knew very well, an Israeli retaliatory air attack on Iraq stood a strong chance of causing the breakup of the Coalition President Bush had carefully constructed. We wanted to prevent that.*

Iraqi Scuds were first launched at Israel on the afternoon of January 17. EUCOM immediately dispatched a U.S. Army Patriot unit to Israel. And an Israeli battery that was then training stateside was rushed home and put into operation; a Dutch battery also joined the force. The operation, called "Patriot Defender," was under the command of a superb U.S. Army colonel, Dave Heebner (later a general).

The Patriots in Israel were then linked to our early warning facilities, whose hub was in the U.S. This system was a complicated, jerry-rigged affair: from satellite indications of missile launchings, to the U.S. base for analysis and determination of the missile's flight path, to the EUCOM command center, and then to the Patriot unit. In seven to eight minutes, the Pa-

triot batteries could be cued to the incoming Scuds for engagement and destruction. Seconds later, the Patriots began actual engagement.

Because of the continuing questions about Israel's commitment to stay out of the fight, a decision was made to send a not-too-senior general officer from EUCOM to Israel to check on our Patriot unit and to provide a friendly presence to reassure the Israelis.

I jumped at the opportunity and was on a jet to Tel Aviv a few hours later.

I moved in with the Patriot unit . . . actually lived in the tents with the young troops in the Patriot battery, observed their operations in the command and control vans, and watched them go through their procedures when they shot.

I also spent time at the Israeli battery, and of course paid calls on a number of senior Israeli commanders . . . not always an experience I'd care to repeat. In their view, America was holding them back from the retaliatory attack that was their right and their obligation. They were incredibly determined and incredibly frustrated, and they really beat up on me about it. Though they understood why we'd asked them to refrain from retaliating, this did not sit well with them, and I felt they would not sit back much longer.

Meanwhile, the Patriot crews had learned from each Scud attack.

There've been a lot of misconceptions about the Patriots and their capabilities . . . and about their perceived failures. Some reports even claimed—falsely—that they didn't work at all, as though all the Scud warheads got through untouched. Let's set the record straight.

First, the Patriots were designed to be point defense systems. That is, they were built to protect small areas like air bases or command centers. So if you're at air base X, and you have your Patriots there, and the Patriots intercept and stop an attacking missile, fine. But whatever's in the sky still has to come down. When all the junk left over from the Patriot and the attacking missile doesn't crash down on the air base, that's a success. But our Patriots had to defend the Tel Aviv–Haifa megalopolis. (We set up our batteries there; the Dutch battery was sent to defend Jerusalem.) When all that junk scatters over a metropolitan area like that, you've got problems. People say, "Wait a minute. What the hell? You obviously didn't vaporize the thing. And a piece the size of an engine block just came through my roof." I don't want to deny this guy's distress. His complaint's legitimate. But we should also be *aware that a Scud warhead going off in the same place would have ruined his day even worse.*

Second, these were new systems. When the Patriots first went in, we had never used them in battle. The crews had to learn how best to engage them. They made mistakes. For instance, at first they put them on what you might call "automatic mode" (which is the fastest way to get missiles into the air against attacking missiles). But when they were on automatic, some of the Patriots were launching on atmospheric clutter. The lessons learned from these Patriot Gulf War experiences led to many needed improvements in the system.

To make matters even more difficult and complicated: The Iraqis were often shooting their Scuds at greater ranges than they were designed for (the Iraqi scientists had hot-rodded modifications that allowed them to reach Israel from western Iraq; some of their Scuds landed in the Mediterranean). But since the Scuds weren't designed to take that kind of stress, they frequently broke up into hundreds of pieces during their descent.

When the lieutenant in the van saw these breakups in his scope, he had to make a choice fast: "What do I shoot at?" He'd pick out a likely piece in all the clutter, and shoot at it. If he didn't pick the warhead, then it would continue on and blow up somewhere in Israel.

I know what the guys in the vans had to deal with. I saw the tape replays of previous engagements.

But these were very resourceful guys.

Later on, as they studied the tapes (they replayed them over and over), they came to realize that it was possible to distinguish the warhead from the clutter. The warhead, they began to see, continued to travel at its original velocity, while the other pieces slowed down. This was not at all obvious to an untrained eye. The difference was almost imperceptible. I couldn't see it. These sharp young soldiers could.

Once they had that little gleam of an advantage, they began to be able to pick out the warhead and hit it. And as time went on, they got even more proficient.

All the noise about the shortcomings of the Patriots did not affect the Israeli public. The Patriot soldiers were their heroes. You could see Patriot logos on signs everywhere; and "Patriot" became the name du jour for all sorts of new products (I saw an advertisement for Patriot condoms). Now that the Israeli Patriot crews were the darlings of the people (my Israeli air defense officer escort, Colonel Romen Moshe, told me), everyone in the Air Force wanted to join the unit, which upset the pilots (who always consider themselves the elites in any air force).

Another learning experience for me took place at an Israeli military base where top Israeli missile experts had been gathered and set up at what they called "the Scud Farm." The experts would go out the instant a Scud impacted, gather up all the pieces they could find, and bring them back and reconstruct what they could. (It was amazing how fast they could do that.) They'd lay them out in a large open area outside like a big 3-D jigsaw puzzle and study the configuration of the missile. There were several possible variations. What they learned gave them insights into Iraqi missile capabilities and how to counter them.

On a tour of the reconstructed Scuds at the Scud Farm (a few partially reconstructed Patriots were also there), I was given insights into what they had learned. "Look," they said, pointing to a collection of Scud pieces, "here Saddam tried to enlarge the warhead." And pointing toward another set: "In this case, he tried to increase its fuel capacity and give it more range."

The Iraqis were running all kinds of science projects, using a long-obsolete Soviet missile as their test bed.

The last shot they took at Israel used an all-concrete warhead, which hit somewhere in the more or less trackless southern desert. Everybody laughed. "Well, Saddam is shooting a practice round," they said. "He's desperate. He's run out of warheads."

A scientist at the Scud Farm showed me a map on the wall with all the trajectories of the Scud shots. All of them were aimed in the general direction of Tel Aviv or Haifa except this one. It had a really weird trajectory, and they were seriously concerned about it. Rumors later floated that an Israeli nuclear plant facility was the actual target. If the concrete warhead had penetrated the plant's containment shield, there could have been a terrible catastrophe.

A few days into my trip, I had visited all the Patriot batteries except the

Dutch battery on a hill outside Jerusalem. "While you're here," my Israeli escort suggested, "you ought to visit the Dutch battery."

"Sure," I said. "It would be a great experience for me." I had never been to Jerusalem before. Here was an opportunity not only to show the flag for the Dutch but to encounter the spiritual home of my own religion.

But when I checked in with the U.S. Embassy to get their okay for the visit, the ambassador turned me down. There was a lot of sensitivity and tension in Jerusalem at that time. The Palestinians had supported Saddam; and the ambassador thought it was best to low-key the American presence until things got quieter in the city. He didn't want any Americans there, especially senior American military.

When I told that to my escort, the Israeli colonel, he was incensed. "The hell with that," he announced. "That's like saying we can't protect you. This is our country. We can take you to Jerusalem. You're safe with us. No problem."

"This is not a security issue," I protested, giving him the ambassador's position as best I could. "It's political sensitivities."

"Well, to hell with that," he said, all fired up. "It's an insult to us." And then he took the issue up with his bosses, who agreed with him: They all wanted Zinni to visit Jerusalem. It had become a matter of face to them.

At this point, I said to myself, "Hey, Zinni, the Israelis are already angry and poised to attack, and you're down here to keep them happy." For the past few days, we'd worked our tails off and I'd subjected myself to a lot of slings and arrows to keep them calm and now this Jerusalem thing could maybe get them upset. I knew I had to go to Jerusalem, but I also knew I had to minimize my footprint there.

"Look," I told the Israelis, "I'll go to Jerusalem, but we have to do it without stirring up anybody. We just visit the battery and come back."

"Not a problem," my escort said. "We'll drive out very quietly, visit the battery, and that's it."

We took our trip out to the Dutch battery on February 28, and it went without a hitch. We met the commander and talked to the troops. Since no Scuds had been fired at Jerusalem, they hadn't seen action, so they didn't have a lot of operational information; but it was a good, friendly meeting. The view *from their hill overlooking Jerusalem, however, was spectacular. This was the first time I'd seen the Old City of Jerusalem, and the religious and historical significance hit me powerfully.*

As Colonel Moshe and I were chatting about this, he said, "Let's go down to the Old City."

"No, I'd better not do that," I thought to myself. "I'm already out here when I shouldn't be; I shouldn't push this thing."

"Look," he said. "Nobody's around. I'll take you to West Jerusalem; the Jewish section. You can see the city's empty."

He was right. Everything was quiet. People were all indoors, hunkered down.

"Listen," he said. "We go into the Old City, go to a cafe, have a little coffee or something, and it'll all be okay."

And that's what we did. We found a little cafe, with all its doors closed and its windows shuttered and taped in anticipation of Scud shots; but we could still get coffee.

We were sitting there with our cups when the end of the war hit.

It was like an angel had passed overhead. Suddenly, there was a rumbling sound. It quickly grew louder, and before we knew it thousands of people burst outdoors and came into the streets yelling. Everybody in West Jerusalem was in the streets cheering. We were swarmed (I was in my Marine cammies). Women ran up and kissed us. "The war's over!" they screamed. "The Iraqis have just surrendered!"

Pretty soon a camera crew showed up. I tried to duck out and get back to our car, but it was no use. When they saw my general's star, they had to ask me who I was and why I was here. I explained as best I could; but of course the embassy had their TVs on; and there was Zinni in Jerusalem where he was not supposed to be.

On the way back to Tel Aviv, I received a call from the embassy telling me to go right to the airport and leave. I notified our aircrew, picked up my gear, said a quick good-bye to the troops, and headed for the airfield.

Israel is the only country I've ever been thrown out of; but I couldn't think of a better place other than Jerusalem to be at the moment the Persian Gulf War ended.

OPERATION PROVIDE COMFORT

Back in Stuttgart, the command was celebrating. And when I came in, so was our staff; they were elated but exhausted. The nearly yearlong twenty-four-hour manning of the CAT and the Battle Staff had drained all of us. Everybody in the EUCOM J-3 shop was just beaten . . . worn thin. And yet there was still a lot to do before we could shut down the Battle Staff and the CAT and get back to normal. We kept targeting a stand-down date, but it kept getting delayed.

Finally, on Friday, April 5, we came to the point when we thought we could actually shut it down.

There was one possible hang-up to that. A situation was developing on the Iraqi-Turkish border that merited concern (much of the following information we did not learn until later): Urged on by promises of U.S. military support (that subsequently was not provided), the Kurds had mounted a revolt against Saddam, which Saddam had brutally crushed. The Iraqi military had then pushed the panicked Kurds into the mountains along the Turkish border, slaughtering many in the process. Just about the entire Iraqi Kurdish population was involved in this exodus; hundreds of thousands of refugees were now pouring over the border, few carrying more than the clothes on their backs, all of them in dire straits. The Turks (who had had a bad previous experience with Kurdish refugees, and have a Kurdish problem of their own) refused to let the refugees down from the mountains; and the harsh winter conditions were threatening to devastate these traumatized masses.

Early on the fifth, we got a call to tell us that Secretary of State James Baker had become concerned about the refugees and wanted to take a first-hand look. (He was already in the region.) He flew into Turkey, and we provided him with a pair of Navy CH-53 helicopters to carry him out to the camps where the refugees had collected.

We were monitoring this developing situation, but it didn't take up very many pixels on our screen.

Later that day, a call came from the Joint Staff at the Pentagon. "Maybe you ought to keep the CAT in place," they advised us, "in case Baker wants to take some action." So we were ready to keep the CAT going. But then they came back: "No, forget it. It's no big deal. Baker's gone up in the helicopters. Nothing much is going to come of it."

That meant we could close down the CAT at last. "At the end of the workday—normal hours," Snuffy Smith announced, "we're going to shut down the CAT." The exhausted staff was in heaven after two solid years of double duty.

Then Snuffy took me aside. "Get Debbie," he said. "I'll get Dotty"—his wife—"We're going down to Pietro's." Pietro's was a little Italian restaurant just outside the gate, one of our favorite places. "We're going to have a big dinner and get shitfaced tonight. Have a good time and celebrate the end of all the crises."

That sounded pretty good to me. In some very real ways, going out to Pietro's was like getting released from prison. Not just because we'd been working hard. Security on the base had been iron tight. Except for flying off to do our jobs, we'd been locked in: German police had discovered terrorists observing General McCarthy's house (located in a nice neighborhood in town where Americans had been living for a long time). This raised serious security fears. There had also been peace demonstrations, and some of the demonstrators had managed to get inside the base. The resulting precautions were necessary, but a burden: All the officers were issued .45s; and guards armed with machine guns had been placed all around the base.

This was going to be the first time we could just go out and relax since the war started (though we still had to have a security detail outside the gates).

Pietro, the owner, and everybody else at the restaurant were all delighted to see us; it had been a long time; everybody was laughing and in high spirits. There were mandolin players; and we sang along with them. We were enjoying a splendid Italian feast; Snuffy and I were drinking a lot of wine; and we were feeling really good.

All of a sudden, the door swung open and the colonel that runs our command center rushed in. "Sirs," he told us, "you have to get back to the base right away. The director of operations at the Joint Staff wants to talk to you immediately. It looks like you need to launch an operation ASAP."

"Holy shit," I said to myself. It was the middle of the night, and we were feeling no pain; but we dropped everything, got our wives out of there, and hurried back to the command center.

When we called the director of operations, this is what we learned: Secretary Baker had spent the day observing the Kurdish refugees, and he was appalled. The refugee situation was developing into a terrible catastrophe. There were already tens of thousands of people collected in makeshift camps; and hundreds of thousands more were in the mountains moving in. Worse, the Kurdish authorities were pointing the finger at George Bush for encouraging them in their revolt. The Bush administration potentially had a lot of egg on its face. If something wasn't done fast, things were going totally to hell.

We were ordered to have relief supplies on the ground in thirty-six hours.

This seemed like an impossible task, given the remote locations where the ravaged people had clustered and the lack of forces in position to react immediately; but we put our heads into the problem.

The first thing we did was call Jim Jamerson at USAFE to give him a heads-up: His guys had to rapidly develop a plan for a humanitarian airlift. Jamerson, who had just returned from commanding JTF Proven Force in southeast Turkey, instantly began piecing together a force to move back into position and conduct airdrops to the refugee sites. The mission would be organized very like Proven Force. Though he'd have a different mission and different kinds of airplanes, the structure and the staff control would be the same. And knowing the area was going to be a big plus. "We'll need C-130s and helos to carry the stuff; and they will need escorts to fly with them. Where will we get all of that? Can we get enough parachute riggers? Where can we get the food?" We spent all that night trying to answer questions like these . . . and at the same time getting the CAT back up and running.

About halfway through all this scrambling, Snuffy said, "We've gotta call Galvin and tell him what we're doing."

"Yes, sir," I said.

Then Snuffy looked hard at me. "Talk to me," he said.

"What do you mean?"

"Go ahead, talk to me."

So I tossed him a few words.

"I think you're sober," he laughed. "You call Galvin."

I called General Galvin and told him what was going on.

The next day, Saturday, the sixth of April, after a rapid coordination effort with the Turkish government, Jim Jamerson moved his USAFE forces into bases in Turkey. On Sunday, U.S. Air Force transport planes, with air cover from our fighters, airdropped thirty-seven tons of supplies into the snow-covered mountain tent camps.

No one really believed that it could be done in thirty-six hours. But we got fired up, beat the thirty-six, and put the first airdrops on the ground, thanks to Jim Jamerson and his USAFE team.

By Monday, we were able to start looking at the longer-term needs of the mission. At first, it looked like the original mission would require about ten days' worth of airdrops; but we realized very rapidly that the problem was going to be much bigger than that.

We initially concluded that given the force we had, we could extend the immediate mission to provide thirty days of support, while we worked to get a better handle on the situation and came up with a longer-term solution. Parachute riggers from all the services were ordered to Incirlik Air Base in Turkey to set up a massive operation to package relief supplies for airdrops. The two CH-53 Navy helos that had carried Baker were ordered to remain to support the movement of the supplies.

Meanwhile, Dick Potter was sent to Turkey with his staff to form a Special Operations component. Potter had commanded the joint Special Operations task force under Proven Force. Now his mission was to get up in the mountains, make an assessment, and then get his SF (Special Forces) troops into the refugee camps, where they could do a great deal of good.

Once this emergency operation was under way, we began planning a more robust response.

What do we do? What do we need? We had no experience with refugees and humanitarian problems. They were all totally new to us. How do we craft a humanitarian operation? Already NGOs (nongovernmental organizations) were starting to head into the area. How do we deal with them? Obviously, somebody senior would have to go down to Turkey to handle that end. Who'd go? We knew we had to send more people down to Jim Jamerson. We also knew this wasn't strictly an air operation. It would grow. But Jamerson's organization was solely designed for air operations. It wasn't going to be able to handle everything else we'd need down there. We'd need a full-blown joint operations center capable of dealing with ground troops, a humanitarian effort, the logistics, the UN, the NGOs, the Turks, and God only knows what else. We knew how to put together a Joint Operations Center, but we'd never done anything like the one this was shaping into.

We were doing all this planning fast and furious, trying to improvise with this unusual mission, when somebody came in and announced, "Sir, there are two Army captains out here. They say they need to see you."

We were too wrapped up in the battle to make sense of the humanitarian task to listen to a couple of Army captains. "I can't deal with them right now," I said. "Maybe later."

Finally, a few hours later, I took a break and went out to where they were waiting. They looked bright, eager, and enthusiastic. A good sign.

"Sir, we're Captain Hess and Captain Elmo," they said, introducing themselves. "We're the EUCOM staff's Civil Affairs guys."

"Okay," I said. "What have you got?"

"Sir, we know what to do in this humanitarian relief situation."

"Oh, great," I said to myself. I didn't think anybody in the world could help with this thing. It was all just totally new. But I didn't want to send them away, either, just in case. And I did like their enthusiasm. "Well, I don't have time for any long discussions," I said.

"Sir, we really ought to brief you," they said. "You need to hear what we have."

"Okay," I said, feeling I'd taken enough of a break and needed to get back into the Op Center, "but give me a minute."

Later, I found a few extra minutes and was able to give the captains a listen. But after they started throwing at me what they could provide, I suddenly realized that they did have something—most of the answers to the questions we'd been breaking our heads over. They had practical solutions for all the operations we were trying to design out of our brains from scratch. They knew what was required in terms of food, shelter, housing; they knew how to set up health-care facilities; they knew how to set up combined civil-military operations centers; they knew how to deal with NGOs and the UN; they knew how to process refugees; and they knew how to organize and staff all this.

"You've got to brief Admiral Smith," I told them.

But when I went to Snuffy, he pushed me off: "I just don't have time for these guys . . . later. I'll deal with them later."

"No, sir," I said. "You've got to hear them now. These guys have got the answer."

"Okay, bring them in," he said, with visible skepticism. But his hesitation didn't last long. "Where the hell have you guys been all day?" he told them when they'd finished.

We took them on then and there, and by the end of the day (Monday) we had a plan. Later, we brought them with us into Turkey, and they were indispensable in getting the operation going and moving it forward.

WITH THE help of Captains Hess and Elmo, we designed a joint task force to fill out Jim Jamerson's operation. Its initial priority was to stabilize the refugees in the mountain camps. Late Monday afternoon, the decision was made to send me to Turkey to function as Jamerson's deputy. Since I'd been in on the planning, I'd be better able than anybody else to get the JTF off the ground and then to make an assessment of how all of it was working.

"You're just going down there for a week to ten days," Snuffy told me. "That's all. You'll stand up these things, make an assessment, see what's needed, and come back."

I left for Turkey the next day.

Seven months later, I came back.

The operation was named "Provide Comfort."

MY FIRST order of business as Jim Jamerson's deputy was to set up a Joint Operations Center at Incirlik that turned his predominantly Air Force command into a joint task force.

I brought with me a few key people from the J-3 staff who physically set up the Joint Operations Center. They took care of all the necessary nuts and bolts—the communications, the internal systems, the planning; and they began to make the assessment of what else we needed.

My next order of business was to connect with Dick Potter, who was just getting out in the field, and see what was going on out there.

My first visit to the camps via one of Potter's MH-53 helos was a shock. In fact, to call the forty-three locations where the refugees had massed "camps" was a real stretch. We had over 500,000 refugees strewn over freezing, desolate hilltops, all with desperate looks on their faces. Most had come with little to help them survive in the snow. Many were city or town dwellers with no experience living in the wild. Nobody had enough clothes to keep warm; everybody was shivering and shaking, not only from the cold but from hunger. Everybody was desperate for food. Children were dying. Mothers were scraping out little graves.

When our two CH-53s made their first lifts of food into the camps, they were swarmed by panicked mothers who desperately threw their babies onto the choppers. (The Kurds were incredibly fertile. We learned later that seventy percent of Kurdish women of childbearing age were pregnant. Infant mortality was high.)

The brutal slaughter along the way by Saddam's troops had only added to their trauma.

The Turkish military had been doing all they could to provide order and security (I have to hand it to them), and they were also providing food, medicine, and shelter, but far from enough to begin to cover what the refugees needed for survival. More important, the Turks were insistent that the Iraqi Kurds remain close to the border (even when that resulted in many deaths from exposure), forcibly preventing them from coming down the mountains into Turkey. In their eyes, the refugees were an Iraqi problem and not a Turkish problem . . . and they did not want to add the Iraqi Kurds to the problems they already had with their own Kurdish population.*

It did not take Dick Potter long to realize the magnitude of the potential humanitarian disaster we faced. He had originally gone in with a single battalion from the 10th Special Forces Group (commanded by Colonel Bill Tangney†); but early that first week he requested that the entire 10th Group (two additional battalions) be sent into the camps to stabilize these sites. His request was immediately granted; and the rest of the group had begun to ar-

---

* Southeastern Turkey is largely Kurdish, and a significant part of this Kurdish majority wants to join their brothers in the Kurdish portions of Iran, Iraq, and Syria in a unified Kurdish state—Kurdistan. In Turkey Kurds have frequently signaled their separatist intentions by means of guerrilla insurrections and terrorist acts.

† Tangney, as a lieutenant general, was later the commander of the U.S. Army Special Operations Command.

rive by the end of the week. This act saved tens of thousands of lives. Though more than 10,000 people perished in the flight from Iraq and later in the camps, this number would have been far larger had the relief effort not have been accomplished so swiftly. The efforts of the 10th Special Forces Group was the most significant contribution to that effort.*

Another pressing order of business was to learn as much as I could about these people: I had never heard of the Kurds before this operation. Fortunately, a U.S. Army intelligence officer, Nelgun Nesbit, who had grown up in Turkey before immigrating to the U.S., was available to fill in our ignorance; she was with us giving expert advice from very early in the mission. Her language capability and knowledge of the Kurds proved invaluable. Nell provided much of the information that we based our planning on. (She later went on to become a colonel in the Army.)

Nell was assertive, self-confident, and knew her own mind. She did not blindly follow the party line, which tended to upset the traditionalists; but I liked her. She got things done.

The point she repeatedly emphasized: We didn't understand how the Kurds' social system worked. As a consequence, we were trying to connect with them in ways that didn't match their culture . . . picking the wrong people to deal with (a fact that I had already started to realize).

In the camps, we initially tried to connect with people we'd have normally linked up with—the ones who spoke English, the doctors, the lawyers, the teachers, the Western-educated. Many of these types came forward and curried our favor, but nothing was coming out of it. So then we looked for the political leadership—the mayors, the provincial executives. Still nothing was happening.

Nell Nesbit made it plain that we had to forget all of that Western thinking and reach out to the tribal chiefs (the Kurds are a tribal society) and figure out how the tribes were structured.

She brought in a Kurdish schoolteacher who answered my questions about social structure and decision making by mapping out the Kurdish tribal and political structures: how Kurds do things, who makes the decisions in the so-

---

* This story is told more fully in Tom Clancy's *Shadow Warriors*, chapter 14, "The Face of the Future."

ciety. These were important issues for us as we tried to determine who were the actual leaders in the camps.

There were two major political factions among the Kurds. One was the Kurdish Democratic Party (KDP), under the leadership of Masoud Barzani (the son of a legendary resistance fighter), and the other was the Patriotic Union of Kurdistan (PUK) under Jalal Talabani, who had broken away from Barzani's group to form his own faction. Each faction had a tribal, political, and geographical base (the KDP—the stronger of the two—had power in the west, while the PUK had power in the east).* Each had its own militia; and each had been contending with the other—sometimes violently—for years. They did, however, cooperate during Operation Provide Comfort.

The Kurdish fighters (the militias of each faction) were called "Peshmerga," which meant "those who face death." They were tough, battle-hardened guerrilla fighters who'd proved more than a match for Saddam's soldiers, man for man, but had been no match for the artillery barrages, air attacks, and gas attacks they'd been subjected to during their many years of resisting Saddam.

We also found others in the camps, including Turcomans, Assyrian Christians, Chaldeans, and Arab Iraqis . . . all fleeing Saddam's brutal regime. Some were defectors from his own government and personal staff.

DURING THE first week, we were really scrambling. Potter and his Green Berets on the ground were taking an assessment of what had to be done in the camps. We were working to connect with the Turks. NGOs were trying to get in with medical supplies; and the UN had also started to move in some teams. We had to set up procedures for working with both of them. All the while, we were setting up the civil-military operations center. But by the end of the week, we had managed to put all this together and were functioning adequately.

As we were working to stabilize the people in the hills, General Galvin

---

* Both leaders maintained ongoing negotiations with Saddam during our relief operation. At one point, Barzani asked for advice about what to settle for that the U.S. might support. He never got an answer from us—in my view, a serious missed opportunity.

and others were soliciting NATO and international support. Soon we were getting offers of medical, transportation, and combat units.

From April to June, we delivered seventeen thousand tons of supplies to the camps, while Dick Potter's guys took control of the chaos. They organized the camps and ended the "survival of the fittest" atmosphere.

As time went on, we began to realize that the airdrops were not the most efficient way to deliver supplies to the camps. The airdrops quickly provided emergency supplies to the most remote areas; but they were highly inefficient, and very expensive. Bundles ended up all over the hillsides; and then we couldn't control the distribution once they were on the ground.

We knew we had to shift increasingly to helo delivery and eventually ground transportation. But that was easier to talk about than to do. The road networks up in the mountains were ghastly. There'd already been serious accidents that had cost us some people. So before we could switch from air to ground, we had to improve the mountain roads and consolidate the refugees in more accessible locations.

Toward the end of April, Ambassador Abramowitz advised us to contract for Turkish food, tents, and transportation. This was wise advice. The change reduced costs by four-fifths—a huge saving. Turkish food was more in line with the refugees' normal diet (they didn't like the relatively expensive MREs we'd been giving them). Instead of the military tents we'd been forced to use in the camps (also expensive, and we never had nearly enough of them), we were able to contract with Turk tentmakers who took tarpaulins and other ready-to-hand materials and turned them cheaply into usable shelters. Several thousand Turkish truckers, who'd been put out of work because of the sanctions against Iraq (most drove oil tanker trucks), took the big oil tanks off their frames, turned them into open-bed rigs, and went back to doing what they did best—navigate the tricky and dangerous mountain roads. They moved the food and supplies into the mountains. All of this gave a big boost to the Turkish economy—badly hurt by the cutoff of trade with Iraq—which encouraged Turkish support for all of our programs.

The embassy sent us an excellent liaison team headed by Marc Grossman, the Deputy Chief of Mission. Their excellent advice and close coordination were invaluable.

. . .

AS WINTER *turned to spring and the snows melted, our problems did not ease. Though we had supplied the refugees with food and shelter, the summer temperatures of up to 120 degrees in these locations would bring diseases and water shortages. The weak and traumatized refugee population— crammed into small areas, drinking, bathing, urinating, and defecating into an already contaminated water supply—was very susceptible to disease. And, sure enough, we began to see cholera, dysentery, and other communicable diseases.**

Some of the Kurds from the towns didn't have a clue about basic sanitary procedures, such as: You don't crap upstream and then draw your drinking water downstream. The Special Forces troops saved thousands of lives simply by educating people about adhering to proper sanitary conditions.

The end of the snow cover also meant the end of most of our water supplies. It was clear that we would soon have no water in the hills—a truly dangerous situation. There was only one solution to both the disease and the water problems: We had to move the refugees down from the mountains. We couldn't keep them up there. Since it was clear that they weren't going to be allowed to move farther north into Turkey, there was only one direction we could safely take them—south.

The initial plan we worked out with General McCarthy was to make an incursion into a valley in northern Iraq and set up huge refugee camps there.

By that time, the UN High Commissioner for Refugees (UNHCR) had set up a liaison office with our JTF. Because they are used to dealing with refugees, they proved to be enormously helpful. Right away, they tossed cold water on the idea of creating refugee camps. "Don't build them," they warned. "They become miserable, and you'll be running them for years. These people have to go home.

"If you have to make camps, make them austere. They should only serve as transient facilities."

Since Washington was not ready to make the political decision to take over

---

* Teams from the U.S. Centers for Disease Control (CDC) came in to help.

northern Iraq, we began to establish a few camps as an interim measure as we worked on plans for a more permanent solution.

After centuries of oppression, the Kurds had learned how to be tough survivors and to keep stoic through their suffering. But, fearing Saddam, they refused to leave the apparent safety of the Turkish border and go down to the new camps. We took videos and showed the Kurdish leaders how they'd have greatly improved quality of life and security in our new camps. They still balked.

But after much persuasion, we convinced them to send a delegation down to check out what we were building.

They didn't like what they saw: We were building the camps like military camps, with everything lined up in lines, grids, and squares. "We can't live like that," they said. Their communities had a very different kind of structure from our "straight line" military alignment. "We build our communities around clusters of cul-de-sacs. We like to have several families facing inward."

They then insisted on redesigning the camps, to make them more reflect their community structure, and on actually taking part in their construction. This was a good idea. It not only gave them the kind of environment they were comfortable with, it let them buy into the whole process. At the same time, it made us realize that the UN was right about the camps. They weren't going to work as a long-term solution.

So then we thought, "Okay, we'll stretch out a little bit more and take part of northern Iraq. At least we can get some people into camps and others into their villages."

In several stages, we took the northern part of the Kurdish areas, stretching to the provincial capital of Dohuk (sixty kilometers south of the Turkish border) and out toward Iran. (There were thousands of Kurdish refugees across the border in Iran, whom the Iranians were taking care of. These refugees also wanted to come back home.)

But the UN was persistent: "If you're going to get a little bit pregnant, get all the way pregnant. Take them all home."

They were right again; and we made an assessment of what it would take to move them there.

. . .

ONCE THE decision was made to enter Iraq, we knew we would need additional forces. We also had to expand our own organization in order to control these new forces and coordinate our operations with those of the UN, the NGOs, the aid and security forces from other nations, and the agencies of our own government that had joined the humanitarian relief effort.

The JTF became a CTF (Combined Task Force), with the inclusion of forces from twelve other nations (including Great Britain, France, Spain, and Italy). Lieutenant General John Shalikashvili (General Saint's deputy at USAREUR, and, later, as a four-star general, the chairman of the Joint Chiefs of Staff) was sent to command the CTF; Jim Jamerson became the deputy commander; and I moved to chief of staff. Shali (as everyone calls him) had the command until June. Then Jim and I resumed our original billets.

A subordinate JTF (JTF Alpha) under Dick Potter's command was responsible for the refugees in the mountain camps and getting them back into Iraq. Another JTF (JTF Bravo) was formed under Major General Jay Garner, U.S. Army, to enter Iraq and secure the Security Zones we were establishing. The Air Forces component was under the command of Brigadier General Jim Hobson. A Civil Affairs Command was formed under Brigadier General Don Campbell; and a Combined Support Command (CSC) for logistics under Army Brigadier Hal Burch. We also put in place a Military Coordination Center (MCC) under Army Colonel Dick Nabb, to work coordination with the Kurds and the Iraqis. There was a DART (Disaster Assistance Response Team) team led by Dayton Maxwell,* and over sixty NGOs and PVOs (Private Volunteer Organizations) were also working with us.

The allied contributions to Provide Comfort were significant. The French, under the command of Major General Maurice LePage, a superb French

---

* DART, which operates out of the U.S. Office of Foreign Disaster Assistance (OFDA), is a civilian agency whose mission is to assess and handle foreign humanitarian relief. They send out teams to make on-the-ground evaluations, and they coordinate with other government agencies and civilian contractors. Dayton Maxwell was a senior-level professional with the OFDA.

Marine paratrooper, provided mobile combat teams that cleared the routes from the mountain camps back down into Iraq. The Royal Marines, under General Robin Ross, whose units had just returned from Northern Ireland, provided an excellent force for initial entry into the cities in the Security Zone. The Italians, under Lieutenant General Mario Buscemi, provided elaborate hospitals. The large brigades contributed by the French, British, Italians, and Spanish allowed us to give them each a sector of the Security Zone. General Shali ran this coalition brilliantly, with few (if any) written agreements.

We pieced together this highly nontraditional, ever-evolving organization on the go. Though some of its components were first-time structures, they met the task. Even so, these strange new structures bothered many older officers. This made me come to realize that nontraditional operations like ours were best handled by younger, more innovative officers who could think outside the traditional and rigid wartime doctrine with which the older officers had grown up.

General Shalikashvilli, a highly intelligent and capable senior officer and a real internationalist, was extremely effective dealing with the Iraqis and the thirteen-nation coalition. I learned a lot from watching him do that kind of business—persuading people, coordinating at that level. But when it came to the technical, tactical, and operational side of things we were trying to put in place, he was very traditional. He liked to follow standard Army doctrine.

For example, when we were looking at how to handle the Security Zones in Iraq, I said, "We'll create a joint task force, we'll stick it out front, with Jay Garner and Dick Potter in charge."

"No, wait a minute," he protested. "You're going to put a joint task force under a joint task force? Is that doctrinally correct?"

"General Shalikashvilli," I said, "who gives a shit? It'll work. We should not worry about doctrine here."

And when we started to change the refugees' transition camps to reflect the Kurds' cultural needs, he was skeptical. "What's wrong with the way we built them?" he laughed. . . . In time, he came to accept the need for cultural sensitivity (which I thought was essential; we constantly emphasized this in our briefs); but I felt he didn't think it was really all that important.

. . .

OUR AREA of operations was roughly the size of Kansas, encompassing 83,000 square miles of rugged mountainous territory, with little infrastructure. The biggest challenge after the initial crisis was to establish a logistics distribution system in this austere and rugged environment. The transportation system was frail, it was austere; the road networks were extremely limited.

Normally, the services provide logistics support to their own service components, while each nation similarly provides their own logistics to their own components. That's an okay system under normal circumstance. But it did not reflect the realities we faced—an omnium-gatherum of nations, services, and agencies all trying to force their stuff through the fragile infrastructure, all at the same time. We had major humanitarian and military demands on the distribution system (besides our military supplies and equipment, we were handling relief supplies contributed by over thirty nations), and nobody was pulling it together. We had no central management, no prioritization, and very thin security. It was like forcing a gallon of water through a soda straw.

We could see right away that we needed to put in place a centrally designed distribution system, with forward staging bases and interim bases, where we could build up stocks of supplies which everybody could draw from.

The component commanders—Garner and Potter—fought this; each wanted to run his own logistics support. I had constant battles over this issue with them, two of my closest friends. They were shouting at me and I was shouting at them. "Don't mess with our logistics," they kept telling Shali. "We're running our own show. We need our own stuff here."

From the other direction, our logisticians were begging me to convince General Shali to form a Combined Support Command. But when I told him the logistics were going to break, and we were going to see a real disaster, he was reluctant to change the book-dictated system.

Finally, when it was totally obvious that it was either change or endure the world's most embarrassing traffic jam, he made the decision to set up the CSC.

We opened small Humanitarian Service Support Bases (HSSB) in a "hub

*and spoke" system that let us stretch our reach well into Iraq. We brought
down Army Brigadier Hal Burch (a USAREUR logistics commander), and
he set it up.*

OUR UNORTHODOX *command structures eventually caught the attention
of the chairman of the Joint Chiefs. During a visit in May, Colin Powell,
who is a very quick study, was initially impressed with how well the operation was going, but wasn't clear how we had it all organized. The easiest way
to explain that was to show him our organizational chart. . . . The chart was
of course as weird as our organization; but we had done what we could to
draw the lines and links and labels according to the proper doctrinal procedures. So we had lines for "Operational Control" and for "Tactical Control"
and so on. Of course, when Powell looked at the chart, he saw right through
it. "Is this for real?" he asked. "Tell me the truth. What kind of control do
you really have here? What are your real lines of authority? Is it Operational
Control?"*

*"Sir," I told him, "what we really do is HAND CON (Handshake Con-
trol). We work out our problems on the fly and shake hands on the deals. We
don't have time to do anything else."*

*He laughed. He loved that. It became one of General Powell's favorite
stories.*

OUR RELATIONSHIP *with the Iraqis was predictably tricky. Though the
war was obviously over, the Iraqi forces in the north still presented a problem. Unlike units in the south, they had not experienced combat with superior American and Coalition power; and they were not as cowed. Later, after
several units from southern Iraq were moved north, we used to watch with
fascination how the southern and the northern Iraqi units reacted when our
planes flew over their positions. Those who had faced us in the south during
the war waved nervously and looked for cover, while the northern troops were
more frequently defiant, and once in a while even fired at our planes.*

The Military Coordination Center was set up to maintain contact with the Iraqi military; and an Iraqi, Brigadier General Nashwan Danoon, was assigned as our point of contact.* For more important meetings with General Shali, the Iraqis sent a Lieutenant General Saber from Baghdad.

As we moved the refugees back to their homes in the south, we increased the size of the Security Zone and demanded the Iraqi military pull back. They were—unsurprisingly—reluctant to do that; and on several occasions we had to threaten them. A show of force always brought compliance (we had in all sixteen incidents of hostile fire with the Iraqis†).

Eventually, we decided to create a zone that allowed all 500,000 of the Kurds to return home . . . and we also decided to help them repair their homes and make them livable. We not only repaired much of the damage to the areas evacuated by the fleeing population, we provided services and utilities to forty-one communities until their local services could be reestablished.

At this point, we realized that wasn't going to be enough. We just couldn't leave them on their own. We had to make sure the Iraqis didn't return once we pulled out.

To emphasize that point, the Iraqis massed seventeen divisions on the borders of the Security Zone we had formed. These divisions were there to block further expansion and to seal off the zone . . . and to convey a threatening posture toward the Kurds. As a result, we established what was called "the Green Line" as the border of the Security Zone. None of the Iraqis were allowed to pass it. Our air cover in the no-fly zone (which was larger than the Security Zone) further ensured the good behavior of the Iraqi military.

The process of moving the refugees and managing the Iraqis went through several stages. In the beginning, we agreed to allow the Iraqis a police presence in the Security Zone; but it quickly became clear that idea was a nonstarter. The Iraqis' idea of a "police presence" was the Mukhabarat—their secret police.

The Kurds were dead set against any Iraqi government presence, and the Peshmerga set about eliminating it the old-fashioned way—by killing the

---

* He was recalled back to Baghdad toward the end of our initial operation. We heard he was executed for plotting against Saddam.
† We had twelve casualties from land mines, which littered the area and were a constant source of concern both for our troops and the local Kurds. The operation ended up costing the Coalition seven dead and 130 injured from a variety of causes.

Mukhabarat and other Iraqi officials. Eventually, all Iraqi government presence was removed from the Security Zone.

Another agreement that didn't work out was the protection arrangement for Saddam's eight lavish palaces in the region. We had approved a plan that allowed the Iraqis to retain military security over the palaces; but when an Iraqi unit guarding one of them opened fire on a British Royal Marine patrol, the Marines blasted the Iraqis; and that ended the agreement.

Saddam's private airfield at Sirsenk was turned into a logistics base for our operations. Our troops made pen sets from its black marble wall panels and passed them out "Compliments of Saddam."

At one point, I went out to see one of the palaces. It was still under construction, occupying the top of an imposing hill; and it was massive—like a fairy-tale castle. Luxurious villas were scattered down the hillside; and water pumped up to the top flowed down the side of the hill in a system of waterfalls. Underneath the hilltop castle was a vast tunnel complex. At first, we thought this may have been for WMD storage; but it turned out to be for something like a casino. It was shocking to see these grand structures in the midst of the poverty of the local population.

During the same trip, I visited the villages that had been gassed by the Iraqis in 1988 . . . a chilling sight. They were not only empty of people, but the Iraqis had left not one stone upon another. The Kurds who'd made their homes there had asked to return; but when we did soil tests, we found dangerous toxic chemical traces that made return impossible.

THE HUMANITARIAN aspects of the operation were of course its primary focus. Except for our Civil Affairs officers, this was a new experience for most of us; and it led to many coordination problems.

When the NGOs started showing up, most of them had had no experience working with us, we had had no experience working with them, and there was mutual suspicion.* They were all wonderful, well-meaning humanitarians; but they all seemed to think they could do their own thing without much

---

* One big reason they don't trust the militaries: They're used to trying to fix the disasters that result from militaries in conflict.

coordination with the common effort: NGO planes would suddenly show up in our airspace demanding landing permission, unable to understand why we had a hard time accommodating them.

To minimize these problems, we established a Civil-Military Operations Center (CMOC) under Civil Affairs control to coordinate with the NGOs, DART, and the UNHCR. Though friction between the military and the relief agencies continued (on a much smaller scale), the CMOC provided an excellent forum to work out the problems. EUCOM established a Civil Agency Response Element (CARE) at their headquarters that helped a great deal to sort out problems at the Unified Command and Washington levels.

In spite of our mutual problems, working with the NGOs and the various government agencies like DART and the Centers for Disease Control was not at all a bad experience. I learned a lot from the teams advising us. Each of them provided valuable lessons in their specialty areas (water, food, medical care, etc.) that I would use later in missions of this sort.

From the CDC I learned about the nature of diseases—the cycle, the causes, and the treatment . . . the conditions that lead to them, the signs that diseases are spreading, and what you have to do to prevent that. This was a totally unique experience . . . and it's not an instrument you normally find in the military tool kit.

Cholera, for example, is difficult to cure—especially in the case of children. The kids will initially seem to be improving, but they're really not. They'll look like they're getting better; then they'll sink down; then they seem to be getting a little better; and then they sink down a little more. The process is really a gradual decline, but you'll find upswings that give you hope. The upswings can fool you.

I also learned a lot from the teams sent in by Médecins Sans Frontières (Doctors Without Borders). They are not only fine doctors; they are also culturally sophisticated in dealing with refugees and third world peoples. They had serious concerns about the level of care we were providing.

The Kurds needed a great deal of medical help instantly. To fill that need, we brought in what we had—technically advanced military medical units and field hospitals. (I observed a major operation at a Belgian field hospital, where they were doing elective surgery. It was a world-class facility.) Our idea was to come in and lay down a massive effort . . . really flood the place.

But when we pulled out, we'd leave a tremendous void. That is, we were bringing in a level of care that couldn't be maintained after we left.

By way of contrast: when Doctors Without Borders work within a third world environment, they try to leave something behind that can be maintained. It's the old idea: You just don't hand people fish, you try to leave the skill of fishing behind. They know how to leave the skill behind far better than we in the military do. And I took many lessons from this which I used later in Somalia and elsewhere.

RETURNING REFUGEES to their country of origin was no simple task. The large number of international laws and regulations created to safeguard the rights of refugees generate a large administrative and technical burden. This was the first operation at this level of civil-military coordination; and many lessons learned emerged that would be useful in future operations. For example, I had never known before that there's a difference between "displaced persons" within borders and "refugees." Each class has rights, but the rights of displaced people are not the same as the rights of refugees.

Processing all that took a great deal of our time and energy; but it was all necessary. You assume all these people want to go home; but that assumption is not totally correct. Some Kurds did not want to go back. Some were simply too paralyzed with fear to move. We knew they couldn't stay in the hills. But we couldn't just herd them into trucks and carry them wherever we thought it best to take them. We had to convince them we would protect them and take care of them before we could get their agreement. It was not easy.

Every single Kurd had to have written documentation spelling out that they weren't going home under duress and that they understood what they were doing. Forms had to be filled out for each Kurd, and somebody had to fill them. That meant Potter's guys in the camps had to interview every adult among the 500,000 Kurds and take care of all the necessary paperwork.

Later, each Kurd had to be continuously accounted for—where they started from, where they were at that particular moment, where they would end up. We set up a transit system with checkpoints, way stations, and the like, to keep track of everybody; but of course things didn't work out the way we planned.

Some of the Kurds moved out without telling anybody . . . just took their don-keys or whatever and went back down the trails. We were losing count. "My God," Shali told me one day, "I've lost 100,000 Kurds. Where have they gone?" We sent recon airplanes to find out, but we didn't have much luck with that. The Kurds had simply scattered into the hills. We had to trust that they knew their way home.

Over the course of Operation Provide Comfort, eight tasks had evolved for the CTF (and the operative word here is evolved):

1. Provide immediate relief and stabilize the population in place.
2. Build a distribution system/infrastructure for continuous logistics support.
3. Establish a Security Zone in northern Iraq.
4. Construct temporary facilities, i.e., transit centers, way stations, support centers, etc.
5. Transfer the refugee population to the temporary sites.
6. Transition the humanitarian operation to the international relief organizations.
7. Provide continuous security for all aspects of the operation.
8. Enable the ultimate return of the refugees to their homes.

The mission was continually changing. We didn't just get instructions up front, look at the expected end state, and go and do it. We were probing our way through every stage—often thinking when we reached one stage that we were at the end state. But then we'd see other paths opening that we'd have to follow. Once we'd stabilized the refugees in the hills, we realized we had to move them out of the hills; then we realized we had to put them in a sus-tainable area; then we realized we had to bring them home; then we realized we had to protect them from the Iraqis. Tasks emerged from other tasks. We were developing them as we went. And we had no idea what the end state would be until we got there.

By mid-June, the Kurds were back in their homes, and we were able to withdraw our ground forces back to Turkey. There we established a tempo-rary base for a ground reaction force just inside the border at a town called Silopi. Though humanitarian airlift missions were no longer required, con-

tinuous combat air patrols were maintained over the Kurdish areas, and the MCC remained in the Security Zone. The ground troops left Silopi in July.

On July 24, Provide Comfort I ended and Provide Comfort II began. General Shalikashvilli returned to USAREUR, Jim Jamerson resumed command, and I went back to being the deputy. With the ground troops gone, Provide Comfort became an air operation again. Only the MCC and a CSAR capability remained on the ground.

Now that the air operations had transformed into combat patrols, and the Rules of Engagement gave only Jim Jamerson and me authority to order certain responses to Iraqi threats, Jim felt that I needed greater familiarity with air operations. I was not only thoroughly briefed, but I was taken on a flight in a two-seater F-16 to get a hands-on feel for what the pilots faced. And since we had an aircraft carrier in support, I also flew in a Navy A-6—including a series of catapult shots and traps aboard the carrier. This valuable experience served me well in future joint tours of duty.

Later, when Jamerson left and Brigadier General Glenn Profitt took command, I was asked by General Galvin to stay on to provide continuity.

I finally returned to EUCOM in November.

Provide Comfort evolved into Operation Northern Watch, and continued on for well over a decade until Operation Iraqi Freedom in 2003.

OPERATION PROVIDE HOPE

By the end of 1991, it was becoming increasingly evident to Secretary of State Baker that the New World Order was not happening. The twelve republics that had split off from the former Soviet Union—many of them nuclear-armed—were not going to blossom painlessly into democracies and free-market economies. That much-desired outcome faced serious obstacles. Baker concluded that achieving world stability required helping the FSU recover by means of a new international Marshall Plan.

This was a gigantic undertaking, with many uncertainties: Could the U.S. muster the international community, use NATO, bring in the Japanese and other developed nations, and get the necessary resources? And then, how would this undertaking be received in the FSU itself?

Baker's vision was to jump-start this post–Cold War Marshall Plan by means of a humanitarian airlift of food, medicine, and other supplies to the republics of the FSU. The operation, called "Provide Hope," was conducted by the U.S. military during January and February of 1992. Once that was under way, Baker hoped other countries would join the effort. He foresaw down the road not just a humanitarian gesture but a follow-up international effort to reconstruct the economies and political systems of the FSU, to encourage investment, to provide the technical expertise needed to bring them up to international standards, and to show them how to operate in the international community.

The project was headed up by Ambassador Rich Armitage; Congress approved $100 million for the initial effort.

Though the natural inclination of the military is to avoid getting tangled up in such projects, Generals Galvin and McCarthy jumped on the effort right away. It obviously fitted in with Galvin's long-standing inclinations. He saw the importance of supporting Provide Hope, yet it was far from clear how EUCOM would help.

Early in January, the decision was made to keep the Provide Comfort Crisis Action Team going, with a focus on Provide Hope; and a meeting was held at EUCOM headquarters to decide what else to do. Someone obviously had to link up with Ambassador Armitage and find that out.

Tony Zinni got the call.

General McCarthy turned to Zinni: "We're not sure what this is all about, but it looks like a very good thing, and EUCOM needs to be a big part of it. Rich Armitage is in Bonn [on a trip to solicit European assistance]. Get up there and tell him you're there to support him. Figure out what he needs and go make that happen."

To Zinni, these are the assignments he loves best—missions that nobody knows how to define or execute; and you go out with what are called mission-type orders: "Go get it done."

When Zinni arrived in Bonn, Armitage was holding a meeting with German and U.S. officials at the U.S. Embassy. During a break, he was ushered into the conference room to meet Armitage.

Armitage, a Naval Academy graduate and later a Navy SEAL, had had a long history in Vietnam both in combat and working for the State Department. In a long career in government, he had been an Assistant Secretary in the Department of Defense, and then an ambassador-at-large—a troubleshooter. In that capacity, he had brought acceptable settlements to a number of knotty negotiations, such as the Philippine bases contract. All the recent Republican administrations have used him as their front-line troubleshooter . . . the man who can handle the really tough jobs, get done what has to get done, no matter what it takes. He has had vast experience both at the Pentagon and in the State Department. (He became Deputy Secretary of State under Colin Powell.)

Armitage is a big, powerfully built man, blunt, forceful, to the point, and easily intimidating to those susceptible to intimidation. He does not tolerate fools or people who waste his time, and he doesn't tolerate a lot of idle brainstorming. He knows where he wants to go; he wants to see what people can do, not what they can say. At the same time, he's a very smooth and savvy operator on the playing fields of Washington, with fine-tuned political instincts. He makes few wrong moves.

Zinni took an instant liking to him. All his instincts told him he and this hard-driving diplomat would work well together.

But Armitage was not thrilled when he was introduced to the Marine brigadier general from EUCOM. He was polite enough, but his expression said, "Who the hell are you? And what do you want?"

"I'm on orders from EUCOM to report to you," Zinni said, "and get you any military support you need. I'm here to help you."

"I'm not sure I need your help," Armitage answered suspiciously, with an expression that was even less encouraging. His long familiarity with the military—always wary of nonmilitary missions like his—had made him skeptical of generals bearing gifts. It was more than likely that Zinni had been sent to keep an eye on him, and to make sure he didn't tap into military assets.

Armitage knew he did not need EUCOM, and he made that instantly clear (though without saying so directly). His mission was from the Secretary of State; that is, from a level several notches above EUCOM. And Colin Powell was one of his best friends (and remains so). As far as he was concerned, Zinni—and EUCOM—were probably obstructions rather than solutions. "Who needs EUCOM? I can blow EUCOM away and get whatever I need."

Zinni quietly pressed his case: "General Galvin is totally sincere. He did not send me to sabotage Provide Hope, but to offer you everything we have on a silver platter. We want to help you get this thing off the ground.

"Believe me," he assured Armitage, "I have both General Galvin's and General McCarthy's ear: You will get what you want."

After a time, Armitage softened into a "Well, we'll see" attitude. That was enough for Zinni.

Back at EUCOM, General McCarthy set up a joint task force (under a special outfit in the Crisis Action Team) to carry out the airlift mission. The JTF was commanded by Brigadier General Jim Hobson, USAF, who had also worked with Zinni on Operation Provide Comfort, and it was composed of U.S. Air Force airlift units—a logistics component to move, stage, handle, and pack the supplies; a psychological operations unit to translate the instructions on how to properly use the relief supplies provided and convey our messages of cooperation; an information bureau to handle the public relations aspects; and the On-Site Inspection Agency (OSIA), which was tasked to provide advance contact and coordination at the delivery locations.

Though OSIA's mission was normally arms control verification, their capabilities (language, small-team deployability to remote sites, etc.) made them ideal for this task. Many airlift delivery locations were in places U.S. aircraft had never flown into—remote airfields where there was little or no information about fuel availability, field conditions, and navigational aids. The OSIA teams made their way to these locations a week in advance, made the contacts on the ground for handling the supplies, and passed on all the necessary information by means of satellite communications.

The U.S. Transportation Command (TRANSCOM) supported the operation; EUCOM established a Special Projects Team in their command center to run it; and a Disaster Assistance Response Team from the Office of Foreign Disaster Assistance joined the effort.

The relief supplies themselves came from Cold War stocks, prepositioned in Italy, the Netherlands, and Germany—food, medicine, blankets, and medical supplies—much of it in storage since the 1950s. EUCOM units gathered these up and moved them in a massive series of airlifts to places they had never seen before—Dushambe, Almaty, Tashkent, Kiev, Bishket, Baku, and other remote spots in the FSU.

Meanwhile, Armitage's team watched over the JTF, visited countries and organizations in NATO and the European Union (to gain participation and support for the follow-on efforts), and traveled to the various republics of the FSU (to establish contact with local officials, coordinate future activities, and make assessments of needs). Secretary of State Baker chaired a multination donors' conference in Washington to solicit support and resources for the long-term effort.

Secretary Baker kicked off the operation in a ceremony at Rhine-Main on January 23, 1992.

EUCOM had put together a system that would deliver everything Armitage might want. Thus when he came to Zinni and asked, "Can we get a plane to deliver medicine to Kiev?" Or: "Can we move some supplies to Almaty?" Zinni got him the airplanes and set up the deliveries.

Zinni made things happen—contributing to, demonstrating his loyalty to, and becoming part of Armitage's team; and that impressed Armitage. Loyalty and team playing are important to Armitage—probably a legacy from his military background.

Meanwhile, the two men were connecting on a more personal level. They liked each other's company, and they shared deep, bonding experiences—combat in Vietnam, weight lifting. It didn't take long for Zinni to become one of Armitage's right-hand men.

After a time, somebody asked Zinni, "Okay, so what are you now? What do they call you?"

Zinni gave the question a second's thought, and then made up his title: "I'm the Military Coordinator for Armitage," he said. The title stuck.

Zinni was provided an office with Armitage's team at the State Department in Washington, and he had another office at the Rhine-Main Air Base* in Germany, where they were running the JTF. But he spent most

---

* This was the base used in 1948 for the Berlin Airlift; it therefore had an ironic and historic significance.

of his time crisscrossing Europe with Armitage. They flew to Moscow and St. Petersburg, to Ankara, to Brussels. They dealt with NATO and the EU. They coordinated support, participation, receipt, and distribution of the aid and the future larger-scale reconstruction effort. They worked with U.S. government assessment teams on the ground in the FSU and with local officials. They were all over the place.

The airlift operation ran until the end of February and delivered 2,100 tons of food and medical supplies to twenty-two locations.

Zinni spent three months on Provide Hope after the end of the airlift. During that time, Armitage worked tirelessly to transform into reality the vision he and the Secretary of State had put together.

As time passed and the military requirements ended, Zinni's work for Armitage took him increasingly into the economic* and political realm. Though Armitage wanted to keep Zinni around, it had grown obvious that the military aspects of Provide Hope had faded away.

"There's no point in your hanging around here anymore," Armitage told Zinni finally. "Why don't you go back to EUCOM? As things move on, we might get you back in, but there's no sense in your hanging out here."

The need for Zinni to come back never materialized. By the end of spring, the mission was folding. The silence from the international community had been deafening. Other countries did not have the will or share the vision; they were simply not interested in participating in a new Marshall Plan.

What kept them away?

The world of the early '90s was not the world of the late '40s. This wasn't a devastated Europe threatening to collapse into communism. It was a Europe of individual nations who were not only beginning to feel their own oats but had serious problems of their own to solve. The Germans, for instance, had to pay for German reunification.

No one was interested in working under a U.S.-led program . . . or in laying down the necessary resources.

---

* Toward the end of Provide Hope, much effort was put into the problem of stabilizing the ruble.

It was nevertheless a badly missed opportunity; and much of the turmoil and instability that came afterward in Russia, the former Yugoslavia, and elsewhere could have been avoided if the nations of the free world and their organizations (like the UN and the EU) had been more farsighted.

ZINNI'S INVOLVEMENT in "Operations Other Than War"—like Provide Comfort, Provide Hope, Provide Promise, and others while at EUCOM—provided a wealth of experience that he later drew on constantly. These were fascinating, exciting missions . . . like military operations, even combat operations. On these missions, he got to do what he loved best—get out into action in the field, but with the added thrill that he was saving people's lives.

Later he participated in several other Operations Other Than War— such as the one in Somalia—that have been seen as the most advanced models for military-civil operations, peacekeeping, and humanitarian missions. No one has had more experience in these kinds of operations than Zinni.

CHAPTER FIVE

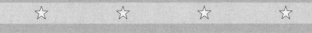

SOMALIA

AFTER EUCOM, Tony Zinni returned to Quantico as the deputy commanding general of the Marine Corps Combat Development Command (MCCDC).*

The MCCDC watches over the Marine Corps requirements and structure in doctrine, organization, material, training, education, and leadership development; and it manages the Corps' career schools for its officers and enlisted (all of which together make up the Marine Corps University).

It was an obvious assignment for Zinni, yet he was not overjoyed to have it. As he saw it, his recent experience could have been better used in an operational assignment. ("Every officer worth his salt always feels he is the best qualified operator in the Corps," he comments.)

On the other hand, returning to Quantico brought him back into the doctrine, training, and education base with which he was familiar. There he'd be at the red-hot center of all the exciting, revolutionary changes that General Gray was creating, and there he himself would be provided with a forum for his own ideas for change. He knew he had a lot to contribute

---

* The Marine counterpart to the Army's Training and Doctrine Command (TRADOC).

to Quantico. His tour at EUCOM had convinced him that U.S. military services would soon be forced to improve their performance significantly in joint operations and to develop programs for handling the messy new third world missions that were clearly on the horizon.

The Marine Corps, specifically, had to examine its organization, its doctrine, and the way it fought, taking a hard look at the tactics, techniques, and procedures needed for nontraditional missions such as peacekeeping and humanitarian operations. The new missions that he had tackled at EUCOM were not aberrations—the Kurdish relief effort, the NEOs, the engagement with former Warsaw Pact militaries. They were the face of the future. And Zinni was convinced that the Marine Corps, with its tradition of flexibility and resourcefulness, could more easily adapt to these missions than could other services, and pioneer the kind of post–Cold War force that was ideally suited to it.

Zinni was granted his wish to explore these new ideas . . . but not, as it happened, in the classrooms and on the fields of Quantico. Instead, he became a major player in the most trying and tangled U.S. military peacekeeping operation until the occupation of Iraq in 2003. It made the Kurdish relief in '91 seem like a walk in the park.

By November 1992, Zinni had been at Quantico for six months. Shortly, he would be in the zone for promotion to major general. The next summer would change his fate one way or another; he'd either be moving up to a new command or out into civilian life.

That month, while working to develop a new war game with the Navy, he learned that President Bush had decided to launch a joint task force to conduct a humanitarian operation in Somalia. Zinni was vaguely aware of the desperate and worsening situation in that country—civil war, famine, disease, anarchy, thousands of innocents dying. The news of the humanitarian operation, however, came out of the blue.

In a few days, it would be decided whether the 1st Marine Expeditionary Force (I MEF) or the Army's 18th Airborne Corps would lead the operation. Even though he was in the dark about the operation's actual nature, Zinni knew his EUCOM experiences in joint and humanitarian operations would come in very handy in the planning if I MEF got the call.

He immediately went to his boss, Lieutenant General Chuck Krulak,* to offer his services.

Somewhat to Zinni's surprise, Krulak was enthusiastic. "Hey, listen," he said, "I don't want the operational force to look at Quantico as a drain. I want them to see us as an organization that's there for them. We look out for them; we support them. So if we've got expertise, I want to offer it up."

Krulak called General Carl Mundy, who had replaced General Gray as commandant, and made the offer. General Mundy, in turn, called the commanding general of I MEF, Lieutenant General Bob Johnston. (Zinni had known Johnston for years, had served under him in Okinawa, and had great respect for him.)

While these discussions were taking place, Zinni was on his way to Fort Leavenworth for a conference. When he arrived, he had a call from Krulak. "I MEF has been chosen for the mission," Krulak told him, "and General Johnston wants you to take part in it. Get back to Quantico as soon as you can, then call Bob Johnston for further instructions."

"The best possible news!" Zinni thought. The news soon got better.

Back at Quantico, he called Lieutenant General Johnston, still thinking that Johnston would want him primarily for the initial planning. What he heard then just about knocked him over: The commandant had recommended him for chief of staff of the Joint Task Force (JTF) that would be formed around the core of the I MEF staff.† Since this meant he would be going to Somalia in a leading operational role, he was ecstatic.

But it turned out that Johnston had a better idea. He wanted Zinni to be the director of operations. Even though the chief of staff was the senior position, he felt strongly that this operation was going to be so challenging and complicated that he wanted someone with Zinni's wealth of operational experience, both in combat and in humanitarian missions, to run it. The practicalities of integrating all the pieces of this mission meant

* The son of a legendary Marine general.
† In the military, the chief of staff is something like a civilian chairman of a board of directors. He's the senior man on the staff who pulls together all its sections—administration, operations, logistics, planning, etc. He's also third in command after the commander and his deputy.

that the chief of staff was going to have to back up the chief of operations (in planning and logistics and the like). Operations was where all the action was going to take place.

To Zinni, this was great news. "I don't care about seniority," he told Johnston. "I want the operations job."

The next day he packed his bags, went up to Washington, and joined the CENTCOM* CINC, General Joe Hoar, for the flight to Hoar's headquarters in Tampa. There they linked up with General Johnston and got a briefing on the operation. Afterward, Zinni was to accompany Johnston back to his headquarters at Camp Pendleton, California, for a week of planning. They were to deploy to Somalia on December 10.

The plane ride from Washington to Tampa proved to be invaluable. Zinni had known Joe Hoar from his first days in Vietnam (he had first met Hoar in the Rung Sat), and the two had remained friends ever since. Hoar was a savvy operator who had earned a tremendous reputation as the CENTCOM commander. For the duration of the three-hour flight, the two men went over the mission.

Zinni had recommendations based on his recent experiences: techniques, tactics, and organizations (like UNHCR) they'd need to employ if they were dealing with refugees or displaced persons; using Civil Affairs to set up a Civil-Military Operations Center (CMOC) like the one created in Operation Provide Comfort to connect with the NGOs and the UN; using psychological operations (such as avoiding military terminology in order to better convey the humanitarian message).

Hoar listened carefully to Zinni's ideas—most of them totally new to him: Refugees? The third world? NGOs? UN? . . . *another universe*! After he'd taken them in, he put his arm around Zinni—he's a large, bearish man—and said: "I'm glad I found you. You're the guy we need out there. This is going to be great."

At CENTCOM headquarters, Hoar, Johnston, Zinni, and the staff went over the situation in Somalia and the planning so far.

The Somali people occupy the actual "Horn" of Africa, and are the ma-

* Somalia was in the CENTCOM area of operations.

jority in northern Kenya, Djibouti, and the now Ethiopian province of Ogaden. They are a clan-based society, with five major clans and numerous subclans, unified in language and ethnic identity, separate in customs, lineage, and history. Somalia became a nation in 1960, following a period as an Italian and British colonial possession and a post–World War Two UN mandate. A weak, fractious postmandate government lasted for nine years, but collapsed in 1969 when the first President was assassinated and a military dictator, Siad Barre, took over. Barre's rule began well enough for the country, though his early alliance with the Soviets did not sit well with the West. It paid many of his bills, however, and brought in modern weapons.

The good times ended in 1977 when Barre attacked Ethiopia to regain Ogaden. This was a tragic miscalculation—not least because Ethiopia was itself a Soviet client state. The Soviets, forced to choose, tilted toward Ethiopia; and the disastrous war and defeat (in 1978) that followed pitched Somalia into a steep decline.

Barre switched sides from the Soviets to the West, and a period of apparent progress followed—only to be eaten up by corruption, and by the increasing repression of clans other than Siad Barre's own Marehan. As the repression grew to violent assault and terror, the Siad Barre government rotted from within. The clans fought back, and the nation drifted into civil war. (The conflict started in 1988, but only became general in 1990.)

Civil war devastated the country. It was a nation awash in Soviet and Western weapons. Most were ultimately used to kill Somalis. Hundreds of thousands of refugees left the country; hundreds of thousands more were killed in the fighting, or died of starvation and disease. By 1992, half the children born since 1987, and twenty-five percent of the country's children overall, had perished. Institutions of government had vanished. Factional feuding among clans only added to the misery.

Millions were still at serious risk.

Siad Barre was driven from power in 1990, but kept fighting in southern Somalia near the border with Kenya, in what was called "the Triangle of Death"—the area between the towns of Baidoa and Bardera, in the interior, and Kismayo, on the coast. Faction leaders controlling the various regions fell to fighting each other. The strongest of these was General Mohammed Farrah Aideed* of the Hawiye clan . . . but there were many others.

In January 1991, Mogadishu, the capital, was divided between Aideed and the businessman, politician, and local warlord Ali Mahdi Mohamed (previously allies against Siad Barre), after Ali Mahdi turned against Aideed. This was a not totally surprising turnaround. Both were members of the Hawiye clan (yet from different subclans: Aideed was a Habr Gidr and Ali Mahdi was an Abgal; significant differences in Somalia's fractious clan system), and both were also leaders of the same political faction, the United Somali Congress (USC)—but in Somalia, betrayal is the mother's milk of politics.

That same month, the U.S. Embassy in Mogadishu was evacuated in a last-minute, dramatic rescue by Marine helicopters launched from amphibious ships participating in Operation Desert Shield.

For several months, the two sides faced off against each other, Aideed in the southern parts of the city and Ali Mahdi in his base in the city's north. Aideed, who was the more experienced and effective military commander and had the benefit of better and heavier weapons (taken from Siad Barre's warehouses), held the stronger position; but fighting between the two warlords was only sporadic. Law and order completely broke down in the city; armed gangs roamed everywhere. No one could control them. Serious fighting finally broke out in September 1991 and raged for several months, leaving little of value intact in Mogadishu.

In May 1992, Aideed finally defeated Barre, who escaped to Kenya, and later found exile in Nigeria. Aideed had proved to be a formidable commander, with powerful credentials to lead his country. He had—as he saw it—liberated Somalia from the dictator Siad Barre, a triumph that en-

---

* Aideed was a highly intelligent man, Western-educated and Western-trained militarily, but also cunning, violent, and brutal. After rising to the rank of general in Siad Barre's army, he had turned against Barre and then had been imprisoned for seven years. After his release and "rehabilitation," Barre made him Somalia's ambassador to India, to get him out of the way. He turned against Barre again after his return.

titled him to take Barre's place as the national leader. Other faction leaders saw things very differently; and fighting continued. This worsened the famine and destruction throughout the southern part of the country, especially in the Triangle of Death. (The northern provinces, at the actual Horn of Africa, were relatively unaffected and in effect have operated as a more or less independent state.)

In 1992, the UN started a humanitarian operation called UNOSOM (UN Operations Somalia), which proved to be powerless and ineffective—too weak to put down the violence . . . or even to provide security for the relief workers. Looting prevented most UN and NGO food and relief supplies from reaching the intended beneficiaries.

In late August of that year, the U.S. also started a humanitarian operation, called "Provide Relief," that airlifted food and medical supplies from Kenya to remote sites in Somalia. Provide Relief aircraft flew nearly 2,500 missions and delivered more than 28,000 metric tons to airfields in southern Somalia. The operation saved lives, but an airlift could not carry nearly enough food and medicine to seriously ease the famine and disease.*

By the fall of 1992, Somalia was a lawless, devastated land ruled by fifteen warlords with their militias and by roving gangs of armed bandits. These traveled around in "technicals," pickup trucks with crew-served weapons mounted on their beds. (They got their name from the relief agencies who had hired out the gangs for protection and charged it off to "technical assistance.") The relief agencies and NGOs were subject to extortion, pillage, threats, and even murder, sometimes by the very guards they hired.

By November, the chaos and violence in Somalia had made some kind of international action inevitable. After much discussion within the Bush administration and the UN, it was decided that a large military force was needed (modeled after the recent Desert Shield/Desert Storm coalition against Iraq), consisting of at least two American divisions, supplemented by other U.S. and foreign forces. This force would operate with UN approval (under Chapter VII of the UN Charter, authorizing peace en-

---

* Operation Provide Relief was absorbed by Operation Restore Hope in February 1993.

forcement using "all necessary means" including deadly force), but it would not be a UN-commanded operation. The operation was called "Restore Hope."

The American concept for Restore Hope foresaw the quick establishment of security on the ground, allowing the relief agencies and NGOs to operate freely, followed by a rapid transition to a UN-led peacekeeping operation (though the U.S. expected to continue to supply logistics and support services and a quick reaction force). But there was to be no attempt to disarm the warlords or seriously alter the political landscape.

However, the UN Secretary-General, Boutros Boutros-Ghali, had different expectations. In his view, Restore Hope's limited time frame and scope would not provide enough security, disarmament, or political change to allow the UN to take responsibility for nation building in Somalia. He wanted the U.S. to embark on a full-scale nationwide disarmament program before there could be any transition to UN peacekeepers.

This ambiguity between the U.S. and the UN understanding of what had to be done came to haunt both the U.S. Restore Hope operation and its UN successor, which came to be called UNOSOM II.

THE FORCE designed to bring initial order to Somalia's chaos was General Johnston's JTF:

The Marine piece would consist of a Marine Air Ground Task Force, centering on the 1st Marine Division, with logistics and air components. The Army had designated the 10th Mountain Division as their part. The Navy was going to bring in maritime preposition ships and a carrier; and naval P-3 aircraft, flying out of Djibouti, would also be available. The Air Force brought in C-130s and a number of other aircraft to augment Marine Corps air. There were also special operations components.

General Hoar was additionally looking at a coalition involvement that would include participation from African, Gulf region, and Western countries. (He called this "a 3-3-1 Strategy.") Because Somalia was both an African and an Islamic country, it was politically important for CENT-

COM to be seen in Africa and in the Islamic world as encouraging their involvement. He also wanted one other Western force as a leavening factor; and the Canadians had already committed to sending a brigade. (Later, the numbers of other participating countries exploded. By the end of the operation, there were twenty-six of them.)

Once the various pieces of the force had arrived in Somalia, they had to be fused together. The CENTCOM and I MEF staffs had already put in much work on that, as well as the more obvious issues of deployment, logistics support, and bases (General Hoar wanted to use regional bases in Kenya and Djibouti as support bases, for example). Sequencing in a large force into the Horn of Africa's slender infrastructure was not going to be easy.

The biggest problem faced by the planners, however, was that they didn't yet understand exactly what had to be done once the forces were on the ground. This was an unusual mission, and few of them really understood its nature. Like General Hoar, they'd had no experience dealing with NGOs and the UN, much less bringing order to a failed third world nation . . . and saving lives there. Though shooting, killing, and destruction were seen as inevitable, this was in no way a typical combat mission. They were groping badly trying to comprehend it.

Here Zinni brought his greatest contribution.

After a day at CENTCOM headquarters, Zinni and the rest of the I MEF staff left for Camp Pendleton. By then, he had a basic understanding of the situation in Somalia and the mission they'd be mounting to deal with it. Yet, at the same time, the situation on the ground was breaking fast, and there was no clear picture of what was actually happening there or what had to be done.

The following week was spent on round-the-clock frantic planning and coordination.

Zinni, Johnston, and key members of their team took off on a C-141 for Somalia on the ninth of December. A Marine Expeditionary Unit (MEU) had meanwhile been positioned off Mogadishu in amphibious ships and would land to secure the port, airfield, and U.S. Embassy that day. The command team's C-141 landed on the tenth.

MOGADISHU

Tony Zinni:

A few hours out of the Mogadishu airport, we received a call that the French government had decided to participate in the operation and had dispatched a general to Mogadishu from Djibouti, where there was a French base; but the French government had insisted that their general be the first on the ground. Bob Johnston's reply was, "Bullshit"; and, as the coalition commander, he ordered the French to stand off as we landed. They complied.

This little show of hauteur had nothing to do with the French military, who were superb troops (and often suffered for their government's arrogance). I knew from operations like Provide Comfort that they were worth their weight in gold on the ground and we welcomed their participation, despite the initial flap. They did not let us down.

It was hot when we landed (Mogadishu is not far from the equator); and the airport was a wreck, with old Soviet MiGs and other wreckage trashed and in piles off to the side, but Marines from the MEU were already in positions to defend it. We were met by the MEU commander, Greg Newbold,* who gave us a quick brief on the situation:

During the night before the MEU's landing, he reported, he had sent in SEALs to recon; somebody had somehow got wind of it and reported this to the Western press who were hanging out in Mogadishu. They came running down to the beach with their klieg lights and cameras for a brilliant media welcome to the SEALs as they swam in. It was a very confused—and later very notorious—moment. (It further convinced me we needed to get a better handle on what was going on here.)

Though Aideed had promised that the Marines would have no trouble during their landing (the airport and port were in southern Mogadishu—Aideed territory), Newbold took no chances.† He immediately seized the port and air-

---

* Newbold had a distinguished career in the Marine Corps, and retired as a lieutenant general.

† There was also a Pakistani battalion already in Mogadishu under UNOSOM I, but they were largely ineffective, with neither sufficient forces nor mandate to make a significant impact.

field and put out security, pushing out looters and vagrants, then flew up to the abandoned U.S. Embassy compound and seized it.

We came in right behind them, and we immediately began the inflow of forces. Troops would soon be flying into the airfield, marrying up with prepositioned equipment, now being off-loaded. Other units would quickly follow. The Canadian ships were on the way. We expected to spend our next days setting up the command post, receiving troops to rapidly begin operations, and coordinating with the other efforts on the ground.

After the brief from Newbold, we moved to helicopters to fly the short distance to the U.S. Embassy compound. The sights from the helo as we flew over the city were overwhelming. The place was devastated . . . like Stalingrad after the battle. The people we could see seemed to be mostly combing through the ruins, searching for food or anything else of value.

As we touched down at the embassy compound, the devastation became more immediate. The effects of the destruction and wanton looting of the buildings and grounds were everywhere. For now, the Marines had set up a hasty security perimeter around the compound, and were in the process of clearing out dead bodies and debris. A few refugees who had taken up residence were also being removed. The embassy itself was completely gutted. The rooms were blackened from fires and full of trash and human waste. Even the electrical wiring and granite floor tiles had been torn out; every window was broken. Though our troops were hard at work clearing the mess, we knew it would be a long, hard task to get this place ready for operations.

We actually had other alternatives. The UN headquarters, for instance, was in a posh, intact housing compound; and one like it had been offered to Bob Johnston, but he had declined. It was our embassy—and a symbol of U.S. determination to reclaim its property.

He also did not believe in special frills or comforts for the command element; we ate MREs like the troops and were the last to receive service facilities such as shower units.

As I curled up the first night on the concrete floor of the room where I was sleeping, I wondered how this country could have fallen into such chaos and self-destruction. We faced a daunting task. The infrastructure was either destroyed or else practically unusable. It would take a major engineering effort to improve the roads, airfields, ports, and storage areas—not to mention elec-

trical and water systems. The crude hospitals in Mogadishu were treating forty-five to fifty gunshot wounds on average per day; but these numbers sometimes reached one hundred fifty.

Outside Mogadishu, food and other critical supplies could not get through to the needy. One convoy of twenty-five trucks had started out from Mogadishu the week before we arrived to deliver food to starving Somalis in Baidoa in the Triangle of Death. In order to get out of the city in the first place, the convoy had had to give up three trucks to pay off extortionists; it had lost twelve trucks to hijackers on the roads; and eight trucks were looted as they arrived. Only four trucks made it back to Mogadishu. None of the starving received the food the trucks had carried.

OPERATION RESTORE HOPE

The mission of Combined Task Force Restore Hope was to secure the major air and sea facilities, key installations, and major relief distribution sites; provide open and free passage for humanitarian relief supplies; provide security for relief convoys and relief organizations; and assist in providing humanitarian relief under UN auspices. Our only role (as I understood it) was to provide an overwhelming security environment so that much-needed relief supplies could flow freely. This was seen as a short-term operation that would jump-start the stalled humanitarian efforts and give UNOSOM a chance to make adjustments and pick up the mission from us. (I learned later that the UN had a different view of our mission.)

We had built our plan in four phases.

The first phase involved establishing a lodgment and securing the major facilities necessary to bring in and store relief supplies. Since the port and airfield in Mogadishu were key to this purpose, and most of the relief organizations had their primary facilities in the capital, Phase I amounted to securing key installations in Mogadishu. Stretching out to the countryside would come later. We thought this would take thirty days, but we actually completed the first phase in seven.

The second phase involved expanding operations to the major relief centers and setting up secure lines of communication throughout the country's interior, allowing supplies to move unimpeded to the eight operational areas assigned to various American and international forces. The total area covered was half the size of Texas—remote, desolate, and with little usable infrastructure. We estimated this phase would also take thirty days, but the addition of numerous international forces allowed us to complete Phase II by December 28, nineteen days after we landed.

The third phase—"the stabilization phase"—we saw as an undetermined period during which we would develop and improve conditions in preparation for the UN takeover of our mission. To our immense frustration, this phase lasted until March 26, as the UN proved extremely reluctant to assume the mission. Though we believed that an understanding had been reached between our government and the UN to make the handoff in mid-January, or at the latest mid-February, the UN command was slow to form and take charge, and in general dragged its feet.

The fourth and last phase—the handoff to the UN—lasted until May 4. The transfer to the UN came about only after strong pressure and compromise by the U.S. government.

OUR FIRST few days were incredibly hectic, with pressure to get everything done at once coming from all sides—the leadership in Washington, the press, the Somalis, the relief organizations, and the UN. All of them had their own ideas about what we should do, and they all wanted it done immediately.

My first order of business was to get our command and control structure up and functioning. Fortunately, my crew of superb colonels overcame the horrible conditions and got the operations center rolling right off the bat. We were able to clean up the piles of crap and run our operation at the same time. There was no exemption for rank; generals through privates all pitched in.

Every staff running a field operation has to quickly and smoothly put into place its "battle rhythm"—its daily routine, schedule of operations, and procedures, all supported by a system of communications and organization for commanding the operation. Traditional combat missions have preset procedures and roles that tend to hold things together even when the operation is fast-breaking. Fast-breaking missions that are nontraditional, and have the additional challenge of integrating coalition and civilian components, make establishing the battle rhythm far more difficult.

In a cycle based on combat operations, you know when you're going to attack and shoot and when the attack aircraft are going to fly. There are always surprises and friction, but the preset procedures help you through them. Here we were throwing all kinds of noncombat factors into the scheduling and timing coordination evolution: We were there to feed people, who need food every day. So when do the convoys have to go out in order to make sure food is delivered every day to the distribution sites? How do we coordinate the security requirements for the convoys? Out of nowhere, an NGO might come up with a plan to set up twenty-three feeding stations. They want security for them. "When are you going to man them?" we ask. "When are they going to open? Where will we meet you for the security?" And then we had to ask ourselves and answer: "How will we fit these requirements into our own capabilities?"

These tasks become part of our operations cycle. Their relation to combat procedures is very slender.

The morning after we arrived, I gave quick guidance on handling these requirements and left the implementation in the capable hands of my staff.

THAT FIRST MORNING, General Johnston wanted us to get on the road right away to hook up with those running the political and humanitarian efforts. We set out in Humvees loaded with armed troops.

Our first meeting was with the President's recently appointed Special Envoy to Somalia, Ambassador Bob Oakley, at the U.S. Liaison Office (USLO), located at a nearby villa. The drive there gave me my first on-the-ground look at the horrific conditions in the city. Buildings were either bullet-riddled or collapsed; hard-looking gunmen roamed the streets, glaring fiercely as we passed; clusters of dazed and traumatized people wandered around poking listlessly in the rubble.

At the USLO compound, we banged on the huge metal gate; two Somalis pushed it back and let us in. A pair of Diplomatic Security guards were in the driveway—the only security I saw. I made a mental note to check on increasing it.

Oakley came out to greet us, a tall, slender, soft-spoken, and very savvy diplomat, with considerable experience in the third world as U.S. Ambassador to Pakistan, Zaire, and Somalia. Earlier, he'd been an intelligence officer in the Navy, and knew and understood the military. He proved to be a brilliant, low-key negotiator, who commanded tremendous respect from the Somalis and the international representatives on the scene. General Johnston and I took to him right away.

What I've always liked about Bob Oakley is his "roll up your sleeves" attitude. In Somalia, he worked the art of the doable, and not some unreachable idealistic dream. He developed every likely avenue, and we'd go down whichever looked most passable. He also understood the necessary cooperation between humanitarian, political, and military efforts, and really went out of his way to make sure everything ran smoothly between them. Military officers were involved in all the serious political and humanitarian negotiations.

The first order of business was security for Oakley's small staff. We immediately agreed to put a Marine rifle squad at the compound.

Oakley then introduced us to John Hirsch, an old Africa hand and friend of his, who'd originally been sent by the State Department to be Bob Johnston's political adviser (POLAD). Later, Oakley asked if Hirsch could serve as both our POLAD and his deputy, and Johnston agreed instantly; this made great sense. It ensured the connection and coordination we all needed and proved an excellent decision.*

Oakley then laid out his immediate plans.

The first would soften our impact in the hinterland when we stretched out beyond the capital. Since we were an eight-hundred-pound gorilla, and a lot of suspicious armed men were out there, clashes were likely. His suggestion was to make advance arrangements with the local warlords and civil leaders.

---

* Oakley and Hirsch have written the best account so far of recent events in Somalia in their book, *Somalia and Operation Restore Hope* (United States Institute of Peace Press, 1995).

He would then move out ahead of us with a small Special Forces security detachment and symbolic food supplies. After the initial contact and food distribution, he'd explain our mission and intent, and then our forces would come in on his heels. His brave proposal worked to a tee.

More immediately, he had arranged a meeting later that morning at the USLO compound with Mohammed Farah Aideed and Ali Mahdi Mohamed. Getting cooperation from them would secure our logistics base in Mogadishu and expedite our move out of the city . . . and advance a further agenda of Oakley's—a plan to anchor political stability by gaining an agreement among the fifteen faction leaders fighting for power in southern Somalia. He would press the two warlords to accept a seven-point agreement he was introducing. Once he had their okay, he would take it to the other twelve faction leaders.

The schedule called for a late-morning meeting with the warlords, then lunch, then one-on-one meetings as necessary, and then a press conference. If we had positive news at the press conference, our operation would get a good psychological kickoff.

AS WE waited for our guests, I walked around the compound to get a sense of the security requirements—and to give my legs a stretch. In the kitchen area to the rear of the compound, I had a chat with some of the cooks—my first direct contact with Somalis. Since many of them had worked at the U.S. Embassy before its evacuation, they spoke English. I learned later that older Somalis often spoke Italian, a legacy from the colonial period, so my own Italian background came in handy.

As I was leaving, I noticed a baby goat tied to a tree. When I stopped to pet the kid, all the Somalis smiled brightly.

"He's a friendly little guy," I said; and they nodded.

Then they added: "He's going to taste good at lunch."

ALI MAHDI'S convoy arrived first, accompanied by an armed escort we'd provided, as well as by his personal security. Since we were in south Mogadishu, Aideed's turf, Ali Mahdi had demanded extra protection.

Aideed's compound was, in fact, directly across the dirt street from the USLO compound, but that did not speed up his arrival. Aideed had a well-tuned dramatic sense. He did not make haste to cross over to Oakley's compound, but kept everyone waiting for his grand entrance.

Ali Mahdi's people emerged anxiously from their vehicles. Once they'd satisfied themselves we weren't part of an Aideed trap, Ali Mahdi stepped nervously out of his vehicle and greeted us, sweating heavily. Inside, his conversation was fast and rambling; and prayer beads were in rapid motion in his hand.

Aideed continued to keep us waiting. "Is he coming at all?" everyone wondered.

And I wondered: "Might he make a move on Ali Mahdi, now that he has his enemy on his turf?"

I stepped outside to see if our troops were alert, then radioed our op center to make sure we had other troops moving around the area showing our strength.

When Aideed finally made his appearance, striding into our little company with a confident grin on his face, Ali Mahdi seemed close to paralysis from fear. But he quickly perked up when Aideed heartily embraced him like a long-lost friend.

After introductions and initial explanations from Bob Oakley, the two warlords made conciliatory speeches. Aideed emphasized the importance of the meeting after more than a year of separation and conflict, and made a couple of small, symbolic, starter proposals to help move the reconciliation along. He said: "We must end the division of the city by removing the green line"—the north-south line separating his turf from Ali Mahdi's—"and we must end our propaganda war against each other."

He closed with a hope that Somalia would again be a viable country.

This man was a formidable personality, I quickly realized—no penny-ante thug. He was articulate and statesmanlike, and obviously had no doubts that he was the natural leader of his country—he saw himself as nothing less than its George Washington—and that our purpose was to benefit his ambitions.

Ali Mahdi was not so impressive. His speech essentially confirmed and seconded Aideed's.

. . .

IT WAS time for lunch. My little goat friend came out well cooked and cut into chunks on a platter. As this was passed around, I noticed one huge piece—the leg, from shank to hoof—sitting in the middle of the pile. Since I was at the end of the table, the last piece left was this gigantic goat drumstick. Everyone was delighted when I pulled it off and began to gnaw away clumsily.

The lunch turned out to be very friendly . . . and useful.

Aideed proved especially helpful. It was obvious that he wanted to be seen as part of our operation . . . and to co-opt it to his benefit, if he could. Yet, he agreed to cooperate on security measures in his areas of Mogadishu and the outlying regions; and his advice was sound. He confirmed, for example, Oakley's plan to enter new areas carefully. "If the militias and gangs know you are coming," he told us, "they will get out of the way and won't cause trouble.

"And make sure," he went on, "that the first troops in arrive with food and medicine to give directly to the people. In this way they won't see you as just another armed band to be feared, but will associate you with good things."

We incorporated this advice into our planning.

A couple of "Oh, by the way" comments also emerged: one having to do with the formation of political committees, the other with the need for a national police force. I didn't pay much attention to either of them at the time; but they greatly affected me later.

Oakley then sprang his seven-point agreement and pressed for acceptance.

The key points were as follows: Immediate and total cessation of hostilities and restoration of unity of the USC; immediate and total cessation of negative propaganda; and the breaking of the artificial lines in the capital.

In Somalia, negotiation means endless talk with minimal conclusion, with any agreement reached today up for discussion again tomorrow. Aideed and Ali Mahdi were thus reluctant to reach any conclusions; they wanted a series of further meetings.

Oakley pushed back. "We have press outside waiting for signs of progress," he told them. "We need something positive and concrete to give a boost to our negotiations. We have to give the people something to hope for."

After hemming and hawing, they agreed to three of the points. (Oakley succeeded in gaining complete agreement within a few days.)

Bob Johnston and I also insisted that technicals be taken off the roads of Mogadishu to prevent any problems with our forces; and both agreed.

We then left Aideed and Ali Mahdi to talk privately as we prepared for the press conference. Once that was over, Bob Johnston and I left, feeling confident that the first meeting with the warlords had gone exceptionally well, and that we had in Bob Oakley a great and politically astute partner. The security cooperation that came out of this meeting allowed us to reach our first phase objectives in seven days, rather than the anticipated thirty, and hastened completion of the next and most crucial phase.

NEXT ON our schedule was a meeting back at the embassy compound with Phil Johnston, the immensely capable, creative, and energetic head of the Humanitarian Operation Center (HOC). Johnston, the president of CARE, was on loan to the UN. HOC's function was to coordinate the humanitarian effort in Somalia for that organization.

Like Oakley, Johnston was an open, can-do guy who focused on the mission and not on prerogatives. Also like Oakley, he was familiar with the military, understood how to work with us, and did not have to be convinced about setting up a solid coordination mechanism. He instantly embraced our plan to set up a Civil Military Operations Center to coordinate our efforts with his HOC, the NGOs, and the relief agencies, adding a suggestion that we co-locate the CMOC with his HOC.

This was a great idea. It was not only logical, but it made life easier for the NGOs and relief agencies, many of whom did not want to be closely associated with the military; and some, like the Red Cross, were actually forbidden association with the military by their charter.

One of our colonels, Kevin Kennedy, who was already involved in Operation Provide Relief and knew the humanitarian side of things extremely well, was designated as head of the CMOC. Two other superb officers, Colonel Bob MacPherson and Lieutenant Colonel Buddy Tillet, were added to the team, along with a handful of Civil Affairs personnel assigned to our task force.

Our meeting with Phil Johnston bore immediate fruit. The next day, we

were able to successfully get off the first protected relief convoy. The first re-
lief ships full of supplies landed and off-loaded in the port of Mogadishu the
day after. These initial steps marked the actual start of our Phase II.*

FOR MANY *reasons our relationships with NGOs and relief agencies proved*
to be mixed—and sometimes tense.

Coordinating these disparate organizations is often like herding cats. Their
culture is sharply different from ours in the military—and often infused with
a built-in dislike for us . . . rising more often than not out of the part they
are called on to play in healing the devastation of armed conflict. Because
they can easily be overwhelmed by the vast capability of the military, they fight
fiercely to protect their identity and their own distinct contribution to the
larger effort. And because they vary greatly in size, areas of expertise, charter,
and sponsorship (religious, private, governmental, international, etc.), they
often have a particular orientation about how or where they will function that
may not be compatible with the kind of broadly coordinated plan the mili-
tary likes to produce. More practically, their people do not respond to rigid
direction and organizational structure, while their organizations often com-
pete for resources and support. There is little natural tendency or interest to
cooperate.

More than sixty relief agencies were operating in Somalia. Of these, sev-
eral came out of the UN; the U.S. government's Office of Foreign Disaster
Assistance (OFDA) had on-the-ground presence in the form of its Disaster
Assistance Response Team (DART); there was agency representation from sev-
eral other countries; and there were many NGOs—all of them working under
Phil Johnston's able coordination mechanism. But coordination was at best
still a difficult task.

To begin with, there was resentment of the military intervention. Many

---

* Our problems in Somalia were greatly compounded when medical problems forced
Phil Johnston to leave for two months. Though he was sorely missed, our officers in the
HOC/CMOC did a great deal to fill in the gap left by his absence; and I did what I could
to stay close to CMOC operations, to meet with relief workers to hear out their concerns, and to work out problems before they grew too great. We made the system work,
but it took a lot of effort from everyone.

agencies feared the military would get credit for any success, even though they themselves had been working in Somalia long before the military. And some agencies opposed military participation at all in humanitarian relief, on the grounds that we did not understand how to do it and would screw up their efforts.

Relief workers also tended to develop views about who were the bad guys and who were the good . . . views as often as not based on partial, local experience and friendships, and not on the big picture. In a culture of blood feuds, it's easy to take sides based on proximity. Armed with such biases, relief workers would strongly urge us to get rid of "their" particular enemies, and fight our efforts to bring everyone to the table. It was our view that Somalis themselves had to decide the who and the how of their governance. Many agencies thought they knew a better way . . . without realizing that in so doing they were treating the Somalis like children.

We had our biggest dispute with the agencies over the security mission. The agencies tended to expect us not only to improve general security for everybody, but to actually replace their hired guns and provide them with both full-time mission security for their organizations and full-time personal security. We could not possibly do that. Certainly not without major—and unacceptable—changes on their part.

For starters, there were well over five hundred facilities and residences in Mogadishu alone. Consolidating these would have made security feasible; but NGO culture put such consolidation out of the realm of discussion. The agencies also liked to maintain a "youthful" lifestyle, with a lot of free and easy movement around town at night for parties or other social events. In New York, L.A., London, or Paris, this kind of travel is perfectly safe. In Mogadishu, you'd be crazy to do that without armed protection; and they expected us to provide it. They refused to change their lifestyle, and we refused to provide individual protection. Tempers ran high.

At one point the UN threw an amazing costume party. They were disappointed when we did not accept their invitation to attend.

IF FARMERS *and cowboys can be friends, so can relief workers and military. The great majority of relief workers are fine people who bravely do God's* work; yet their culture remains far apart from ours; they tend to see the world from another, though equally valid, perspective.

In the military, we often have little patience for "save the whales" types—especially when they seem timid and poorly organized. Yet neither do we normally have sufficient understanding of their special expertise, or of how actions that seem logical to us can be counterproductive to their efforts. I had already learned from past experience, and would learn again in Somalia, that we both had to work much harder to understand each other and coordinate our efforts better. The good news: In Somalia, our day-to-day experiences taught both the relief agencies and the military how to do exactly that—such functions as sending out convoys under security, manning and securing feeding stations, constructing facilities, vetting local hired security, and many others were accomplished through the selfless efforts of both sides.

AT THE END of the first day on the ground, General Johnston and I sat down to assess the situation before he made a report to the CINC. Both of us were encouraged. The meetings with Bob Oakley and Phil Johnston had gone extremely well. ("The Johnston and Oakley team is a definite winner," I said to myself.) The general's guidance was to stay close to both of them, making sure I coordinated the security, political, and humanitarian efforts directly with them. This was fine with me. It made perfect sense. He also asked me to communicate directly not only with his own staff but with the CENTCOM staff; and General Hoar later instructed me to extend my direct communications to the Joint Staff as well. All of this also made perfect sense, though it was highly unusual to grant such access to someone at my level, and meant they had significant trust in me. I was determined to use the access wisely and keep everyone involved well informed. In fact, it allowed us to avoid many potential misunderstandings.

After this wrap-up meeting, I got an update from my guys in the op center: They were making terrific progress setting up our command and control facilities. But reports from our units moving out into the tense streets of Mogadishu were giving me serious concern. There were too many heavily armed men out there. Our guys did see encouraging signs, however. Many people waved and smiled when they saw U.S. Marines.

• • •

THE NEXT DAY *turned out to be less positive.*

To start things off, the bad guys decided to test us quickly, to see if we were made of sterner stuff than the UN troops, whose rules of engagement had made strong response to provocation close to impossible.

We had put up both fixed-wing aircraft and helicopters over the city and its immediate surroundings as a show of force and to provide a source of intelligence, reconnaissance, and cover as we began reaching out beyond the city. That morning, two of these helicopters were fired on by technicals. Though the helos immediately destroyed them, we were not happy that the bad guys were willing to take us on. That was of course a big mistake on their part. The quick and decisive response of the helos demonstrated that we meant business and would not tolerate attacks.

We were not the UN.

This event sparked a widely quoted statement to the press: "Things have changed in Mogadishu," I told them. "Wyatt Earp is in town."

The key meeting that day was with the special representative of the UN Secretary-General, Ismat Kittani, a veteran Iraqi diplomat and senior member of the UN Secretariat, and the military commander of the UN forces in UNOSOM, Pakistani General Mohamed Shaheen. Bob Oakley accompanied us to the UN headquarters, located in a villa in the center of the city that was decidedly more comfortable than our own gutted embassy. The meeting went badly.

Inside the headquarters, the air was thick with resentment. Kittani, confrontational from the start, was clearly infuriated that the U.S. military had been called to pick up after UNOSOM's failure. And if we then managed to achieve positive results, UNOSOM's failure would seem that much greater. Up until that moment, I'd imagined that the enormous size of the job ahead would make taking credit for success easy for everybody. There was, after all, plenty of work for everybody, including UNOSOM. And if we all together succeeded in making life better for the people who were actually suffering, then we could all go home happy. But for the first time I began to realize how far apart we were from the UN's concept of what had to be done.

Several points of contention emerged.

In general: If the U.S. wanted to take on the job of fixing Somalia, fine. As far as the UN was concerned, let the U.S. do the whole thing.

Specifically: The UN did not intend to take over the mission from us anytime soon; neither did UNOSOM intend to work with us beyond a minimal coordination effort to de-conflict our forces; and they were very reluctant to honor any agreements we made or programs we put in place. We proposed setting up a Somali-led and -manned police force, for example. But UNOSOM was opposed—for all practical purposes—to Somalis leading anything important. They made it equally clear that our agreements with the factions would in no way be binding on UNOSOM.

As a final indignity, Kittani demanded an operational name change. For some reason known only to him, and perhaps to the trackless depths of the UN bureaucracy, our operational name at that point—"Combined Task Force," the standard military title given to coalition commands—was unacceptable to the UN; and we would have to change it to "Unified Task Force" (UNITAF).

Such a name change is in fact no big deal . . . such things have little practical importance. But in demanding it, Kittani's arrogance stuck in our craw, and did not help relations that were already starting to get frayed. Still, we did not want to do anything to give the UN an excuse for accusing us of not cooperating, nor did we want to harm efforts to eventually hand the mission back to them; so we accepted the change.

Kittani never let up his hostility, and never lost an opportunity to obstruct our work—even when his obstructions harmed Somalis.

Some time later, Bob Oakley and I worked out a plan with the UN High Commissioner for Refugees, Sadako Ogata, for resettling in Somalia the 350,000 Somali refugees then in Kenya. To the immense chagrin of Madame Ogata (whose job was to try to resettle the almost one million refugees scattered around the region and the half-million displaced persons in the country), the UN rejected our plan—without substituting another; they simply stonewalled. This kind of thing happened all too often.

In time, I began to learn some of the reasons behind the UN obstruction policy . . . though I still believe they were wrong not to try to work more closely with us. Cooperation and coordination would have helped all of us—not least the Somalis. But I now see that their hesitations were based on genuine fears.

Primarily, they were afraid they'd be left holding the bag if chaos and anarchy returned after the eight-hundred-pound gorilla left town. A good point: Chaos and anarchy returned after we left.

As one UN official explained to me: "Boutros-Ghali is afraid you'll hand him a poisoned apple. He won't take the mission from you until he has wrangled as much as he can from the U.S."

What they seemed to want from us, then, was to clean up the country and leave it in a condition that would greatly lessen the ability of the warlords to wage factional war. A worthy goal. But hardly possible without total war.

The big demand from Kittani and Boutros-Ghali was total disarmament of all the Somalis.

Thanks a lot!

There was simply no way we—or anyone—could disarm the Somalis except at the cost of enormous bloodshed. Weapons were everywhere, and most were portable and easily hidden.

This issue became a major bone of contention between the U.S. and UN leadership.

Our thought had been to establish a secure environment, while the UN simultaneously did the things they did best—working on peace agreements, setting up voluntary disarmament programs, reinstituting a national police force, resettling refugees and displaced persons, and eventually assuming the security mission. But it was evident from this first meeting that they would do nothing beyond sitting there without a new mandate and Security Council resolution.

Up to this point, everybody had made it clear that we were all working together. "Hey, we're all one team" was the constant message. "We have one objective. Let's figure out how to work together." Suddenly, we'd hit a wall. The idea that this would be a kick-start operation of short duration was fading fast. It now looked like we had inherited the whole problem.

After the meeting, I would have been blind to miss General Johnston's and Ambassador Oakley's frustration. Theirs mirrored mine.

More bad news came that day: French troops in Mogadishu had shot up an unarmed bus, killing two Somalis and seriously wounding seven others, after an evidently confused bus driver had run a French roadblock. An angry Somali mob had gathered around the French positions, and we had to move in, negotiate some kind of peace with the warlords, and calm things down.

Later, other complaints about French troops in Mogadishu eventually led us to move them out to an area near the Ethiopian border, where they did great work. This location was no less difficult than Mogadishu, but it was politically less sensitive.

We spent the next days getting the operation rolling.

I had already broken our area of responsibility into eight Humanitarian Relief Sectors* (or HRSs)—a term we'd invented to avoid using traditional military terms (like "Sector of Operations" or "Zone of Action"). We wanted to convey the intent of our mission to the people, press, and relief workers as "softer" than a normal military action. Each HRS was unique, with boundaries based on factors like clan and tribal boundaries, political boundaries, geography, military span of control, capabilities of our forces, established distribution sites, security threats, and lines of communications.

Early on we had absorbed the Provide Relief operation out of Kenya and integrated it into our efforts. Soon other U.S. and international forces were flowing in at a rapid rate.

The Marines from the MEU, who'd led the way into Somalia, were quickly joined by additional Marines we flew in and married up with equipment from Maritime Prepositioning Ships that arrived in Mogadishu's port on the twelfth of December, our third day on the ground. The 10th Mountain Division's arrival shortly afterward allowed us to move out quickly to complete the second phase.

Though General Hoar had originally envisioned seven allied forces joining the U.S., following his 3-3-1 Strategy—three African national forces, three Arab national forces, and one Western national force—that went out the window the first day, as forces from all over the world started clamoring to join up. Forces from twenty-six nations ended up participating in UNITAF; and as many as forty-four nations had lined up when we had to shut the door.

These forces were a mixed bag. Some came with limited capabilities, some came burdened with restrictive political direction, some came with big de-

---

* I later added a ninth HRS as our forces increased.

mands for U.S. support, and a blessed few came with highly credible and capable units ready to take on any mission. My job was to find a place to put them, integrate them into the operation, and assign them missions. This was no small task.

My staff took to calling me "the Century 21 man" after I somehow found places where a rapid and unanticipated succession of international troops could lay their heads and set up camp. I'd get a call out of the blue that troops from someplace like Zimbabwe or Botswana had landed unexpectedly at the airport and were looking for direction. I'd then slip on "the yellow jacket"—as my staff put it—and try to "sell them some real estate." I'd go out to meet their commanders—or their advance team, if we were lucky (some militaries were not aware that it helps to send an advance team before they launch the whole force). The "choice lots" were obviously out of harm's way and near major facilities. The less desirable "lots" were in the HRSs out in the bush, where the austere environment and high threat made a "sale" difficult.

Since individual contributions—such as a transport unit, say, or a field hospital—often came in bits and pieces, we devoted considerable creative energy to the marrying up of these with other forces, taking into account factors like language, cultural affinity, political compatibility, and military interoperability.

As the operation evolved, the State Department continued to solicit new contributors for UNITAF. The variety of international troops making up the Coalition staff very quickly turned our headquarters into the bar scene from Star Wars. At its peak, Provide Hope had 39,000 troops under UNITAF command—though not in every case the same troops who started the operation. Troops came and went, and, where possible, were replaced with specialized units, more suitable for the later phases of the operation. Thus, an infantry unit might be replaced by an engineer unit.

This dynamic flow required careful assignment and management, as did issues such as Rules of Engagement, logistics support, and area assignment; and the job of assigning and managing fell on me. The law of diminishing returns set in.

I got a lot of strange requests for support. Some of the strangest included fresh food (that is, live goats, sheep, and chickens); full medical support, to include medical malpractice coverage; and, naturally, money to pay for the troops. We politely declined all of these requests.

For all the difficulties we had to deal with—or put up with—it was great to have this wonderful rainbow of Coalition forces working with us. We had enormous respect for them. I especially enjoyed visiting the Coalition units to coordinate operations . . . or just to check on how things were going. This often brought the added benefit of a delicious, and often exotic, meal.

The African troops were particularly impressive. They asked for little or nothing, and were willing to take on the toughest missions. Our Marines always gave them the highest praise possible for their courage and skill: They wanted them assigned to their sectors.

Since the embassy compound was quite large (it once had, in better times, a nine-hole golf course, for example), we were able to co-locate liaison teams from the various coalition forces close to our headquarters.

One night, as General Johnston and I were walking around the headquarters compound, we happened to pass the row of tents occupied by the African liaison teams. Except for a dimly lit bulb wired to our field generators, each tent was totally bare: no field desks, no cots, no folding chairs, nothing to make the tents livable—much less workable or comfortable. The contrast with the other coalition facilities was stark.

We quickly had our engineers build them makeshift desks, tables, and other field furniture.

"We're eternally grateful for your kindness," the liaison teams told us.

"You've more than earned it," I assured them.

THE PRESENCE of the liaison teams was not an unmixed blessing.

Our policy was to have coalition personnel clear their weapons near the compound entrance as they entered. The idea was to remove magazines or live rounds from the weapons, and then to confirm they were safe by a test firing into a barrel of sand. The sentry and clearing barrel were just below the blown-out window of my small second-floor office, which made me sharply aware of any mistakes. There'd be one or two accidental discharges a day, as the sentry tried to explain how to clear weapons to the often clueless coalition troops. One of these accidental rounds zinged by my feet as I was enjoying a late-night cigar near a ruined fountain in front of our gutted headquarters. So much for my pleasant, peaceful moment.

We got occasional rounds from firefights outside the compound as well. One night as I slept, three heavy, .50 caliber machine-gun rounds hit the concrete window frame of my office. This got my attention. Another time I was pinned down at our piss tube when a firefight broke out nearby and made my location the impact zone for the fusillade that erupted. I zigzagged back to the cover of our building, hitting the deck more than once. My appreciation for indoor plumbing considerably increased after that.

ALL THE WHILE, I spent as much time as I could watching over our operations outside Mogadishu.

General Johnston and I traveled constantly out to the units in the field, to get a firsthand sense of what was happening and what was needed. At other times, I went on patrols with the Canadians, visited feeding stations guarded by the Pakistanis, accompanied Marines on weapons searches, and visited orphanages with our Civil Affairs units.

I particularly remember a trip to our Marines in the south, working our most remote and desperately needy sector. As we drove up to this dusty, arid camp, with only scrub trees and bushes to break up the reddish brown terrain, I couldn't help noticing a remarkable sea of bright yellow in the distance. As we got closer, I realized that every one of the suffering multitudes who had drifted into the camp on their last legs was wearing a yellow T-shirt and yellow sarong. The Marine commander had come up with a scheme to brighten up the spirits of these poor people with color. At his request, his wife back at Camp Pendleton organized a drive for the families back home to contribute anything yellow—material or clothes. It worked. As people came in for food, water, medicine, and shelter, they were given their yellow garments. You could see the immediate effect in their weak smiles. But the pickup in their morale had long-term effects as well. It actually helped them get physically stronger.

.   .   .

FROM VIETNAM ON, *I've had the habit of immersing myself in the people and cultures of the countries where I've been stationed. I kept up this long-standing tradition in Somalia—sucking up everything I could about Somali society and culture. I read anything I could get my hands on; I met frequently with Somalis, both individuals and groups; and Somalis from the States, whom we had contracted to translate and liaise for us, provided additional insights.*

One of these last turned out to be Aideed's son, a student in California and a corporal in the Marine Corps Reserve when we called him up to come home. Though his surname, like his father's, was Farrah, we didn't actually make the connection until we had him in Mogadishu. Once we knew who we had, it was obvious that using him as a translator or liaison would be difficult, so we kept him at the headquarters (where the two of us had occasional friendly conversations). After his father's death in 1996 (he was killed in a firefight in Mogadishu), young Aideed returned to Somalia and took over his father's organization. Years later, when I commanded CENTCOM, he and I maintained a sporadic correspondence. (Again, Somalia was in my AOR.)

Though I could never hope to reach Robert Oakley's deep familiarity with the Somalis' complex culture, I did achieve a basic understanding:

There is a single key difference between Somalis and Westerners: Until very recently, the former have been nomads, while for many generations we have lived the more stable life of cities, towns, and farms. This difference has serious practical consequences. Somali time sense, for example, is vastly different from ours—more fluid, less logical and precise. In negotiations, we like to achieve conclusions, and to build on past agreements. We like to move forward in a progressive, linear manner; to get the damned thing over with, and move on. They don't. They love meetings and committees . . . talking for its own sake; and they love to let talking take its own time. They don't have our imperative to reach endings. Or, as I would later tell an audience: "The good news with the Somalis is that everything is negotiable. The bad news is that everything is negotiable all the time. What we agreed yesterday is still open to negotiation today."

Their tribal, clan, subclan, and family unit system drives their entire culture. Everything is accepted as a group responsibility. Everything is settled by the clans, and only by the clans. There is no strong concept of individual responsibility. Thus, for example, there is a strict "blood tax," or dhia, system. Wrongs are righted by paying for them. If payment is not made, violence often follows.

This system is central to Somali loyalty, not the nation or a state. Unless you understand that, you will never understand the Somalis.

MY GROWING knowledge brought additional responsibilities. Ambassador Oakley found duties for me beyond my operational mission—working more directly and personally with the Somalis. Soon, with General Johnston's okay, I was representing Oakley on a series of Somali committees he had set up; and at his request, I started dealing directly with the faction leaders.

I welcomed both duties.

Thus, I was on the political, security, judicial, police, and other committees; and I frequently met with Aideed or one of the other faction leaders on one matter or another. I also met with women's groups, schoolteachers' and other professional groups, to hear complaints and get cooperation for projects.

These encounters were hardly ever easy, given the Somali approach to negotiating; and my frustrations quickly grew. At one point, I had to ask Oakley what these endless meetings were accomplishing.

"When they're talking, they're not fighting," he answered. "We need to keep them engaged in a lot of talking."

He was right. But it took me a while to realize that.

In time, my presence on the Security Committee allowed me to get to know Aideed's and Ali Mahdi's security chiefs, General Elmi and General Abdi. These relationships headed off a lot of problems and potential disasters as the operation went on.

Another prominent Somali I got to know well was Aideed's financier Osman Atto. Atto was an old-fashioned wheeler-dealer entrepreneur. His hands were in all kinds of pots. Because continued fighting would inevitably harm the many deals he always had working, he did his best to keep Aideed on an even keel and prevent fighting. "Don't upset him," Osman kept urging me. "Bad for business." (Osman and I kept in touch after I left, and he proved to be very helpful when I returned to Somalia in 1995.)

The most important of my working relationships was with General Aideed himself—not easy, given the general's mercurial personality. Today, we'd probably call him "bipolar"—manic-depressive. I could never be sure which mood I would find when I arrived at his compound. When he was in his "statesman" mode, he was articulate and expansive, making grand pronouncements about Somali and international affairs. When he was in his "alderman" mode, he harped about petty problems and complained about our operations. But in his "dark" mode, he was scary. His own men often warned me not to provoke him when he was in this mood.

For all the uncertainties of working with him, he was far and away the one person who might have led his country. His organization was actually a minigovernment, with all the bureaucratic trappings (including— improbably—a Minister for Tourism). Like Washington bureaucrats and used car dealers, Aideed liked to hand out ballpoint pens imprinted with his political party's logo.

"You need administration, bureaucracy, and detail to run a country," he answered when I queried him about such things; "and only I have it." He was right. None of the other warlords had anything like it.

Without doubt, he was a dangerous character who required constant attention, but I believed he could be handled and controlled. There were times when he was relatively easy to work with him; there were times when you had to lay the law down to him; and there were times when I had to wait out a dark mood. But I could live with all that as long as we were making real progress . . . and we were.

Because he was a dangerous, very high-maintenance character, many people thought we ought to just threaten him—and if that didn't work, use force—to make him toe the line. As the UN found out later, doing that opened up lots of problems. They thought they could handle him—without having any idea what they were biting into. I thought there were other ways to deal with him.

MY VISITS to Aideed's lair (or to one of the other warlords' compounds) required forming up a small convoy of two or three Humvees, with security. My driver, Corporal Watts, would usually gather up eight to ten Marines from the staff, have them don their battle gear, and mount them up for the trip.

Inside the compound, the buildings were all layered with the porches that are typical in tropical countries. Dozens of heavily armed men always swarmed about, staring brazenly at my Marines from every level of the buildings. During my meetings, the Marines stood beside the vehicles returning the stares of the cocky Somali gunmen.

Our entrances and exits to and from the compound were normally without incident—which was just as well, considering the possibilities. But one of our entrances proved to be deliciously memorable. As we were stepping out of our Humvees on this particular occasion, I was greeted by shocked faces on Aideed's men. I turned to the second Humvee in line, which seemed to be the source of all the excitement: An African American woman Marine was standing there in her battle gear, with her M-16 at the ready, looking tough as hell.

I left to conduct my business. Forty-five minutes later, when I came back out, the stir was still at high pitch. It was obvious the Somalis couldn't believe their eyes—an armed woman in Marine battle dress.

On the way back, I turned to Corporal Watts. "You brought a woman Marine, huh," I said; I knew he'd set this scene up.

He smiled. "She'll kill you just as dead as any man," he said.

I laughed. He loved jerking the Somali tough guys' chains.

Back to our headquarters, I drew the woman Marine aside for a quick chat. Corporal Watts was right. She'd kill you just as dead as any man could.

MEANWHILE, Ambassador Oakley was moving the peace process forward. By early January 1993, he had arranged a conference in Addis Ababa, attended by all the faction leaders; and in mid-January, they'd all signed a peace agreement. He then convinced the reluctant UN to sponsor another conference in Addis in mid-March, where all the factions signed on to a plan for a transition government, the disarming of the militias, and the establishment of a national police force.

It had become increasingly clear that Oakley was essential if the Somalis were going to settle their differences peacefully. Only he commanded the trust, confidence, and respect of the Somalis. Yet even this was a long shot.

AS FOOD *began to flow, and we had begun to reduce the violence and chaos in Mogadishu, an unexpected phenomenon just sort of broke out here and there in the city. The old policemen started coming back onto the streets, all decked out in their musty uniforms, to include batons—directing traffic, controlling minor problems, and promoting order. It was one of those seemingly minor events that was actually a very big tipping point. Where they appeared, vendors' booths and makeshift markets set up. The police were security magnets, and people flocked to these newly "safe" areas.*

In Somalia, the police have always commanded great respect. They never took part in Siad Barre's oppression, never took sides in the bitter civil strife that followed, and even somehow maintained the goodwill of the warlords.

The reemergence of the police presented us with a splendid opportunity to turn a large piece of the security pie over to trained, competent, and respected Somalis—an opportunity the UN was reluctant to support. We were concerned that we'd lose momentum while waiting for the UN to move ahead. But when Oakley tried to persuade the UN to take on the reestablishment of the police, they refused. And when the UN decreed that it would not accept a police force that was under Somali control, Oakley dropped the job on me.

Though U.S. law has strong prohibitions against U.S. military involvement in this area, Oakley was undeterred, and he convinced General Johnston to let me help put the police back on the street. As a result, I became the head of the oversight committee formed to reestablish the force.

A superb U.S. Army military police officer, Lieutenant Colonel Steve Spataro, single-handedly put together a plan and worked with the old police leadership to vet the former police, rebuild their academy, set up the training program, arrange for equipment and uniforms to be provided, and reestablish the prisons. The Italians and Japanese contributed vehi-

cles, uniforms, and equipment; and we arranged for weapons ("donated" in the name of Ali Mahdi, from whom we seized them) and a control system for them.

We ended up with a national police force of 4,400 personnel, operating in sixteen cities, while Oakley worked with our lawyers to establish jails, and to set up a judicial committee that put in place judges, legal representatives, and a legal code.

THOUGH BY January 1993 UNITAF had achieved its mission to create a secure environment for the conduct of the humanitarian effort, Somalia was still a dangerous place, with violence ready to explode at a moment's notice. Obviously, in the best of worlds, the Somalis would have gladly given up their arms, turned them into plowshares, and lived blessedly in peace and harmony. Since that was not going to happen, we had to consider some less than ideal ways to pacify a warlike society awash with weapons . . . while somehow or other grappling with UN Secretary-General Boutros-Ghali's demand that UNITAF forcibly disarm the factions. Still impossible, in our view. If we attempted it, the warlords would fight; Mogadishu would become a combat zone; and the bloody fighting would put an end to humanitarian operations.

An alternative proposal was to offer "incentives" for weapons. We'd throw money at the problem . . . offer them a "buyout." On the face of it, this was a pretty good idea. But in fact, it was as much a fantasy as Boutros-Ghali's. Not only would it have cost us a fortune, it would have fed an arms market that would have brought in even more weapons.

The solution we came up with was a program to reduce arms gradually, basing the program on increasingly tight controls on weapons, a formal agreement for their voluntary cantonment* by the militias (with an inspection requirement), and an active effort to search for and confiscate uncantoned weapons.

It worked. We removed all visible weapons from the streets, cantoned the weapons belonging to the faction militias in Authorized Weapons Storage Sites (AWSSs) that we watched and inspected, and disrupted the two arms

* That is, the collection of weapons in secure locations.

markets in Mogadishu. Our sweeps captured thousands of weapons and millions of rounds of ammunition. Within days, the price of weapons skyrocketed; the gunshot wounds treated daily at the hospitals were reduced to low single digits; and the faction leaders began to participate in Oakley's political process without fear of attack.

PUTTING A *permanent lid on violence was of course not in the cards. There was no way we could avoid violent confrontations.*

One incident with long-term consequences occurred in February at the southern coastal city of Kismayo.

Following Aideed's victory over Siad Barre, General Hersi Morgan, a graduate of the U.S. Army's Command and General Staff College and Barre's son-in-law, took charge of the remnants of the former dictator's army near the Kenyan border. Early in 1993, Morgan started conducting probes in the direction of Kismayo, one of which provoked a major counterattack by U.S. helicopter gunships and Belgian light armor (Kismayo was in the Belgians' sector). After losing several technicals and some heavy weapons, Morgan's forces scrambled back into the bush.

They came out again on February 22. That night, Morgan conducted a raid on the city (in violation of an agreement brokered among the warlords to freeze forces in place until negotiations on a peace plan were worked out). He infiltrated his fighters, picked up weapons he'd previously stashed (undetected by the Belgian troops), and attacked and drove off Colonel Omar Jess, an ally of Aideed's and the ruling faction leader in Kismayo. Jess, who had committed many atrocities, was not popular; and the residents welcomed his expulsion.

Aideed naturally insisted that we expel Morgan from Kismayo and return Jess to power. Though Oakley and Johnston gave Morgan and Jess an ultimatum that essentially had them revert to the situation before the raid, and the two warlords essentially complied, Aideed staged violent protest demonstrations in Mogadishu in front of our embassy compound and near UN headquarters in Mogadishu. We had to put them down.

These demonstrations had a serious impact on UNOSOM, the NGOs, and the press, who feared a renewal of civil war. Press reports, based on an in-

complete view of the situation, were overblown and inaccurate. In fact, the demonstrations were more annoyances than battles.

Though Aideed was a master of political theater, his violent demonstrations were not normally directed toward UNITAF. Most of the time, he saved them, and the accompanying shooting sprees, for Egyptian forces and the visits of Boutros-Ghali. The Egyptians were not liked by the Somalis, while the UN Secretary-General was hated. In his days in the Egyptian Foreign Ministry, Boutros-Ghali's policies in support of Siad Barre had—in the Somali view—kept the dictator in power. (Since Siad Barre was in exile in Nigeria, there were also demonstrations against the Nigerian troops.)

Meanwhile, the U.S. Marine commander of the Mogadishu sector, Colonel Buck Bedard, ran the security of the city with an iron hand and responded quickly and decisively to all of Aideed's provocations.

One of his more effective measures was to station Marine sniper teams in taller buildings around the city. When over the course of several nights, armed gunmen had tried to move into ambush positions near our compound, all of them were picked off by our snipers. The remaining ambushers decided to find a better way to spend their time.

Later, gunmen from an Aideed AWSS started taking potshots at passing troops. When my warnings failed to stop the shooting, the Marines attacked the compound with helicopter gunships, tanks, and infantry. The AWSS was captured with no friendly casualties.

I called a security meeting for the next day. It was a tense, confrontational encounter. "You have to make a decision right here," I told Aideed's generals. "Are we at war or not? Decide now. We'll take our next actions based on your decision."

I then threw on the table several rounds that had landed in our embassy compound from a random shooting that had originated in the AWSS we'd just attacked. "We won't tolerate this any longer," I told them.

The generals went off to talk, and returned much chastened. "Let us put this behind us," General Elmi announced. "There will be no war." He went on to explain that a difficult-to-control rogue militia had been manning the AWSS. "We regret the problems they've caused," he said. "We'll put pressure on them to stop."

We had no more trouble from them.

• • •

MUCH OF *the violence on the streets of Mogadishu comes in midafternoon, when young thugs have started feeling the khat they've been chewing all day. Khat leaves (a mild, inhibition-removing narcotic) were flown into dirt airstrips each morning and quickly moved to market stalls to sell before they lost their potency. All morning, we'd see chewers' bulging checks all over town. By three in the afternoon, the gangs of hostile young men were feeling they could take on the world. The occasional violent confrontations with our patrols ended badly for the khat-chewers in every instance.*

Thugs and shooters weren't the only security problem. We also got thieves—incredibly brazen thieves who'd risk their lives to steal anything, no matter how little it was worth.

One night, thieves came over a wall near a squad of Marines. The thieves were gunned down before anyone realized they were unarmed.

We later turned over the perimeter security of our compound to a less effective coalition force. But then another band of thieves came over the wall at night and made their way into our building. Voices whispering in Somali woke me up. I grabbed my pistol, ran into the corridor, and watched two men fleeing out of the building. Moments later, I heard shouts and scuffling; our sergeant major and General Johnston's aide had seized one of them.

I quickly made the commander of the coalition force responsible for compound security aware of my displeasure. Though he assured me that he'd fix the problem, I didn't sleep well after that, and checked his positions often.

Much more frustrating were the young street urchins. Some threw rocks at our convoys and patrols—not a smart idea, given our advantages in firepower. But worse were their attempts to grab loot by swarming our trucks as they passed through the streets. Intelligence reports that kids might be used to place bombs on the trucks made a bad problem worse. After our security troops had to shoot and kill a few of the young thieves, we started looking for ways to block the kids without hurting anyone. "There must be some way to apply less than lethal force," we told ourselves. Nobody wants to kill kids.

One day, I was walking past our makeshift motor pool at the embassy and noticed troops gathered around a truck, testing a strange device. It only took me a moment to figure out what it was—a jury-rigged electric prod attached to the truck's battery.

I gave them credit for their innovation, but not for their judgment. The prod was not a workable solution to the nonlethal problem. I could see a CNN shot of a Somali kid getting zapped. We needed a better, more permanent answer. But when we asked the Pentagon for some sort of approved, nonlethal capability, the best we could get was small cans of pepper spray. Though these were no more potent than the pepper spray you might find in a lady's purse back home, they came—unbelievably—with an exhaustive training program and rules of engagement. Our troops had to implement the program and familiarize themselves with the ROEs before they could use them. Bureaucracy at work . . . a spray can is a spray can.

I knew this problem would surely come back to haunt us in future operations and made a mental note to address it.

Though security was our primary mission, other demands were hardly less pressing: We ran the ports and airfields, conducted extensive psyops and civic action programs, undertook major engineer projects to repair and rebuild the infrastructure, and provided medical support.

Our medical units also had a tough task keeping our own force healthy in this harsh and dangerous environment. By the end of the operation, we had suffered eight killed in action, twenty-four non-battle deaths (one from a shark attack), twenty-four wounded in action, and 2,853 illness and injury cases (including snakebites).

ONE OF my responsibilities was to coordinate our psychological and tactical operations.

Though there were plenty of sources of "information," the Somalis had little access to accurate news accounts. Most Somali news sources—notably, Aideed's—were nothing but propaganda . . . much of it inflammatory. We published leaflets and a newspaper, and set up a radio station, to counter the lies. The paper and radio station, which were called "Rajo"—"hope" in Somali—made Aideed very unhappy; and he counterattacked through his own radio station. A period of "radio wars" ensued.

When he summoned me to his compound to complain about our broadcasts, I told him we'd tone down our broadcasts when he toned down his own inflammatory rhetoric. He agreed.

Another victory for nonviolent engagement.

The months to follow would show that the UN had failed to learn this lesson. Instead of countering Aideed's hostile media blasts in kind, they tried to close down his radio station. Freedom of the press has to work both ways; we don't shut down radio stations just because we don't like what is broadcast. The resulting confrontation was the opening of the violent war between the UN and Aideed.

ALL THE WHILE, we did not want for VIP visitors—including President George Bush.

President Bush visited us on New Year's Day, a few days before he was to leave office. It was a grand sendoff.

General Aideed even sent a huge cake as a welcoming gift, all adorned with a portrait of the President and Aideed standing side by side beneath U.S. and Somali flags. The cake, uneaten, stayed in our admin office for several days until one of the troops noticed that it was the only thing around the place that never had flies on it. He was right. I told him to get rid of it.

The best moment of Bush's visit came when he visited our troops. The President really connected with our guys. As he walked through their ranks to a microphone, their enthusiastic cheers visibly moved him, leaving him visibly close to tears.

I'll never forget that scene.

Unfortunately, the President did not bring with him the news we'd hoped for—plans for the UN to assume our mission. Though we'd been led to believe that talks had been going on, we were disappointed to learn that nothing had been arranged with the UN. The Clinton administration would have to pick up on the transition from us to them. This was not a job you want to drop on a brand-new administration.

AS FEBRUARY turned into March, our efforts were increasingly focused on stabilizing the positive environment UNITAF had created and promoting the *political agreements Oakley was skillfully piecing together. During this time I met frequently with Aideed, the other warlords, and the various committees, trying to keep things calm and to hold agreements together.*

The UN, meanwhile, continued to fight us hard on the transition and handover front. While this process dragged on, I worked on the plan to turn over the mission to them.

The Secretary-General had presented us with a series of nonnegotiable demands. Unless we agreed to them, there'd be no transition. For starters, he wanted UNITAF to stay after UNOSOM II took over. He wanted full U.S. involvement in any follow-on UN operation. And he insisted on a U.S. Quick Reaction Force, U.S. logistics support, and a senior American leader to act as his special representative to head the operation. He got everything he asked for.

Even so, the UN was painfully slow to take the reins of the operation. In February, Boutros-Ghali appointed a respected Turkish lieutenant general, Cevik Bir, as the UNOSOM II force commander. An American Army major general, Tom Montgomery, became his deputy. Another American, Jonathan Howe, a four-star admiral and President Bush's former Deputy National Security Adviser, took over from Kittani the job of Boutros-Ghali's special representative. Robert Oakley left Somalia on March 3 in order to make way for Howe. Oakley was sorely missed.

The official handover date was March 26, but we continued to run the operation until we finally left on May 4. In effect, the UNITAF staff commanded the new UNOSOM II force. The UNOSOM staff simply sat on their duffs, refusing to accept command, but kibitzing over all our decisions and actions. It was weird to have two staffs officially overseeing the same force. In fact, we were actually commanding both forces, ours and theirs, while they were sitting there trying to set policy for future operations.

The UN plan that they intended to implement was vastly different from Oakley's. Where Oakley was steering a course that encouraged the Somalis to determine their own fate, UNOSOM II had a specific political outcome in mind. They sought to rebuild the nation of Somalia into a thriving democracy of their design, with the UN dictating who would participate in the political process. (They intended to exclude General Aideed, for instance.) We saw trouble on the horizon. In our view, the UN plan was overly ambitious, and grossly underestimated the power and support of the faction leaders, as well as the historical Somali animosity toward the UN. It was a recipe for disaster.

By the time Oakley left in March, the atmosphere on the political front had drastically changed.

We turned over the command to UNOSOM II on May 4, 1993. UNOSOM arranged a grand ceremony with dancers and singers.

After the ceremony, I drove with Bob Johnston to the airport. As our two Humvees wound through the narrow streets, he was very quiet, deep in thought. Suddenly he ordered a stop, and had the vehicles pull over to a nearby curb where several children were standing. At his direction, we got out of the vehicles, and he gathered all our pens and pencils and gave them to the kids (who all seemed pleased to get them). After his little act of charity, he slowly swung his gaze around. Something was obviously weighing on his mind.

"What are you thinking about?" I asked.

He looked up at the bright sunny sky. "I give this place thirty days," he said, "and then it's all going to go to hell."

Thirty-one days later, his prediction came true.

BACK TO QUANTICO

Zinni quickly resettled into his job as the MCCDC deputy commander at Quantico, but with events in Somalia never far from his thoughts. As he resumed the old routines, he stayed in close contact with Bob Oakley, participating with the former ambassador in Somalia-related speaking engagements and conferences on humanitarian and peacekeeping operations.

His Marine Corps career, meanwhile, continued to advance. Back in Somalia, he had been selected and frocked as a major general. That is, he was entitled to wear the rank but would not receive the increase in pay or the actual grade until his number for promotion actually came up several months later. The promotion meant he would be reassigned sometime within the year—hopefully back to the operational forces and possibly command of a division.

. . .

ON JUNE 5, 1993, a clash in Mogadishu between mobs loyal to General Aideed and Pakistani troops under UNOSOM resulted in the deaths of twenty-four Pakistanis and an unknown number of Somalis. Aideed was instantly blamed for the tragedy; and blame soon escalated into demonization. The UNOSOM II leadership stepped up their policy of marginalizing Aideed and putting the squeeze on his followers. Within days, UNOSOM II and Aideed forces had plunged into a raging war, with high casualties on both sides.

The growing conflict called into question the credibility of the U.S. mission in Somalia; Congress and the media went on the attack. General Johnston's prediction was coming true: the tragedy of Somalia was growing worse by the day; and Zinni could do nothing but watch from the sidelines.

A FEW weeks later, Zinni attended a course at Maxwell Air Force Base for new two-star generals and flag officers, with much of the classroom discussion centering on the growing conflict in Somalia—as representing an emerging form of serious U.S. military involvement. The final class featured a distinguished guest, Representative Newt Gingrich, who continued the debate. The congressman was obviously concerned about the U.S. part in the Somalia tragedy. After it came out that Zinni had been the UNITAF director of operations, Gingrich drew him aside and picked his brain. This casual meeting had consequences. It was to lead to Zinni's return to Somalia.

Several weeks later, on October 3, news came of the horrific battle in the streets of Mogadishu between Special Operations Forces and Aideed's militia. Rangers and Delta Force operatives had snatched several key Aideed aides in a surprise raid. Aideed's militia had counterattacked with automatic weapons and RPGs, pinning down the Rangers and Deltas and shooting down a pair of Army Black Hawks. An attempted rescue by the Quick Reaction Force got bogged down, and in the firefight that followed, eighteen U.S. soldiers were killed and seventy-eight wounded. Hundreds of Somalis lost their lives. An American helicopter pilot, Chief Warrant Officer Michael Durant, was wounded and then captured by the militia; and a dead U.S. soldier was brutally dragged through the streets. The American public was outraged.

Within hours of the battle, Zinni received a call from Congressman Gingrich: There was to be a bipartisan meeting at the White House. "What do you think we should do about Somalia?" the Congressman asked. "Should we pull out, or should we send in significant forces to continue the fighting?"

"If those are the only choices," Zinni replied, "then we should pull out. Sending in more combat forces just means more casualties—civilians included—and a lot more destruction. It's not worth it."

"What other options do we have?"

"The best option is to get the fighting stopped and move the situation back to where it had been when UNITAF closed down."

"Who could possibly accomplish that?"

"Bob Oakley."

Two days later, Zinni was up late watching the baseball playoffs when a call came in from General Mundy, the commandant. "You're to report to Andrews Air Force Base tomorrow morning at six," Mundy said. "By order of the White House, and at the request of Ambassador Oakley, you are to accompany the ambassador on a special mission to Somalia."

"Yes, sir," Zinni answered. "I'll be on the plane."

"By the way," General Mundy asked, "do you know how this came about?"

"Newt Gingrich got it in his head that I know something about Somalia; he called the other day and asked who could make things better over there. I told him 'Bob Oakley.' "

"Good luck."

Zinni ordered up a car, packed his bags, then made a quick call to Oakley. "It looks like I'm going to Somalia with you," Zinni said.

"Well, you got me into this," Oakley answered, "so you're coming along."

"How long will we be gone?"

"I'm not sure. But plan on several months."

Zinni repacked his bags.

The next morning, October 7, he met Oakley at Andrews AFB.

"What's the plan?" Zinni asked.

"We'll work that out on the plane."

BACK TO SOMALIA

Tony Zinni:

After the Air Force C-20 took off, Oakley told me that our first stop was Addis Ababa, Ethiopia, to solicit President Meles Zenawi's help. Meles and the Eritreans had connections in Mogadishu who could communicate with Aideed's faction.

Later, Oakley described his meeting at the White House. It was clear that he'd been given little guidance. The President expected him to use his own judgment.

For the remainder of the long flight to Addis Ababa, we worked out tasks we wanted to accomplish. We had no doubt that we'd run into other pressing problems on the ground that would change them—or render them obsolete; but these would give us a starting point.

The first two steps were absolutes. Accomplishing them was a necessary condition for further progress:

First, get a cease-fire in place to stop the violence and allow us to open the dialogue.

Second, get the prisoners released.

In addition to Warrant Officer Durant, Aideed also held Umar Shantali, a Nigerian soldier captured in earlier fighting. "These prisoners have to be released unconditionally," Oakley told me. "America does not negotiate for hostages."

We knew this would be a tough sell; the prisoners gave Aideed a lot of leverage. We had to convince his people that giving them up was in everyone's interest.

Once we'd gotten through that hurdle, the third task was to reestablish a Security Committee like the one that had so effectively de-conflicted problems during the UNITAF operation.

Fourth, organize another humanitarian conference in Addis Ababa, possibly as soon as the following month (November 1993).

Previous conferences had successfully gained agreements—though these had never been fully accepted by UNOSOM II.

Fifth, explore the possibility of reducing the UNOSOM II force presence in southern Mogadishu, Aideed's turf. During the UNITAF operation, we had tried to set up our logistics lines elsewhere, but without total success. The road, port, and airfield facilities in Mogadishu were unfortunately the only viable infrastructure that could handle the demands of the operation. We decided to look at this again, anyway.

Sixth, the Aideed problem. How much of the current fighting was his responsibility? How much should he be held accountable for it? Should we work with him? Could we work with him?

Admiral Howe, the Secretary-General's special representative, had put a $25,000 reward on Aideed's head after the June 5 battle, and had followed that up with attacks and raids on Aideed and his key people. Aideed had fought back. As long as these actions continued, there'd be little room for reasoned discussion.

In Aideed's defense, the question of his actual guilt was very much open. The UN was in fact contemplating investigations to look into this question, while Aideed himself was calling for "independent inquiries"—outside the UN—to investigate the circumstances of the conflict.

In the light of all these questions, we decided to delay a decision about Aideed.

Seven, the press problem. As word of our mission began to circulate, the media began descending on Mogadishu in droves. They had to be handled carefully. Not only did Aideed remain a master at using the press to his advantage, but an angry and confused American public and congress were watching our every move with careful scrutiny.

IN ADDIS, Meles's insights, advice, and strong views proved to be extremely helpful. On our two key issues, he had good news and bad:

Aideed had recently declared an unconditional, unilateral cease-fire.

Though the UN had not accepted it (preferring, as usual, to ignore him), this was still a positive first step.

But Meles was not so optimistic about getting the prisoners released. The UN at that point held eighty-plus prisoners from Aideed's side on an island off the southern coast. An unconditional release of Durant and Shantali would be difficult without some sort of exchange for the UN-held prisoners.

As for other issues that concerned us: 1. He thought another conference was a good idea; and he was willing to support it in Addis Ababa. 2. It was his view that an independent tribunal was the best way to deal with the Aideed problem. 3. Most tellingly, he made it clear that UNOSOM was not working well; and the fighting had strengthened Aideed among his followers.

On the tenth of October, we left Addis for Mogadishu.

BECAUSE THE direct route was risky from the airport to the former U.S. Embassy—now the UNOSOM compound—our helo took a circuitous path. As we approached the embassy, we could see improvements UNOSOM had put in after we left. Comfortable trailers had replaced our tents; and I learned later that "real food" had replaced our MREs. On the face of it, UNOSOM personnel were living a lot easier than we did. However, landing gave us a shock. We found a force under heavy siege. All the troops were dug in or protected by stacks of sandbags. All the new trailers were sandbagged into bunkered positions. Virtually nothing was moving outside the gates.

Oakley and I gave each other a sharp look.

After a series of initial briefs by the U.S. Liaison Office, we met with Generals Bir and Montgomery, who provided a good sense of the military situation. It was clear that the environment on the ground was extremely tense; a fragile and uneasy cessation of fighting was holding, but only by a thread.

It was equally clear that they were not glad to see us. In their view, UNITAF's "failures" had made it impossible for UNOSOM to succeed; and they took every possible opportunity to pin responsibility on UNITAF for anything that had gone wrong. So it did not sit well that we had come back to attempt a fix.

Our presence did not sit well with Admiral Howe, either, we learned when we met him. As far as he was concerned, our mission was going to be neither helpful nor productive; nor would he yield any of the concessions we thought would smooth negotiations. "UNOSOM II's strategy must remain as it has been," he explained, "to isolate, marginalize, and minimalize Aideed, check the intimidation and domination of the other faction leaders, and encourage democratic processes among the ordinary people." He continued to refuse to declare a cease-fire, as Aideed had done. In his view, Aideed's cease-fire was nothing but PR—psyops. (Howe did agree, however, to "suspend offensive operations" . . . a cease-fire under another title. We could live with that.)

Howe's strategy may have been high-minded; and yet it was also a recipe for war. The factions could only be dealt with through a political process that directly involved them. Their power had to be gradually reduced through cooperative agreements to disarm, followed by organization of a transitional government acceptable to all. A process that replaced the rule of the gun might follow . . . or so we hoped and prayed.

The UN was moving too fast. They had underestimated the warlords' power, and had challenged it too soon.

WE COULD *not at that point set up a meeting with Aideed himself; he was too unacceptable to UNOSOM. So Aideed's representatives met us at Oakley's old USLO compound. Since the Marines protecting the U.S. mission in Mogadishu were not part of UNOSOM, Aideed's party agreed to let them act as our security. His people treated everyone from UNOSOM like plaguebearers.*

The drive through the city was Stalingrad again. The police were absent from the streets, the market stalls had vanished, the buildings more blasted than ever. Everything accomplished after we came nearly a year before had been lost.

Aideed's men arrived at the compound in a state of high distress. The war had taken a toll on their accustomed arrogance.

Oakley let them vent awhile, then laid out the issues, concentrating on our two key demands. "Your cease-fire and UNOSOM's cessation of offensive operations are a good start," he told them. "They provide the environment we need in order to proceed. The next step must be to restart engagement and dialogue. But," he cautioned, "nothing can move forward without an unconditional release of the prisoners." When, as expected, they bristled at this, Oakley remained adamant. He knew they wanted an exchange of prisoners, but there'd be no negotiations for the captives.

"At least agree to the release of the UN's prisoners after we hand over the captured soldiers," they implored.

"That's impossible," Oakley said. "We can't proceed on anything until there's an unconditional release."

After two emotion-packed hours, the Somalis agreed to take the issue back to Aideed and then get back to us.

While all this was going on, a helo passed overhead spreading psyops leaflets calling for Aideed's arrest. Aideed's men went ballistic. The leaflets almost derailed the talks. Thanks a lot!

I had earlier checked to make sure no operations would be run during this very sensitive time, but the leaflet drop fell through the cracks. Amazingly, the military operations on the ground were going on with little or no coordination. All the various UNOSOM commands were, as they say in Washington, stovepiped. Everything lined up top to bottom, but nothing connected side to side.

Fortunately, we got things calmed down, and the Somalis left pacified.

Later, when I jumped on the psychological operations officer, he turned out to be totally in the dark about what he should have been doing—and, far more tellingly, who was responsible for it. Under UNITAF command, he'd had a clear line of authority; but now no one coordinated with him, and he had no one to go to for approval.

The following day, he actually tried to get me to approve his leaflets; but I had to tell him I had no authority for that; he had to connect to UNOSOM.

OVER THE next days, several conversations confirmed what I already knew—Somalia was a mess, and it didn't have to be.

That evening, I talked with Colonel Kevin Kennedy and some others I knew from the NGOs. (During UNITAF, Kennedy had run our Civil-Military Operations Center. Now retired, he had returned to Somalia to *work for UN relief agencies.) Their very outspoken take on the current situation was not encouraging: "UNOSOM creates problems; it doesn't solve them," they told me. "Their leadership is either culpably blind to what actually goes on in the streets of Mogadishu, or they're lying: Most mornings, the relief workers get a briefing from UNOSOM—just like the briefings that used to go on in Moscow back in Soviet times. They're laughable . . . except that everything here is too terrible for laughter. They invariably report quiet—no military operations the night before—while we all know that special operations missions went out; we all heard shooting; and we all see the Somali casualties in the hospitals.*

"Meanwhile," they explained, "each stovepiped command has its own intelligence (if you can call it that). Mistakes have proliferated. It's no surprise that UNOSOM forces searching for Aideed or his henchmen have attacked innocent civilian compounds. But they've even hit UN facilities by mistake."

Sleep didn't come easy that night. The terrible cost of the war was beginning to sink in. Since the June 5 flare-up that precipitated the four months of war, 83 UNOSOM troops had been killed in action (26 of these Americans) and 302 wounded (170 Americans). But thousands of Somalis had lost their lives. I thought it was a gross exaggeration when Aideed's people informed us that they had lost 10,000 killed—two-thirds of them women and children—but reports of relief workers at Somali hospitals and our own intelligence sources later confirmed that these numbers were not that far off. I simply could not believe the level of slaughter since the fighting began.

Each side had a different version of the June 5 clash:

The monthlong period after UNITAF turned over operations to UNO-SOM saw a constant worsening of the never-friendly relationship between the UN and Aideed. Differences over the role of the factions in the political process (the UN wanted to marginalize them), Aideed's radio station (the UN wanted to shut down its inflammatory broadcasts), the police and judiciary (the UN was not convinced Somalis could run either), and participation in political conferences (the idea, again, was to marginalize certain factions by inviting only UN-approved delegates) had created a tense and hostile environment that the slightest spark might set off. That spark came on June 5.

By early June, rumors were everywhere (the rumors were accurate) that UNOSOM intended to shut down Aideed's radio station, Radio Mogadishu—

located, as it happened, on the site of one of the AWSSs. UNOSOM, meanwhile, had a policy of no-notice, or short-notice, inspections of the AWSSs. Late in the day on the fourth of June, a Friday, the Moslem holy day, a bad moment to make demands, two UNOSOM officers appeared at Aideed's headquarters to deliver notification that an inspection would take place the next morning. As luck would have it, the responsible officer was away, and the subordinate who took the message was not cooperative. "An inspection on such short notice is impossible," he told them. "We need more time to prepare for it."

The UNOSOM officers stood firm. "The inspecting force will arrive at the AWSS in the morning."

The Aideed lieutenant grew more belligerent. "If they come, it will be war," he replied.

Early the next morning, the inspectors arrived at the AWSS, accompanied by a force of Pakistani soldiers. Moments later, they were confronted by an angry mob. When the soldiers tried to enter the radio station, a scuffle broke out, and a Somali was shot and killed. Word of the fighting quickly spread, and angry mobs sprang up elsewhere in town. One of these swarmed a feeding station guarded by Pakistani troops, and a number of Pakistanis were killed or captured. Another large mob engaged the Pakistani force returning from the inspection site, and more soldiers were killed, wounded, or captured. At the end of the day, twenty-four Pakistanis were dead, fifty-seven were wounded, and six were missing.

At this point, the truth gets murky. Tempers flared. Reason got tossed aside. The big question: Did the mobs rise up spontaneously? Or, as UNOSOM claimed, did Aideed's people plan the ambushes? Aideed's faction—and most other Somalis—claimed that the attacks were spontaneous responses to a real threat to the radio station that was compounded by the killing of the Somali. (It's very possible that the mobs had been urged on by Aideed's leaders, though without advance planning.)

Aideed didn't help matters the next day when in a radio address he praised the people who had risen up to fight the foreigners (further provocation and an admission of guilt in the eyes of UNOSOM). Yet, at the same time, he offered a surprisingly reasonable proposal for an impartial inquiry into the causes of the confrontation, followed, hopefully, by a peaceful resolution.

UNOSOM II would have none of that: Aideed and his lieutenants must be brought to justice; and Admiral Howe placed the $25,000 reward on Aideed's head.

A series of battles followed. UNOSOM conducted air strikes; the Aideed forces executed ambushes. The fighting escalated until the U.S. sent in special operations forces to capture Aideed and his chief lieutenants. They conducted several operations, with mixed results, until the tragedy of October 3 brought Bob Oakley back to Somalia.

MEANWHILE, Oakley and I kept in close touch with Ambassadors Lissane and Menharios, the Ethiopian and Eritrean liaisons who were our contacts with Aideed. We waited anxiously for word about the prisoners.

Word finally came that Aideed had agreed to release them. However, he would only release them directly to us, not to UNOSOM.

This was not a good idea.

Since Oakley knew a release to us would create further problems with UNOSOM, he worked out an arrangement to have the prisoners turned over to the Red Cross. To emphasize our noninvolvement and to minimize our media presence, he had us pull back to the airport. As soon as word came that the prisoners were released, we'd leave Somalia for a few days and return after the news flurry had calmed down. The moment that Durant and Shantali were released, we boarded our C-20 and headed for Asmara, Eritrea, Addis Ababa, and Cairo, for meetings with President Isaias of Eritrea, President Meles, and the Egyptian Foreign Minister. (The Egyptians had troops in Somalia; the refueling stop in Cairo was a good opportunity to connect to senior Egyptians.)

We returned to Washington on the sixteenth of October. Next day at the White House, we briefed the National Security Adviser, the Secretaries of State and Defense, and the ambassador to the UN, among others. Later, at the Pentagon, we briefed the new chairman of the Joint Chiefs of Staff, General Shalikashvili. Though Oakley presented both a superb description of the situation and a clear plan for our best possible way through the Somalia mess, I had a foreboding that the Washington leadership was looking to disengage from Somalia and write the country off. Despite my misgivings, we were given the go-ahead to pursue Oakley's plans.

A few days later, we were off again to Somalia.

After another stop in Addis to see President Meles, we flew on to Mogadishu, arriving on the first of November for a planned visit of four days. Our primary purpose in Somalia was to put in place a revised plan we had worked up since our last visit. It called for reestablishing the Security Committee; reestablishing a viable police force; getting the cease-fire and disarmament agreements back in place; getting the factions back to the process of forming a transitional government; involving in the process other nations and political organizations in the region; scheduling another conference in Addis; establishing agreed-upon sectors and security zones in Mogadishu to prevent confrontations; and several other proposals designed to put the humanitarian, political, and security situations on track.

During an intense four days of negotiating, we met with the UNOSOM leadership, the other faction leaders, and various Somali groups seeking agreement on our proposals; and we successfully persuaded everyone involved to accept a renewal of our original mission.

Sticking points remained—chiefly, the question of the UN-held prisoners and the question of Aideed's war crimes guilt.

Aideed had accused UNOSOM of abusing the prisoners they were holding on the island; and wanted their release. In fact, there were some health problems among the prisoners (who now included Osman Atto, my contact from the UNITAF days, who had been snatched up in a Special Operations roundup). Eventually Aideed got his wish, and they were released.

Since the question of Aideed's personal guilt was still far from being settled, we decided to continue our policy of keeping distant from him. For the time being, we dealt only with his lieutenants.

WHEN WE LEFT, we made the regular round of African stops (adding Kampala, Uganda), returned briefly to Washington, and were back in Somalia by mid-November—this time, for direct talks with Aideed. A new Security Council resolution (Resolution 885), accepting Aideed's party as legitimate, had eased tensions with Aideed and greatly lessened the danger of continued violence. It was time to bring him into the process and persuade him to sign on to Oakley's program.

Aideed (still UNOSOM's most wanted man) was hiding out in the labyrinths of Mogadishu. Getting to him was not going to be easy.

On the day of the meeting, our armored SUV was escorted by Marines to the old UN headquarters, where we were to be turned over to Aideed's security. As we were waiting for Aideed's gunmen to appear, a large, excited, and very curious crowd gathered around us. Though they made our Marine security nervous, they didn't actually threaten us.

We soon had other things to think about, when Aideed's hard-looking, heavily armed fighters came speeding into the intersection, hanging from technicals. Their leader was the largest Somali I'd ever seen, at least six and a half feet tall with bulging muscles. A man of very few words, he directed us to pull our vehicle between the technicals; and we raced off at high speed through a maze of back alleys and side streets. It was like a movie: Keeping up with the speeding technicals required blasting through intersections, countless near misses, and breathtaking two-wheel turns.

We suddenly found ourselves rushing into a large plaza, heading straight toward a screaming multitude of Somalis.

"What do you think?" Bob Oakley asked.

"Ambassador," I said, "they're either going to kiss us or eat us."

As we got closer, we realized they were actually cheering us. The gathering in the plaza had obviously been staged by Aideed.

Eventually, we turned into a compound and came to a stop in front of Aideed's temporary headquarters, where his chief lieutenants and a broadly smiling Aideed were standing ready to greet us. A bank of cameras off to the side videoed every move. As we stepped out of the SUV, the giant, taciturn security goon came up and put together what for him must have been a major speech. "No more shooting," he said, with evident emotion, grabbing me by the hand. "No more. Too many people will die." He had clearly had his fill of fighting.

"We'll all do our best," I answered, as the hugely grinning Aideed wrapped his arms around me like a long-lost relative and then ushered us down the ranks of his officials for their greetings. I hoped the cameramen didn't catch all that. Taking photo ops with Aideed would not make us popular back home (where the media had followed UNOSOM's lead in demonizing him).

Inside the headquarters, we followed Aideed into a large conference room. His party's banners were hanging on the walls; pens and stationery with his logo were neatly placed at each seat. After an exchange of small talk, we got down to business with a group of people who were surprisingly somber. I'd expected them to be upbeat at the very least; and I wouldn't have thought twice if they'd been gloating. They'd been hit hard, but had hit the U.S. and UN even harder; and now we were again treating them like leaders with a legitimate place in the political process. And yet they did not rejoice in their triumph; they were subdued and solemn. They recognized the terrible tragedy we had all suffered. It was clear that the loss of ten thousand Somali lives during the past four months was weighing heavily on all of them.

Aideed maintained the serious tone—though without altering his long-held positions: The release of the UN-held prisoners was still a pressing concern, and so were the big questions about his own status and UNOSOM's unceasing accusations against him. He made it abundantly clear that UNOSOM and the Secretary-General were as evil in his eyes as he was in theirs (though he pointed out that he did not oppose the UN itself). He welcomed the U.S. back into the peace process, and would further welcome an independent commission to look into the causes of war—headed by former President Jimmy Carter and with members who were not appointed by the UN Secretary-General.

Following an in-depth debate of the program Oakley had put together earlier that month, Aideed gave it his reluctant consent, adding that he hoped to work within the earlier Addis agreements. Oakley's policy was correct, he said in conclusion: Governing Somalia should be left to the Somalis.

What form that governing might take still remained a very open question, as was the part the UN and the U.S. would take in the process of answering it.

BEFORE WE LEFT, I wanted to satisfy my curiosity about the fight on October 3 that became known as the Battle of Mogadishu (dramatically captured in the book and movie Black Hawk Down).

"Could you tell me the story from your side?" I asked Aideed.

He was more than willing to do that.

As he began his account, his respect for the military skill of the special operations force—"those dangerous men at the airfield,"* he called them—was obvious.

The special operations forces had focused their attacks on Aideed's meetings with his top staff. As a protective measure for his meetings, Aideed had ordered machine guns and RPG launchers to be positioned on neighboring roofs, with orders to concentrate fire on the helos if the Americans attacked. He knew American forces would rally around a downed helicopter and be easier to fix in the fighting. He had furthermore put out a standing order to attack any reaction force coming out of the airport. The UNITAF Marines had multiple reaction forces that could respond from several directions, but now the principal reaction force always came from the airport. For that reason, it was important to cut that off if he was attacked by the special operations forces.

Aideed's tactics had all been purely defensive . . . but that's not the way they'd played on television. Even worse in the eyes of the world, they'd worked.

This did not excuse Somali atrocities; and Aideed acknowledged that no apology could make up for Somali mobs brutally dragging dead soldiers through the streets. But he also was careful to point out that he had immediately taken control of the prisoner, Warrant Officer Durant, and had adhered to Geneva Convention requirements in his treatment of him.

It was obvious that there were two widely different versions as to what happened and who was responsible for the violence. Even investigations and inquiries have presented different views.

Our return ride to the rendezvous with our Marine security force took us through another screaming crowd. Soon after that, we returned to the States.

And so my practical involvement in Operation Continue Hope, as the U.S. had named the UNOSOM II phase, ended.

In the coming days, Oakley was busy planning the Addis conference and working out implementation of his overall program. Though he asked me to be ready to return, the focus was shifting from security (which had been my

* The Mogadishu airport was their base.

responsibility) to politics and humanitarian relief. In his mind, the security situation was under control.

I returned to Quantico to watch developments from there.

It quickly became clear that the Clinton administration wanted out of Somalia. The final nail in that coffin came when they announced that all U.S. forces were to be pulled out by March 1994. In my mind, Oakley had been used to achieve a cease-fire and provide a decent interval to allow the administration to cut its loses and pull out. The U.S. was not going to follow through on the Oakley program to put the peace process back on track.

On a more positive note, at least the fighting had stopped and the ravaged country had a few quiet moments to catch its breath.

As for the question of Aideed's war crimes guilt: Months later, in February 1994, a UN commission of inquiry into responsibility for the June 5 clash published its findings. It concluded that both sides had been at fault.

I MEF

At Quantico, Zinni received good news: He was slated to take command of the 1st Marine Division at Camp Pendleton the following summer. This was exciting; he couldn't wait to move on to the division.

He didn't know that other plans were in the works.

In the early spring of 1994, he was made president of a Reserve General Officer Promotion Board at Marine Corps headquarters. At the conclusion of their work, the board members took their recommendations to General Mundy. When they were done, he asked Zinni to stick around.

"What do you want as your next assignment?" he asked, after all the others had left.

This seemed an odd question, since he had already been told he would get a division command. "Is the question just a formality?" he asked himself.

"I want a division," he told the commandant, bearing that last thought in mind.

"Which one do you want?"

"It doesn't matter," Zinni answered. "Any Marine division is just fine with me."

At that point, the commandant handed Zinni a folder. "Well," he said, "I think there's a division in here somewhere."

Zinni, who was by then enormously confused, opened the folder: It was a nomination for promotion to lieutenant general and appointment as commander of the 1st Marine Expeditionary Force (I MEF).

He was shocked. He'd *just* been promoted to major general, and here he was moving immediately to three stars . . . and skipping over division command. That was a bummer; he'd wanted to command a division. On the other hand, it was a very big honor to command I MEF—and also pretty exciting.

Zinni's recollection of his next moments is blurry. He mumbled his thanks to General Mundy, then left his office wrapped in shocked confusion.

A few months later, in June, he assumed command of the largest Marine operational force, I MEF, at Camp Pendleton, California. I MEF had in its ranks over 45,000 Marines and sailors, with its main components being a Marine division, an air wing, and a logistics group. Units were spread over bases in California and Nevada, but many of its forces were constantly deployed all over the world. The MEF had responsibilities that involved six different Unified and Sub-unified commands from Korea (where they were given a major new commitment), to the Western Pacific, to Latin America, to Europe, to the Middle East, and to the United States itself. During Zinni's two years in command, the MEF had forces involved in security and counter-drug operations in Central and South America; in humanitarian operations in Africa; in peacekeeping operations in Bosnia; in human remains recovery operations in Vietnam; in sanctions enforcement operations in the Persian Gulf; and in disaster relief and counter-drug operations in the western United States. They were involved in over one hundred major military exercises around the world and in hundreds of smaller training events.

The MEF's most substantive new effort was a crisis response assignment in Korea. Though the Okinawa-based III MEF already had a commitment there, they were now greatly augmented by I MEF. The new role was particularly challenging in that the joint and combined forces they'd be assigned in their envisioned Korean missions would be significant. According to the war plan, the MEF in Korea would become a combined Marine Expeditionary Force. That is, Zinni would command two Marine divisions—the 3rd Marine Division would be added to his own 1st Division—two Marine air wings, a Korean Marine division, a Korean Army division, and the U.S. Army's 101st Air Assault Division.

The commander in chief in Korea, U.S. Army General Gary Luck, was a brilliant operator who taught Zinni a great deal about war fighting at this highest level of operations. Fighting a war in Korea would be much like fighting Desert Storm, but on a much larger scale. The whole business of theater logistics, movement and integration of forces, the relationships between air components and ground components, working with coalition forces, fighting a strategic battle with deep strike and close combat, and integrating all these on a large and difficult battle space, took on for Zinni a new and far larger significance.

MEANWHILE, he continued to exercise his growing skills in peacekeeping and humanitarian interventions. He had become one of the few senior-level military experts on "Operations Other Than War" (OOTW).

For obvious reasons, General Binnie Peay, the new commander of CENTCOM (one of the Unified Command CINCs the MEF answered to), gave the MEF the mission to respond to peacekeeping and humanitarian crises in his theater. To better accomplish that mission, Zinni retooled a major exercise, called "Emerald Express," to develop his unit's humanitarian and peacemaking capabilities. Since he didn't have to worry about tactical-level field capabilities (his MEF had those down pat), he reshaped Emerald Express into a comprehensive conference to address issues like planning, coordination, and integration, especially at the operational and policy levels, and to direct special emphasis to coordination with relief agencies, international organizations, coalitions, and political organizations.

In a short time, Emerald Express became the most significant and effective effort to promote integration of military, political, humanitarian, economic, and reconstruction functions in Operations Other Than War.

Zinni's growing OOTW expertise brought him to testify frequently be-

fore the Senate Foreign Relations and Senate Armed Services Committees. His testimonies on specific interventions (such as in Bosnia), on U.S.
humanitarian and peacekeeping policy, and on the nature of OOTWs in
general, were not always encouraged by the administration or particularly
the Pentagon leadership: General Shalikashvilli, the chairman of the Joint
Chiefs, did not relish OOTW missions. Zinni did his best to steer clear
of problems with the chairman and other superiors, but he had strong feelings about these missions that he did not hesitate to express. He began
to earn a reputation as outspoken—a reputation he thinks is undeserved.
He has always maintained he has only done what Marines always do: Tell
it like it is.

BY THE TIME he took command of the MEF in June 1994, U.S. forces
were out of Somalia, and the UN mission was sputtering out. Though
Zinni did not forget the lessons of Somalia, he didn't expect to return to
that country.

In a few months, he was thrown into the Somalia disaster for a third
time.

UNITED SHIELD
Tony Zinni:

*During the summer of 1994, the UN decided to end the UNOSOM mission
and withdraw UN forces from Somalia. The date set for the withdrawal was
March 1995.*

*This was going to be a complicated move: Since forces from several coun-
tries would be involved, there would be coordination problems; since the
pullout would be phased, the last forces to leave were vulnerable to attack;
and credible—though unsubstantiated—reports of handheld surface-to-air
missiles made a withdrawal by air risky. As a result of these threats, the UN
requested U.S. protection for the withdrawal. Though the Clinton administration was not excited about renewing its involvement in Somalia, the in-*

ternational forces on the ground had accepted the mission at our request. The administration felt responsible for their safety.

That August, less than two months after I took command, I MEF received a warning order that we were to lead a Combined Task Force to protect the UN withdrawal. I MEF was the obvious choice for the mission: We already had responsibility for crisis response in their portion of Africa; the SAM threat required an amphibious withdrawal; and I MEF had conducted Operation Restore Hope in 1993, so the staff was already familiar with the situation.

We knew it would be a difficult assignment. The international forces would have to execute extremely complex tactical tasks (tough even for U.S. units); and interoperability problems with doctrine, procedures, equipment, and language could compound the difficulty.

The good news was the planning time. We'd have five months to plan, coordinate, and practice the mission.

"Plans are nothing, but planning is everything," Eisenhower said, possibly apocryphally. Whether he said it or not, the saying is true. We had a lot of time. I wanted to use it all to plan exhaustively, think through every possibility, and cover every contingency (or branches and sequels, in military terms). One innovation in our contingency planning was to produce a "playbook" that gave us a course of action if one of the possible scenarios occurred. At the end of the operation, I reviewed the playbook and found every event that occurred covered by a contingency plan.

The entire five months, from August to mid-January, was devoted to planning and coordination. This was the first phase of the operation. The second phase, deployment, rehearsal, and positioning, was scheduled from mid-January to the beginning of February. Phase three, setting conditions for the withdrawal and assuming of control of UN forces, was scheduled for February 8 to 28. Phase four, the execution, was scheduled for February 28 to March 3. Our fifth and final phase, the redeployment of our forces, was planned to last from March 4 until the end of that month.

The operational tasks during the execution phase were extremely complex. We would conduct two night amphibious landings at the Mogadishu port and airfield; two reliefs in place of UN forces; a withdrawal and passage of lines by the Pakistani Brigade through our coalition lines (U.S. and Italian Marines); a day and night defense of the air- and seaports; a Non-combatant Evacuation of UN, media, and civilian agencies personnel; and two night amphibious withdrawals. These difficult tactical evolutions were tough enough, but the mix of coalition forces, the nighttime executions, and the prospect of doing these under fire compounded the difficulty exponentially.

We had another serious concern—civilian crowds, mobs, and looters . . . always a possibility in Somalia. Mobs especially were always a major problem . . . and they were one of the warlords' most effective weapons. They could effectively block many of our actions, yet they were only very rarely a physical threat to our troops. A response using lethal force was obviously unjustified; but nonlethals had been very hard to come by. That situation was about to change.

Early in our planning, I pressed for a more substantial nonlethal capability . . . a search that yielded surprisingly good results. We were able to gather a significant and varied arsenal of gadgets, ranging from rubber bullets to sticky foam guns to high-tech acoustic devices, microwaves, and lasers. During the coming months, we trained our forces in these capabilities, while the lawyers developed new rules of engagement for them. (They prohibited some of the more experimental devices, since there were no details on their effects.)

Our attempts to prevent unnecessary loss of lives actually sparked controversy. "You're disarming our Marines!," claimed alarmed op-ed articles. Other articles by military professionals claimed: "Our troops will be confused. They won't know the difference between 'lethal' and 'non-lethal' weapons." When I threw this question at my Marines, they told me, "Don't worry, sir. We know the difference." They all wanted and needed this capability.*

We took the plan to General Peay on November 8; and to the Joint Chiefs a little over a week after that. Quick approval came. Though the chairman of the Joint Chiefs, General Shalikashvilli, remained opposed to OOTWs and was in no hurry to get reengaged in Somalia, he knew this was an obligation the Clinton administration had to take on. One month later, on De-

---

* The nonlethal issue stuck with me. After I returned from Somalia, there has been a major effort to develop more sophisticated capabilities. And over the years, I have been called to testify before several congressional committees and attend numerous conferences and study groups on this subject.

cember 16, President Clinton approved the plan and gave the go-ahead for the operation.

In early January, we held our final planning conference at CENTCOM; and on the fourteenth the joint task force United Shield was formally established. That day I gave the CINC a final brief, at which point General Peay added a highly unusual wrinkle to the command structure. Normally, the JTF commander reports directly to the CINC. But for this particular operation, General Peay decided that I would report to his naval component commander, Vice Admiral Scott Redd, rather than directly to him.

Peay's decision raised a serious question: Was I going to be running the JTF or was Admiral Redd? And yet I appreciated the CINC's logic: This operation required a large number of supporting U.S. and coalition ships (during the actual operation we had twenty-three); directing this large seaward component was potentially a huge—and unnecessary—distraction.

In the event, the arrangement presented zero command problems for either of us. Scott Redd felt strongly that United Shield was my operation, and his role was to ensure that I got what I needed. He and I worked closely and productively together. When the time came, Scott attended the final CENT-COM planning sessions, and then I flew with him back to his headquarters in Bahrain, where I received a firsthand experience of another rationale for General Peay's command arrangement. Scott's was the only CENTCOM headquarters near our AOR, making his people more quickly responsive to our needs. During the operation, he was able to instantly respond to several immediate requests for support, not the least of which was the rapid dispatch of a U.S. cruiser to provide us a last-minute naval gunfire capability.

I was also fortunate in having Rear Admiral Lee Gunn (from the U.S. Third Fleet) as my deputy commander and the commander of my JTF naval component. Because Lee and Scott were able to work all the ship issues, we were able to keep our total focus on the withdrawal.

After Bahrain, I went to Nairobi, Kenya, to meet the military chief of staff, General Mohamed, and other government officials. We intended to use Mombasa as a base for our AC-130 gunships and as a logistics and staging base (to stage forces that would link up with ships sailing in from the Pacific).

In Nairobi, we picked up Ambassador Dan Simpson, the President's special envoy to the Somalia mission, and Ambassador David Shinn, the State

Department's Africa bureau head, and then flew to Mogadishu to coordinate with the UNOSOM forces and meet with warlords.

In Somalia, General Aboo Samah, the Malaysian commander of the UNOSOM forces, and Ambassador Victor Gbeho, the special representative of the Secretary-General, were professional and cooperative; and the initial meetings with warlords were also encouraging. Essentially, our message to the warlords was: "Look, we'll take you on if we have to, but that's not the point. We're not looking for trouble. We just want to get these people out of here. So lay back. It's over. Let's get these people out of here without making waves." And they all bought that.

But our visit to Aideed was a near disaster.

Aideed was never the most punctual of men, and, true to form, he was a little late that day. But when he came rushing in, he was in a very up mood—in his statesman mode, which was fine with me. He'd just been to a political rally, which had gone well; the UN departure favored his interests and objectives; so he seemed happy to see us.

For some reason, however, from the very start of our discussions, Ambassador Simpson took a very provocative line with Aideed. He clearly wanted to get in Aideed's face (and, God knows, there was plenty of bad blood between our people and Aideed); and here was his chance to show Aideed that he was a very hard-ass guy who couldn't be pushed around by a two-bit warlord. The discussion quickly grew heated; threats were tossed back and forth; and the whole situation seemed headed for a bad crash.

By then, Aideed had switched into his black mode; my brain was working on all cylinders; and I was really pissed. "What in the hell are we doing?" I was thinking. "We don't need to piss Aideed off and take on more enemies than we need. We just want to get these troops out of here and avoid confrontation."

Somehow we got through the rest of the meeting without a renewal of open warfare.

At the conclusion of the meeting, we stepped outside with Aideed for a photo at the bottom of the building steps. Afterward, as the others were preparing to leave, Aideed grabbed my arm and drew me aside.

"Zinni," he said, "you look worried."

"You're right," I told him. "We don't need a confrontation at this point," I *continued. "I'm here to protect the UN, and I will; but we don't need more casualties on any side."*

"Don't worry, I will not attack the UN or interfere with the withdrawal," he promised. "But," he added, "I don't control all the militia or gangs; and the militia and gangs at the end of the airport will fight you. I will try to control things where I can."

It was good to know that Aideed had sense enough not to be thrown by the provocations. He knew he was getting what he wanted—the UN's departure; he'd have been nuts to jeopardize that success. His warning, meanwhile, proved accurate; but he also delivered on his promise to control whatever his forces were able to control.

I immediately left Somalia for wrap-up meetings back in Bahrain, then flew on to Pakistan to brief General Abdul Waheed, the chief of staff of the Pakistani military. Since his forces had suffered more casualties in Somalia than any other national force, he wanted to be sure the scheme for withdrawal was sound. His support meant we were now completely on track.

I then headed on to Kenya, to board the USS Belleau Wood, which would be my command ship.

In addition to our twenty-three ships, the force we assembled for United Shield included and totaled 16,485 soldiers, sailors, airmen, and Marines from seven nations. It also included the Pakistani Brigade and Bangladeshi Battalion that would be the last UNOSOM forces that would hold the airport and port and would be put under my command for the final withdrawal.

We sailed from Mombasa on the first of February; stopped off the coast of Malindi, Kenya, for rehearsals of our landing and withdrawal; then moved north to begin our third phase—setting the conditions for the withdrawal and assuming control of the UN forces.

We arrived off the coast of Mogadishu on the seventh of February and began setting the stage for the final withdrawal. For the next three weeks, the UN drew down its presence until they controlled only the port and airfield. Meanwhile, United Shield forces prepared for the final withdrawal. This would take four days. During this period, I began taking increasing responsibility for functions like medical care and fire support, as we moved toward the moment when General Aboo passed command of the UN forces to me.

In addition to our physical preparations (defensive positions, barriers, and the like), we conducted a series of sand table exercises, thoroughly rehearsing our plan with the UN forces, to ensure everyone knew his role cold. Again, we had time—the rarest commodity—and I intended to use every second to our advantage.

Mogadishu's airfield is located near the seashore and south of the port. Just south of the airport is a wide expanse of beach. Our plan was to land our forces, take control of the port from the Bangladeshi Battalion, then hold it and move them out by ship. The Pakistani Brigade which held the airport would then withdraw through our lines to the port, where we would also move them by ship.

During these operations, United Shield forces would maintain control of the beach areas east and south of the airport. After the UN forces had departed, we would move out of the port, then off the high dunes overlooking the airport, and finally off the beach south of the airport. We would, in effect, pull back from north (the port) to south (the beach below the airport). This would be the most dangerous phase of the operation, since we expected militias, gangs, and mobs to close in rapidly behind us. Our physical preparations involved extensive engineer work; we erected barbed-wire obstacles and huge sand mounds to cover our withdrawal.

Though our headquarters for the Combined Task Force remained aboard the Belleau Wood, my Special Operations component established a forward command post ashore (called "the Advanced Operating Base"). The special ops forces also provided Coalition Support Teams to each of the allied forces to ensure close coordination and communications. As soon as we arrived off Mogadishu, a shipboard heliborne Quick Reaction Force was activated as a reserve. Another critical component was the Explosive Ordnance Disposal unit, whose task was to destroy the considerable amount of ammunition and captured weapons that the UN forces had amassed over the years. Though the daily explosions from the EOD were necessary, they were often unnerving.

My landing force was composed of U.S. and Italian Marines. The U.S. Special Forces and U.S. SEAL units also provided valuable capabilities to the forces ashore as well. Each of our four forces had sniper teams; these proved to be key assets when the withdrawal began.

On the ninth of February, Kofi Annan, then the head of the UN peacekeeping organization, arrived to review the plans for the withdrawal, and also to visit our forces and ships. It was clear that Annan understood the complexity of the operation and appreciated what we were doing. To symbolically mark the entrusting of UNOSOM forces to our protection, he presented me with a UN beret.*

Several days later, a formal ceremony at the airport passed control of the UN forces from General Aboo's command to mine.

By then, I was greatly impressed by the competence and professionalism of the Pakistani and Bangladeshi units. We had loaned armor and other equipment to the Pakistanis for their mission in Somalia. Now we had to recover and evacuate this equipment. When our U.S. maintenance personnel recovered the tanks, armored personnel carriers, and other equipment, they found the gear in terrific condition. "This stuff is like new," a maintenance guy told me. "Every single tool in every single kit is there." The pride of these coalition units gave me confidence that their parts in the operation would go without a hitch.

The media was not so easy to handle. They bristle at any form of control; convincing them to form a press pool proved to be particularly difficult; and loose media were running around Mogadishu unencumbered by pool restrictions. I was determined that the media who joined the pool would be rewarded: They were at all the significant locations during the operation and were denied access to commanders only when that could interfere with the mission. I spent a great deal of time briefing the pool and providing them background. By the end of our operation, the relationship that had developed with the pool was superb, benefiting both sides—the best cooperation between the media and the military I had ever experienced. This took a lot of effort and trust on both sides, but we made it work.

As the three weeks of the preparation phase came to a close, we could see the problems forming that we would face during withdrawal. The port and airfield were full of material soon to be abandoned by the UN; and these "prizes" were beginning to tempt the desperate Somalis. Soon they were

---

* Annan is a tremendously impressive human being, with a rare intellect and the common sense to handle the most complex situations. His selection as UN Secretary-General was a splendid choice—and a much-needed change.

gathering ominously in growing numbers around the reinforced gates and walls of the port and airfield. Militias were already jockeying for control of entry points, hoping to be the first to claim the facilities and spoils for their warlord.

In the hope of heading off more trouble, I called a meeting with the heads of these militias and my old police commanders, to be held in the open, on a small hill overlooking the city just above the airfield. Everybody showed up, with the exception of the leaders of groups that were especially hostile to us, and everybody was eager to cooperate, quickly agreeing to our plan to set up a thousand-meter buffer, marked off with warning signs and barbed wire, to keep Somalis separated from our forces. Yet like Aideed, they warned that they could not control the more hostile groups (such as the gang at the southern end of the airport).

Because these guys threatened our last position on the beach as we withdrew (no other beach area would do), we were going to have to do something about them.

It was a successful meeting; but I was particularly glad to see my old policemen, who offered to take and defend the port for us as we pulled out, if we could give them ammunition, guaranteeing we'd have no problems there. Despite opposition from our political side, who shared the UN's distrust of the Somali police, I gave them the ammo. I knew they were anxious to prove once again that our faith in them had not been misplaced.

They lived up to their word; the port area was never a problem for us as we pulled out.

Another encouraging development at the meeting came from Aideed's one-time financier, Osman Atto. After his release from the UN's island prison, Atto had a falling-out with Aideed and then carved out his own faction and militia. Now, during the meeting, he offered to help with security. I took him up on his offer a few days later, when a particularly nasty armed gang outside the main gate of the airport started giving the Pakistanis trouble. They subsequently shot up an Italian news crew and killed the photographer. I called Osman, who rolled out his super-technicals (big, military-type trucks armed with heavy crew-served weapons such as quad fifty antiaircraft guns) and engaged the rogue militia. After a fierce fight, his troops defeated the bad guys and drove them from the area, and then took control of the gate area.

Later, I had to ask him to pull his super-technicals out of there, since they made our helo guys nervous. Osman gladly complied.

As the meeting was breaking up, an old militia leader remained seated, staring grief-stricken out over the devastated city and the piles of abandoned UN material around the port and airport. "A lot of resources and lives have been wasted," he told me, his face close to tears. "For what? We'll be abandoned by the world and left on our own to suffer more years of killing and devastation."

I didn't have much hope to offer him as he left.

ON THE *twenty-eighth of February, we began the fourth phase—the final withdrawal.*

That morning, we took control of the port; and the UN contracted ships which were to evacuate the Bangladeshi Battalion arrived. The condition of the ships was appalling. Yet when I raised this issue back up the line, I was told that they were the best available. Still, I was bothered that these fine soldiers were subjected to such horrible conditions. The Pakistanis, it turned out, were going to get a worse deal.

Appalling conditions or no, the Bangladeshis began their move out.

As they were boarding the ships, we began to receive sporadic firing at our positions guarding the port, and the crowds at the gate started to get more restless, hostile, and threatening.

We meanwhile evacuated the final group of 112 noncombatants to our ships—UN contract employees, non-pool media requesting evacuation, and a few civilian relief workers—for transport to Kenya. Our normal procedure is to search such people before we bring them on board our ships, but in this case I waived that requirement. After we dropped them off, however, I learned that a few of them were carrying drugs, illegal wildlife, and other contraband that had to be confiscated by Kenyan customs. This taught me a lesson about trust.

When these operations had been completed, the time had come for the passage of lines of the Pakistani unit and their move from the airport to the port. Because this operation was sure to unleash the hordes into the airport, I wanted to get the ship carrying the Pakistanis loaded and gone as soon as pos-

sible. That way we could quickly leave the port and collapse our lines to the beach south of the airport for our pullout. If everything worked according to plan, we'd be on the beach by nightfall.

The Pakistanis executed a flawless passage of lines and closed on the port in good order. We recovered their equipment and very quickly loaded it on our ship. We then waited for the ship, which the UN had contracted to carry them to Dar es Salaam, Tanzania, from where they would fly back to their country. The ship arrived late, having nearly run aground coming into port. When the ship finally pulled in and tied up pier side, it was clear it was too small for the number of troops it was to carry. Worse, the first officer was reporting that the master of the ship was drunk and there was no food or water aboard. It was to be a trip of several days.

It was easy enough to transfer pallets of MREs and water from our ships to the UN ship, but the careless treatment of brave and highly professional troops by the UN was unforgivable.

We were now way behind schedule, and a flood of people, technicals, and looters was pouring onto the airport dangerously close to our lines. There was firing everywhere as friendly militias attempted to take control and chase off the looters. Though the police had taken effective control of the port, we were now taking fire all along our lines. Somali translators shouted warnings and our snipers fired warning shots. This got the attention of the militias, and they started to gain control.

Late that afternoon, Aideed suddenly showed up to claim the airport, breaking an agreement among the warlords to share control. He simply blew in with his people and grabbed it; and the other warlords could do nothing to stop him.

Meanwhile, my hopes to be on our exit beach by dark were fading. It looked like we wouldn't be moving there until later that night.

As dusk set in, Aideed was not yet in full control of the airport, and rogue gunmen with rifles and RPG launchers were taking up hiding places behind abandoned container boxes and other piled material scattered around, then popping up to take potshots at us. Though we called out warnings with loudspeakers, and close-aimed shots from our snipers were driving them back, my Marine commander, Colonel John Garrett, reminded me that we couldn't let them stay nearby into the night; it would be very tough to track them then.

He was right, and I had to order the snipers to take them all out. They did. Later, when the press got wind of the story, they wanted to know how many were killed. My response got a lot of coverage. "I don't count bodies," I told them. "This isn't Vietnam."

Meanwhile, the Marine units holding the last exit beach to our south reported increasingly heavy fire from the militia there. Though helo gunships helped cover the beach area, the militia fighters were well hidden. Because it was growing ever more clear that the last troops off that beach would have a hell of a time, I decided that I would have to leave that night with them.

During the move down to the beach, we put obstacles prepared by the engineers in place behind us. They had also created huge sand dunes that covered our large air-cushioned vehicles rapidly moving our forces and equipment out. At the beach, we evacuated all but the last two companies; these would pull out by amphibious tractor.

Around midnight, I joined Lieutenant Colonel Phil Tracey, the battalion commander of these troops and an old friend. The intensity of the firefight was picking up. The militia was now sending squad-sized units at our lines, but the Marines were instantly cutting them down. I listened on the company tactical nets as young lieutenants and captains directed their troops in the fight—taking me back to Vietnam. One of these voices on the radio net sounded familiar, and Phil confirmed that it was the son of a close friend, a fellow Marine general. Another generation had come to take our place and go through our passage to manhood.

The plan for the final pullout called for the troops on signal to rapidly board the tractors, our AC-130 and helo gunships would keep up their covering fire, and the armored amphibians would make a quick rush for the water before the bad guys could react. Though we had rehearsed this maneuver many times, I worried that a lucky RPG shot could hit a tractor racing for the water. The close quarters fight that followed could be messy.

As the signal flare was fired, my aide, my chief of staff, and I jumped into the back of a nearby tractor. The hatches quickly closed, and the tractors raced in a line to the water. Soon the rumbling down the beach gave way to the gentle ride through the waves. Though the track seemed to jerk and shudder as we rumbled down the beach—as if the transmission had problems—I didn't worry about it once we hit the water.

I'd heard no explosions, but I told my chief of staff, Colonel John Moffett, to check on the tracks.

"They're all in the water," he reported, "and none have been hit by fire."

I sat back in relief.

By that time, we found ourselves in huge swells, and the swaying of the track and the water pouring through the overhead hatches started to make the Marines sick. A helmet they passed around soon filled. I think I was the only one who did not silently "donate" to the pot. I guess the tremendous feeling of relief kept me straight.

Earlier, I hadn't worried much when the track hesitated and stuttered as it roared down the beach. But now we were losing power, and smoke was starting to fill our track. John poked his head up into the commander's cupola, then came down and reported that we had a transmission problem and were going to be taken under tow by another track. I put my hand down on the deck: if incoming water was kept no more than about a foot deep, the bilge pumps were working. . . . It wasn't and they were.

Soon we could feel the tow, and we all relaxed some. But then it stopped. John poked his head back into the cupola, soon reporting that the tow vehicle was now also dead in the water, and we were both drifting back to the beach.

I stuck my head out and could see the headlights of the technicals back there.

Just then, Corporal Deskins, the track commander, stuck his head down into the troop compartment. "Sir," he said to me, "here's the situation. We are on fire and drifting back to the beach. The track that's towing us is also on fire and drifting back with us. The other tracks have headed back to the ship and we can't raise anybody on the radio. We have fired flares but have not seen any safety boats. We can see the enemy on the beach." He then paused and smiled. "But don't worry, sir. Our machine guns work better on the beach."

We then popped the overhead hatches and all the Marines climbed on top of the tracks. It was very tricky there, with the swells crashing over the vehicles, but, eventually, a small Navy safety boat responded to the flares, spotted us, and came alongside. Moving troops in high seas from the track to the cramped boat was a sporty event. It was quickly overloaded, and a larger craft had to come to help. After the troops were safely transferred to the other boats, I turned back toward the beach looming against the dark horizon. There the lights of Mogadishu silhouetted the technicals, signaling each other with their headlights.

The four-man crew led by Corporal Deskins were the last troops aboard the track.

"We have to get them aboard so we can move out," the safety boat officer was telling me, "or else we might be swamped."

But when I asked Corporal Deskins to abandon the track and get into the boat, he scurried away from us. "Sir, we will never abandon our track," he said.

I looked at John. He smiled and shook his head. I turned to the boat officer. "We're just going to hang on," I said, "and hope a larger landing craft gets here before we hit the beach."

It did, and so did a number of tracks racing out to rescue us. We had managed to avoid an unplanned return to Somalia.

Earlier, the other tracks had gone on to the ship, thinking we were under tow; but when they were told of our situation, the entire track platoon raced to the well deck and splashed their tracks back out to the sea to come get us.

As I was climbing from the boat to the larger craft, I was handed a hot cup of coffee from the Navy chief in command of the craft. For the first time that night, I realized I was soaking wet and cold and bone-tired. I looked at my watch. We'd left the beach five hours ago; the intensity of the events afterward made that time seem like minutes.

The craft pulled into the well deck of the Belleau Wood early in the morning. As the ramp went down, I realized I'd have to wade through waist-deep water up the ramp. At the top of the ramp was the massed press pool, with cameras snapping. I smiled at the chief. "You're going to make me wade up to those cameras, aren't you?"

He smiled back. "Just like MacArthur, sir."

LATER, up in the command center, a briefing confirmed that we were all accounted for. I then reported to Scott and General Peay, "Mission accomplished."

I went to my stateroom, showered, and collapsed in my rack. When I woke the next morning, the ship was gently rocking. We were on our way to Kenya. The fifth and final phase, redeployment, was under way. Remarkably, we had suffered no casualties in this operation. The exhaustive planning had paid off. I was proud of all my forces.

We docked in Mombasa on the sixth of March; and I flew off with my staff back to Camp Pendleton.

Two weeks later, Secretary of Defense William Perry spoke at an awards ceremony at the Pentagon. "We live in an imperfect world and we can never make it perfect," he said, "but we can attain moments of perfection. Operation United Shield was such a moment."

LEAVING SOMALIA *was an emotional moment. We left a lot of sacrifices and dashed hopes on that beach . . . but learned significant lessons from the Somalia experience. I am convinced it could have been better had we run this complex undertaking with more skill and thoughtfulness.*

CHAPTER SIX

CENTCOM

IN AUGUST 1996, the new commandant of the Marine Corps, General Chuck Krulak, nominated Tony Zinni as deputy commander in chief (DCINC) of U.S. Central Command,* located at MacDill Air Force Base in Tampa, Florida.

Leaving command of I MEF was hard, yet Zinni welcomed the opportunity to continue to serve. At the higher levels of the military hierarchy, it's either move to a new position or retire. CENTCOM was in fact a particularly welcome assignment. . . . "It's where the action is," he thought. "It's operationally oriented; and I'm already familiar with the command from my Somalia experiences and I MEF," which was assigned to CENT-COM as a responding unit when required. He quickly supplemented his initial store of knowledge by plowing through more than fifty books on the history and culture of the region.

When Zinni arrived at CENTCOM headquarters early in September, he did not find a happy place. The command had just suffered the worst

---

* Zinni was replacing General Butch Neal, one of his oldest, closest friends in the Corps. After extensive experience in CENTCOM (three tours of duty in the command), General Neal had been selected for promotion and assignment as the assistant commandant of the Marine Corps.

terrorist attack on U.S. facilities since the 1983 Marine barracks bombing in Beirut. A suicide truck bomb had killed nearly twenty Americans
at Khobar Towers, an Air Force barracks in eastern Saudi Arabia (CENT-
COM had also suffered a bombing of one of its security assistance facilities in Riyadh). The tragedy weighed heavily on the command, cast a dark
cloud over the remainder of General Binnie Peay's tour as commander in
chief of CENTCOM . . . and directly affected Zinni as DCINC when
General Peay tasked him to oversee the implementation of the hundred-
plus recommendations put forward by a fact-finding commission chaired
by retired Army General Wayne Downing. It was clear that the terrorist
threat was growing ever more dangerous and that force protection was becoming a dominant theme for America's military leaders.

The Downing Commission recommendations ranged from the reloca-
tion of units to the establishment of more stringent security; and there was
a lot of pressure to get them implemented. Some of the recommendations
were straightforward, such as adding security forces, putting up barriers,
and other forms of physical security. Some took more time. For example,
the commission recommended reducing the number of "accompanied
tours" in the region, which are tours of duty for which military personnel
can bring their families. This recommendation was not well received, especially for those in assignments such as security assistance billets, which
require people to stay in one place for at least two or three years to be effective. Nevertheless, a blanket decision was made to drastically reduce
the number of accompanied tours. Most people would now be rotating out
after a year . . . which was about the time it took to get up to speed. (This
policy was eventually partially reversed.)

Downing had also recommended moving CENTCOM headquarters
out to the region. But when the command looked hard at setting up a
major headquarters in that part of the world—at all that it would take to
make the move; to set up the security; to take care of the military construction, the politics, the families and schools—the expenses were so
great that the issue was deferred.

Instead, CENTCOM settled on setting up a rapidly deployable forward
headquarters, with forward elements of the headquarters of its subordi-

nate commands—ground, air, naval, and special operations—in place. (For the invasion of Iraq in 2003, General Tommy Franks set up his forward headquarters in Qatar, which was one of the locations that had previously been designated for a CENTCOM forward headquarters.)

Good or bad, the Downing Commission recommendations could be dealt with in a straightforward, professional way. But the commission report went further than that; it assigned blame, which took the fact-finding process into more questionable territory. There is a fine line between assessing responsibility, assessing blame, and scapegoating. When the report was issued, blame for the "failures" that had allowed the attack to succeed was dumped primarily on CENTCOM and the commander at Khobar Towers.

This was not a completely irrational judgment: The commander has to carry ultimate responsibility for what goes on in his command. The buck has to stop somewhere.

On the other hand, the military exists to handle situations that are by definition high-risk. You want to reduce those risks as much as possible, but there is a point at which reducing risks also greatly reduces the effectiveness of the military. Total safety and total security are not conditions of the military life.

You can reduce risk to the point of absurdity: "Don't cross streets. You've got lousy drivers out there." And you can build—and cower in—impregnable bunkers.

Tony Zinni:

During the Downing Commission's investigations, the commission's approach to the command was open and nonjudgmental. But the Downing report was another thing. The tone of the report was much more fault and blame assigning than was warranted. And worse, many of the security steps that we were forced to implement impacted negatively on our mission.

What bothered me about the report (but the problem goes far beyond that, as I have made clear in later testimony to Congress) is its failure to understand that we live in a risky world. We have been stalked by terrorists. And they're still after us. Yet in order to do our mission, we have to take risks. The only one hundred percent safe way to avoid them is not to go there. But if we're going to be in the region, and we're going to do our job, there is risk involved. We're going to expose troops.

The mood back in the United States has been deeply frustrating, and that is: We have to make our force presence in the world one hundred percent safe for our soldiers, sailors, airmen, and Marines. And if one soldier, sailor, airman, or Marine is injured or lost to a terrorist activity, then we have to find somebody on our side to blame for it.

I can't think of a more dysfunctional way to run military operations.

The job of implementing Downing Commission findings consumed much of Zinni's time during the next year—and after.

IN THE MEANTIME, CENTCOM was a beehive of activity.

Containing Iraq was always a primary order of business; several flare-ups with Saddam after the Gulf War had required military responses. Usually these occurred while enforcing the no-fly and no-drive zones in Iraq. Iraqi tankers, however, were also smuggling sanction-busting oil down the gulf. U.S. Maritime Intercept Operations had grabbed a number of smugglers; but most had proved very hard to stop; they avoided American naval patrols by using Iranian territorial waters (and paying tolls to the Iranians).

The command had continued the longtime U.S. containment policy toward Iran (the other regional hegemon); and tensions there remained high. U.S. naval forces in the Gulf daily confronted hostile and aggressive Iranian Islamic Revolutionary Guard naval forces; their harassments and provocations could easily have sparked major confrontations.

The Gulf was not the only hot spot. There were others in East Africa and Southwest Asia. And the forever-crisis between Israelis and Palestinians impacted every country in the region, though it was not itself in CENTCOM's AOR. The command constantly had to reevaluate and adapt itself to ever-changing realities and challenges.

After the Gulf War, Marine General Joe Hoar, the CENTCOM CINC who followed General Norman Schwarzkopf, launched a major effort to create strong relationships between the U.S. and friendly nations in the region; and built a solid foundation for military cooperation.

General Peay added to this foundation by enhancing America's force presence in the region. This had to be done carefully; basing U.S. military forces there jarred local sensitivities. He skirted that problem by structuring a force that combined prepositioned equipment and rotational units,* spreading the forces throughout the Gulf area, using joint facilities to conduct operations,† and placing a select few headquarters of subordinate commands in the region to run day-to-day operations. These actions demonstrated America's intent to share the military burden and gain local cooperation and support for its military missions . . . while *not* building U.S. bases in the region or basing dedicated forces there. As an added benefit, they allowed flexibility in the size and composition of U.S. forces.

These new directions created far greater capabilities for meeting the emerging challenges in this vital area of the world. Tony Zinni was the beneficiary of the innovative and tireless work of Generals Hoar and Peay.

FROM HIS first day on the job, Zinni got himself up to speed militarily by immersing himself in briefings, intelligence reports, and conversations with commanders who had experience in the region. But he knew this was not enough. There was nothing like being there. He already knew how important it was to see a place firsthand, and to spend enough time there to build critical relationships.

General Peay made frequent trips to the region. While he was away, Zinni stayed behind, keeping the home fires burning, as the nature of his job dictated (the CINC goes forward and the DCINC stays back). Yet each time Peay returned, his increased insight and wisdom amazed Zinni. You can't acquire such things from briefings and readings at headquarters.

Several months after his arrival at CENTCOM, Zinni at last made a trip to the region. His primary orientation was to check out the forces— what were out there, what they were doing, seeing them on the ground,

---

* Units that were not based permanently in the region but which rotated in and out from other U.S. bases.

† Facilities operated jointly with the local governments.

getting briefs. But he also visited senior military commanders and national leaders.

During his visit, he attended a number of social events with Arabs . . . he would attend many others over the next years. People in that part of the world don't sharply distinguish business from social.

Zinni:

In the Arab world, they conduct business far more casually than we do at home—or in Europe, the Pacific, and other places where I'd served. In America or Europe, the meetings are structured. There's a timetable and an agenda. You limit small talk—and feel guilty when you indulge in it. You tick off items that must be covered. And once they're covered, you instantly move on.

That's not the way Arabs like to do business. They don't jump directly into the "big issues"; they prefer a far more casual mix . . . and not because they don't understand the issues. Rather, it's the way they connect and take the cut of a man. Personal relations and trust built out of friendship are more important than just signing paper agreements. They'll sit around a room and drink coffee, eat some nice food, laugh a little, and have an easygoing conversation about their families, hunting, the weather, or anything else that doesn't seem terribly important. In time, they'll subtly work their way toward the business at hand and deal with it. But don't try to rush them.

When Westerners have tried that—even CINCs—it's led to problems.

Our way of conducting business just doesn't work there. When we try it, we're not well received. Yet politeness, graciousness, and hospitality are so inbred in Arabs that we may not recognize that they've turned off to us. They will always be polite to guests. Hospitality is more than just a nice civility in that part of the world; it's a duty and obligation. To be inhospitable or impolite is a sin. On the other hand, they really take to people who like their kind of personal interaction. But doing that right is truly an art.

An art I've always enjoyed practicing.

It's interesting to watch Washington insiders out there dealing with Arabs. In Washington, everyone is comfortable with formality. That's how they do business. It goes with the pin-striped suits.

During one of our crises with Saddam Hussein, Secretary Cohen and I went to several countries in the region to obtain permission to bomb Iraq.

Okay, our way of doing things: You hand them the paper and they read the fine print and sign on the dotted line. No problem. . . . Only, that's not how Arabs operate. They don't directly tell you yes or no. They have ways of signaling their intention, but the signals aren't clear unless you understand them.

In one country, Secretary Cohen pressed and pressed and he got nowhere; they didn't want to give an answer. But as we were leaving, they said, "You must always know we are your friends."

After we walked out, Cohen said, "Did we get an answer?"

"Yes, we did," I said. "We can do it."

"I didn't hear that."

"Yes, in the end when they told you they'd always be our friends, that was their answer. That meant they were telling you to go ahead and do it. Don't make an issue of it."

In another country, we were told, "Please, don't ask us to do this."

This really meant: "Do what you've gotta do. No one's going to interfere. But don't ask us the question that we don't want to answer, either way."

Americans are of course always looking for the hard-and-fast no-yes.

In many other cultures, such as the Israelis', people are frank, blunt, and to the point; and they see anything less than that as a sign of less than full friendship. With good friends, you should be that honest and open. You're only polite to people you're not close to or don't like.

Each culture ticks differently. It isn't that the basic values are different, it's that there are cultural subtleties and cultural sensitivities that you really need to understand.

Early in 1997, General Peay was approaching the end of his tour as CINC. Though it was customary to alternate the job between Army and Marines, Zinni did not expect to be offered the job. No one ever before had risen from the DCINC position at CENTCOM to become commander. So Zinni was knocked off his feet when General Krulak told him he was nominating him as General Peay's successor. . . . It was a surprise; yet there was no job in the world Zinni would rather have had. It was the part of the world where his fighting experience, cultural experience, personal connections, and knowledge could be best used by his country.

But first a big obstacle had to be passed.

Zinni was informed that General Shalikashvilli, the chairman of the Joint Chiefs of Staff, opposed his nomination, supporting instead his good friend Butch Neal (whose credentials for the job were superb), on the grounds that Zinni was far too "outspoken" and could not be "controlled." Zinni had a hard time understanding the chairman's objections (they had worked well together during Operation Provide Comfort), but he took a stoic approach to the situation: If the chairman didn't support his nomination, it wouldn't go through. Live with it.

That meant his career was effectively over. He told his wife to make quick retirement plans; he took the transition course for retiring military personnel; they bought property in Virginia, and talked to architects and contractors about building their retirement home.

General Krulak and the Secretary of the Navy, John Dalton, submitted both names, Zinni's and Neal's. Zinni was grateful, but convinced it wouldn't matter. He went through what seemed to be a pro forma interview with the Secretary of Defense, Bill Cohen, and waited for the inevitable moment when he would call Butch Neal with his congratulations.

A few weeks later, Zinni got hit with another stunner: Secretary Cohen called to tell him he was the administration's pick for CINC of CENTCOM; his nomination had been forwarded to the Senate for approval.

Tony Zinni:

After getting over the shock, I set about gathering advice about the emerging challenges of the command and its future direction in the dynamic environment we faced in our AOR. In time I expected these ideas would contribute to a new CENTCOM strategy for our region; I had thoughts on that score that I wanted to develop.

Of all the advice I received, three people—Joe Hoar, Binnie Peay, and Ed Fugit—gave me the wisest counsel.

General Hoar emphasized relationships. "In that part of the world, personal relationships are often more important than formal agreements," he told me. "Remember our days as advisers in Vietnam. There we knew the value of building trust and friendship."

The outgoing CINC's political adviser (POLAD) reinforced General Hoar. Ed Fugit, an experienced diplomat and deeply familiar with our region, advised me to connect personally with both the leaders and the people. "But you can take that even farther," he continued, "by showing interest in their culture and society. Do that and you build trust and confidence."

I warmed to this approach. Too often we get caught up in crises, rushing around with requests, programs, and policy positions, without taking the time to listen to the concerns of the people who have to live with our decisions.

"And choose your POLAD well," he concluded. "It's the most important personnel decision you'll make." He was right; and I had the good fortune to select as my POLAD Larry Pope, a former ambassador, Arabic speaker, and brilliant diplomat . . . and my right hand for the next three years.

General Peay's advice came on the final day of his command. "Be your own man," he told me, "and don't feel obliged to follow my strategy. The AOR is dynamic. You'll have to reevaluate and update the command's strategy and policies. You must take a fresh look, as all new CINCs should, and put your own personal touch on our tasks."

I was grateful for his encouragement . . . and his blessing. Binnie Peay had become a friend and mentor. He had sought my input on every issue, trusted me to make critical decisions, and left me with a command in excellent condition to meet the many crises and threats we later had to face. His focus on building our war-fighting capabilities is still paying off.

ON AUGUST 13, 1997, I became the sixth commander in chief of the United States Central Command.

STRATEGY, POLITICS, AND THE NEW AMERICAN EMPIRE

Tom Clancy: Tony Zinni will take the rest of the chapter.

My immediate priority as CINC was to reshape our strategy in the light of our ever-changing AOR and the emerging global strategy of the

Clinton administration. We needed a structure, a horizon, and goals to meet the many challenges in this most risky part of the world. Without these, our day-to-day work would have no focus.

CENTCOM had twenty countries in its AOR (soon to be twenty-five)—a diverse region that spanned an area from East Africa through the Middle East to Southwest and Central Asia and into the Indian Ocean. Yet the command's near-total focus was on the Persian Gulf and our long-standing problems with Iran and Iraq—our major threats in the region. We were operating under a national security strategy called "Dual Contain-ment," whose objective was to protect Gulf energy resources, contain both Iraq and Iran, and maintain local stability. We were the only unified command with two major "theater of war" requirements (as we say in the military): fight Iraq, or fight Iran.

These threats were not about to go away. Yet other parts of the AOR were heating up, requiring us to broaden our focus beyond the Gulf States.

Weapons of mass destruction were proliferating all through the region. The Iraqis had used them in the '80s. The Iranians were acquiring them. Pakistan and India were in serious conflict over Kashmir and tossing ever louder threats at each other (Pakistan was in CENTCOM's AOR; India was in PACOM's); our relationship with Pakistan had soured for all sorts of political reasons; and both countries were nuclear powers.

Afghanistan was a catastrophe.

East Africa—Somalia, Sudan, Eritrea, Ethiopia—were trouble spots.

Terrorist activity was picking up.

We'd had little recent contact with Iraq, Iran, Afghanistan, Sudan, and Somalia. Developing relationships with Yemen, Ethiopia, Eritrea, Djibouti, and the Seychelles required new engagement programs. Long-standing re-lationships with Egypt, Jordan, Kenya, Saudi Arabia, Kuwait, Bahrain, Qatar, the United Arab Emirates, and Oman had to be maintained and strengthened. We had to rebuild our shaky relations with Pakistan. And a little later, most of the Muslim states of Central Asia that had split off from the Soviet Union—Turkmenistan, Uzbekistan, Kazakhstan, Tajikistan, and Kyrgyzstan—were added to CENTCOM's AOR. Each had its own special problems (including a civil war in Tajikistan).

CENTCOM found itself in a bubbling pot of crises from one end to the other. We had to develop a CENTCOM strategy to handle them . . . without necessarily using military force—or else only as a last resort. We needed to help build stability in this troubled region, in my view, or we would pay the price in the long run.

A regional conference was scheduled at CENTCOM headquarters for early 1998, and I wanted to firm up the strategy by then.

We were not approaching this process with a blank slate. Since ours was probably the most volatile region in the world, we were starting with thirteen preexisting war plans, an exceptionally large number for a unified command. These come out of taskings from the Secretary of Defense to prepare to counter either a specific threat or sometimes more generic situations, like what we call "consequence management." Let's say somebody explodes a nuclear device or uses other WMD. We had operational plans to police up these situations. Other plans dealt with Iraq or Iran. Others were aimed at generic missions such as "keeping the Gulf open for the free flow of oil." And so on. Each plan had a real possibility of execution, given the nature of the region.

These plans gave us a war-fighting orientation that we were well postured to deal with, thanks to the work of General Peay. We now needed to expand and broaden the strategy beyond that dimension.

In order to get a better fix on all the issues, I talked first to my commanders, then sought input from friendly leaders of the nations in our AOR and from U.S. diplomats with expertise in the area, to ensure that we were all working in sync.

For the bigger picture, we turned to President Clinton's emerging National Security Strategy, with its stress on engagement and multilateralism. The military implementation of this strategy is the job of the Secretary of Defense, whose National Military Strategy looks at the National Security Strategy from a specifically military point of view. Every four years, the Secretary of Defense presents to Congress and the President what is called "the Quadrennial Defense Review," which offers still more specifics about how the military side of defense is going to execute the National Security Strategy. It directs the Unified Commands to build new strategies for our assigned regions based on these concepts. The QDR directed the CINCs to "shape, respond, and prepare." This reflected not only the war-fighting responsibilities (respond, prepare), but the new charge to "shape" our areas of responsibility.

The Secretary of Defense also directed the CINCs to prepare Theater Engagement Plans for our AORs. This is our strategy for engaging with the countries with whom we have relations on a day-to-day basis. Specifically, it is our plan for helping friendly countries build their militaries, for cultivating and building coalitions for security cooperation, and for welding together viable multilateral teams to deal collectively with the chronic problems we face and to better stabilize the region. In other words, it is the "friendly" side of our overall strategy.

THE FIRST problem CENTCOM had to fix was the near-total focus on the Persian Gulf. To that end, I decided to "subregionalize" our strategy, by breaking the AOR into four subregions—East Africa, the Persian Gulf, Central and Southwest Asia, and Egypt and Jordan—and developing a strategy and programs for each. This approach would ensure that our Gulf-centric tendency did not detract from the programs and relationships we developed in other areas. Though I knew this would not be a clean separation—many interests overlapped—I felt we could accommodate that.

Because the nations of each subregion had their own problems, we also had an articulated strategy for each country. In addition, I assigned each of our military components "focus" countries that fit their capabilities and their compatibility with the militaries of these nations. This spread the burden and balanced the span of control in managing our various engagement programs and crisis response requirements.

I then broke down our strategic goals into three areas: war fighting, engagement, and development.

The war-fighting goals were designed to have in place the right plans, forces, and basing options for any possible crisis. We also built a basis for responding to crises cooperatively with regional allies through training, exercises, military assistance, intelligence sharing, military schooling, and the like.

Three more practical war-fighting issues also had to be dealt with.

The first was agreement on a Joint Fires standing operating procedure

(SOP) to coordinate fires on the battlefield. Up to this point, the services had been unable to agree on a joint doctrine for battlefield coordination, direction, and procedures for our air and ground-based fires systems. This may have seemed to be a mere intellectual issue back in the States, but for us it was life or death. In our AOR, war was always a near possibility. If war broke out, without coordination of fires we could expect serious friendly fire casualties or even battlefield failures. We couldn't wait for the services to work through their bickering and rivalries. I therefore directed my component commanders to work together to produce the CENTCOM Joint Fires SOP (if they hit issues they couldn't resolve, I told them I would make the call). These superb professionals delivered, providing an SOP that their services and service chiefs accepted (although only for the CENTCOM AOR).

My second objective was to finish work already started under General Peay to set up a command element, or small forward headquarters, in the AOR for each of my components, providing them command facilities they could rapidly fall into if the balloon went up. When I became CINC, the Navy already had its full headquarters in the region, and the Air Force had its air operations center there. But I also wanted the Army and Marine Corps to establish a forward element for the Joint Force Land Component Command (JFLCC), which would run the coordinated ground battle in Kuwait. As a result, we established Joint Task Force (JTF) Kuwait; and I had the CENTCOM Special Operations Command establish a forward command element in Qatar. This gave me a base to build on for all the functional component headquarters (air, ground, naval, and special operations) if we had to quickly respond to a crisis. Though this was controversial and caused grumblings among rear echelon doctrinal purists, who didn't understand the purpose of these JTFs forward, we ignored their criticisms.

My third objective—never fully accomplished during my tenure—was to create one logistics command for the theater, to control and coordinate the massive logistics effort we would have to undertake in a major crisis. The system of separate and competing service and coalition systems, all putting stress on the limited lines of communications and infrastructure in the region, would really cause us problems if we didn't have one um-

brella organization to pull all the support needs together and ensure security for our rear area networks.

Though the components developed a basic design before I left command, and the U.S. Army was chosen to be the core of this joint/combined
Theater Support Command for CENTCOM, the plan drew criticism and
resistance again from doctrinal traditionalists, who didn't understand the
realities of the battlefield; and I was unable to accomplish this innovation
before I left.

OUR ENGAGEMENT goals were designed to build strong security relationships and allied capabilities, and to enhance the education of military leaders and familiarize them with principles and values that drove our
military system. Though much of this area was related to war fighting, it
went beyond that to work in cooperative areas that were not strictly military, such as environmental security issues and natural disaster responses.
This built the day-to-day military relationships and capabilities needed to
respond to crises and work as a combined team.

OUR DEVELOPMENT goals were objectives for establishing new relationships, improving regional stability, and countering emerging threats.
They were also related to the development of CENTCOM itself as it
evolved to meet future challenges and a changing defense environment.
These were the primary "shaping" efforts directed by the QDR.

In designing this ambitious strategy, we cooperated closely with the
Joint Staff, the Office of the Secretary of Defense, and our State Department partners at embassies in the AOR and at the regional bureaus in
State's Washington headquarters. Our strategy also reflected ideas contained in the Clinton administration's new global strategy . . . and from
my own lifetime experience in the military, in conflict resolution, and in
peacemaking.

The Clinton strategy represented a significant shift in the way the
United States related to the rest of the world. Though the administration
did not always handle this shift as effectively as they could have, their over-

all approach was, in my view, correct. Unfortunately, the Clinton strategy lacked the resources to be fully and effectively implemented.

In America, we look at the world from two powerfully opposed angles of vision. We are either "engaged" or "isolationist."

The engaged—people like Wilson, Marshall, and Truman—believe we can prevent conflicts by actively shaping the environment that produces them, by directly involving our military, diplomatic, and economic capabilities in the world to make conditions better, to stabilize the various regions, to build partnerships, and to do it collectively—by using the UN and regional (or larger) multilateral coalitions and institutions. In the long run, they see engagement as less costly than any of the alternatives.

The isolationists fight this view. They see the world as so big, so messy, so out of control, that nobody can fix it. And even if we could help a little here or there, dozens of other hopeless cases lie festering. And besides, who says we have any responsibility for the rest of the world anyway? Who made us the policemen of the world? We should be bringing troops home, not committing them to useless foreign "engagements." Who said we have to suffer all the risks and shoulder all the costs of making the world better? Foreign aid is just another way to throw good money down a bottomless hole. We could use it better at home tending—and protecting—our own garden. Yes, we have friends whom we will continue to support. We have interests that we will protect. But that's all the involvement in the world that we want or need. During the Clinton years, Congress generally tended to back the isolationist side and was not supportive of providing resources for engagement.

"Engagement" was not an airy concept (though many portrayed it that way). It came with nitty-gritty specifics (though these varied, depending on whether the country in question was an adversary, a friend, or potentially a friend). We had very formal ways to "engage" both militarily and diplomatically (the two had to work in tandem). And we expected these to lead to clear and specific results.

For example, in a form of military engagement we call "Security Assistance,"* specific components—foreign military sales, foreign military fi-

---

* Just as the term implies, we help other nations improve their security situation by improving their military and security forces.

nancing, provision of excess defense articles, training, education in our school system, intelligence sharing, and so on—were expected to create a formal and developing military-to-military relationship.

Thus when we embarked on a new relationship of engagement (as we did in my time with the Central Asian states or Yemen), we'd usually begin programs informally, in a small way, and later we'd make them more formal . . . put them into one or more of the categories, set up a program to develop their actual resources, set up and fund joint training programs, and the like. In other words, engagement might start informally, but it was expected to grow into a more formal relationship. I felt that if we were more aggressive and planned and coordinated engagement programs better—military, diplomatic, economic, cultural, etc.—we could truly "shape" a more stable, secure, and productive environment in troubled regions of the world.

THE CLINTON administration's engagement policies had the added effect of building on a process that the Goldwater-Nichols Act and the end of the Cold War had already started—the expansion of the role of the CINCs in their regions. Goldwater-Nichols, passed in the mid-'80s, gave more power to the CINCs, but primarily as war fighters. By the end of the '90s, Goldwater-Nichols had come into bloom; the CINCs had become far more than war fighters; and the Clinton administration gave the CINCs all around the world a mission to shape their regions and use multilateral approaches in ways that went beyond the CINCs' traditional military role.

This was not simply a wish. The administration strongly promoted and stressed this change; and they made it very clear that they wanted the CINCs to implement it.

But not everyone welcomed it, including the CINCs themselves. The change came because there was no other choice. No one else could do the job.

When I took over as commander of CENTCOM, I found a tremendous void in the diplomatic connections in our AOR. There was a void in expanding the personal relationships that Generals Hoar and Peay had worked hard to create. There was a void in establishing and implementing policy.

The void came from several causes.

One, the State Department had not been given the resources they needed to do their job. The neo-isolationists had cut foreign aid, leaving the State Department without the wherewithal—the people, the money, the programs—to make the impact they should have been making.

Two, while the end of the Cold War had greatly diminished any chances of a world-spanning conflict, crises had begun to pop up all over the place; and the military found itself involved in confronting all of them, even those that were not totally military problems.

Three, the CINCs now had resources the State Department did not have; the power of the CINCs was now growing (a reality recognized throughout our region); and the CINCs soon became the chief conduit to personal connections and to the resources State did not have. Much of what got done was done through the CINCs.

During my time as a CINC, I was asked to carry out presidential and other diplomatic missions that would normally have fallen to diplomats. I'm sure such things frustrated the State Department, but I don't think they disapproved. In fact, they were very supportive. It was more a case of: "Well, if we can't do it, at least somebody is taking care of it. If it's the CINCs, then God bless them."

Like most CINCs, I tried to work very closely with the State Department. In every country, our ambassador is the President's representative. I never did anything that an ambassador did not know of and approve.

Moreover, the CINCs often had more personal presence and far more connections than the ambassadors. In many countries in CENTCOM's region, for example, the senior government leadership is also the senior military leadership. This is not our system (and the downsides are obvious), yet the fact had practical consequences. They were usually more comfortable with soldiers than with diplomats in many cases.

In fact, more often than not, the ambassadors were very glad we were there. We not only brought them the connections we'd made, but we provided them with the ability to get things done they couldn't ordinarily do . . . some small, some larger.

Anything we did for the ambassadors had to have some military over-lap. We couldn't simply blatantly set up an aid program. But even here we had some room to maneuver. In Africa, for example, we might be engaged in teaching a country's military how to conduct peacekeeping or human-itarian operations, and we might set up training exercises in the villages. I would send out my military veterinarians, dentists, and doctors (who needed the training; they needed to practice these kinds of operations) to go into the villages with the African country's military, and they'd conduct the exercises together. In the context of the military exercise, we'd build an orphanage or paint a school or set up a clinic as a Civic Action proj-ect. We'd be providing our guys with useful training while showing the African troops actually how to do it; and at the same time, we were ben-efiting needy people. When the exercises were over, we would have the American ambassador cut the ribbon for the new clinic. It was important, in my mind, to always demonstrate civilian leadership of our military and the close cooperation between our diplomats and soldiers.

The countries of Central Asia are prone to frequent and often devas-tating natural disasters such as earthquakes and mud slides (made all the more devastating because buildings are often made from mud bricks). When disasters hit, the normal procedure in these countries is to call in the military to preserve order and help pick up the pieces. We take care of this mission in a very different way. Our national military normally does not get involved. Rather, our National Guard units in the states are trained to handle the aftermath of earthquakes, floods, hurricanes, and the like.

We decided to hold conferences on disaster assistance in some of these countries. They brought their fire, police, emergency service units, and military; we brought experts from the U.S., who showed them how to in-termix the civilian and military and cooperate with each other; and we did all this in the name of the U.S. ambassadors.

We held other conferences in the region on environmental security issues—justifying them from the point of view that the military had to be good stewards of the environment, too. (We actually have many restric-tions aimed at protecting the environment; and, of course, military training can damage it.) And sometimes the military is called in to police the environment—oil spills, violation of protected fisheries, hazardous waste, and so on.

In organizing environmental security conferences, the term "security" was key. An "environmental" conference on disposing of hazardous waste, for example, would not have played well back at the Pentagon. We had to have a "military" or "security" connection. Armed with that, we could bring in the EPA to talk about how to deal with hazardous waste material. Then I could bring in the ambassador and expand the conference to other issues—even human rights. (Human rights issues are very important militarily when you are trying to teach the importance of "winning hearts and minds" to military forces with no history of these considerations in their operations.)

All of these forms of engagement build strong relationships with the various countries. They tie in important military and nonmilitary programs. And from there we are able to move on to more sophisticated joint training and military assistance projects that promote strong military-to-military relationships and build better capabilities. Everybody benefits.

Not everybody back home saw things that way. The struggle went on and on between those longing to lean forward into the world and to do what we could to shape it, and the isolationist passion to block all that.*

DURING THE nearly fifteen years since the end of the Cold War, talking heads and op-ed writers have spilt a lot of words on the "emergence of the American Empire."

We are the last-man-standing superpower. No other nation or combination of nations can seriously threaten the existence of the United States (though people who can grievously hurt us are working night and day to accomplish that aim). History suggests that the eight-hundred-pound gorilla among nations will eventually yield to the temptation to defend itself,

---

* The current Bush administration has seriously limited the powers of the CINCs; and Secretary of Defense Rumsfeld, who has a passion for centralized control, has changed their name. They are no longer CINCs; they're "Combatant Commanders."

protect its interests, maintain stability, and keep itself on top by gradually taking ever greater control (direct or indirect) beyond its immediate borders. It begins to impose its will by direct force, unilaterally. Because it has the power to change distasteful situations or governments on its own, it asserts that power. The gorilla metamorphoses into an octopus, with ever-stretching tentacles. It becomes an empire.*

"Is that the destiny of the United States?" many have asked.

In my view, it's not likely. . . . I pray not.

The truth is more subtle and complex.

True, the United States is now in a situation that is historically unprecedented. No nation has ever wielded such physical power, and the capability to project that power *quickly* anywhere in the world.

Yet, also true, no great power has ever before existed in such interdependence with so many other nations. No nation today can go it alone—economically, politically, diplomatically, culturally, or religiously.

The word *empire* does not cover this case. I don't know of any word that does. We are not an empire of conquest, occupation, or colonies. We are in a new relationship with a new kind of world. If I were to risk putting a label on America's new position in this world, I'd call us "an empire of influence."

FOR THE CINCS, our strategies are operational models—policy where the boots hit the ground. Once the CINCs have drawn their regional strategies out of the realities of their AORs and the global strategy of the President, they then have to implement them. Since doing that depends on the vicissitudes of Washington politics and the often dysfunctional Washington bureaucracy, and not on the intent of the President, executing our strategy was, at times, a frustrating process. We'd have a charter from the President that told us to go out somewhere and

* Some journalists have accused the CINCs of becoming the proconsuls of this new American empire. This opinion is flattering, but far from the truth. Dana Priest has developed this point of view very well in her interesting and provocative book *The Mission*.

do such and so, and then we'd get our knees cut out from under us before we could go out and do it. Since the Congress tended to fall more in the isolationist camp, they usually resisted the President's engagement policies . . . meaning, practically, that we didn't get the resources we needed to do what the President wanted done or we would get ill-thought-out sanctions or restrictions that were counterproductive and limited our ability to engage.

Though I've had many disagreements with the Clinton administration, its basic global strategy was right. I was out in the world and saw the needs, the newly emerging conditions, and how we can help to change them. I also saw that if we failed to change them, we were doomed to live with the tragic consequences.

I believe that military force does not solve every problem, nor is it our only form of power. There are other kinds of pressure and other kinds of support. In order to achieve our national goals, we have to combine every capability in our national bag in the most artful mix possible. But that's hard when the political infighting spills over into the implementation end of policy.

The Washington bureaucracy was too disjointed to make the vision of all the strategies, from the President's to the CINCs', a reality. There was no single authority in the bureaucracy to coordinate the significant programs we CINCs designed. The uncoordinated funding, policy decisions, authority, assigned geography, and many other issues separated State, Defense, Congress, the National Security Council, and other government agencies and made it difficult to pull complex engagement plans together.

To further complicate matters, the CINCs don't control their own resources. Their budgets come out of the service budgets; and these are controlled by the Service Chiefs (who are also double-hatted as the Joint Chiefs), who, understandably, don't want to give up their resources to the CINCs. The Service Chiefs have minimal interest in, and little insight into, engagement programs. They're trying to run their services, and that job's hard enough without other burdens. Their purpose and function is to train, organize, and equip forces for the CINCs, but what they actually want to do is provide these forces where, when, and how they see best. In other words, CINCs are demanding forces and resources for purposes that the Service Chiefs may not support. Thus the CINC is an impediment—and even a threat—and the rising power of the CINCs reduces the powers of the Service Chiefs. It's a zero-sum game.

Looking at the problem from the other side, the CINCs see the Service Chiefs as standing in the way of what they desperately need; and they are frustrated by the chiefs' inability to fully cooperate with them or support their strategies. The CINCs want to see their money identified and set aside in a specific budget line, so they know what they have. For all kinds of reasons, the Department of Defense is reluctant to do this.

The result is constant friction between the CINCs and Washington.

This is *not* a case of good guys and bad guys. The CINCs and the Service Chiefs are all fine men, doing the best jobs they can do. The Service Chiefs have a legitimate case. They're responsible for training, organizing, and equipping their forces. The CINCs have a legitimate case. They're responsible for employing or fighting their forces and for finding the resources to implement the President's policies out in the world day to day. These two responsibilities don't come together. The Washington bureaucracy has not been able to devise a coherent, cohesive way to make the system work.

This frustration was often voiced by the CINCs at their conferences in Washington, but to no avail. Washington issues and Service Chiefs' issues seemed to take priority over the CINCs' concerns.

I'D LIKE to suggest changes that might fix the system.

First, I would change the composition of the Joint Chiefs of Staff. I'd make them truly "joint."

Currently, the Joint Chiefs are simply the Service Chiefs wearing another hat now and again during the week. They're not really "Joint" Chiefs; they're Service Chiefs. Their first priority is to look out for their own services. Most of them have had no real "joint" experience in actual joint operations.

A better way to select Joint Chiefs would be to create a separate body, choosing it from former Service Chiefs and former CINCs, after they've served their tours. That would allow people with top-level experience from both worlds to pull the system together.

Looking at this idea more closely, you obviously can't have serving CINCs as Joint Chiefs of Staff. They're already all over the world doing their thing. Service Chiefs likewise have a full-time job in Washington as Service Chiefs (though they'll fight hard to keep their Joint Chiefs hats, because a lot of power comes with the job). But by selecting the Joint Chiefs of Staff out of the pool of former CINCs and former Service Chiefs, you would create a full-time dedicated organization without most of the temptations to which both CINCs and Service Chiefs can fall victim. Yet you would benefit from the enormous wealth of knowledge and experience they all represent. And they would be truly joint. This body would advise the Secretary of Defense, testify before Congress, and bring together all the relevant issues.

Two, where the CINCs' resources and their engagement programs are concerned, I think we ought to bite the bullet and identify the money and set the budget for whatever we want to call engagement. It should be out there, transparent, and separate from the service budgets. That way the CINCs would know exactly what they have, and the services would know exactly what they have.

Three, we need mechanisms to pull all the separate elements together. We need a body to oversee coordination, set priorities, and manage results. That way, if somebody comes in with a program (a CINC, an ambassador, etc.), that body reviews and approves it, and is responsible for making sure the other agencies of government meet the time lines and the commitment to get it done. Thus, our programs would no longer be disparate and fragmented, we'd be looking at them in a holistic way.

In other words, we would be doing for government what the Goldwater-Nichols Act did for the military. We'd be making government joint.

IN LATE January 1998, my CENTCOM conference in Tampa put the final touches on the new strategy. Attendees included our commanders, staff, security assistance personnel,* and diplomats assigned to the region and from the State Department. Many U.S. ambassadors were present, as were the Assistant Secretaries of State who directed the regional sections at the State Department that involved our AOR.†

By the end of the conference, we had full agreement on the new strategy.

My concluding direction to all was to make the strategy real. It couldn't be a nicely worded document that sat on the shelf and had no relationship to our daily actions. We had to live it day to day. Everything we did had to be related to our articulated strategic goals.

PUTTING OUT FIRES

My years at CENTCOM ranged from eventful, to hectic, to tumultuous— with crisis as our "normal" operating condition. We had the WMD inspectors' crisis with Iraq; India and Pakistan tested nuclear weapons, fighting continued in Kashmir, and a coup in Pakistan brought General Pervez Musharraf to power; Ethiopia and Eritrea went to war; Al Qaeda swaggered onto the world stage with embassy attacks in Nairobi and Dar es Salaam (followed up by the bombing of the USS *Cole* in Aden, Yemen, soon after I left CENTCOM); the running sore of the Israeli-Palestinian conflict directly affected every country in the region; and the region

---

* There were hundreds of these military and civilian personnel in the CENTCOM AOR—all worth their weight in gold to the CINCs. They administered the extensive programs of military assistance to the friendly countries in the region. They coordinated and administered foreign military sales, military exercises, military school attendance, training, and other cooperative efforts with local militaries. Along with the military attachés at American embassies, they provided the CINCs and diplomats with a vital link to local leaders. They were the day-to-day connections to the local militaries, and were an invaluable means of communications to the military and political leadership in the various countries. The job they do has never been valued by superiors, and promotions for those in the military have never come easy.

† One problem we were never able to adequately tackle was the differences in assigned geographical areas from one government agency to another. As an example, the assigned AOR for CENTCOM overlapped four regional bureaus at the State Department, while State's assigned regions had countries that were not in the CENTCOM AOR.

was simmering with lesser destabilizing crises such as border and ethnic disputes.

I met with local people from all levels of society to get a variety of
views on issues. I didn't just want the views of leaders. Our ambassadors
were very helpful in getting me these contacts and arranging the meetings
that gave me a full sense of the key issues in the region.

Managing the many crises we faced often required my presence close
to the scene. But I also traveled frequently to the region on "listening"
trips, building personal relationships, and experiencing the various cultures firsthand (following Joe Hoar's advice). I spent over seventy percent
of my time as CINC on the road; and I truly enjoyed my trips to the region. My visits to Washington were not so enjoyable; though the meetings with Pentagon staff, the Joint Chiefs, the Secretary of Defense,
Congress, and the President were necessary . . . and sometimes productive. But it was always good to get back to CENTCOM after Washington trips. I couldn't have asked for better bosses or supporters in D.C.
(especially Secretary of Defense Bill Cohen and Chairman of the Joint
Chiefs Hugh Shelton); but, as ever, the system, bureaucracy, and politics
were not for me.

My first trips as CINC to the AOR were dedicated to building relationships. I insisted on taking no issues to the regional leaders on the initial trips (and fought off those with lists of demands, requests, and points
to be made). I was not going out there to talk business. I wanted to listen
to the concerns of the people and hear their views of our role. It was an
enlightening experience: Meetings with heads of state such as President
Mubarak of Egypt, King Fahd of Saudi Arabia, and King Hussein of Jordan were a novelty for me, but I found it easy to engage these personable
leaders.

I found on my journeys that our commitment to stability in the region
was widely appreciated, but our policies and priorities were sometimes
questioned. Views of the threats varied greatly, as did opinions about handling them. The principal complaint was our failure to consult with them
not only during but *between* crises. The first was a bad lapse, though un-
derstandable; the second was more serious, though far less obvious. What
they were saying is that building trusting relationships as a normal state

of affairs would make working together in crises far easier and more productive. I promised to remedy that situation at my level.

Another—and related—complaint (echoing Ed Fugit and Joe Hoar): American leaders only blew in and out of the region when they had business to conduct, leaving no opportunity to establish the personal relationships that are critical and necessary in that part of the world. I also promised to do what I could to remedy that. Here I was thankful for Bill Cohen and Hugh Shelton, who accepted my request to come to the region often and establish the close, personal relationships we needed. Regional leaders were appreciative of their visits and personal connections. This paid dividends during crises when we needed regional cooperation.

As the coming months turned hectic, I was glad I had made my "listening" tours. It made the cooperation we badly needed from regional leaders far easier to gain.

ON THE twenty-sixth of November 1997, I was called to the Pentagon to hold a press briefing on the Iraq crisis, the first of many press contacts as CINC.

Though I don't bask in the glow of press attention (I can take it or leave it), I know how important it is to deal honestly and honorably with members of the media, the vast majority of whom are responsible professionals who provide the window of transparency without which a democracy cannot exist. With only a few exceptions, they have treated me fairly. Their interest on the whole has been based on a desire to report and understand, and not to promote a particular agenda. . . .

But a few of them can be pains in the ass—or, worse, irresponsible, shallow, dishonest, or hypocritical. I imagine the ratio of good to bad is not different from any other community.

The Washington bureaucracy has always been more frightened of the media than those of us with field commands. Washington knee-jerks to daily consolidated press clippings, put together each morning by the various government departments' public affairs offices. For DOD, the consolidated morning clippings were called "the Early Bird." I could be virtually certain that any questions, ass-chewing, or directions I was going to get on any given day had been driven by the Early Bird.

I quickly learned that leverage with the media came from the access I could grant or withhold. If a reporter reported accurately, even if the resulting story was not favorable, I made sure I granted as much access as I had time to give. If the reporting was not accurate, that ended my contact with the reporter. To this day, there are a handful of reporters, newspapers, or even networks that I won't deal with.

At press conferences, I've always tried to answer questions with short declarative sentences. I hate rambling, vague, bureaucratic answers that avoid direct responses to questions. This era of "spin" sickens me. I would never have accepted a White House "spin doctor" being assigned to my command to run our public affairs effort, as was done during the Iraq war.

NINETEEN NINETY-EIGHT was a year of nearly continuous turmoil.

It started in Africa.

Though many in Washington see little in the way of vital national interests there, I had long felt that we have important concerns in that continent that merit using our national resources—not to mention our obligation to help the enormous humanitarian needs. Our efforts in Africa have been woefully short of what we should be doing.

On a trip I made to Africa early in January, our ambassador to Kenya, Prudence Bushnell, briefed me on a developing crisis in that country. Severe flooding was washing out roads and bridges, and several hundred thousand people were in danger of being cut off from their sources of food, potable water, and medicine. Because the Kenyans were ill equipped to meet the emergency airlift demands to move emergency supplies, I agreed to send our Special Operations Command (SOCENT) team, supported by a USAF C-130, to assess the situation and then to deploy a Humanitarian Assessment Support Team (HAST) to handle the humanitarian crisis. I had tasked SOCENT to establish a trained HAST ready to go on a moment's notice if a humanitarian crisis developed.

The situation in Kenya quickly worsened; the floodwaters continued to rage; and over 300,000 people were in immediate danger of starving or succumbing to disease. But the Pentagon was reluctant to help them; the mission cost too much, and they didn't want to use our military. I persisted, the "Five-Sided Labyrinth" eventually yielded, and I ordered CENTCOM's Marine component to deploy a task force to Kenya. I had also tasked our Marine component with the responsibility to respond to humanitarian and peacekeeping missions in East Africa. This mission, known as "Operation Noble Response," saved the lives of hundreds of thousands of Kenyans and cost $800,000. Saving so many lives has rarely come so cheaply.

AT THE END of March, I made a trip to the region, primarily to attend a Gulf Cooperation Council meeting in Bahrain. My purpose was to bring the six GCC countries* together to work security issues collectively. Previously, we had almost always done business with each country individually. I wanted to change that. I wanted our regional allies to begin to think collectively about security issues.

Since our biggest obstacle was the reluctance of the Arab countries to embark on a collective security relationship with the U.S., I knew it would take time to develop what I hoped to achieve. Nevertheless, I felt that if I could put issues of common interest on the table as starting points, and get agreement on these, we'd at least be moving down the right path. I found two such issues—theater missile defense, and environmental security.

The members of the GCC could not fail to be aware that the growing missile proliferation in the region was a real problem, and they all knew they needed a coordinated regional defensive capability to deal with such threats. We had therefore proposed that the U.S. provide the technology and organization skills to pull it all together, and they had agreed to discuss this at the conference.

But first we had to steer through their instinctive suspicion of our motives. Some saw our proposal as an attempt to rope them into buying high-cost U.S. systems, while others saw it as a scheme to pull them into an arrangement that specified a particular enemy. Yet once these suspicions

---

* Our six closest friends in the Gulf.

were allayed, the conference really took off . . . especially when we offered to share early warning information. Since we obviously had the best information against missile and air threats, it made sense for us to provide it in a cooperative defense arrangement. Though some of the council didn't believe we would actually give up this information, I explained that this was not only a matter of trust but in our own interest, since it would help protect our military in the region.

Though we had a few rocky moments, the conference was a success. It was followed by a series of other conferences to further develop the initial concepts and capabilities.

In order to keep this momentum going, I decided to schedule another conference on a different issue—environmental security. The Omanis agreed to host it. Again, it was a success.

After the conferences ended, I visited Qatar, where the foreign minister, Sheik Hamad bin Jassim, persuaded me to give an interview to the notoriously controversial Qatar-based network, Al Jazeera. Since I didn't want to be baited or set up in an unfriendly interview broadcast throughout the region, I was reluctant to do it.

Hamad didn't deny that the interview could be rough, yet he explained that the region badly needed to see the "human face" of the U.S. military. So I went ahead with it . . . with no regrets. The interview was tough but fair. And the interviewer's probing questions about ethical considerations in our military operations allowed me to show that human face. Afterward, I agreed to do several more interviews. One interview was videoed by an Iraqi crew who gave me a thumbs-up from behind the camera every time I blasted Saddam.

DURING THE second week of April, I attended the annual Emerald Express Conference (which I had started when I commanded I MEF). What I hoped would come out of the conference was the start of a cooperative regional capability for peacekeeping and the humanitarian mission.

Since Africa has never received much attention from Washington, and it was split between CENTCOM and EUCOM, progress was not going to come easily. When my early attempts to start a coordinated, more expansive program for African engagement did not work out, I decided to piece together a CENTCOM program, focused on peacekeeping and humanitarian capabilities developed with the African countries in our AOR.

This program had three major elements.

The first was the African Crisis Response Initiatives (ACRI), set up earlier by our government for low-level (small unit and individual) training and equipping of African military forces for peacekeeping and humanitarian missions. This program was very rudimentary, and its value was overinflated by our government. It was a solid beginning; yet it wasn't enough. We needed a larger operational element, consisting of major exercises and significant field training at the battalion level and for the staffs; we needed to work in a real environment; and we needed actual applications, using, for example, real veterinarians, dentists, and doctors in real situations.

With these thoughts in mind, I decided to build on ACRI by adding an annual brigade-sized exercise with African and U.S. forces. The exercise, called "Natural Fire," was designed to bring together regional forces in a realistic peacekeeping and humanitarian operations task that they would work in conjunction with NGOs and international relief organizations. I further combined into this our medical, dental, and veterinarian training, in order to gain the goodwill these provided in the African villages in the exercise area.

Then we needed a third element at the strategic, policy level. That is, we needed to bring in senior political officials, senior NGOs, and senior military to talk about how to make the big operational strategic decisions, and bring the different elements into cooperation on the ground. This was supposed to be the function of Emerald Express.

Once these elements were in place, I hoped to broaden the program into a model for all Africa, and tie it in with the newly formed (and U.S. DOD–sponsored) African Center for Strategic Studies (ACSS)* to further

---

* DOD has set up several centers to deal with regional security issues. For example, the Marshall Center focuses on Europe, Eastern Europe, and Russia. The Asia-Pacific Center focuses on that area. The Near East, South Asia Center focuses on that area. And the African Center for Strategic Studies focuses on Africa. Some of these centers, like the Near East and the African, had only just recently been formed.

develop policy issues and reinforce Emerald Express. The truly superb director of the ACSS, Nancy Walker, enthusiastically and skillfully supported our efforts.

Among the attendees at Emerald Express for whom I had special hopes were General Tsadkan of Ethiopia and General Shebat of Eritrea, the heads of the militaries in their countries. These two old friends (and friends of mine) had fought and won the two-decade "Long Struggle" against the oppressive Menguistu regime in Ethiopia; and both had wonderful tales of their rough days in the bush during the guerrilla war.

I was keenly interested in helping their two militaries, and saw a further opportunity to stabilize their portion of the troubled Horn of Africa if I could persuade them to sign on to our proposed cooperative regional initiative. But neither showed much interest in that. I figured they were still consumed with their internal issues after emerging from twenty-plus years of warfare and devastation.

A few months later, their two countries staggered into a tragic war; and the two old friends became enemies.

The one nation that took to my plan was Kenya. General Tonje, the strong and impressive leader of Kenya's military, had instituted deep reforms that had transformed that organization into a noncorrupt and professional force. At the conference, he and President Moi proposed that we run the program through the East African Community (EAC), a regional political organization that included Kenya, Uganda, and Tanzania. This was a good idea, but unfortunately unworkable, since Uganda and Tanzania were not in CENTCOM's AOR. When I asked if they could be assigned to us, EUCOM objected. And when we then tried to run the program jointly with EUCOM, it only barely got off the ground. . . . Those parts of the program that were run in Kenya through the EAC were very successful.

Meanwhile, confusion had crept in about the directions and goals of Emerald Express.

Pacific Command and the Marine Corps (for various legitimate reasons) were claiming part ownership of the conference, while providing very little in the way of funds to support it—most of which were coming from CENTCOM. Their idea was to shift the focus of the conference to their own particular areas of interest. Though I didn't object to their participation, I was not happy to see the shift away from the areas where CENTCOM had concerns.

I therefore decided to make changes to Emerald Express that would reorient it into a solely CENTCOM affair, focused on Africa, and held somewhere in our African region. I MEF agreed to keep sponsorship and run the conference, which was renamed "Golden Spear." It provided a high-level, intergovernmental forum for discussions on planning and lessons-learned development for several types of engagement missions. Kenya agreed to cohost the first Golden Spear conference.

WHEN I returned from Emerald Express, I learned that the CENTCOM AOR had grown. We'd been assigned the Central Asian region that included the countries of Kazakhstan, Uzbekistan, Kyrgyzstan, Tajikistan, and Turkmenistan. We soon began taking on new challenges presented by this assignment.

LATER IN APRIL, Senator Ted Stevens led a seven-senator congressional delegation (CODEL) to the Gulf to look at gaining more burden-sharing support from Persian Gulf nations, particularly Saudi Arabia, for our ongoing military enforcement of sanctions against Iraq.

I picked up the CODEL in my plane (an ancient Boeing 707) and took them to Jeddah, Saudi Arabia, where we met the Saudi Minister of Defense, Prince Sultan, and the Saudi ambassador to the U.S., Prince Bandar. Since I was certain that the CODEL was unaware of the support we were actually receiving from the Saudis, I prefaced the meeting with a briefing that covered the hundreds of millions of dollars of direct support we received each year in fuel, food, water, etc., as well as the additional hundreds of millions the Saudis had spent to build a state-of-the-art housing facility for our forces. We also received indirect support from Saudi purchases of U.S. defense equipment. And, finally, Saudi Arabia and other Gulf nations had provided troops and funding support for our missions in places like Somalia. This information (obviously unexpected) satisfied the

CODEL; the Minister of Defense followed this up with a show of personal support and friendship for CENTCOM.

EARLY MAY. In response to an Indian nuclear weapons test, Pakistan was scheduled to test their own nuclear weapon, an act that would drastically escalate tensions in the region—and the world.

In an effort to persuade the Pakistanis not to test, the State Department planned to send Deputy Secretary of State Strobe Talbot and the Assistant Secretary for the region, Rick Inderfer, to meet Prime Minister Sharif and the senior Pakistani leadership. I was to accompany them.

The mission was not going to be easy. Relations between the U.S. and Pakistan were already tense. The Pakistanis had backed our efforts in Afghanistan during the Afghan rebellion against the Soviets; there were now a large number of refugees—and a state of chaos—on their western border as a result; and we had (in their view) dumped them.

Their bitterness had increased when we imposed sanctions over their WMD program. Specifically, we had refused to deliver F-16s they had bought and paid for, or even to return their money; and then we'd deducted storage fees for the planes from what they had paid. No surprise: They were enraged. (The anger was compounded after many pilots flying older planes were lost, which wouldn't have happened if they'd had the F-16s.)

Our treatment of Pakistan was working against our interest. This was a state on the edge; the government was shaky and badly corrupt; and politically powerful Islamists inflamed the population. If Pakistan failed, or turned into an Iranian- or Afghan-style theocracy, we would have major problems in the region . . . and beyond. We did not want nuclear-armed Islamist radicals. Then or now.

The delegation flew to Tampa to join me on the twenty-two-hour flight to Islamabad. As we prepared to board the CENTCOM 707, word came that the Pakistani government had decided not to approve the visit. This triggered a flurry of diplomatic calls from the waiting room at our air base . . . made more urgent by the approach of our drop-dead takeoff time. If we didn't get in the air within two hours, our crew time would run out.

When the calls kept getting negative results, I decided to propose to Secretary Talbot a back-channel approach. If I called General Jehangir Karamat, the chief of staff of the Pakistan military, I thought he would okay the trip. Karamat was a man of great honor and integrity, and a friend. Relations with Pakistan hung on the thin thread of a personal relationship that General Karamat and I agreed to maintain.

"Go ahead," the Secretary told me, though his face was skeptical.

But when I called General Karamat, he promised to take care of the problem; and a few minutes later we were in the air . . . further proof, if the Secretary needed it, that the relationship between our two militaries remained strong, in spite of the strained relationships elsewhere. Though Washington had severely limited the military-to-military connections I could make, I had insisted on maintaining that personal connection to General Karamat.

In Pakistan, we met several times with Prime Minister Sharif and his ministers, but were unable to convince them not to test. The domestic pressure to respond to the Indian tests was too great.

As we left, I had a few private moments with General Karamat, who shared with me his frustration with his corrupt government. Pakistan's military leaders had more than once seized power from the elected government. Though others in the military had urged him to follow that tradition, he assured me he could never do that. He kept his word; but that did not stop a military coup later that year.

IN MID-MAY, shooting incidents in Badime, a disputed border area between Ethiopia and Eritrea, had caused the Eritreans to attack in force and seize the area. The Ethiopians were mobilizing for a counterattack.

On the eighteenth, I called General Tsadkan, to get his take on the situation. According to my Ethiopian friend, his old friend General Shebat had been visiting him to celebrate the belated graduation of his wife from college (after leaving college decades before to join the political struggle, she had finally returned to complete her degree). According to Tsadkan, Shebat had abruptly walked out of the celebration; and the attack had come the next day. It was a stab in the back. He was predictably outraged.

Needless to say, when I called General Shebat on the twentieth, he gave me a different version of these events. He claimed the attack had come in response to a series of violent incidents staged by the Ethiopians.

Wherever the truth lay, it was tragic that these two old friends, who had suffered so much side by side, couldn't work out this quarrel peacefully.

As tensions worsened, Susan Rice, the State Department's Assistant Secretary for African Affairs, asked me to intervene; and she and I worked together to try calm everybody down . . . but with no success. Over the next months, the crisis grew to critical mass and exploded. All we could do in response was plan a precautionary Non-combatant Evacuation Operation.

HAPPILY, many of our relationships in the region were actually improving—some after years of conflict. One of the more notable turnarounds came from Yemen. After years of civil war had devastated the country, the nation was now united. But a stupid decision to support Iraq during the Gulf War had soured relations with the U.S. Earlier that year, however, Yemen's president, Ali Abdullah Saleh, had sent word that he was looking to mend fences and begin a cooperative military-to-military relationship with the U.S. This was good news. Yemen was a strategically vital country in serious danger of becoming a failed state. Helping Yemen was critical to our security interests in the region.

I visited Yemen on May 22, spending several days with President Saleh and his ministers. Because he had no ability to control his borders and coast, or to effectively act against the terrorist groups who freely transited the country and used it as a base, Saleh desperately needed help in training his counterterrorist forces. And of course, he desperately needed a Coast Guard.

I added several other Security Assistance programs to his wish list, as well as an intelligence-sharing program.

Again, these actions brought forth little support from Washington. I was nevertheless determined to build this relationship. It was in the region's, and our own, security interests.

While I was in Yemen, I toured the port of Aden, where new construction and refueling sites were being examined by our naval component as a potential replacement for the refueling stop at Djibouti, where there were significant security problems. I liked what I saw. The refueling site was away from any piers; the actual refueling could be accomplished out in the harbor at a secure distance from sea traffic; and initial reports from the DOD experts about fuel quality and quantity were encouraging.

IN JULY, we received two notable visitors at CENTCOM headquarters— Prince Abdullah of Jordan and General Altynbayev, the Kazakhstan Minister of Defense.

A bright, vibrant young leader with innovative ideas, Abdullah was at that time the head of the Jordanian Special Forces. Inevitably, our conversation turned to the failing health of his father, King Hussein, who had long been fighting cancer. The cancer was worsening; it was clear the king would soon be dead.

For many years, Hussein's brother had been designated as next in line to the throne; but that was soon to change. Though the king was about to change his pick to Abdullah, the prince had had no indication of that. It was a splendid choice. He has proved to be one of the most enlightened leaders in his part of the world.

General Altynbayev was the first Central Asian official I had met since the five former Soviet states were assigned to the CENTCOM AOR. As he and I talked, I quickly realized that these states were going to pose very different problems from the other subregions of our AOR—problems that were more related to their former rule by Moscow than to their religion or ethnicity (though these issues were also very much present). I looked forward to a visit to the Stans later that year.

AT THE END of July, on another trip to Pakistan, I visited some of the more remote and rugged parts of the country—the Line of Control Area of Kashmir and the nearby Siachen glacier, and the fabled Khyber Pass on the western border with Afghanistan. In these wild mountains, Pakistani and Indian troops had faced off against each other for decades at altitudes in excess of twenty thousand feet. If the fighting didn't kill you, the weather and altitude did. To my surprise, the two countries had, for the most part, succeeded in containing the fighting to this dangerous and volatile, yet well-defined, area. But that "happy" situation was going to change in a matter of months.

At the Khyber Pass, I gained a greater understanding of Pakistan's rugged western border with Afghanistan-remote hostile tribes, a territory not fully subject to Pakistani law or control, and a truly tough mountainous terrain. By then, I had a solid sense of how the ruinous rule of the Taliban was destroying that country and the sanctuary they provided extremists like Al Qaeda presented a growing and exceptionally dangerous threat.

WE LEARNED how serious it was on the seventh of August, when our embassies in Kenya and Tanzania were hit by suicide truck bombs. Twelve Americans (including three members of our CENTCOM Security Assistance team) and 234 locals were killed in the attacks, and over 5,000 were wounded. The attacks were conducted by Osama bin Laden's Al Qaeda terrorist group.

We immediately sent a Fleet Antiterrorist Support Team (FAST), from the Marines, Navy engineer units, and medical units to meet the emergency needs; and I dispatched a team to Nairobi from our headquarters to function as a Joint Task Force Command Element to determine what else was needed. All of this became "Operation Resolute Response."

The attack did not come as a total surprise. We had already learned from President Moi several months earlier that Muslim extremists were operating in his country and in neighboring Somalia, and that terrorist activities were becoming a grave threat to East, Central, and West Africa.

In February, acting on a request from our ambassador in Kenya, Prudence Bushnell, I had sent a message to the Secretary of State warning of the vulnerability of the Nairobi embassy to car bomb attacks (it was located on one of Nairobi's busiest thoroughfares) and offering to help with a security assessment and recommendations. The State Department reply essentially told me that my help was not needed—the same message the ambassador had got when she'd tried to catch Washington's attention before coming to me.

When a reporter somehow dug up the basic contents of the message, there was a small crisis in Washington; but, to my amazement, the State Department just blew it off, and the issue died.

This was just as well. We had a much larger question to answer: What to do about Osama bin Laden and Al Qaeda? In those days, we knew that they were a growing threat, but we did not know how dangerous they would become. Yet on the evidence of Nairobi and Dar es Salaam, "dangerous" might be too mild a word. Clearly, we had to counterattack. But that was not going to be easy. Al Qaeda has never been a "place" that we could easily target; it's a network, a web. And Osama has always been elusive. We did know that Al Qaeda had facilities in Afghanistan; and our intelligence agencies knew Osama was then located somewhere near these facilities; but there was no way we could locate his day-to-day position.

By mid-August, additional intelligence suggested that bin Laden might be visiting one of his terrorist training camps in Afghanistan. I was ordered to prepare Tomahawk missile strikes on the camp and on a target in Khartoum, Sudan. (According to our intelligence, this was a pharmaceutical plant that produced a precursor used to develop toxic chemical agents for terrorist organizations.) The strikes were scheduled for August 20.

The Sudan target was new to me; I had not yet seen them mentioned in our intel assessments, but the evidence of its terrorist use seemed highly reliable.

The training camps were rough-and-ready facilities that did not offer high-value targets in terms of infrastructure, and the odds of getting bin Laden were not good, but in my mind it was worth the shot. If he was there, and we hit him, great. If he wasn't, then at least he'd know we could reach him. I knew it was a long shot and that if he wasn't there we would be criticized, but I felt we had to take the shot.

The day we fired the missiles, I cleared my desk of everything but a card of thanks from the parents of Sergeant Sherry Olds, a remarkable NCO who had been killed in the Nairobi attack, for a letter I'd sent them and for our honor guard at her funeral.

This strike was called "Operation Infinite Reach."

It did not actually do much damage, and we did receive a lot of press and political criticism for it, but in my mind it was worth doing. Intelligence came down with several other targets after these strikes, but, again, they never had the specificity or reliability that I felt warranted launching missile strikes or special operations missions. The risks to our forces or the assured collateral damage were not justified by the sketchy intel we saw in the strikes executed.

On a visit to Nairobi on the twenty-ninth of August, I promised Ambassador Bushnell that our FAST security forces would not leave until a new embassy was established—work that could not be completed for several months. I was therefore shocked a short time later when the Pentagon started pressuring me to withdraw the Marines before a new, more secure location for the embassy had been acquired.

According to the Pentagon, keeping the Marines there was too expensive, and security at the embassy was a State Department problem anyhow. "We did our part. Now it's their business."

"We can't pull out," I told them. "There is no way, shape, or form we can leave Americans exposed and in jeopardy out there."

"Well, that's the State Department's problem," the Pentagon kept saying. "They should be taking care of their people. Not us."

I wasn't going to let interagency bickering get in the way of protecting Americans. So I got tough. "Bullshit," I said. "I'm not going to leave Americans in danger. Those Marines are going to stay out there until they get a suitable place to move the American embassy. I'm going to protect the Americans where they live and work. They're still vulnerable."

I got a lot of mumbling and grumbling from the Pentagon, but no one was going to challenge me on this.

BY EARLY September, the crisis between Ethiopia and Eritrea had grown even more alarming. It looked like war was soon coming to the Horn of Africa. In an effort to ease tensions and find a peaceful solution to the crisis, the President had designated former National Security Adviser Tony Lake to be a special envoy; and I was tasked to work with him. This effort became known as "the Tony-Tony Strategy."

I traveled to Ethiopia and Eritrea during the first week of September. In meetings over several days with Prime Minister Meles and General Tsadkan of Ethiopia and President Isaias and General Shebat of Eritrea, I tried to convince everyone that a war over Badime—a desolate and barren patch of ground on the common border—was senseless and would lead to a needless bloodbath. Everyone listened politely, but neither side was willing to compromise. It was clear they were already committed to military action. I returned to the States extremely discouraged, convinced a bloody war was approaching.

Still, I had to keep trying to prevent it.

LATER IN September, when I made my first visit to the Central Asian states, I found all these societies in a state of post-Soviet shock. After seventy years of communism, Kazakhs, Uzbeks, Kirghiz, Tajiks, Turkomans, and the other ethnic groups in what had once been the southern parts of the USSR had significant economic, security, political, and social problems. Now that the communist weight had been lifted from their backs, they were trying to figure out their true identity and search for the best way forward. Naturally, each looked at our new U.S. involvement as a chance to gain the support they needed to make necessary changes. And, naturally, the U.S. was once again unwilling to invest in this new region of engagement.

But the U.S. wasn't the only barrier to progress. Each state had its own set of problems and view of the way ahead; and there was little interest in the collective, regional approach that we preferred. Thus it was clear to me that we had to begin with bilateral arrangements.

For starters, their militaries had a dire need to reform the old Soviet system, while their security concerns about the threats (extremism, drugs, and crime, primarily coming out of Afghanistan) were real. Once again, we'd be creating an engagement program with few resources, but I was determined to work with what we had. These were frontline states, extremely vulnerable to the growing forces of extremism and chaos in South Asia. It was becoming ever clearer that these threats were not just directed at them; they were also directed at us. We *had* to help them.

I had begun to hear the same warning from all the leaders in the region—from President Moi of Kenya to President Karamov of Uzbekistan. They were all alarmed over the spreading menace of religious extremism and terrorist activities.

Nineteen ninety-eight marked a major transition in the institutional nature of terrorism. Before 1998, terrorist bands tended to be small, disparate, and haphazardly managed . . . or else run by charismatic leaders. They were more likely to be gangs with gripes than organizations with plans, programs, and strategies.

Al Qaeda* changed all that.

The genius of Al Qaeda was to pull the disparate terrorist groups together, create a network to link them all, and provide the resources, training, command and control, and global reach to make this threat international. Al Qaeda had created what was in effect a virtual state whose base was its global network. Each part of the network was relatively weak, insignificant, and vulnerable; but because of the invisibility and security of the links, the threat from the network had soon reached an unprecedented level.

This was far from the threat of world annihilation that we had endured for the nearly fifty years of the Cold War; yet the dangers from an Al Qaeda allowed to grow unchecked were far from small.

IN CONNECTION with an October 21 trip to Washington for Senate testimony, I was asked by the DOD public relations office to hold a press conference at a Defense Writers' Group breakfast.

During the session, I took questions about some exiled, London-based Iraqi opposition groups that had become the apple of Congress's eye. The most prominent of these, the Iraqi National Congress, was led by Ahmed Chalabi. Chalabi had conned several senior people into believing that he could spark a guerrilla movement that would sweep Saddam Hussein and the Ba'athists from power—if only he had a lot of money and a little spe-

---

* The name in Arabic means "base" or "foundation."

cial operations and air support. I thought this idea was totally mad (our intelligence had reported that nothing the INC said was trustworthy and none of their plans were viable).

The October press conference was not my first encounter with this idiocy. On the twenty-sixth of March, I had traveled to Washington for my annual congressional testimony.

CINCs are required to give annual testimony before the Senate Armed Services Committee, House Armed Services Committee, and House Appropriations Committee,* but are often also called during the year to give testimony on specific issues as they come up. At our annual testimony, we'd generally provide a status of our command and region and respond to questions. Most questions related to pet programs or issues that individual legislators wanted to promote or challenge; but some made a political point about the administration's policies.

The issue at the March sessions was the administration's policy in Iraq. Congress was brewing its own strategy, cooked up by a couple of Senate staffers, promoting the Iraqi National Congress and Chalabi's guerrilla plans. I testified then that there was no chance that this operation could succeed. Saddam was too firmly entrenched to be dislodged by a handful of guerrilla bands, and Chalabi's organization was a sham.

Naturally, my reluctance to get on board a boat I didn't think would float did not endear me to Chalabi's backers, many of whom, such as Senator John McCain, were powerful in Washington. And when I offered these views, I could tell Defense Secretary Cohen was not comfortable. Though the Clinton administration was extremely leery about dealing with Chalabi, any plan that promised to get rid of Saddam played in the media like motherhood and free speech, so the administration was not eager to seem to oppose it. That evening, out on the steps of the Capitol, Secretary Cohen told me to stick to military execution of policy and stay out of policy development. The rebuke was polite, but I got the message.

Congress had passed the Iraqi Liberation Act, which applied $97 million to Iraqi opposition groups, including Chalabi's.

---

* Before becoming CINC, I had testified several times before these committees, and also the Senate Foreign Relations Committee.

The administration still did not want to touch this issue. But they had no intention of spending the money on the Iraqi opposition (except for minor administrative support). They were not about to actually buy them weapons.

But by October the two Senate staffers I'd run into in March, now working with a retired Army general, had actually come up with a crazy plan to arm the "military branches" of these dissidents and insert them into Iraq with promises from us of air cover and special forces support. It was a recipe for disaster, which I referred to at the press conference as "the Bay of Goats," adding further insult by calling the exiles "Gucci Guerrillas."

These comments caused a furor, and during my Senate testimony later that day I faced several angry Senators who supported this ludicrous proposal.

Though I was severely chewed out by my bosses afterward, I received hundreds of letters and calls, and several articles were written, in support of my position.

The story does not end there. Washington is a vindictive town, and the two staffers swore revenge. They did not take it out on me, but on my political adviser, Larry Pope. When Pope was nominated for Ambassador to Kuwait, they were able to block a Senate vote on it. This petty act against a man who had nothing to do with my opinions was typical of the Washington politics that sickened me.

NINETEEN NINETY-EIGHT ended with a bang with Desert Fox.

I knew we'd get no respite from the constant high-level tempo of operations in 1999.

IN EARLY JANUARY, the administration directed Tony Lake to make another effort (which we supported) to broker peace in the looming Ethiopia-Eritrea war; yet I knew we were not going to stop the impending fight. When the war actually began in the spring of 1999, we conducted an evacuation of American citizens (called "Operation Safe Departure").

The war was bloody. World War One–style trench warfare and massive frontal attacks caused thousands of deaths.

After an Ethiopian victory at Badime (by which time the two belligerents had exhausted themselves on the battlefield), we worked with Tony Lake and the State Department to establish a peacekeeping force there. By the end of the year, a UN force provided a boundary demarcation team and peacekeepers to try to help resolve the dispute.

ON THE twenty-first of April, I traveled to Pakistan for several days of meetings with the new chief of staff, General Pervez Musharraf. The two of us connected quickly and easily. He was bright, sincere, and personable. A fervent nationalist who nevertheless leaned toward the West, he was as appalled as General Karamat over the ever-worsening corruption within the civilian government. He also understood the various, powerful Islamist currents running through his country, and saw them as the threats they were to bringing his country into the twenty-first century; yet he also understood that his country would never modernize and solve its myriad ills without the emergence of some kind of religious accommodation, and hopefully religious consensus.

It was a great meeting, despite the chill cast by our sanctions. As I was leaving, we both agreed to stay in close touch (we exchanged our home telephone numbers). Our friendship would later prove to be enormously valuable to both our countries.

IN MAY, Pakistani forces made a deep incursion into an area called Kargil, on the Indian side of the Line of Control.

Though there was normally "fighting" near the Line of Control, the area for a long time had been quite stable. There'd be probes and shooting during the good months of the year, but nothing ever changed much; and in wintertime, everybody would pull back down into the valleys, and the two sides would create a "no-man's-land." As spring came, they'd go back up into their positions.

Every so often, somebody on one side would be a little late getting up to their spring position, and the other side could grab an advantage of a kilometer or so. It was like "Aha, I've gotcha!" on a tactical level. But it didn't really change things.

This time, however, the Pakistanis waylaid the Indians and penetrated all the way to Kargil. This was such a deep, significant penetration that it wasn't tactical; it threatened Indian lines of communication and support up to Siachen glacier.

The Indians came back with a vengeance. There were exchanges of fire, there was a mobilization of forces, there were bombing attacks, planes were shot down. Then the two sides started to mobilize all their forces all along the line; and it was beginning to look like the opening moves of a larger war. It got alarming.

I was therefore directed by the administration to head a presidential mission to Pakistan to convince Prime Minister Sharif and General Musharraf to withdraw their forces from Kargil.

I met with the Pakistani leaders in Islamabad on June 24 and 25 and put forth a simple rationale for withdrawing: "If you don't pull back, you're going to bring war and nuclear annihilation down on your country. That's going to be very bad news for everybody." Nobody actually quarreled with this rationale. The problem for the Pakistani leadership was the apparent national loss of face. Backing down and pulling back to the Line of Control looked like political suicide. We needed to come up with a face-saving way out of this mess. What we were able to offer was a meeting with President Clinton, which would end the isolation that had long been the state of affairs between our two countries, but we would announce the meeting only after a withdrawal of forces.

That got Musharraf's attention; and he encouraged Prime Minister Sharif to hear me out.

Sharif was reluctant to withdraw before the meeting with Clinton was announced (again, his problem was maintaining face); but after I insisted, he finally came around and he ordered the withdrawal. We set up a meeting with Clinton in July.

IN OCTOBER 1999, the tension between the civilian and military leadership of Pakistan finally came to a head. The government was freely elected but outrageously corrupt. The military found itself between a rock and a hard place. If they let the situation continue, the rot could grow bad enough that the country would collapse—a very real possibility. But there was no way to change this situation according to the normal liberal democratic rules.

Sharif set in motion his own downfall by trying to fire General Musharraf, while Musharraf was out of the country, and to put the chief of intelligence in his place. He had originally given Musharraf the job under the misperception that Musharraf would be easy to control. He had not reckoned on the general's integrity.

In response to Sharif's move, the Pakistani army executed a coup.

While the coup was moving to its climax, Musharraf was flying home; and for him, success was a very near thing. His aircraft came back into the country low on fuel; but the airports, still under the control of Sharif's forces, were closed to him. At the last possible moment, forces friendly to Musharraf took over the airport and the general landed.

Prime Minister Sharif was soon placed under arrest, and Musharraf declared his intent to clean up governmental corruption and install true democracy.

The coup did not play well in Washington, and I was ordered to cease communications with General Musharraf. Though I thought the order was stupid, I complied.

EVERY OTHER YEAR, we conduct a joint exercise with Egypt called "Bright Star." It is the largest military exercise in the world.*

In November, I was in a reviewing stand with Secretary Cohen, participating in Bright Star, when my communicator announced that a call from General Musharraf had been patched through to my satellite phone (which was with me at all times).

I turned to Cohen. "What do you want me to do?" I asked.

---

* The Bright Star exercise was key to pulling together a major coalition operation, and was our major preparation for any future repeat of Desert Storm. Nowhere else in the region did we have the land, air, and sea space for exercises of this scale.

"Take the call, but don't make any commitments," he said.

It was a personal call between friends, Musharraf explained (though, of course, we both knew that any conversation we had would have wider ramifications). He wanted me to know what had led to the coup and why he and the other military leaders had had no choice other than the one they took.

The point he made then was a powerful one: "Democracy and the ballot are both a sham when any government that results can offer everything they control up for sale. We've had a democracy of form, and not a democracy of substance. I want democracy in substance, I'll work for that, no matter what it costs me.

"And there's one more thing I have to make clear," he told me. "I don't care what most others think about my motivations or intentions; but it's important to me that you know what they are."

I thanked him for his candor, and wished him well.

When I briefed Cohen on the call, I made it clear that it was more important than ever to stay connected to Pakistan. He understood what I was saying, but he didn't think Washington would be convinced.

IN DECEMBER, Jordanian intelligence uncovered a massive plot to kill American tourists at the turn-of-millennium celebrations in Jordan and throughout the Middle East. The captured terrorists, who had links to Osama bin Laden, revealed that their immediate leaders were in Pakistan.

Calls soon came from the State Department and National Security Council: "Please call Musharraf and ask him to help."

In response to my requests, Musharraf arrested the terrorists (and gave us access to them and to their confiscated computer disks) . . . and threw in several other favors.

"Now do something for Musharraf," I told Washington. "Or at least let us reconnect."

The answer was no.

I called Musharraf and told him how disappointed I was. "I know that cooperation isn't popular in some circles of your own government and people, as well," I explained. "I know what courage it took to do what you did for us. So it's doubly embarrassing for me that I can't give you anything in return."

"I don't want or expect anything for what I've done," Musharraf replied. "Tony, I did it because it was the right thing to do."

ON MY final trips to the region in the spring and summer of 2000, I was deeply moved by the reception I received from my many friends. Their expressions of appreciation for what we had done and the relationships we had built made me feel we were well on our way to stabilizing this volatile part of the world. I knew, however, that we had a long way to go. This was a dangerous neighborhood. The region needed to make many political, social, economic, and security reforms, but it needed time, space, and support (and, in some cases, prodding) to get these done. I felt we could help effect these changes by providing this help.

During my time at CENTCOM, every country except the Seychelles was continually under a terrorist threat. We had conducted a series of military actions against Iraq, while continuing to enforce sanctions against that nation. We had contained Iran and opened new relations with Yemen and the Central Asian States. We had dealt with wars in Sudan, Somalia, Ethiopia, Eritrea, and Tajikistan. Our responses to crises in Pakistan, Africa, and elsewhere had ranged from humanitarian assistance, to evacuation of U.S. citizens, to mediation of disputes.

It was an incredible experience.

In the summer of 2000, I transferred command of CENTCOM to Army General Tommy Franks, and my thirty-nine-year career as a Marine ended.

BUT IT was not the final chapter of my CENTCOM story.

On Thursday, October 12, 2000, Al Qaeda terrorists suicide-bombed the American destroyer USS *Cole,* then refueling in the harbor of Aden, Yemen. Seventeen young Americans were killed, and the *Cole* was out of action for years. Somebody had to take the blame for allowing this tragedy to take place. The buck had to stop somewhere.

Some people looked at an obvious target, the ship's captain. But the folks who like to point fingers whenever bad things happen to our soldiers, Marines, airmen, or sailors wanted to hang somebody higher up. The finger landed on me.

Fine. That's where the buck stopped.

So when the chief of naval operations tried to pin the bombing on me, I wasn't surprised. He accused me of setting up the refueling station in Aden because I wanted to improve relations with Yemen.

That accusation brought on a call from Senator Warner of Virginia, the chairman of the Armed Services Committee. "Look," he said, "I'm getting hammered by my constituents. They're asking questions about the *Cole*. The American people need to learn the truth. We need to have the hearings. We've asked the Secretary of Defense and the top military to testify, but they will not appear. We can't get them to come. That leaves you, Tony." He apologized for that. "You need to come testify.

"It's going to be hard," he continued. "We're going to put you through a lot. . . . I'm going to put you through a lot."

"I'll do it," I said. It was the only right thing to do.

I was grilled by fourteen senators, three hours under klieg lights (a lot of press was there), with no break (not even to piss). And I got hammered with questions.

Before I went in, I'd decided I would take full responsibility for this thing. I was the CINC and everything that happened in my AOR was my responsibility. If I didn't, they'd dump it down on some poor son of a bitch like the captain of the ship. Somebody senior had to stand up. I remembered how hard they had hit General Peay for the Khobar Towers attack. When he tried to explain what happened during his testimony, they took it as waffling and not standing up to his responsibilities (which was far from the case). I was tired of admirals and generals trying to pass the buck. I was really upset with the chief of naval operations for trying to pin the blame on anybody else . . . it didn't matter who. And I was enraged at the Washington blame game.

So I decided, "What the hell. The buck stops here." And that's what I said in my testimony: "I was the commander in chief who made the decision that we would refuel in there," I told the senators. "I'm fine with that. If it was the wrong decision, you can hold me responsible for it.

"Now I'll give you the circumstances, I'll tell you what happened, and why I made the decision:

"Yes, it's true that I wanted to improve relations with Yemen, but that was not the reason we chose to refuel in Yemen. We chose to refuel there for operational and not diplomatic or political reasons. It was the only practical port for our naval component to refuel their ships.

"The Navy has rules about fuel levels on their ships," I explained. "In normal operations, they don't let that level go below fifty-one percent.

"Ships traveling out of the Mediterranean could of course refuel in the Persian Gulf, but in many cases ships didn't have enough capacity to get there without exceeding the fifty-one percent limit. That meant they had to find a refueling port between Suez and the Gulf. These were the possibilities: Djibouti, Eritrea, Jeddah, and Aden. That was it. Djibouti had been the Navy's refueling port, but it was now a no-go. Eritrea was out because of the war with Ethiopia. Jeddah was out because we'd just had the bombings in Saudi Arabia. So there was no other choice.

"We looked hard at Aden. The Navy went in and vetted it, inspected it, and cleared it; and the Navy component for CENTCOM had the responsibility for security. We refueled twenty-eight ships during my tenure as CINC, and all without incident.

"Yet, having said that, there's no getting around the risk. There is no risk-free place in that part of the world to refuel ships.

"If we're going to have people out there, if we're going to have people traveling around doing security assistance work, if we're going to have forces on the ground training and exercising, if we're going to have a presence out there day to day, responding to operations, in an environment that's really hostile and where people are out to get us, and they're watching our every move looking for an opportunity to hurt us, we're going to have times when our people are going to get hurt."

The senators walked out of that meeting satisfied with what I'd said; and it all ended there.

Later, to Tommy Franks's credit, he stepped up to the plate and said, "I agree with General Zinni's decision. I would have made the same one. It made military sense."

The CENTCOM experience taught me a lot about the world and the role of our great nation in it. We could make a difference if we were committed to stand up to our obligations, not only as the last remaining superpower, but also as the last beacon of hope for many people on this planet.

Forty years as a Marine taught me that the only place to be is in the center of the arena. You get knocked down out there and you make mistakes. But you also realize that it sure beats sitting in the grandstands criticizing those who have the guts to be out there. And every once in a while you can make a difference.

I adjusted, with some difficulty, to civilian life and retirement after four decades of service. I missed the Corps and the arena that gave me a tremendous sense of fulfillment. Little did I realize that another form of service awaited me.

CHAPTER SEVEN

WARRIOR PEACEMAKER

AFTER NEARLY FOUR DECADES in the United States Marine Corps, Tony Zinni found it hard to adjust to a different life. He knew he had to move on to another phase, yet months passed before the new phase happened. Until it did, he briefly tried the usual occupations open to retired generals—memberships on boards of directors, consulting on military and foreign policy matters, senior mentoring, teaching college courses, lecturing at military schools, speechmaking.

These early pursuits brought in a comfortable income; all of them were interesting, and a couple were personally rewarding. Despite these satisfactions, however, he knew something was missing. He was no longer taking part in the significant events he watched unfolding every day on the news. He had moved from the heart of the action to virtual irrelevance.

The media networks offered positions as an analyst and commentator; their offers were tempting—a chance to keep a hand in. But he rejected them, preferring not to be a military Monday-morning quarterback. He didn't want to be yet another retired general blathering on the screen about the state of the universe.

"I really believe that once you retire, you retire," he comments. "The way is forward, not back. So for me, I really felt that the worst thing I could do is try to semi hang on. I wanted to cut the cords and get on with a different life. Just put the old life aside."

The day he packed up his uniforms for good—a chore he had put off for months—was one of the bleakest of his life. The uniforms went into his attic; his sword went to his Marine officer son during his retirement ceremony. Yet this was a liberating pain; it was the opening he needed to finally accept that he had to move on.

About this time, wise counsel came from an old and respected Marine Corps friend, Paul VanRiper, a retired lieutenant general who had settled near Zinni's new home in Virginia:

"The best way to manage your time is to divide your life into thirds," he told Zinni. "One-third has to pay your mortgage, put food on the table, and cover whatever else you need to keep your household and family going. You're not that old"—Zinni retired in his late fifties—"so look at doing work that you're okay with, and brings home a decent paycheck.

"The second third comes from doing work you love, where the pay isn't all that important. You might get some compensation; but that's not the point. Whether these things bring in good money or not, this part of your life is about doing things you enjoy doing, things that excite you, inspire you. You can't wait to do more.

"The final third is about whatever you want to put back. It's work you do pro bono, because it's the right thing to do; you have an obligation to do it. You feel required to give the service to your country, or to institutions—like the Marine Corps—that you have a close affection for."

And that is exactly what Zinni tried to do.

After trying those various "normal" occupations open to retired generals, he moved on to more satisfying ways to pay the bills. He took care of the first third primarily by carefully choosing positions in businesses that had ethics, practices, and leadership of the highest caliber.

For the second third, he began teaching at William and Mary College. The pay wasn't great, but he loved the wonderful faculty, loved being around the students, loved teaching, and loved passing on his experience to another impressive generation.

Early in 2001, he was contacted by Professor Steven Spiegel, the director of the Institute on Global Conflict and Cooperation (IGCC) at the

University of California San Diego. The IGCC ran a series of workshops, sponsored by the Defense Department, that brought together prominent people from the Middle East to discuss arms control and security. Spiegel asked Zinni to join this effort as a consultant; and of course Zinni accepted. It was an opportunity to reconnect with the peacemaking and conflict resolution process that had grown into a significant part of his life during the second half of his Marine Corps service. A dream began to emerge.

At the end of July, he took part in the first of what would become several IGCC workshops. Held in Garmisch, Germany, it brought together an impressive group of serving and retired government officials and academics from Middle Eastern countries to discuss the peace process. Though, of course, Zinni had followed these issues when he was CINC at CENTCOM, and discussed them at length with regional leaders, he found himself gaining significant new insights.

And then for the third third—the "putting back" into the people and the institutions that were important to him—Zinni made sure he gave talks and classes at the Marine Corps University at Quantico, and at local high schools whenever the opportunity arose.

The thirds plan allowed Zinni to put some structure into the life of a retired general, but it did not yet solve the problem of filling what was still missing—some way to take positive part in significant events out in the world . . . without butting in. He was ready if he was needed and called.

The call came. And another.

The first, in the summer of 2001, was from his old friend and boss, and now Deputy Secretary of State, Richard Armitage: "Would you be interested in taking on a peace mission in Indonesia?"

This was followed a few weeks later by a second call from another State Department official: "Would you be interested in taking on a peace mission in the Middle East?"

THE WISE MEN

In Indonesia, a bloody dispute had been under way for twenty-five years between the national government and an independence movement in the

oil-rich province of Aceh on the northern tip of Sumatra. The call from
Armitage was an invitation to take part in a mission under the guidance
of the Henri Dunant Centre for Humanitarian Dialogue (HDC) in
Geneva, Switzerland.

The HDC realized a dream of Henri Dunant, the founder of the Red
Cross, to establish a humanitarian center devoted to conflict resolution
and mediation. It gave special attention to internal conflicts—problems
within and not between nations. The latter are normally best handled by
international organizations such as the UN or regional collectives of nations, but sovereign states get nervous when international bodies meddle
in what they take to be internal affairs—as in the case of rebellions or separatist movements. Such conflicts are probably best resolved by private organizations, which have no agenda and no ulterior interests.

Though Zinni was unfamiliar with Indonesia and its multitude of
troubles, and had never heard of Aceh or the HDC, he was eager to take
on the mission. This was interesting. It could add a significant new
angle of vision to what he already knew about peacemaking and conflict
resolution.

Tony Zinni:

*I learned long ago that finding new angles in peacemaking really matters,
because—paradoxically—each peacemaking situation is unique. No matter
how much experience you have, each conflict brings its own unique requirements. You have to develop a process distinctive to it. Sure, you can
maybe call on or modify previous experiences, but there are no models, for-
mulas, or formats that will necessarily help you reach your goals.*

*A lot of people think you can know exactly how to go about the process
and become predictive. I learned you can't. You can't take some model off
the shelf and hammer it to fit. It doesn't work that way. What happens is
this: Gaining more experiences builds up your experience base and your understanding of the possibilities, and that shows you how to combine, mix-
match, develop, and modify from past experiences to fit the unique situation
you're in. Experience doesn't give you any big answers. It shows you how to
be creative.*

• • •

HE TALKED over the mission at a meeting with Armitage and Karen Brooks, a member of the National Security Council. There he learned that the State Department and the NSC had come up with an innovative idea to create a new element in negotiations: a group of Wise Men—people of significant international stature, senior diplomats and military men—who would stand above the negotiating process and advise all sides.

In tough negotiations, mediators always get dragged into the process. They become viewed as biased by one or both sides, or sometimes become too deeply involved in contentious issues to "step above" the heated exchanges. No matter how hard mediators try to maintain and protect their neutrality and objectivity, both sides transfer fears and hopes onto them, attack them, and blame them. It always happens.

The function of the Wise Men was not to change the process but to back it up. If the mediators were getting hit by stones from all sides, they lived with it, rolled up their sleeves, waded into the mud, and did the dirty work. The Wise Men stood above it all, there to be called on by both sides or by the mediators for advice, recommendations, consultation, or intervention.

The HDC jumped at the idea.

At that point, they had chosen three Wise Men for the Indonesia mission—Surin Pitsuwan, a retired Thai Foreign Minister; Budamir Loncur, a retired Yugoslav Foreign Minister; and Lord Eric Avebury, a Member of the British House of Lords. They now wanted a fourth, an American with military stature—someone with peacekeeping experience, who could handle issues such as how to monitor mechanisms and observers on the ground, and who could talk to the Indonesian military—who everyone thought would be the toughest group to bring into the peace process. Zinni was the obvious choice.

"This is great!" Zinni told Armitage and Brooks. "It's just the kind of thing I want to do." He agreed to take on the mission with State Department support, but only as an unpaid private citizen working with the HDC, thus ensuring his independence.

That set the machinery moving.

State Department briefs followed, detailing the history of the struggle, current intelligence about what was happening on the ground, the state of the negotiations, the U.S. position on the issues, and background on the HDC.

Zinni followed up on that by reading everything he could find on Aceh online and from local bookstores and libraries. He was surprised at the amount of information that was out there:

Indonesia is unique among nations. For one thing, it's *big*. It spreads across thousands of islands, some of them among the largest in the world, that cover thousands of miles from east to west and many time zones. It's extremely diverse in geography, population, and ethnic identity. In religion it's predominantly Muslim (usually of a moderate kind), but there are also many Buddhists. All of these factors would make the country very difficult to govern; but add to that corruption, dictatorships, all kinds of divisive political issues, and a blanketing atmosphere of turmoil; and further add to that internal struggles with provinces in distant parts of the country—like East Timor (now independent), Papua New Guinea, and Aceh—that want to break away and gain independence; and you have a nation that's never far from catastrophic fission.

In spite of the confusion and diversity, the political scene in Indonesia is surprisingly straightforward—more or less evenly divided between hardliners and moderates. On the issue of separatism, the moderates wished to end the struggles through peaceful negotiations that would eventually allow areas such as Aceh some freedom and autonomy from the central government. The hard-liners—including much of the military*—would have none of that, and preferred an increased crackdown to end the conflict once and for all. Already, the military and police operations in response to the uprising had turned the beautiful and resource-rich province into a battle zone.

The fight for independence had been led by the Free Aceh Movement, or GAM, directed by its government in exile in Stockholm, Sweden. Now an agreement had been reached to conduct negotiations between them and the government, with the HDC as mediator.

* Though even the military has its complement of moderates.

The United States had taken a carefully moderate position in these negotiations. That is, it supported a resolution of the problem within the context of the state of Indonesia. In the U.S. view, the independence of Aceh had to be off the table. The U.S. was not going to support a breaking up of that nation. By the same token, they sent a strong message to the Jakarta government: "You've got to do better for the people of Aceh. They are in a special situation and deserve special treatment. You have to find a reasonable way to give them that."

There were several compelling reasons for the American position; but the most compelling was practical: Indonesia is fragile. The U.S. didn't want to see it fragment, and create a constellation of potentially nonviable states. God knows what could happen if these failed or incapable states started harboring extremist movements.

There was a second, no less practical reason: Independence movements provoked governments to take a hard-line approach, and this almost inevitably ended in bloodshed. If ways could be found to moderate demands for independence, while delivering many of the material benefits that independence promises, and if all this was coupled with moderation of the central government's hard-line approach, then everybody got a win. But getting there involved a lot of ifs.

Zinni was not involved in developing the U.S. government position in the Aceh-Indonesia conflict, nor was it his place to support or oppose it during the negotiations. His place, as he saw it, was to find a road to peace.

When I became involved with the HDC, I was clear up front to all parties in the negotiations: I'm not making judgments here, I'm not here to judge. I'm here to help you resolve this fight peacefully. My government's position is clear; that's what it is. But I am not part of the government in this respect; and it's not my job to come in and sell my government's line. I don't have a line. I don't have a position.

I learned a long time ago that a negotiator has to be nonjudgmental.

Later that year, when I became involved in trying to mediate the Israeli-Palestinian dispute, I was immediately hit from both sides to take a position. There was no way I could do that.

Who's more right? The Israelis? The Palestinians? Who has greater justice on their side? Who has suffered more? How can anyone measure these things? And even if you could, how could you shape these measurements into the perfect balance that will result in a peaceful settlement?

As a mediator, you reach peace by finding a position that both sides can agree to and practice on the ground. We'll never get there by trying to determine which side is more righteous or "deserving" than the other. It's important to speak out about unacceptable actions, but your task is to help the parties find a lasting solution that all can live with over time.

So when Israeli Prime Minister Ariel Sharon asked me, "How do you weigh this issue? Where do you put the weight in terms of this situation?," I said:

"I don't do that."

Sharon did not reply. He didn't like the answer.

"I don't make judgments," I continued. "There are things that are unacceptable to me, such as terrorist acts where innocents are killed. I reject that. I condemn those things. But in the process of negotiation, the mediator can't allow himself to be put in a position where he starts to form or make judgments. I am here to facilitate both sides finding a workable solution to this situation. One that they and their children can live with."

Obviously, judgments will inevitably creep into your thinking; but you have to resist them. You have to be really hard on yourself and reject taking any positions that come out of these judgments.

And even when you don't form judgments, you're still going to get hit by both sides.

IN MID-JULY, Zinni flew to Geneva for his introduction to the HDC staff and his first meeting with the Indonesian government and GAM officials.

The Centre was located at a mansion on the lake, Henri Dunant's former home, and was a truly international organization, receiving support from private donations from several countries. Its small staff of about twenty (most of them young) came from all over the world. The director and chief negotiator, Martin Griffiths, was a former foreign service officer in the United Kingdom who had worked with the UN in Africa and elsewhere. Griffiths had a wealth of experience in peacekeeping and diplomatic missions. His deputy, a Canadian named Andrew Marshall, had long experience working with NGOs and the UN in third world nations. Both of these men impressed Zinni.

The HDC had brought in other experts in conflict resolution and negotiation as well, but they had also come up with a really innovative idea: They brought in "civil society" to "speak for the people."

At this point, the government said, "Wait a minute, *we* speak for the people."

And the GAM said, "No way. *We* speak for the people."

But the HDC said, "Why not let the people speak for themselves?"

And so they communicated with village leaders, civic leaders, and other prominent people in the community to get their views. What the "people" had to say often shocked everybody. They had a plague-on-both-your-houses attitude: The sentiment often was that neither the government nor GAM had done right by them. This strong sentiment eventually helped bring about an agreement.

When Zinni arrived in Geneva, he learned that the negotiations had proved difficult so far, with both sides feeling that they were expected to give up more than they were getting.

For the government representatives—moderates—it was an extremely high-risk situation. If the special autonomy status they were offering Aceh worked, fine. But if it didn't, or if the negotiations failed, or if the special autonomy offer set a precedent and other provinces demanded a similar status, they knew they had dug themselves into a deep and escape-proof hole.

For the GAM, who had been fighting for independence for decades, special autonomy presented them with a serious crisis. Accepting it meant abandoning their struggle for full independence.

Divided views on these issues within the government and GAM further complicated the negotiations.

Despite the problems and obstacles, Zinni came away from this first meeting greatly encouraged. "This thing can work," he said to himself. "Both sides are sincerely committed to finding a peaceful solution, and the first-rate HDC staff is dogged in its determination to bring that about."

He was ready to plunge back in—when he got another call that changed his life. For the moment, Aceh would have to be put on the back burner . . . though he would return to it later.

THE MIDDLE EAST PEACE PROCESS

The call came from Assistant Secretary of State Bill Burns, a friend from Zinni's time at CENTCOM, a few weeks after he returned from Geneva. "Could you meet me for lunch to discuss a project that's brewing?" Burns asked. Zinni's answer, of course, was yes.

Tom Clancy: Tony Zinni takes the story the rest of the way.

Burns, an Arabic speaker and Middle East expert, was head of the Near East Affairs Bureau at State. When I was at CENTCOM, he had been U.S. ambassador to Jordan—and one of our finest ambassadors in the region (greatly trusted by King Hussein and later by King Abdullah).

We lunched on August 27, 2001, at a Washington restaurant. There, my friend dropped a bomb: The Bush administration was about to sail against the conventional wisdom and seriously attempt to reengage in the Middle East peace process.

According to that wisdom, the Bush White House wanted to distance themselves from the Mideast snakepit. In 2000, the Clinton administration had failed to bring negotiations at Camp David between Yasser Arafat (the Palestinian leader) and Ehud Barak (the Israeli Prime Minister) to a successful conclusion. They had no desire to repeat that failure . . . or to suffer the resulting disastrous political fallout.

After the Camp David meetings broke down, the situation in the Mideast crashed. Barak lost his job and was replaced by Ariel Sharon; and Clinton failed to get the process back on track during the last days of his presidency. In September 2000, the Second Intifada reignited the cycles of violence that had plagued the region before the series of talks begun in the late '90s had raised expectations.

As Burns and I continued our conversation, I came to understand that the President's position had not in fact greatly changed; he was still understandably cautious. The inspiration for this new initiative, I gathered, was coming from Colin Powell, the Secretary of State, who clearly saw that it was critical for the United States to reengage. He was supported in this initiative by a core of senior people, like Bill Burns, at the State Department.

The Secretary had taken his concerns to the President, who had approved cautious and tentative moves at a very low level. (We were then only a few days from the 9/11 terrorist attacks, which would change everything.)

In the recent past, the American approach had been to send high-visibility special envoys to mediate between the Israelis and Palestinians, with attendant media attention and inflated expectations. After the collapse of the Clinton-sponsored peace talks, former Senator George Mitchell had traveled to Israel with a political plan, and CIA Director George Tenet had followed with a security plan.

Tenet's aim was to bring the security situation on the ground back to where it was in September 2000, at the beginning of the Second Intifada. The Israelis would pull out of the areas they had occupied since then, they would move checkpoints, and the Palestinian workers would come back into Israel. For their part, the Palestinians would crack down on extremists, make arrests, and confiscate weapons.

Once everything had been restored to the September 2000 position, the two parties could then move forward on Mitchell's more political plan, which was designed to build confidence and move forward on political issues such as freezing the settlements the Israelis had been building on the West Bank and in Gaza. Eventually, they'd return to final status issues, like the status of Jerusalem, the right of return, the final status of the settlements . . . all of the issues on which President Clinton, Barak, and Arafat had locked horns at Camp David.

Both Israelis and Palestinians had "agreed" to these proposals "in principle," but implementing them had gone nowhere. As I was to learn, you could paper the walls with agreements. Getting them implemented on the ground was another matter; both sides disregarded them.

This time the approach was going to be softer and less visible. There would be no special envoy. Ambassador Burns was going to quietly run the

mediation mission out of his own shop. Since he had to run the whole region, not just this one process, he was looking for someone he knew and
trusted, with knowledge, experience, stature, and solid personal relationships in the region, who would become his semiofficial assistant, working closely with him and filling in when he had to turn his attention
elsewhere. This person would become a part-time right hand, who could
take over and oversee the process when he was away.

The goal, Burns went on to explain, was to reengage without making a
big deal of it. Everyone knew what needed to be done and where we
needed to go; and the Mitchell and Tenet plans already went a long way
toward spelling all this out (as did the various agreements, near agreements, and accords already reached in Madrid, Oslo, and elsewhere).
There was no need to create another big plan or to launch another big effort. What needed to be done was already out there. It had to be won or
lost on the ground.

Burns and Powell wanted a few people to go over there and work out
with the two parties how to actually structure the existing agreements, and
to find the best way to set these up and implement them. These people
would start up the process, feel it out, and then oversee it.

What I think Burns had in mind for me was to start the initial movement; and then, as the process moved along, if a bigger player was
needed in there to close deals or whatever, he would come and take the
lead. When he was not able to be present, but they still needed somebody with clout who could ride herd on this thing, then I would fill in
for him.

"Are you willing to take this on?" he asked.

How could I not be excited? This was a job worth doing. Even if nothing lasting came of it—which was all too likely.

"Great!" I told him. "I'm not real familiar with all the issues or many of
the people involved in this thing; but I'd really love to get involved in it."

"I'd love to see you involved," he said. "Let's see what we can do to make
it happen."

And he continued: "What I'm talking about is a kind of unusual setup
here at State. We'll have to figure out how we structure our arrangement."

"Well, look," I said, "I have some thoughts on that. First of all, I don't want to be paid for this thing. That way I can keep some measure of independence. I want to be able to do what I have to do, say what I have to say, and not feel that somebody's going to accuse me of doing this for gain.

"Second, I don't want a title. I don't want to be called envoy or anything else.

"Third, we ought to keep this low-key. There shouldn't be a lot of publicity about me doing this. I'm just a part-time special assistant who happens to be there with you.

"Let's absolutely do this thing. But let's do it with no pay, no title, no press, no media attention, and no making a big deal of it."

He agreed that was the best arrangement. "I'll take these ideas to Secretary Powell and see what he says."

"Great," I said.

DAYS PASSED. I waited restlessly for Bill Burns's call, which would take us to the next step. I was very eager to find out my actual function and the nature of my mission—all still unclear.

As I waited, I did my usual thing when I took on something new; I read everything about the Israeli-Palestinian problem that I could get my hands on.

During the same period, I worked with Bill Burns's people to structure my official relationship with the State Department. The lawyers drew up a contract. It turned out that even a no-pay employee is still bound by conflict-of-interest and ethics rules, which rightfully limited other things I might have done.

I have to confess that my refusal to take pay did not totally spring from altruistic motives, such as my wish for independence, or from my hope to be a wonderful servant of the nation (though these motives were important). This job was going to be part-time; and I was involved in other work that brought in paychecks. If I accepted pay from State, I'd have to give up these other positions. The ethics and conflict-of-interest rules still prevented me from taking on certain jobs; and everything I did had to be vetted and cleared by the government and the State Department. Was it worth it? Absolutely.

. . .

TWO WEEKS after my initial meeting with Bill Burns, on September 11, 2001, the world changed drastically.

In the aftermath of the terrorist attacks, the Bush administration looked anew at reengagement in the peace process. Their approach changed, and expanded. According to Ambassador Burns, the rate of these changes was accelerating. He couldn't be specific, but the nature of the peace initiative was no longer what we had discussed. I sensed that my own part in all this was also changing.

On the twenty-third of October, I attended a series of briefs at the State Department on the background of the peace process and an update on the current situation; and I was instructed to stay ready to travel quickly after the design of my mission was firmed up. How exactly it was going to be firmed up was still not clear to me.

On November 10, 2001, President Bush delivered a historic speech before the UN General Assembly in which he committed to the establishment of a Palestinian state—the first time a President of the United States had done that. The objective of the peace process, he told the delegates, is two states, Israel and Palestine, living side by side. This was a very controversial and bold statement.

I was very impressed. The reengagement effort we were about to start promised to be more momentous than I had first thought.

The President's speech was to be followed by a major speech from Secretary Powell on the nineteenth at the University of Louisville that would add specifics to the President's general principles.

Shortly before the Louisville event, Ambassador Burns called to tell me that Powell's remarks would trigger our departure for Israel, though he couldn't actually tell me what this meant for me and what we were going to do. . . . He was not keeping this from me; he truly didn't know the answer. All he—or anybody—did know was that Powell's speech would be the defining moment; yet right up to the eleventh hour, nobody was sure what the moment would define.

The day before the speech, Burns faxed me a rough copy of the speech, but with a caveat attached: These pages are not yet final—but they are close.

I read the pages, and, bang!, I got knocked off my feet.

"Holy cow," I said to myself. "There's a big piece in this thing about me: I've got a big new title now! I'm the Special Advisor to the Secretary of State for the Middle East! So much for all our hopes about not making a big deal of my mission. There goes our no-title and no-publicity agreement." (They kept my no-pay arrangement.)

Suddenly, for all practical purposes I'd become another special envoy. Powell had inflated my position into something I didn't want it to be—not because I am all that modest, but because I wasn't convinced it would work (an opinion later justified by events). On the other hand, I was excited to learn that the administration's level of commitment and involvement had moved way up. I really liked it that Secretary Powell had showed what was called the path: We'd try to put the Tenet and Mitchell plans in play on the ground, and this, we hoped, would lead to the final status agreement, and then finally to the Palestinian state. We now had a horizon. The peace process was beginning to look promising.

The speech generated a lot of media excitement; my phone rang off the hook; and there was nothing I could tell anybody. I just didn't know any answers. What was my job?

ON NOVEMBER 21, I visited the State Department for further briefings and administrative processing in preparation for my initial trip, scheduled for the twenty-fifth; but my most important business at Foggy Bottom that day was the marching orders I got from Secretary Powell and Deputy Secretary Armitage. They gave me tremendous latitude:

My mission was to achieve an immediate cease-fire in place, to be followed by implementation of the Tenet and Mitchell plans. They wanted these to be accepted on the ground rather than just in principle. How I did it was up to me. I was expected to use my head, and my own initiative.

"We don't like to lose," Secretary Powell told me. "We like to win. You get out there and make it happen, use your judgment. You've got a lot of latitude, a lot of freedom in action. But don't hesitate to pick up that phone and call me directly if you need something."

It was gratifying to hear the Secretary express such personal confidence in me. Yet taking on that kind of responsibility always makes you a little tense. I knew what kind of burden had fallen on me.

Ambassador Burns would travel out with me on the first part of the trip; and Aaron Miller would be assigned to assist me—a great choice.

Miller was the State Department specialist on the Middle East peace process. Years before, he had joined the Department as a historian, but somehow the peace process itself had captured him. It became his life. His total personal commitment was to bring peace to the region. In time, as the specialist, he'd worked for all the secretaries of state and presidents, becoming over the years the government's corporate memory on that subject.* He knows everybody, and he's known by everybody. He knows every issue, every event, and every betrayal. Nothing in that part of the world stays hidden from Aaron Miller.

In Israel, he was involved in everything I did, and was totally there for me—without in any way trying to impose his thinking or his way of doing things. He provided background, recommendations, support, ideas; and then encouraged me to add my own thinking. "We need fresh thinking," he explained. "A lot of people in this business think they know how to do it, and they'll never skip an opportunity to pass on their wisdom. But the truth is, no ideas have worked so far. So fire at will, and find something new."

He and I became very close; it was just a wonderful fit of two different personalities. He was intense and full of nervous energy. While I'm not exactly easygoing, I try to be more relaxed and good-humored at work. He had started out as a liberal academic, and had never experienced a military guy before we met. I was a complete alien to his country. Yet he found that fascinating, and I found him fascinating; and so we somehow complemented one another. When he was down, I could pick him up; when

---

* He has recently left the State Department, and now heads Seeds of Peace, an organization that brings young Palestinians and Israeli kids together.

I was down, he'd pick me up. And in the end, our friendship really helped the team.

EARLY ON the twenty-first, Secretary Powell, Bill Burns, and I traveled to the White House to brief President Bush, Vice President Cheney, and National Security Advisor Rice.

When the president asked me about my mission—essentially to see how I understood what I was supposed to do—I let him know that I wanted to get the Tenet and Mitchell plans into play. This seemed to satisfy him. He wished me luck and told me he appreciated my doing this for the country. My sense was that he was giving this thing his blessing, but from a distance; this was Colin Powell's baby. Still, we were good to go, and that was enough for me.

AS I prepared to leave for Israel, I tried to keep a low profile and avoid distractions—such as encounters with the press. Better to leave the press interaction to the State Department. This caused resentment in the media and resulted in minor disruptions when some of the media retaliated; but I knew public diplomacy on my part would be counterproductive.

After the struggle to make the U.S. Constitution had been won, James Madison remarked that the twenty representatives who'd put it together had made an agreement to hold the process in confidence and not talk to the press. If that had not been done, he went on to say, if the fathers had failed to keep the process private and it had become naked to the media and the scrutiny of the public, we would never have had a Constitution.

If every step of the way, every consideration, every possibility, every proposal, every tentative glimmer of an idea, every thought put on the table suddenly got into the open where it could be endlessly analyzed or attacked or mauled by the press (and it didn't matter which press—Al Jazeera, the *New York Times,* the *Jerusalem Post,* the *Guardian,* the *Wall Street Journal*), we'd never have moved anywhere. You can't go forward in an emotional, involved, complex process like the Middle East peace process if the spotlight is on you.

Public diplomacy and transparency are a good thing. But these don't work well in some places, under some circumstances, and with some issues. Often a process hits critical moments when private negotiations are necessary to work through sensitive issues or proposals. If these are made public every inch of the way, they can make it impossible for the parties to explore and develop possibilities. This was clearly one of those places.

As I prepared to take on the peace mission, I sounded out friends who were familiar with the Israeli-Palestinian nightmare, looking for advice and insights. Their predictions were gloomy: "You know, you ought to really think about this before you sign on to it. The chances of this thing going south are right up there with night following day. And when that happens, you're going to be saddled with the failure." Even the people from the State Department who solicited me for the job kept asking me: "Are you out of your mind? Do you really want to be actually stuck with this?" . . . Thoughts that were jokingly echoed by Rich Armitage: "Are you crazy?" he asked. I knew, though, that he appreciated my willingness to do this. One reason I was excited about this mission was the chance to work for Rich and Secretary Powell once again. These two great men have always been inspirations for me.

How could I not look hard at the slim chances of success? Yet I also had to face myself and my own conscience. "It's not this or that failure that matters," I told myself. "You know, if you save one life, you have to do it. But more important, if there's even a point one percent chance of success, you've got to try. You can't give up trying in these situations."

The number of times you're successful in these mediations is low. It's like baseball. You get a hit every third time up, you're in the Hall of Fame. You have to answer your country's call to service regardless of personal interests or the likelihood of success.

I had one other strong motivation—Colin Powell's personal commitment. If he was ready to put his ass on the line for this, then I was glad to be part of it.

I have a tremendous respect for Secretary Powell. I don't know many people with greater honor, integrity, and ethics. The distinction between

right and wrong is not a trivial thing with him. I have personally seen
Colin Powell take actions that in no way benefit him, actions where the
personal and political risks are high, actions that calculating people or
those looking at their own personal benefit would avoid. He does them
anyway, without calling attention to himself, because they're the right
things to do.

Powell was not standing back and letting the peace process take its
course. He was pushing it. It wasn't popular. It wasn't politically expedient. Within the administration, he had enemies. I learned that the Defense Department opposed my selection for this mission. While I was at
CENTCOM, I had disagreed with positions taken by many policymakers
there; and now I had few friends at the Pentagon. Powell knew this, yet
pushed on with what he felt was right.

ON NOVEMBER 25, 2001, Bill, Aaron, and I departed for Israel.

ROUND ONE

Our plane touched down at Ben-Gurion Airport in Tel Aviv on the evening
of November 26.

I spent the first night getting briefings from the U.S. Embassy in Tel
Aviv and the U.S. Consulate in Jerusalem (which was our official point of
contact with the Palestinians).

In the past, friction had developed between these two posts. Embassies
tend to get "clientitis," which meant that their staffs, if they're not careful, begin to take the side of locals they see and live with day to day.

Fortunately, when I came to Israel we were blessed with two of our best
diplomats—Dan Kurtzer and Ron Schlicher—running the embassy and
the Jerusalem consulate. Kurtzer, our ambassador to Israel, is absolutely
one of the finest diplomats we have ever created in the United States. He
had been ambassador to Egypt when I was at CENTCOM, so I knew him
well. In Jerusalem, we had Ron Schlicher, a career diplomat with extensive experience in the Middle East and in the Arab world, whom I had not
met, but his reputation was splendid.

These two brilliant professionals made it work and made their people cooperate. Although they both had strong personal feelings on the issues, they made it absolutely clear that their job was to promote the interests of the United States of America, and they made it equally clear that their first and foremost priority at that moment was to cooperate and find a peaceful resolution to the calamitous conflict between the Israelis and the Palestinians. These attitudes took hold of everybody in the embassy and the consulate. And it was the force of their leadership that made it work.

THE INITIAL BRIEFS (and press reports) painted a bleak picture. No surprises here. The level of violence had steadily increased since the Second Intifada had begun in September 2000. All trust and confidence between the parties had evaporated, and peace talks were almost nonexistent. For the Israelis, the first priority was security, and in particular stopping the suicide attacks from extremist groups. Once that goal was achieved, they might begin negotiations and consider making concessions. For the Palestinians, the first priority was political commitment by the Israelis to Palestinian statehood, and removal of all Israeli troops from their territories. The gap between these views was huge.

The only ongoing talks were in the Trilateral Committee meetings. This committee—consisting of security experts from Israel, Palestine, and the U.S.—was set up by George Tenet to deal with security coordination and de-confliction issues (that is, where forces rubbed up against one another). Since it was then the only point of engagement between the two parties, it seemed to be the best venue for any attempt to get the Tenet plan into effect on the ground and a cease-fire in place.

AT THE END of the day, I retired to the King David Hotel in Jerusalem, where we set up our headquarters and living spaces. Because 9/11 and the Intifada had dried up tourism, there was very little occupancy. We set up in one wing of the hotel. My suite, which I used as office and living quarters, was at a corner that overlooked the Old City. It was a beautiful setting, a couple of floors up.

As I hit the sack after a long and exhausting first day of travel and briefs, dark thoughts swirled through my mind.

The task ahead was daunting. I knew I had a lot to learn about the situation, the personalities, the issues, but I couldn't afford to take a lot of time to get up to speed, while at the same time getting the negotiations started and a process moving. I had to hit the ground running. Aaron Miller, Bill Burns, and the others on the team were certainly available with their considerable experience, but much of the responsibility still weighed on me. Expectations were already raised, people had begun to hope again; I didn't want to see the momentum or the hope fade. Progress had to be evident right off the bat.

I had an additional gut feeling that we were going to get heavy pressure from the terrorists and extremists, like Hamas and Islamic Jihad. According to our own and Israeli intelligence, the pattern with these groups was to pick up the level of violence whenever negotiations looked like they were making progress. Inevitably, the violence would box in the mediation effort. The Israelis would retaliate against the perpetrators of the violence. The Palestinians would hit back. And everybody would break off from the negotiations—always the goal of the extremist groups. So I expected that they would come at this one with a vengeance and would hit with a lot of violent events. If I was right, it meant we would have a very limited time frame in which to make progress. How much time depended on our ability to operate through the violence . . . or, better, to prevent violent events, catch a break, and get something done before the violence overshadowed our efforts. Unless I was very off the mark, we were going to be taking a roller-coaster ride . . . whipping from crisis to hope over and over again.

Unfortunately, I couldn't have been more right. When the violence came, it was horrific. It eventually brought an end to the negotiations.

Hamas and Islamic Jihad are committed to the destruction of the State of Israel. Since neither of them, in my view, seriously buys the two-state solution, it's hopeless to think they will compromise. With them, it's all or nothing. That means they will simply continue to generate destructive violence to punish the Israelis and block any kind of peaceful resolution and compromise.

Their history is interesting: When Hamas was initially organized, it was encouraged by the Israelis as a counter to the PLO. It later took a more radical turn and now gets support from Iran, Syria, and elsewhere (Iraq, for example, before the fall of Saddam Hussein). When Islamic Jihad emerged, it was even more religiously fanatic, but just as skilled in the evil arts. It has never quite had the same clout as Hamas, however. Hamas is the big player. It is much better organized, has strong tentacles in the Palestinian population (cleverly put in play by charitable organizations), and has a powerful political wing. Hamas has much better reconnaissance than Islamic Jihad's; and their attacks are far more sophisticated and achieve much greater effect, with far greater casualties. (They were responsible for the Passover bombing and all the major bus bombings—blowing up busloads of school kids, for example.) Their attacks strike right at the heart and soul of the Israelis. They really know how to jam the blade home.

Other Palestinian extremists can probably be handled. But Hamas is another thing. It would almost certainly take a civil war in Palestine to break their back—assuming they didn't win the war.

In talks with mediators, the Palestinians will always press for a cease-fire and a compromise with Hamas. I don't see it. It would be great if Hamas actually agreed to all that, and meant it; but it's hard to see how they'd square their objectives with a compromise.

Even if they bought into a cease-fire, I'd be suspicious that it was just an attempt to regroup and rearm. And of course, as they went about doing that, the Israelis (whose intelligence is excellent) would find out about it and strike. The case would then be made that the Israelis had struck for no reason . . . and so on. The spiral of violence would start again.

THE FIRST full day was scheduled for meetings with the Israelis. To begin the day, Prime Minister Ariel Sharon had laid on a helicopter tour, highlighted by his personal perspective on the geography and situation on the ground. This was to be followed by a series of briefs that would last well into the evening.

Some of my State Department advisers had reservations about this, on the grounds that the Palestinians might accuse us of letting Sharon co-opt the agenda; but I told them I could handle any attempt to manage my views. And if the Palestinians wanted to take me on a similar tour, they were welcome to invite me. I thought it was better to be open and transparent with both sides . . . and not tight-assed and overcautious.

Sharon's tour gave me a strong sense of the land of Israel. We saw all the major sites—Bethlehem, Nazareth, the Jordan River, the Dead Sea, the Sea of Galilee. We flew down to look at Sharon's farm in the south. We flew up to the Golan Heights, stopped at a military position, and talked with their people.

What was most interesting that day was Sharon's own take on all this. He was a battle-tested soldier (1967, 1973), a farmer deeply attached to his land, and an Israeli convinced of his birthright, as well as a wily politician. His running dialogue during the trip came from all of those perspectives. He stressed security issues in relation to the terrain, the way any soldier would to another soldier. But there was open joy and pride in his voice as he dwelled lovingly on the agricultural aspects of the panorama that unfolded below us. And there was a similar joy and pride as he pointed out sites of historical significance to Israelis—ruins from Roman times and earlier.

"Look at those terraces up there in the rocks," he'd exclaim with a simple passion that was very touching. "My ancestors built those thousands of years ago!" Or: "Look at this piece of terrain. You're a military man. If we don't control that, we're vulnerable." Or: "Look at this land. It was desert. Look what Israel has done here. We have greened it. Look at the orchards. Look at the fruit we produce. Look at those beautiful cattle down there."

These three elements—soldier, farmer, Jewish roots—really sum up the man. Everything he is flows from these. His commitment to them is passionate and total. The man is committed with his entire soul to the land he'd grown up in: "We have returned from the Diaspora. This is our land, this is our birthright, this is our history."

Before I met him, I was led to expect that I was going to run into some kind of big bully soldier. That characterization does not exactly fit. He is certainly a hard guy, who grew up in a tough environment—direct, frank, blunt, tells you right out what he wants to say to you, doesn't try to twist words (he's no slick politician)—but he never tried to bully me. What you see is what you get, that's the way he is. If he couldn't do something— make some concession he didn't want to make—he wouldn't weasel around the issue. He'd just say no. Unfortunately, I had the feeling that when we got down the road, when the tough concessions would be nec- essary, I couldn't see him making the kind of concessions some of his predecessors had offered.

As long as I was in Israel, Sharon never stopped trying to get the read of me; or to pry judgments and opinions out of me; and I think he was very frustrated when I didn't show him any of that. He simply couldn't under- stand how anyone could not see what was obvious to him. To him, I think, you have to judge, you have to have opinions. It goes with being commit- ted the way he's committed.

From my angle, any judgment I expressed would close off the other side; and I couldn't allow that to happen. Clearly every thing I said, or al- legedly said, would be in the press the next day. Leaks from both sides were more like deluges. Though the two of us got along together, there was always an underlying tension between us.

Toward the end of the flight, a call came over the radio: A shooting had occurred in the small northern Israeli town of Afula. We immediately changed course and headed up there. Reports confirmed that a pair of Palestinian gunmen had opened up in the town's marketplace, killing a pregnant Israeli woman. Several other Israelis were wounded, and the two gunmen were dead.

When we arrived overhead, we could see the security forces and med- ical personnel busily taking control of the scene. We hovered for a time, taking it all in, and then flew back to Jerusalem.

Later, I got a fuller account of the story—which leaves lots of unan- swered questions. Earlier that day, as a good faith gesture at the start of my mission, the Israelis had taken down a checkpoint near Afula so the Pales- tinians could have an easier time moving about. The gunmen had obviously taken advantage of this opening to launch their terrorist attack. The big question is: Was the attack a deliberately planned provocation aimed at un- dermining the peace process? Or was it—as the Palestinians later claimed—

simply a revenge killing? The Israeli military had recently killed a relative of the gunmen; the gunmen shot up the marketplace in retaliation.

Wherever the truth lay, this was clearly one of those violent incidents that tempted me to lose hope in the peace process. I knew I could forget about having a quiet start to my mission. My sense that this would be a roller-coaster trip from crisis to hope and back to crisis was proving right. Even though both sides had made encouraging statements about cooperating with my mission, I had to wonder how much any of that counted now that a violent event had already cast a black shadow over the first full day.

THE REST of the day consisted of meetings and briefings with Prime Minister Sharon, Foreign Minister Shimon Peres, Defense Minister Ben Eliezer, and Chief of the Israeli Defense Force Shaul Mofaz.*

This brought me up against a complicated situation: At that time, the Israeli government was a unity government, a coalition government . . . which means in practice that it was a divided government. Sharon was from Likud, the party which had the largest number of seats in the Knesset, while Peres and Ben Eliezer were from Labor, the chief opposition party. It was not an easy situation to handle. "Who can actually speak for Israel?" I had to ask myself.

Sharon cut through this confusion: "I'm the only one who can speak for this government," he told me.

It was kind of strange to an American who is used to cabinet ministers who can speak for their boss. But I accepted this condition. It was their system, not ours.

The others I met with were far from unhelpful, even if somewhat marginalized by Sharon. Everyone had a lot of experience in the nitty-gritty of working with the Palestinians, and they all came through with powerful insights and solid advice.

Though Mofaz had a reputation as a tough hard-liner, he was a quiet, thoughtful man, and not immovable, nor totally unsympathetic to the

---

* I'd known Mofaz since 1982, when I was an instructor at the Marine Corps Command and Staff College and he was a student there.

Palestinians. When I met him that afternoon, he made it clear that he wanted to be cooperative, that he wanted me to succeed, and that he did not believe there was a military solution to the problem.

Later, he and I spent a lot of time together, just talking, and the two of us came to a good appreciation of our positions. I understood there was no way he would compromise on security; but within that boundary, he understood that the Israelis would have to give up some things . . . without—again—taking any security risks. He was aware there was never going to be a total and lasting military defeat of the Palestinians, so something had to be arranged to make the peace agreements go right. Yet he also made it clear that he did what he had to do out there in the field, even if it was hard and people got hurt.

PERES GAVE me valuable counsel on how my mission might proceed and on the possibilities that could develop. In these early days of my mission, he was the one person who gained my complete respect as I worked through the peace process.

I will never forget his advice:

"General Zinni," he told me, "you're going to find three kinds of people in this business.

"First, you're going to find the righteous. Don't waste your time with them. You'll find them on both sides, and they're always going to appeal to the righteousness of their cause.

"You're never going to get anywhere with people like that. There's no negotiating with righteousness. Yes, it's their right to believe what they believe. But you're not going to change them. They interpret facts from their religious angle, and they ignore any facts that don't support that.

"The second group you're going to meet," he went on, "are the collectors of arguments, the debaters. You see them on TV with all the talking heads. They're going to outdebate the other guy and score points. But where making real progress toward peace is concerned, these people are useless. If you want to get into the debate for academic purposes, that's fine. But it serves no other purpose.

"The third group you're going to meet are the ones that count. These are the ones who want to figure out a solution on the ground. These are the ones who ask themselves over and over: 'How the hell are we going to make this ghastly situation work and get out of this terrible nightmare?'

"Focus on them," he said, "and focus on what needs to be done, and then get it done."

It was the best advice I got in Israel.

The other briefs were devoted to the security situation—the overriding issue, in the Israeli view. Their first order of business was to stop the terrorist suicide attacks. They were convinced that Arafat and the Palestinian Authority could stop, or at least control, most of the violent attacks, but chose not to. Or, to put this more bluntly, Arafat supported and condoned much of the violence. If the peace process was going to move forward, they made it very clear, he had to make a strategic decision to abandon violence and return to a negotiated settlement of the issues. They doubted his willingness to do this.

The Palestinian Authority couldn't bring themselves to do that. If they did—if they confronted Hamas and Islamic Jihad, cracked down on the extremists, made arrests, confiscated weapons—there'd be blood in the streets. But if they did not confront Hamas and Islamic Jihad, the Israelis weren't about to make any of the concessions outlined in the Tenet plan (and other plans)—such as removal of checkpoints, withdrawal of security forces to previous positions, and readmission of Palestinian workers to Israel. And there was no way we'd see any progress toward a Palestinian state.

At first the Israelis took a very tough line on how the Palestinian Authority had to demonstrate their good faith: Sharon insisted on one hundred percent compliance, including at least seven days of quiet, before he would approve any talks.

If we could not even get talks started for at least a week (if we were lucky enough to have no attacks), my job was clearly going to be impossible. In time, however, the Israelis backed away from their more absolute positions; and Sharon agreed to participate in the Trilateral Committee talks that I had decided to use as the venue for the initial meetings. But their bottom line remained the same: The Palestinians had to show good faith in stopping terror attacks.

．．．

THE FIRST day ended with mixed results. On the one hand, the terrible and tragic attack at Afula had cast a dark cloud over our hopes; but we had at least gained an agreement from the Israelis to meet in the Trilateral Committee. I had met with the Israeli leadership, we had connected well, and they had indicated that they would give, at least, cautious support for my mission.

I SPENT the second day with the Palestinians. Since it was the Islamic fasting month of Ramadan, my meetings took place in the evening, beginning with the Iftar meal* with Chairman Yasser Arafat and the Palestinian leadership in the West Bank town of Ramallah, where the Palestinian Authority had one of their headquarters (called "the Muqatta'a"; their official seat of government was in Gaza).

On the way there, our consular people took me on a tour of the Israeli settlement areas in the West Bank, where, contrary to agreements, significant settlement expansion was going on. During the tour, we passed through Israeli security checkpoints and witnessed the frustrating and humiliating process Palestinians had to endure in order to travel from place to place.

In our talks the day before, the Israelis had acknowledged that these checkpoints caused problems, but they were necessary to prevent attacks (such as the Afula incident). It was obviously a difficult situation. Young soldiers who could not compromise on security subjected Palestinians to time-consuming and humiliating security procedures. I was told checkpoint stories of the birth of babies, of people dying unable to reach hospitals in time, of senior Palestinian officials held up and embarrassed, and of many other incidents that inflamed the people.

My meetings with Arafat were cordial. He has always been hospitable, and very expressive, with abundant assurances of cooperation (always echoed by the people around him).

* The Iftar meal breaks the daily Ramadan fast.

By then, meeting with Arabs came easy to me; I was comfortable with their ways. And though I didn't yet know these Palestinians very well, they certainly knew me. Arafat had already talked with President Mubarak, King Abdullah, and the other major Arab leaders, all of whom had advised co-operation. "They all told me that you are a guy I could trust," Arafat explained, "who can help me do what I want to do." He strongly stressed that, and assured me that this was marvelous. "I'm totally committed to the success of your mission," he went on to tell me. And when I brought up the Trilateral Committee as a venue for further discussion, he went along with that as well, though he added that he wanted to open up discussions in areas other than security—a far more loaded issue than it might have seemed.

On the whole, he was always agreeable, always quick to promise co-operation, but not so quick to deliver on his promises.

It became increasingly evident to me, as Yasser Arafat and I met again and again over the next weeks and months, that this wily old revolutionary could never really bring himself to make the compromises that would lead to a lasting resolution of the conflict. He could never look at concluding a deal that risked his own place in history and his personal legacy. He saw himself as the leader who had never given an inch in compromise, and this was more important to him than concluding and implementing an agreement that caused him to make serious compromises. He's at the point in his life where he clearly sees his own mortality, and he wants to go out as defiant. "I'm the only Arab general that's undefeated," he said to me at one point. "You're not going to walk behind my funeral like with Sadat and my partner Rabin."

I began to realize toward the end of my piece of the process that he wasn't the guy who could bring home the bacon. He wasn't going to take the risks for peace that Sadat, Rabin, Hussein, Begin, and Barak did. Not when his own legacy and history were at stake and he saw their fate.

Of course he knew he would have to make compromises. And Barak put on the table at Camp David a lot of compromises. The deal might not have been perfect, and he probably could have negotiated a better one; but he didn't seem to try. He walked out.

I once asked Arafat about that. "Were you close to a deal at Camp David?"

"Oh, yes, very close."

There are a lot of versions about what happened at Camp David or Taba. Was the deal on the table good or bad? Could it have been further negotiated? I don't know. Still, I could never fathom why the process ended so abruptly. When you're close or at least have a process going in the right direction, why do you cut it off?

AFTER MY talk with Arafat, I met privately with other Palestinian leaders, including Mahmoud Abbas (Abu Mazen), the then number two man and later Prime Minister; Ahmed Qurei (Abu Ala'a), the Speaker of the Palestinian Legislative Council and Abu Mazen's successor as Prime Minister; and Sa'eb Erekat, the Palestinian Authority's Chief Negotiator.

Abu Mazen had been involved in the process for a long time, did not agree with Arafat on many issues, was opposed to the Intifada, and clearly saw what had to be done on the ground pretty much the way we did. He wanted to move to negotiations. But it was clear that he didn't have any real power; his position as number two didn't give him much clout. He was not living as the number two guy.

The pecking order was always fuzzy after Arafat. Like every revolutionary leader, he spread out the guns and the authority; he didn't let anybody who could challenge him have real power. Abu Mazen had stature; he openly disagreed with a lot of the steps Arafat had taken; but there was nothing behind him—no guns, no money, no popular support, no political clout. Yet he said the right things, I thought he meant them, and he had a tremendous reputation; and I thought, "Jeez, too bad this guy doesn't have a lot more. He makes sense. He's committed. He's a realist."

I had the same impression of Abu Ala'a, the Speaker of the Assembly. Abu Mazen did not last long as Prime Minister. And Abu Ala'a has not had much greater success.

Sa'eb Erekat is the mayor of Jericho—heavyset, balding, highly intelligent, easy to like. Sa'eb is constantly talking. A collector of arguments, he loves to debate (he's on CNN all the time). He's been in this process a long time, and by all accounts he is a very honest man. But

I wonder if he hasn't been in the process too long; maybe he's too caught up in process. He and I got along very well, and I spent a lot of time with him and with his wonderful family at Jericho. (I enjoyed dinner at his home.)

I also got to know the security chiefs from the West Bank and Gaza, Jabril Rajoub and Mohamed Dahlan. These were practical men who could take the security steps necessary IF they were given the authority and backing from the top. Unfortunately, that would not happen.

None of these leaders had real power. Arafat called the game.

FROM THESE MEETINGS, I gathered that the Palestinians' priority was political issues, and their chief concern: Would the Israelis really make political concessions down the road once the security issues were resolved?

I also gathered that there wasn't much stomach from these leaders to take on the extremists who were perpetrating the horrific suicide attacks. They wanted the Israelis to "end the occupation" and move out of their areas, and then they would deal with the extremists . . . but through negotiations rather than confrontation.

According to the Tenet/Mitchell plans, taking action against the extremists was the necessary condition for progress on the later steps leading to Palestinian statehood. Failure to take action would thus violate the principles of Tenet/Mitchell that Arafat claimed to have accepted.

For the Israelis, of course, this was an unacceptable risk, not only militarily but politically. No Israeli leader wants to be seen to yield on a point of security without unbreakable guarantees.

ALL OF these roadblocks and potential roadblocks notwithstanding, by the end of the second day I was cautiously optimistic. My personal connections with both sides were good; they'd both be easy to talk to; yet I had no illusions about the probability of success. Each side viewed the problems differently. Worse, they each saw a different path to resolving them.

. . .

BILL BURNS left on the third day. I was on my own.

We held our first Trilateral Committee meeting shortly after he left. To avoid press and security problems, we held back our announcement of time and place until the last minute for this and all our later meetings.

The crews from each side were the security chiefs from the various Palestinian military forces and their intelligence services and from the Israeli Defense Force and their intelligence representatives. These old rivals were all pros, who knew each other well and seemed to share mutual respect. I didn't realize how well they all knew each other until they all gathered at our first meeting place. It was all hugs and kisses there, cheery jokes, questions about families, good fellowship.

And then they sat down and started screaming.

At breaks, they'd return to good fellowship.

The screaming bothered me. It's no way to conduct a negotiation. But there seemed to be a need to vent, and I let it go for the first couple of meetings; after that, I demanded serious discussion and constructive sessions.

Even after they quieted down, results from these initial sessions were mixed. Both sides were reluctant to get serious; for every small step forward we had to suffer through hours of screaming recriminations and accusations; and I left meetings exhausted and frustrated. Yet, with a few exceptions, I came to like these negotiators. They could make it happen, I realized, if they had the support and authority from their political masters. I had to get that. Meanwhile, I needed them to do the painfully difficult work of hammering out the detailed measures that had to be accomplished on the ground.

We made a little progress—at least on one side. The Israelis eased up on their insistence on seven days without attacks and one hundred percent results. They now asked for forty-eight hours of quiet and one hundred percent effort.

But the Palestinians still seemed reluctant to act against the terrorists and take real action (arrests, weapons confiscation, etc.). Despite Arafat's promise to cooperate, no serious orders to act had been given to his security forces (they privately acknowledged this to me). This was not encouraging. Without Palestinian action against the terrorists, there would be no cease-fire. And without a cease-fire, we could not move forward.

Even more discouraging, our intelligence and Israeli actions indicated that Hamas and Palestinian Islamic Jihad were stepping up suicide bombing attacks in an effort to derail our mission.

The Israelis actually had great success blocking these attacks, but it was impossible to stop them all. For every ten attempts they foiled or countered, one got through. About every third day during this initial trip, a suicide attack would set back our progress and bring on retaliation attacks, sometimes with tragic collateral casualties, by the Israelis. It was obvious that these attacks would eventually cause the process to collapse. I felt like we were shoveling sand against the tide.

As casualties on both sides mounted, and the inevitable retaliation attacks destroyed Palestinian Authority facilities, anger grew in Israel and the streets of the Palestinian areas. I visited some of the sites of the attacks. The pointless murder of innocents sickened me.

AS ALL this was going on, I worked on the Palestinian security forces to take action to break the cycle of violence: Arresting terrorist leaders would demonstrate their good faith and compliance with the Tenet/Mitchell plans.

They wanted that more than I did, they told me; but the Israelis were screwing them up by tossing on the table not one but many different lists of people they wanted arrested. Palestinian security claimed they were eager to pick up all the bad guys, but only if they had a single, authoritative list to act on.

"Fine," I told them, "I'll provide one list, compiled by our [not Israeli] intelligence, that will benchmark your effort."

I gave them a list of thirty-three men who were on every list of bad guys; nobody had any doubt of their guilt.

Very little happened. Arrests were made; but only a few of them, at best, were real; and many of the "arrested" were actually either free or living under loose house arrest.

It was clear that the security heads would not—or could not—take any real action without a major commitment and direct order from Arafat. And Arafat was not about to give that order.

DURING THE next three weeks, I continued my Trilateral Committee meetings, I met frequently with Sharon and Arafat and their lieutenants, but I also met with international leaders and representatives from numerous organizations and nations. All of them offered support.

The "Quad," or "Quartet" (the U.S., the UN, the European Union, and Russia), was an especially important and helpful group. The UN, EU, and Russian representatives—Terje Larson, Miguel Moratinos, and Andrei Vdovin—became friends of mine, and provided tireless support for my mission. The EU representative Javier Solana visited several times to offer assistance and encouragement.

I also talked frequently with leaders from the region, particularly old friends from Arab nations. Both their frustration and their strong desire to see our mission work were evident.

On a more personal level, I tried to get a sense of ordinary people on both sides. I really wanted to know them and to understand their situation and views. I attended ceremonies and observances in Israel and in Palestinian areas. I ate meals with Israeli and Palestinian families. I ate dinner in both East and West Jerusalem. Everywhere, I was deeply touched by the desperate desire for peace. "Don't give up," everyone pleaded, with one voice. People on the street came up to me to beg me to hang in there. I visited Gaza and saw the awful conditions in the crowded refugee camps. On one occasion, I met with the kids from Seeds of Peace. "Why can't the adults figure it out?" they asked with heartrending openness. "We have."

FOR MY own sanity and well-being, I worked out at the Marine House that billeted the Marine security detachment at our consulate in Jerusalem; and I sometimes dined with these hard-charging Leather-necks to keep my spirits up. Through them, I met Father Peter Vasko, an

American Franciscan (the order has responsibility for the care of Christian sites in Jerusalem for the Catholic Church). Father Peter, the Marines' unofficial chaplain, decided to look after my spiritual welfare as well. I sometimes ate with the Franciscans at their monastery, attended Sunday Mass with them, and enjoyed evenings talking to these dedicated and devout monks. Father Peter gave me a fascinating tour of the Old City.

One evening, the *Custos* (the Vatican custodian of the holy sites and the Franciscan superior in Jerusalem) presented me with the Papal Gold Cross for my efforts for peace in the region.

"Thank you from the bottom of my heart," I told him when I accepted the award, "though I'm deeply distressed that we haven't been more successful."

"It's important that we try," he said in response. "That's justification enough."

I also met the Christian patriarchs from the sixteen other denominations who shared responsibility for the Christian sites. These holy men never failed to remind me that the Christians in the region had serious and long-standing concerns that the major combatants often ignored.

DURING MY frequent meetings with Sharon and Arafat (never together; these two old rivals couldn't stand each other), I tried to organize a senior-level political committee below Sharon and Arafat to oversee our efforts and provide a high-level group where we could open other areas for discussion besides security matters. I saw this committee as being made up of people at the ministerial level, like Abu Mazen and Abu Ala'a, the senior Palestinians, and Shimon Peres and Ben Eleazar, on the Israeli side, with me, perhaps, as the U.S. representative. This oversight body would oversee the security measures taken on the ground, and (I hoped) resolve differences, disagreements, or reports of violations. But on top of that, it could also open the political dialogue; and in so doing we might square the circle—satisfy the Palestinian demand for political progress without compromising the Israeli demand for security before negotiations on political issues could begin. That is, we might not make political commitments; yet a beginning of talk on these issues would give the Palestinians a sense that we were fulfilling expectations. This in turn would build confidence. In this way, we'd be opening a two-track approach: On one track, security. On the second, parallel track, political issues. I thought this parallel approach might get us around the sequentialism issue that was proving to be such a stumbling block.

Sharon was a little unsure about all this. "Why should we make political commitments up front?" he told me. "It looks like we're caving in to terrorism and doing it under the pressure of violence." He was leery of big political steps. Big political steps would show his hand; and he never showed his hand. Neither did Arafat. I never actually knew what either of them was really after or what they saw as a long-term solution.

Sharon would surely take security steps up front. And I'm convinced that if he had the right security cooperation from the other side, he would withdraw from certain areas, move certain checkpoints. I think he could implement the entire Tenet plan without a problem. Now when he got down the road, would he make the kind of political commitments on settlements and other more difficult issues (such as Barak offered)? That remained to be seen.

The Palestinians were very leery that he could or would do any of that. They were convinced that he'd be glad to move forward on Tenet and get the security concessions out of the way; but he would stall on political progress once the security situation leveled off.

In my mind that was always a possibility. I simply wasn't sure. Would he move forward or not? I can't say. He could definitely start a process. I wasn't sure whether he could finish one.

As for the other side—I don't think Arafat could even start it.

Sharon and Arafat eventually came around and agreed to set up the committee; but for one reason or another, we could never get it off the ground.

For three weeks we tried to get something started, to get an agreement working on the ground and to get the violence tamped down. It didn't work.

I knew time was running out and we were close to it all falling apart.

The attacks and retaliations escalated. Targeted assassinations by the

Israelis sometimes spilled over and killed nearby innocents. The Israelis had suffered a large number of casualties; innocents on buses or in cafes were brutally slaughtered by suicide bombers—young brainwashed Palestinians, agonized by the plight of their people. We were one event away from collapse.

It came on December 12 when a suicide bomber blew up a bus near the settlement town of Emmanuel. Ten Israelis were killed and thirty wounded. This brought the total killed since I'd arrived to forty-four, and it ended the Israeli willingness to continue the talks. They were now going to retaliate big-time. Arafat's headquarters in Gaza, his helicopters, and many of his government facilities were bombed.

I was deeply dismayed that things had not worked out.

Many nights I had stood on my small balcony at the King David gazing at the softly lighted Old City of Jerusalem. I knew of no other place on earth that had seen so much glory and triumph and so much sorrow and violence, all in the name of religion.

It was decided that I would come back to the States for consultations, rather than stand helplessly by while the spiral of violence continued, and there was no immediate hope of talks.

Before we left, I was joined by Bill Burns; and on the way home we passed through Jordan and Egypt to talk to King Abdullah and President Mubarak. Since I knew both of them well, it was not easy to call on them after our failure to make progress. Both of them had high expectations and hopes for peace; and I felt their disappointment and frustration.

I arrived back in the U.S. on the seventeenth of December, and debriefed the President and Secretary Powell on the twentieth. They were still determined to make this work—a most encouraging development. The President thanked me for my efforts, and the Secretary told me to be ready to reengage when things settled down.

"I'll be ready to go back at any time," I told him.

In the days following, both Sharon and Arafat sent letters to the President asking for my return. In his reply, the President insisted on more action on the ground to curb the violence; but the news from Secretary Powell was slightly more positive. He asked me to prepare to go back after the holidays . . . if the situation improved.

. . .

OVER THE Christmas and New Year's holidays I reflected on my trip: It seemed to me that the extremists were calling the shots. If it looked like we were making progress or creating hope for a peaceful resolution, they would attack with a vengeance, knowing retaliatory strikes would follow and talks would break down. Unless Palestinian security forces put genuine effort into curbing these attacks, there was no hope.

On a personal level, I knew that both sides had tested me at every opportunity, trying to measure my commitment and impartiality. On a more positive note, I felt I had made connections on both sides and had the trust of key people; and with the exception of a few members who felt compelled to create political theater (outrageous political statements, heated diatribes, screaming), I liked the makeup of the Trilateral Committee. Yet if I went back, I was determined to put an end to the screaming and the diatribes. The time for venting and posturing was past.

My greatest conviction: We could make progress if we could get a break in the violence.

As I followed the daily news, I sensed that things were quieting down.

The Palestinians had grown desperate. The Israelis had destroyed their headquarters in Gaza; Arafat was pinned down in Ramallah (the Israelis refused to let him go anywhere); things were coming apart; and they didn't know what the Israelis would do next. Was Sharon going to take out Arafat?

The Israelis were also in a bind. Sharon had tried negotiating; and when that broke down, he'd tried a powerful military incursion. Now he seemed to have spent most of his options. He had to be asking himself, "What do I have to do to get this monkey off my back?" He was under a lot of political pressure, and hadn't produced anything. He was getting a lot of bad world press as a result of the heavy retaliatory attacks.

So I think that for different reasons they were both desperate to get this thing restarted.

The decision was made for me to return immediately after the holidays. But this time there would be a different approach: Our visit was to be short, only four days. We would convene the Trilateral Committee, and give them very specific tasks and goals to accomplish over the course of two to three weeks. During that time, Aaron would return to determine whether or not there was significant progress. If there was, I would return to move to the next phase.

There were several reasons for this approach: First, we had to take the "theater" out of the meetings. With me out of the way, the temptation to waste time in heated rhetoric would be gone. Second, we had to force both sides to put more effort into bilateral communication and coordination, and not to rely on us to arbitrate every issue. Third, we wanted to take away our high profile, which drew press focus that was frequently disruptive. Fourth, low-key talks (unburdened of my continuous, direct involvement) might reduce the extremists' will—and opportunity—to use terrorist attacks to break up the talks.

ROUND TWO

Aaron and I left for Israel on January 2, 2002, and arrived on the third.

As soon as we landed, we were briefed by the Israelis on an impending takedown operation: A ship in the Red Sea, the *Karine A,* had sailed from Iran with fifty tons of illegal weapons and ordnance ordered by the Palestinian Authority—a serious violation of the Oslo Agreement. Under that agreement, the Authority was permitted certain weapons and ordnance for their security. Though they actually had more weapons than the agreement permitted, the Israelis had looked the other way, as long as the excess weapons of the security forces were limited to small arms. But on the *Karine A* were Katyusha rockets, 120-millimeter mortars, and other high-caliber weapons systems, as well as explosives, mines, and demolitions. All this went way beyond Oslo.

The Israelis were planning to grab the ship when it moved into international waters, which would be around noon the following day. (The operation had to take place in international waters, rather than, for example, Saudi territorial waters.)

This news put me in a fury; it was a total surprise to me. No one had briefed us on it before we left the States, and now it threatened to derail our efforts before they even got off the ground. . . . Later, to my immense relief, both the Israelis and the Palestinians kept their cool and did not use the takedown as an excuse to back away from the Trilateral Committee meetings or our proposed plan. Still, my mission was once again off to a less-than-desirable start.

The next morning at Prime Minister Sharon's farm in southern Israel, I received more information on the pending operation: It would occur at noon during my first scheduled meeting with Chairman Arafat in Ramallah. Before I left the farm, I asked Sharon if I could break the news of the *Karine A* to Arafat. I wanted to see the look on Arafat's face when I told him about it.

"Yes," he said, "but don't do it before noon. That's when we're going to run the takedown."

Later that morning, I met with the members of the Quad, who recommitted to working with us. Since they had significant influence on the Palestinians, they proved to be invaluable in facilitating progress on confidence-building actions during my return to the U.S.; their permanent representatives added greatly to the undertakings of our embassy and consulate.

I FLEW to Ramallah, where I had a typically pleasant meeting with Arafat; he once again promised to take the actions necessary to implement the Tenet plan.

Noon came and we began preparing for lunch.

"Umm," I asked myself, "should I give him the word during lunch?" I thought on that. "No," I concluded, "I'll wait till afterward."

About halfway through the meal, people all of a sudden started running around with panicked looks, cell phones were firing up, aides were whispering in Arafat's ear. I can understand enough Arabic to pick up on alarms and excitement. They had gotten word of the *Karine A* takedown.

I watched Arafat across the table, trying to gauge his reaction. He seemed both confused and dismissive. (One of his defense mechanisms is to deny bad news and seem indifferent to it, both at the same time.)

Finally, I asked him, "What's going on?"

"It's nothing. Forget it."

"Well," I said, "I know about the *Karine A,* I know about its cargo, and I know the Israelis were going to mount an operation to take it down. It looks like they've done that."

"That is not true," he shot back. "This was not our ship. It's an Israeli plot. This is an Israeli setup."

I gave him a skeptical smile and a shake of the head.

But later, after the ship's master admitted Palestinian Authority involvement and the TV news was filled with pictures of the ship and the huge amount of weapons aboard, Arafat vowed to investigate. The investigation never happened.

Meanwhile, I gave Arafat's top subordinates a warning. "Look," I told them, "you better think hard about how you want to respond to this thing. I'm not sure it will be a good idea to try to shift the blame . . . or claim an Israeli plot. There's evidence that leads right back to you. We and the Israelis know that Chairman Arafat made payments to the Iranians, bought the weapons, and chartered the ship; we know that the captain of the ship is a Palestinian Authority guy; and he is now spilling his guts."

The situation was obviously looking bad for the Palestinians.

At this point, Arafat dumped the blame on one of his own people. It was an obvious scam. The guy could never have put out that kind of money without Arafat knowing about it.

There was no doubt that Arafat had his hand in the cookie jar big-time, and I was in fact just a little shocked that the Israelis didn't just say, "Screw the talks."

So the Israelis really surprised me by ignoring Arafat's trickery. They just let it pass. They now had a tremendous military success, and they were proud of it—not only because it was a well-executed military operation but, more important, it put them at an advantage over him. "No, go on with the talks," they said. "We're not going to do anything." Yet every day they released more pictures of the *Karine A* and the weapons they found in its hold.

For a change they had cleverly handled a potentially messy event. Usually they just went in there with brute force. This time, they put the Palestinians on the defensive in a really slick way.

I spent the next day in Jerusalem and Jericho with Palestinian officials, urging them to take serious action against the extremists who were responsible for the violence and to make a genuine commitment in the Trilateral Committee to implementing the Tenet plan. As always, they seemed willing to move forward, but were unable to take real steps in that direction because authorization had not come from the top.

On the sixth, at our initial Trilateral meeting of this session, I laid out our plan . . . pleasantly surprised at the absence of the usual theatrical outbursts. Everyone immediately accepted our proposals to work with each other and with our representatives on the ground to meet our timetables and goals. I began to think that our new approach to the talks might succeed. The takedown of the *Karine A* just may have had a sobering effect on everybody. My hopes were up.

The next day, Aaron and I left for the States with renewed hope. I couldn't wait for the next trip.

OVER THE next two months, my heart sank. The spiral of violence grew more horrific. The continuing violence, together with Arafat's failure to do more to stop it, diminished President Bush's faith in the peace process. In his view, the *Karine A* affair had taken the credibility of Arafat to a new low. It was hard to see how he could rebuild it. Members of Arafat's own political movement and security forces were now taking part in the attacks against Israel.

As a result, the plan for me to go back was put on hold.

In February, a small measure of hope returned when Crown Prince Abdullah of Saudi Arabia made a truly remarkable offer: If there was a peace agreement, the Saudis would recognize the State of Israel. Twenty-two other Arab nations supported this initiative.

It started to get a momentum of its own; and the President decided that it represented an opening. In a Rose Garden speech on March 7, with Vice President Cheney and Secretary Powell by his side, he announced that I would return to the region for another attempt to get a cease-fire and implementation of the Tenet plan. During this time, the Vice President and Secretary Powell would also visit the region. The Vice President would travel to ten countries and link up with me at the end of his journey. This was a high-level effort to get things moving. I was scheduled to leave in mid-March.

ROUND THREE

We took off on March 13. As our Continental Airlines jet approached Tel Aviv, the passengers began to sing songs of peace. They knew I was on board; they were singing encouragement.

Since our last trip, there had been an endless series of attacks and counterattacks. The Israelis had occupied most of the Palestinian territories and Arafat remained restricted to his Ramallah headquarters. The U.S. had pressed Sharon to withdraw his forces as I arrived, in order to establish a positive environment for my mission. One of my first pieces of business was to determine Sharon's reply.

After I deplaned, I went through the now-standard briefings, then went immediately to see Prime Minister Sharon. He had positive news: He would withdraw his forces from Area A, the areas in Palestinian territory previously agreed to be under their security force control.*

The good news meant the trip was off to a positive start, but I knew that gestures of goodwill didn't last long in this environment.

The second day brought things back to reality as nine Palestinian kids were killed by a mine in Gaza near security positions protecting Israeli settlements. It was almost certainly planted by the Israelis to take out people trying to sneak up and fire onto these positions. What happened, I think, is the kids got in there to play, something went wrong, and the mine went off. Accusations flew: Was this a remotely detonated mine controlled by the IDF? If so, did the IDF deliberately kill the kids?

Wherever truth lay, the incident gave the Palestinians a club to beat the Israelis with. Inevitably, the controversy made my mission harder.

Yet in my meetings over the next few days with senior Israeli and Pales-

---

* The Oslo Agreement broke down the occupied territories into three areas: A, B, and C. Area A would be policed by the Palestinians; the Israelis would not go into it. In Area B there would be some kind of interim security. Area C contained the settlements and the areas immediately around them. When violence broke out, the Israelis made incursions into Area A. Though these violated the agreement, they claimed they had to do it for their own security reasons.

tinian officials and key members of the Trilateral Committee, I sensed a far more serious focus and readiness than ever before to make the process work. I had given all the participants homework in my absence, and they had actually done it: I had asked them to list what they could agree on and how they understood the agreement. And then I wanted them to list their disagreements, so we could focus on these.

To my enormous surprise, they weren't that far apart. I'd expected a debate on every issue. I'd expected they'd be all over the map. But that didn't happen. They were actually pretty close. Right at the beginning, there was a lot they could work with.

The first Trilateral Committee meetings were extremely encouraging. There were no political statements, heated accusations, or theatrics. Every member was ready to work. Each side developed a first cut at "a Tenet Work Plan," detailing their take on the measures and timelines needed for implementation.

In subsequent meetings, we succeeded in dramatically reducing the differences. I was able to report to Washington that progress was exciting. If the attacks didn't derail us before we gained agreement, I felt we just might start the process I had been sent out to put in place.

The third day brought the first terrorist attack. "Oh, shit," I thought. "Now the Israelis will hit back. And we can forget about progress."

But the Israelis, surprisingly, held back. They did not retaliate. And that gave us a small opening. . . . I knew this would close if attacks continued.

Vice President Cheney visited on the eighteenth and nineteenth of March. We had meetings with the Israeli leadership, but decided Cheney couldn't meet with Arafat until he had done more to curb terrorist attacks. I delivered the message to Arafat that Cheney was willing to meet with him in Cairo on as little as a week's notice, once we saw real progress in stopping the attacks.

Arafat was disappointed that Cheney was avoiding him. He loves the big time. He loves the red carpet and the cameras. He loves to be out there on the world's stage meeting heads of state. And here he was, pinned down by Sharon in Ramallah for four long months. So when I offered him a chance to go to Cairo to meet Mubarak and Cheney, his face lit up. He'd be out from under this crushing restriction.

We thought we might encourage Arafat to order real actions, such as arrests and weapons confiscation. We were wrong. In the next two days, suicide attacks killed a number of Israelis in a bus and street bombing. He had done nothing.

In Washington, meanwhile, the President and Vice President made statements that I would be the one who determined if Arafat should get the meeting with Cheney. "Thanks a lot!" They both knew Sharon was set against the meeting; and there was a lot of pressure at home against a meeting with Arafat. So they pinned that rose on me.

Okay, I'm a big boy. But I knew I had to be careful.

I looked at Arafat and I told him what he had to do; and when it came down to the crunch, he didn't do it. On the twenty-second of March, I delivered the news to a sullen and disappointed Arafat that there would be no meeting.

SOMEHOW, we managed to work through the attacks and setbacks, and the progress we were making encouraged everyone to refrain from retaliatory action. We were apparently very close to agreement.

On the twenty-fourth, I made a decision I was later to regret. Since we were down to only a few differences, I wanted to close the deal. But it was clear time would run out on us eventually, as long as the attacks continued. So I decided to put forth my own proposals to expedite the process and resolve the remaining issues. When we started, I thought I had written in stone that there would never be "a Zinni plan." There were already enough plans out there. All the possible issues were already covered. Everyone knew what had to be done. The problem was doing it. I had always been convinced that the Israelis and Palestinians had to work that out themselves.

Still, I couldn't resist the temptation to close the last gap.

The plan, known as "the Zinni Bridging Proposals," was intended to do just that—bridge the remaining gaps and differences.

I tried to make it absolutely clear that these proposals were not a make-or-break thing. "I'm putting suggestions on the table, not demands," I told everybody concerned. "You don't have to accept them. If you can't, there's no harm, no foul. This works for either side. We'll simply take them off the table, and then go back to working things out together."

As we were initially presenting these proposals, preparations were under way for the annual Arab Summit, to be held in Beirut starting the twenty-fifth. Two big issues were then in the air. But the first—would Sharon allow Arafat to attend?—was dominating the media and political exchanges to the detriment of the second and far more important one—Crown Prince Abdullah's proposal to recognize the state of Israel. The proposal was to be formally presented at the summit; its acceptance would be a giant step.

We were under a great deal of time pressure. If we could conclude an agreement before the summit, Arafat would be allowed to attend, make a speech, and be in his glory; and the summit's focus would be on Abdullah's historic proposal and not on the problems of Yasser Arafat.

Meanwhile, the Israelis had a number of reservations to my bridging proposals, but promised to study them and get me a quick response. After they looked at them (and it didn't take them long), they came up with thirteen objections—all of them serious. They didn't think they'd be able to accept them. "We're going to think about all this for a bit," they told me, "but it looks like we can't go for it." I waited. They thought about it; and some of Sharon's top advisers (including some hard-liners like Mofaz) went to the Prime Minister; the debate went on late into the night, but they finally came up with a position: "Even though we have serious objections, let's go with Zinni. Let's just accept his plan as is. Let's not be the ones accused of holding back peace. Let's move on this."

On the twenty-sixth, the Israelis called to tell me they had accepted the proposal with no reservations. I was astonished. I had expected it would be really tough to get agreement from the Israelis, and they would take a hell of a long time to negotiate. But somehow they had found a way to accept the deal.

The Palestinians had only three reservations. Two were minor administrative matters that we dealt with easily; but the third was a showstopper: We wanted to reestablish the security situation as it was prior to the beginning of the Second Intifada in September 2000; and the bridge proposal had a phased approach to this goal. The determination about whether or not to move into the subsequent phases depended upon performance measures monitored by teams we proposed, which would then be approved by the Trilateral Committee. The proposal additionally called for the establishing of a senior committee of leaders from the U.S., Israel, and the Palestinian Authority who would arbitrate any disagreements arising from this process. Finally, the two committees could agree to move ahead, even if some measures had not been achieved according to the timelines outlined, as long as good faith was shown.

The Palestinians did not want to be held to measurable actions—such as monitored arrests and weapons confiscations—and this came through very clearly. Privately, some of them told me that Arafat would never order action against terrorist groups, regardless of what he told us. Without that order, no security force commander could take action.

I hoped we could work through this issue; but I was beginning to sense that Arafat never intended to carry out the actions described in the Tenet plan, which he had agreed to in principle. I believe the Palestinians hoped the Israelis would be forced to accept measurable steps that they had to execute—such as withdrawals—while they could get away with just trying to talk the extremist groups into a cease-fire.

The pressure was now on the Palestinians; but I couldn't get them to reply.

"Okay," I told them, "then you don't accept the proposals. That means they're off the table. Okay, let's go back to the committee negotiations with no hard feelings. But let's move on."

"No, they're not off the table," they countered; they didn't want to turn them down because of the negative reaction they anticipated. "We are not opposed to them. We just need to talk further about them."

"We've got to hurry!" I said. "We've got to hurry! I need an answer!"

Meanwhile, the other Arabs got wind of the proposals, and they were putting a lot of pressure on Arafat to accept the bridging proposals.

All the while, the Palestinians were caught up in the question of Arafat's trip to Beirut. Since Sharon was not inclined to let him go, they were looking at alternative means, like videoconferencing, for him to address the summit. The issue occupied their attention to the exclusion of everything else. The bridging proposals got shunted to one side.

Sharon was making a hero, a martyr, and a victim out of Arafat. The American government pressed him to let Arafat go, but the gut hatred between those two is so bad he couldn't bring himself to do it. Of course, this enhanced Arafat's stature on the street and played into everything that he was doing. It was a mistake. The conference started as scheduled on the twenty-fifth without Arafat. Even the teleconferencing option fell through.

Time was running out.

March 27 was Passover, and I had accepted an invitation to a Seder dinner with an Israeli family. During the meal, news came of a horrific suicide bombing at a Passover celebration in a hotel restaurant, with heavy casualties. This bombing had a tremendous effect on the people of Israel. It was their 9/11.

I knew immediately we had come to the end of our road.

Soon afterward, I talked with Ben Eliezer, the Defense Minister. "I don't know what we'll do," he told me. "But we're ready to retaliate. And if we do, we're going to have to do something big. That will probably end peace talks for now. The only thing that can save this thing is if Arafat accepts the bridging proposals."

I called Arafat. "You've got to condemn the bombing in the strongest terms," I urged him. "And you've got to make a decision on the proposal. You've got to give us something to keep the talks alive. Otherwise, the Israeli retaliation is going to be severe."

He hemmed and hawed, and I never received a reply on the proposal. Other Arab leaders continued to press him to accept the proposal; they knew what was coming if he did not.

The displeasure of the other Arabs presented Arafat with a problem. Since he didn't want to get in hot water with them, he had to dump blame on somebody else (he is not inclined to accept blame himself), and blamed me (which was quite a shock)—accusing me of conspiring with the Israelis. "The bridging proposals are part of a plot to force unacceptable terms on us," he told Arab leaders. His Palestinian leaders repeated these charges on TV.

I was incensed. I called some of the Palestinians who were making these accusations (people I thought were friends who knew better), and really unloaded on them. "Hey, it's only business," they answered. "We know none of this is true, but don't take it personally. It's just stuff that we have to say." They really pissed me off.

My anger was somewhat lessened when I received reassuring calls from Arab friends, like Prince Bandar, the Saudi ambassador to the U.S. They did not believe the Palestinian accusations; they still trusted my honesty and appreciated my efforts. These calls greatly lifted my morale.

Now we had to wait for the Israeli attack. I knew it wouldn't be long in coming. As I waited, a couple of lights dawned on me, really hit me hard: First, I realized that we had never been close to an agreement. Arafat was never going to rein in Hamas. Second, the Zinni bridging proposals were a terrible idea. By putting forward proposals of my own, I gave Arafat a target he could lay blame on. (The Israelis could have done the same thing.) And that's what he did. He said the proposals were pro-Israeli (though if anything, the Israelis had more objections to them than the Palestinians; they were very apprehensive about agreeing to the proposals). I ended up giving them an excuse for failure that they could peddle around the Arab world. I should never have given them that excuse. Without it they would have had to sink or swim on their own.

At this point, Washington made the decision to keep me in place and not bring me home, which would have been the normal thing to do under the circumstances. It was a wise decision.

OVER THE next week, the Israelis unleashed a devastating attack on the Palestinians; really hammered them hard. We watched helplessly as virtually all Palestinian Authority government buildings and facilities were destroyed. Casualties mounted, and Arafat's headquarters, the Muqat-ta'a, was under siege and half destroyed. There were other sieges at the Church of the Nativity in Bethlehem and the Palestinian security head-quarters for the West Bank. The town of Jenin was under systematic de-structive attack.

For us it was a period of crisis management, dealing with desperate calls from Palestinians asking for help in handling all sorts of dramatic hu-manitarian situations. We tried our best to respond to each request. And we were constantly asking the Israelis to pull back from some incursion, to let help through where people were desperate, to de-conflict forces, or to provide emergency aid; but of course the Israelis were not in a very good mood to cooperate. Still, we could always find people in place and put pressure on them.

We had a lot of questions about what we were doing. Was it our job? The answer was nobody else was doing it. "Yes, we have to," I said. "If it saves lives, we've gotta do it." So we ended up becoming like a 911 emergency coordination team, and I think we did save lives.

Meanwhile, we worked for a quick end to the Israeli attacks. President Bush and many other world leaders called for restraint, an end to the attacks, and a withdrawal.

As the siege continued, it looked increasingly likely that Arafat himself might become a casualty, or if that didn't happen, forcibly expelled from the region.

By then, Arafat's Muqatta'a headquarters had been turned into Berlin in the spring of 1945. It was now surrounded by Israeli tanks and soldiers. Everything was blown down, the compound walls crushed, the cars in the parking lot destroyed. A pall of smoke and dust covered everything.

And nobody was talking. Sharon wanted to totally isolate Arafat. No outsider could see him. In retaliation, Arafat had refused to allow his leaders to meet with anyone until the siege was lifted or they came to see him first.

Sharon had stonewalled President Bush's demand to end the attacks and incursions. It was therefore important for me not to sit idly by, but to keep pushing for meetings and contacts to signal our mission was not dead. I decided to break the impasse and visit Arafat, with the hope of restarting our meetings. Sharon didn't object. So my security guys saddled up in their SWAT gear—black helmets, Kevlar, the whole deal—and off we went.

It was tense crossing the five-hundred-yard no-man's-land between the IDF forces and the bombed-out building complex where Arafat and his security forces were barricaded. When the media heard I was going in, they came rushing out; but the Israelis shot at them and drove them off (some cameras were able to get pictures).

I walked the last yards and came to barricaded windows, the walls were blasted by tanks, Palestinian gunmen were at the doors, and I had to walk through this rubble to see Arafat.

Peace activists from the States and Europe had somehow made it in through Israeli lines. The hall- and passageways, where the activists were living, were overcrowded; there was hardly room for all of them. There was no electricity, no phone lines (and I'd noticed an IDF communications-jamming van outside to cut off calls), little water, and only sporadic food. The place smelled bad. Things were grim.

I met Arafat in a dimly lit little room; there was a semiautomatic weapon by his side. All of his aides looked like drowned rats, stressed out and beaten; but he was in his glory, upbeat and animated, more alert and fired up than I had ever seen him. The siege had brought out the fighter in him.

"I am under siege," he announced dramatically, enjoying the hell out of the moment. This was what he lived for. This was an old revolutionary in his element.

That was okay. If he was having a great time, fine. But my aim in visiting him was to break the impasse with Sharon. Thankfully, that happened. Arafat agreed to let his people meet with me, and so I was able to keep up our contacts.

I met with some Palestinian leaders at a onetime casino in Jericho (now shut down because of the conflict). It was a somber meeting. We discussed where to go and what to do next. We made some progress. Defused some bad situations. Got some sieges lifted. Probably saved some lives but not much more.

But I knew the process was dead.

ON EASTER SUNDAY, I attended Mass with Father Peter at the Tomb of the Holy Sepulcher and walked in the Garden of Gethsemane where Christ had prayed before His betrayal and crucifixion. The olive trees in there—huge, gnarled, old things—went back to the time of Christ.

All this gave a much-needed spiritual boost . . . though I've got to say that I have a pretty good idea how Christ must have felt in the garden.

. . .

SECRETARY POWELL came to the region on the eleventh of April to try to stop the Israeli attacks. The impact of that Passover bombing had struck at the core of the Israelis' psyche. That was when Sharon finally wrote off Arafat. There would be nothing to do with Arafat, nothing. He refused absolutely to back down from that position.

The Secretary and I met with Israeli leaders, then went out to see Arafat in his gutted compound. We worked hard to arrange a relief of the siege. The stumbling block was two men inside the compound who were wanted by the Israelis. The pair had killed the Israeli Minister of Tourism Ze'evi months before; Arafat had refused to give them up; and the Israelis were close to a decision to storm the buildings. If anything bad happened to Arafat—and it didn't matter what, death, injury, capture, or exile—it could end up being a disaster. We worked out a deal. The pair were to be jailed in Jericho by the Palestinians, but under U.S. and U.K. monitors. We also worked with others to relieve sieges in other West Bank areas.

For the next few days, Secretary Powell, Bill Burns, and I tried to find ways to salvage our mission, but the immediate future was looking terribly grim. By the end of these meeting, I believe that Powell had also lost faith in Arafat's will to move forward on the peace process. Soon after his return to the States, the President reached a decision that we couldn't deal with Arafat; he was a lost cause; and the Palestinian Authority had to be re-formed. By June, the United States made that position clear. Unless the Palestinian Authority was re-formed, and somebody other than Arafat was in charge, we weren't going to do business.

Meanwhile, one of my daughters was about to be married, and I wanted to return home for her wedding. When nobody came up with objections, I prepared to leave, promising to return if needed. I left on the fifteenth of April.

FOR THE next year, the process went nowhere. I remained under the contract with State Department; but it was clear the administration wouldn't call on me again.

I did meet with Israelis and Palestinians on a number of occasions, especially at IGCC sessions in Brussels and Athens in the months after my departure. Each time I was asked when I would return. I had to answer, sadly, that I doubted that I would be sent back.

On March 1, 2003, I resigned my position with the State Department. It was pointless to remain under contract and keep the title of Special Advisor to the Secretary of State knowing that I wouldn't be called upon again. By then, concerns I had voiced about the impending Iraq war made me persona non grata with the administration.

WHAT COULD we have done that was different?

For starters, there should not have been another special envoy. The expectations and media attention become a detriment to progress with a high-visibility envoy. Also, it was time to get away from personalities. We needed worker bees.

Second, and more broadly, what we were trying to do was take that very small match, light a very narrow fuse, and hope it burned evenly all the way along. We were trying to construct peace by taking sequential steps along a path. Everything hinged not only on the sequence but on each very fragile and vulnerable step. All the focus went on these steps—media, people, leaders. And it's all too easy to disrupt. Too easy to break. Too easy to attack. And peace fails.

What we need to do instead is put a large delegation on the ground, with a political component, a security component, an economic component, and a monitoring component. The delegation should come from the United States, the Quad, and any others from the international community that we can interest in the process. We should light a thousand fires instead of one fuse with one match. We need to find small positive actions, tiny cooperative measures. We need to go into towns like Jericho, where there aren't many problems, and start some projects. We also need to start some joint model projects—a joint economic project here, a security arrangement there. While we continue trying to build on the Tenet/Mitchell plans or the President's "Roadmap to Peace" (which was put forward in June 2002 and covers much the same territory), we'll have other things generating activity, and giving a sense of momentum or progress to build hope. This is all going to be slow, but it will also go forward on a broad front. It'll get there in time.

Third, the Palestinian Authority must be re-formed. But those that step up to the challenge like Abu Mazen and Abu Ala'a have to be given support and clout. This can only come from tangible U.S. support for them and from serious negotiations with them by the Israeli leadership.

ACEH

My involvement with the HDC as one of their Wise Men did not cease during my time in the Middle East.

During the first week of February 2002, we held a session in Geneva with representatives of the government of Indonesia and the GAM. The government of Indonesia's chief representative was retired Ambassador Wiryono and the GAM's chief representatives were Dr. Zaini Abdullah and Malik Haythar Mohmood. These negotiators were civil and cooperative. I did not see the kinds of theatrical outbursts I had seen in the Middle East; I had a sense that each wanted a successful and peaceful resolution to the issues.

Still, it was a tough meeting with intense negotiating periods. The two sides and the HDC mediators made considerable use of the Wise Men— in addition to me: Surin Pitsuwan, Budamir Loncur, Lord Eric Avebury. These brilliant and experienced statesmen added a great deal to the negotiations. Each negotiating party called on us to provide advice on developing issues and recommendations on constructing points for agreement. We were most effective when discussions hit an impasse and needed a "push."

The Wise Men were also joined by an additional pair of outside experts in the art of negotiating, who provided valuable insights on procedure and processes.

This new approach (designed by the Henri Dunant Centre) of bringing in multiple parties beyond the traditional three has caused me to look hard at other nontraditional approaches to conflict resolution. This is a critical area that must have a great deal more study and development.

. . .

THE ACEH process went through several steps.

The first session was aimed at achieving an agreement to accept the political process and get a cease-fire. Though this was far from easy (for all the reasons and issues discussed earlier), we got that.

In the second session we worked with the government to persuade them to make an offer on special autonomy, and then to draft a proposal. Once that had been achieved, we worked with the GAM to get them to understand it.

The third session put together what we called a cessation of hostilities agreement, which was the mechanism through which they would turn this into a political and a peaceful process.

The February meeting ended with the parties signing an agreement titled "Points for Further Consideration." This was an agreement to continue to meet and a commitment to a peaceful resolution to the problems in Aceh. This was progress. I had learned that signing meant commitment.

We met again in early May outside Geneva, with much larger delegations from both sides, in a beautiful Alpine Swiss estate offered to us as a venue to provide privacy (there was growing press interest). It was an environment conducive to constructive negotiations.

This session produced a more substantive agreement to cease hostilities and pursue a political process to resolve differences. We Wise Men earned our keep—struggling with precise wording of the agreement that would satisfy each party.

All was not sweetness and light, however. I sensed a major roadblock that would later on prove fatal.

The government had proposed a political process with elections; but these elections did not include independence as an option. In the government's view, the GAM would be no more than one political organization among others that might represent the people in the context of special autonomy.

The GAM leadership could not live with that. They could not bring themselves to publicly disavow their aspirations for independence. The best they could do was accept a nonviolent political process, with elections at the end, that allowed the people to decide whether to accept the government's offer of special autonomy or opt for independence.

This was a serious impasse, with Jakarta pressing GAM to formally disavow independence as a goal, and GAM refusing to take that step. (They could not even tacitly accept special autonomy without formally acknowledging it, knowing with certainty that independence was not in the cards.)

All that aside, the agreement for a process and a cessation of hostilities was enough to move forward. It seemed to me that if independence didn't become an immediate issue, we might resolve the block down the road through further negotiations.

Special autonomy was itself no small matter, from the government's point of view. It set a precedent that could cause problems with other provinces (which is why hard-liners in the government continued to want to resolve the issue with greater military force). Meanwhile, the moderates, headed by the Coordinating Minister for Political and Security Affairs, Susilo Bambang Yudhoyono, worked to convince President Megawati to accept this peaceful measure.

As the session closed, the mood was upbeat and positive; and I hoped we could sidestep the independence issue until constructive actions started happening on the ground in Aceh.

IN AUGUST I traveled to Singapore and Indonesia, where I met with Minister Yudhoyono, General Sutarto (the chief of staff of the Indonesian military), and other government officials. They all expressed a strong desire to produce a comprehensive proposal on special autonomy and a process for implementing a peaceful resolution to the conflict. We agreed to work with them on this effort.

I also traveled to Aceh to get a firsthand sense of the situation there. There, I met with local government officials, GAM members, and ordinary people who were caught in the middle of the struggle. Over ten thousand of them had been killed so far, and many more had suffered from atrocities committed by both sides. They were tired of this painful conflict.

A drive through the countryside and jungle areas with HDC representatives brought on an eerie sense of déjà vu; it was like going back to Vietnam.

I had a great deal of respect for the small HDC staff on the ground in Aceh and their local employees. It took courage and commitment to work in this environment; and I could sense their determination to work for positive change.

I left the region encouraged that a peaceful resolution could be achieved there. Though I knew progress would be difficult, I felt the momentum would rapidly grow if we could get a process going on the ground.

IN SEPTEMBER, we met at Versailles to advise the government on the drafting. (The French government had offered the palace as a venue after the Indonesian government had expressed a desire to add significance to their proposal by drafting it in "a historic setting.") Their proposal was then forwarded to the GAM, and over the next two months issues were worked out through the HDC.

In December, we convened in Geneva, where both parties signed "The Cessation of Hostilities Agreement Between the Government of the Republic of Indonesia and the Free Aceh Movement." The agreement laid out a detailed process, which covered disarmament, political procedures, elections, monitoring mechanisms, and many other aspects of the peaceful path to resolution of their conflict. The HDC was designated as the monitoring agency, with countries in the region contributing personnel to support the effort. Things got off to a wonderful start and everyone involved was ecstatic.

Soon after the signing, President Megawati traveled to the province to kick off the process, and expectations and hopes continued to be high.

For a few months, all went well. But when the independence issue again reared up in a series of heated exchanges in the press, the situation rapidly deteriorated. The angry words triggered violence on the ground; the HDC monitors were threatened and forced to withdraw.

The HDC tried to get the two parties back on track, but arguments over dates and venues scuttled their efforts.

With the agreement breaking apart, President Megawati, under pressure from the hard-liners, dispatched troops to the province to commence a large-scale military operation.

IN MAY 2003, I received urgent calls from both the State Department and the HDC asking me to fly immediately to Stockholm to encourage the GAM leadership to recommit to the agreement. This might possibly convince the government to call off, or postpone, the impending military action. I took a Concorde flight to London and reached Stockholm only hours after I left Washington.

As I arrived, I learned that the U.S., European Union, and Japanese ambassadors had issued a demarche to the GAM and another to the Jakarta government, making it abundantly clear that these governments could not support independence for Aceh; the outstanding issues between GAM and Jakarta had to be resolved within the context of the Indonesian state.

My side of the mission proved successful, but the Jakarta end of things was stickier. The GAM agreed to issue a statement recommitting to the agreement and requesting the government to join them in trying to get the provisions of the agreement back on track in Aceh. But the Indonesian government was not favorably inclined to accept the GAM's offer. President Megawati did, however, agree to postpone military action for a week to give peace one more chance.

The U.S., European Union, and Japanese governments, together with the HDC, hastily arranged a meeting in Tokyo to get the two sides together (which, regrettably, I could not attend). It collapsed almost immediately when the government insisted on a statement disavowing independence as a nonnegotiable condition. The GAM refused.

Within hours of the collapse, government forces launched a full-scale military operation. Thousands of troops were involved.

I was tremendously disappointed.

In spite of the disappointment, the HDC and the Wise Men are still committed to the effort and standing by to help. I also committed to work with the HDC on emerging peace efforts in Africa.

THE PHILIPPINES

In early June 2003, the members of HDC, the Wise Men, and the monitoring teams that had been on the ground in Aceh all gathered in Geneva to discuss lessons learned and the possibilities of reengaging. Everyone agreed to remain ready to salvage the peace agreement or to begin a new round of negotiations if the opportunity presented itself. At this session, Martin Griffiths asked me if I would be willing to participate as a Wise Man in other peace meditations that the center was considering taking on.

"Absolutely," I answered, "but I'd have to look at each situation and get a State Department okay, even though I'll still be undertaking these missions as a private citizen."

He of course understood that I would need the Department's blessing.

Two weeks later, eighteen of the most prominent peace negotiators, post-conflict supervisors, and writers (the foremost experts and practitioners in conflict resolution) came together in Oslo, Norway, in a Norwegian government–sponsored conference they called "a Mediator's Retreat." I was flattered to be included in this group.

At the conference, Martin Griffiths discussed with me efforts to settle the decades-long guerrilla wars between the government of the Philippines and several separatist groups. The parties had approached HDC as a possible mediating body; and Griffiths was wondering if I'd like to be involved as a Wise Man. I agreed to participate, contingent on State's okay.

On June 16, after my return to the States, I called Deputy Secretary of State Rich Armitage, who, it turned out, had also been directing attention to the Philippine conflict. During a visit to Washington in May, Philippine President Arroyo had asked President Bush for his support in peace negotiations with the Moro Islamic Liberation Front (MILF), a group that seemed ready to come to the peace table after long resisting that course. Though Rich was positive about the help I might offer the process, there were questions about which organization would be handling negotiations; and he was not aware of HDC's possible connection. He wanted to get back to me about that.

A week later, Tom Cymkin, a State Department official I had worked with during the Aceh negotiations, called to clear up the issue. The U.S.

Institute of Peace (USIP), he explained, would be the designated "facilitators" for this process, and this had been squared with HDC. State wanted me to join a group of Wise Men being formed at USIP to engage in that process. The Malaysian government had taken on the role of mediator; the USIP Wise Men would augment and support the effort, as a follow-up to President Bush's public commitment to support the peace process.

The USIP was established by Congress "to support development, transmission, and use of knowledge to promote peace and curb violent international conflict." The institute's primary work was in education, training, and research to promote peace and the resolution of conflicts. The mandate to establish a team of Wise Men to facilitate the mediation effort was a new role for them. The team they formed—seven others in addition to me—was impressive. All were highly experienced and well-regarded diplomats. Four had been U.S. ambassadors to the Philippines.

Ambassador Dick Solomon, the head of USIP, called me later that day to welcome me to the group and to set up meetings and briefings over the coming weeks. On the first of July, I visited USIP offices in Washington, met with the other Wise Men, and received detailed briefs on the situation and the approach we would take.

The conflict we were dealing with, begun over three decades ago, had its roots in the long-standing friction between the Muslims of Mindanao and the Christian majority in the rest of the Philippines. In 1968, non-Muslim soldiers had massacred Muslim soldiers in the Philippine Army. This outrage led to the formation of the Moro National Liberation Front (MNLF); their aim was independence. In the mid-eighties, the more religious and ideological MILF broke away from the MNLF.

In 1996, the MNLF reached a peace agreement with the government (which was not accepted by the MILF). Though it has had a rocky implementation, it has been holding; and recently, the MILF had indicated that they too were ready for talks. The government under President Gloria Macapagal Arroyo had declared its intention to join these negotiations.

In response to President Arroyo's May request, President Bush issued a statement promising support. This was welcomed by chairman Hashim Salamat, the leader of the MILF.

Following our initial briefings, we were briefed by representatives from the Malaysian Embassy in Washington. We reassured them that we were truly there to support them and not to replace them as mediators.

Our next step was a fact-finding trip to the region to get a firsthand sense of the situation on the ground and meet some of the key players. On August 10, four of us left for the Philippines, just as the MILF announced the death of Salamat, their leader. The death of their longtime leader caused the MILF to undergo internal adjustments, but his heir apparent claimed that he too was committed to a peace process.

We spent the first days of our visit in Manila calling on President Arroyo and other government officials. The President was a truly impressive leader. Her self-confidence, intellect, knowledge of details, and obvious leadership ability, together with a sincere commitment to the peace process and honesty about past government failures, clearly came through. The members of the congress, ministers, military leaders, and the chief negotiator for the government seemed equally committed. Though there were hard-liners in the government who did not favor negotiations, the majority seemed to support them. Everyone we talked to acknowledged that there was no military solution to this conflict.

In Manila, we also met with members of the Muslim community, the media, Christian church representatives, NGOs, and our own embassy officials. Our Ambassador, Frank Ricciardone, was an old friend from my CENTCOM days. We also met with our USAID officials who were working in Mindanao. They had started a series of impressive projects there, whose incentives and rewards helped keep the '96 agreement together. The promise of more of these was a big reason for the MILF's motivation to reach an agreement.

On our third day, we traveled to Carabao, Mindanao, the small port city that served as the capital of the autonomous region set up by the '96 agreement. There we met representatives of the MNLF, the MILF, and members of civil society. Mindanao is a beautiful Pacific paradise . . . with striking poverty and little promise of a brighter future. The Moros (as the locals were called) described centuries of oppression, injustice, and suffering; and gave mixed reviews on the fulfillment of the '96 agreement and the programs it had promised.

In the hinterland, we presided over the opening of a USAID project that provided training and facilities for former MNLF guerrilla fighters, now trading their weapons for farm implements. It was another country-side that eerily reminded me of Vietnam—thatched huts, water buffalos, rice paddies, and bamboo clumps, all familiar sights. At the site of the ceremony, a small grain-storage building and training area in a jungle clearing, I studied the faces of the wiry, tough former guerrillas as they sat through the speeches and ribbon-cutting ceremonies in the hot sun of midday; I had seen thousands of such faces before. I wondered what was going through their minds. The security was heavy with Philippine military and police, and MNLF security forces all around us.

We returned to Carabao and continued our meetings with local USAID representatives.

On my last day, we had sessions in Manila with Lieutenant General Garcia, the deputy chief of staff of the Philippine Armed Forces and the chairman of the Coordination Committee for the Cessation of Hostilities, the element established to implement the '96 agreement. General Garcia was an impressive man, honest and experienced, with exceptional insights about the practicalities of implementing the agreements on the ground (always the tough part of conflict resolution). He taught me invaluable lessons.

I left the Philippines on the fourteenth of June with a real sense that this effort could work. It was going to be difficult, but enough pieces seemed to be in place to encourage hope.

The process continues . . .

WORKING TOWARD a peaceful resolution to long-running, bitter conflicts can be difficult and thankless. Your successes are few. But along the way, you save lives or better the lot of poor souls caught up in conflict. And on those rare occasion when you fully succeed, every effort becomes worthwhile. I have experienced firsthand the pain and devastation of war. I know I have to work to find alternatives to it where I can.

CHAPTER EIGHT

THE CALLING

TONY ZINNI REFLECTS.

At the very beginning of the twentieth century—a time when the daring and brave from many nations struck out for the promised land—two men from the rugged, mountainous province of Abruzzo in central Italy set off to achieve that promise. One of the men was a peasant farmer named Francesco Zinni; the other was a tailor named Zupito DiSabatino. They were my grandfathers. They had never met, and would not for many years.

Their trek followed the pattern followed by thousands of others. They came alone, found jobs, established themselves in this strange, raw, bustling land, and a few years later sent for their families. With the same courage and apprehension, my grandmothers, Christina Zinni and Cecilia DiSabatino, packed up the kids, headed to the Italian ports, and sailed across the seas to join their husbands. With Christina in 1910 was her fourteen-year-old son, Antonio, my father; and with Cecilia in 1906 was her three-year-old daughter, Lilla, my mother. I often look at faded old pictures taken around that time and wonder what my parents and grandparents were thinking as these great changes unfolded.

Neither of my parents had an easy life growing up. Like all young immigrants of the time, they managed only a few years of education before they had to go to work. My father worked in mills, and then in landscaping, and eventually became a chauffeur; my mother worked in garment factories.

Our family military tradition in America started with my father, who was drafted to fight in World War One—the War to End All Wars—shortly after he arrived from Italy. He got here and he was drafted. Later, I looked into it and found that twelve percent of America's infantrymen in World War One were Italian immigrants. Their new homeland did not forget their wartime service. My father, who served in the 101st Aero Squadron in France, received his citizenship papers along with his discharge papers. He came out of the war as a full-fledged citizen of the United States. Just imagine what that meant to him!

Meanwhile, his family had settled in a mill town called Conshohocken on the outskirts of Philadelphia; and my mother's family had settled in the Italian neighborhoods of South Philadelphia. These places were the center of my universe for the first two decades of my life.

They met during the 1920s, married, and raised four children: Frank, Christine, Rita, and me. I entered the wonderful, loving world of large Italian families on September 17, 1943, when my parents were well into their forties.

The people with whom I grew up were from working-class families. The mothers were full of love and caring, and raised the brood. The men worked hard, and most served their country in time of war—all as enlisted men. Besides my father, I had cousins who served in World War Two; my brother served in the Korean War; and my sisters married men who served. I listened to the stories these men told with fascination and envy. To them, service was an obligation of citizenship and, more important, a rite of passage to manhood. That obligation was engraved on my young brain. It was part of what had to be done as you grew into adulthood. If you were fortunate, I thought, you might even see action.

In my neighborhood were ethnic families that included Italian, Irish, Polish, African American, and "Mayflower" Americans. I don't remember much friction between these groups. The mixed neighborhoods, schools, and workplaces tended to bring everyone together. I attended public school for the first five grades, then switched to Catholic school for the upper grades and for high school. The good sisters ran a tight ship. We learned self-discipline and a strong work ethic, mixed with a good dose of right and wrong.

THESE ARE the particular influences that have shaped me. Other, larger events shaped my generation. Those of us who survived those changes, and were able to advance more than we retreated, may have had advantages not shared by many young people starting out today. Of course it always helps to have good genes and DNA, and to come from families that function normally. But we also grew up in school systems that actually taught us something and imprinted us with a code, which helped move us along the path toward being useful citizens. And for most of us, our religious upbringing gave us an acceptance of a Higher Being in one form or another, at the core of our beliefs.

Of the events that shaped us, some came to us as a legacy; some we actually lived through. One of the biggest was World War Two, which has proven to be both a blessing and a curse to my generation. The blessing was that the Greatest Generation preserved our freedoms and our way of life, lifted us out of a severe depression on a wave of prosperity, and moved us into a role of world leadership. The curse is that it was the last Good War—the last with moral clarity, an easily identified and demonized enemy, unprecedented national unity in mobilization and rationing, pride in those who served in uniform (shown by the blue star flags hung by the families of those who fought and the gold star flags by the families of those who died), and welcome home victory parades for those lucky enough to return from overseas. Every war should be fought like that.

After World War Two, I learned about war at the knees of my cousins, who'd fought at the Battle of the Bulge in Europe and all over the Pacific— on the ground and in the air. A few years later, my older brother was drafted and fought in Korea. Their war stories were remarkable: sometimes gory and horrible, but always positive in the end. It was like winning the Big Game against your archrival—always clean and always good. So this was my generation's legacy: World War Two was the way you fight a war. And all throughout our four decades of service, this notion kept getting reinforced. Former Secretary of Defense Caspar Weinberger's famous 1984 statement of doctrine about the six criteria for the use of military force* is a recipe for refighting World War Two—not for fighting the Operations Other Than War (OOTW) that we face today. In fact, if you read the Weinberger Doctrine and adhere to every one of its tenets, you will be able to fight no war other than World War Two.

I JOINED the Marines in 1961 and officially retired on September 1, 2000.

I'd like to shine a spotlight on who we were—the military generations who went through the past four decades, from the 1960s up to the new millennium. If you looked at a snapshot taken when I first came into the service, all the generals looked the same—distinguished older white males with Anglo-Saxon names and Southern drawls—while the troops they led came from lots of different places. Let's just say that the generals didn't speak Philadelphia the way I speak Philadelphia.

But things were changing in the 1960s. Marine Corps officers were still coming in from the service academies and military institutes, yet more and more were coming in from Catholic colleges in the Northeast (as I did), from state colleges and universities around the nation, and from other schools with strong NROTC units or other strong military traditions. At the same time, we were seeing people coming up through the enlisted ranks to become officers—not just the tough old mustangs or limited-duty officers with midgrade terminal ranks, but young people whom we would send to school as an investment in the future. Back then, whatever our various backgrounds, we all came into the service with a code imprinted on each of us by family, school, or church. Those who had come from military schools received the imprint from their officers. One way or another,

---

* In its essentials, the Weinberger Doctrine is very close to the Powell Doctrine: We should not consider using military force unless we are prepared to field decisive/overwhelming force; to have clear objectives; and to obtain the full support of the American people.

all of us were programmed to believe that we were not just doing a job, or even a profession, but were pursuing a calling.

It was never a drag for me to go to work. The troops, the leaders and mentors, the day-to-day experiences, always gave me a charge. I just loved it from day one. Don't get me wrong. It wasn't always fun. There were bad times. And some of the times were truly harrowing. But I never tired of engaging with the challenges. I could wrap my entire self around them— body, mind, and spirit. I never once regretted that I took that course through life.

AROUND THE TURN of the millennium, I had occasion to talk with old World War Two vets. It was often unnerving to face the old guys who'd look at me and seem to say, "How in hell did you screw it up? We had it right and we did it right and we fought and we understood and we left this country an incredible legacy, and now look at where we are . . ."

It's hard to escape the feeling "God, I've let them down," because the second major challenge that affected us was the Vietnam War—our nation's longest and least satisfactory. It was my second-lieutenant experience, and I was pretty green (that changed fast). I didn't see then all the problems we see now—the war was fought in the wrong way; it was badly led. I went through serious pain and suffering. I was sick; I was badly wounded. Yet despite all these problems, I would do it again. We had to do it.

Not because it was a "good" war, but because even in our failure we delivered a message that had to be delivered. We have to understand Vietnam within its context. We were in the Cold War. We were fighting communism. We had to stop it from spreading. We made a stand and didn't hold that line. But communism didn't spread. You can't tell me that the Soviets didn't get the message that we would stand if we had to.

The veterans of that war, in their losing fight, were no less heroes than the veterans of World War Two; and in some ways their heroism goes deeper, because it was never truly recognized and appreciated by the American people.

As my time in Vietnam lengthened, I began asking questions . . . wondering just what in hell our generals—my heroes who fought in World War Two—thought they were doing. Those of us who were platoon commanders and company commanders fought hard, but could never understand what war our most senior leaders thought we were fighting. The tactics didn't make sense and the personnel policies—such as one-year individual rotations instead of unit rotations in and out of country—were hard to comprehend.

Today, of course, we are seeing a stream of apologetic books by the policymakers and military leaders of that era—as though saying *mea culpa* enough will absolve them of the terrible responsibility they still bear.

The third major test we went through was the challenge of the '70s. It was the toughest time for me in my four decades of Marine Corps service—racial problems, drug problems, generational problems, authority problems . . . flower children, peace marches, demonstrations (some of them violent), the loss of trust in the military by a large portion of the American people. But in passing through that tumultuous cauldron, our military has, in my view, put together its greatest achievement during that forty-year period. To name just one example, it is the one segment of society where integration of the races has fully taken hold. Sure, we still run into problems, but nowhere else in American society can a person of color find the kind of opportunity he or she can find in our military. And we in the military are far better off for their presence. I am proud of them. We want the best and the brightest, and we get them.

The fourth challenge that affected my generation was the Cold War—which was actually a forty-year commitment to refight World War Two, if ever the need arose. Once again, we were energized to engage in global conflict, but this time against the evil "Red Menace." Problem was, we could never figure just how this particular war would actually start. After playing a bazillion war games at the Naval War College and other places, I still could not come up with a logical or convincing way such a war would kick off. It was just too hard to show why the Soviets would want to conquer a burning, devastated Europe, or how that could possibly benefit the communists in any way. So we would just gloss over the way the miserable war got started, jump into the middle of things, and play on. The Cold War was ever-present, and it was great for justifying programs, systems, and force structure—but, deep down inside, no one seriously believed that it would actually happen.

Still, it necessarily drove things. It drove the way we thought; it drove the way we organized and equipped; and it drove the way we developed our concepts of fighting. It totally *shaped* us. It totally defined who we were. And when it was all over, we achieved our aim. The war didn't happen. This was *not* a dog that didn't bark. The readiness we worked so hard to achieve for so many years was apparent to the Soviets and their surrogates. They could see the level of our commitment. They didn't want to take us on. Our readiness and commitment acted as a deterrent—exactly what we wanted them to do.

That taught us one other vital lesson: How to contain and how to deter—the use of the military to *prevent* wars. This was the first time in history, to my knowledge, that a great power has taken that course. It's a course we will have to take again and again in the twenty-first century.

Then suddenly, at the end of the 1980s, the Berlin Wall came down, the Evil Empire collapsed, and we found ourselves in the New World Order. It would require a major adjustment. We didn't do that right.

The next influential event was Desert Storm, which, as far as I am concerned, was an aberration. Though it seemed to work out okay for us—indeed proved beyond doubt how enormously powerful our Cold War military really was—it was the final salute of the Cold War military. It left the impression that the terrible mess that awaits us abroad can somehow be overcome by good, clean soldiering, just like in World War Two. In reality, the only reason Desert Storm worked was because we managed to go up against the only jerk on the planet who was stupid enough to challenge us to refight World War Two—with less of everything that counted, including the moral right to do what he did to Kuwait. In the top-level war colleges, we still fight this type of adversary, so we always can win. I rebelled at this notion, thinking there would be nobody out there so stupid to fight us that way. But then along came Saddam Hussein, and "good soldiering" was vindicated once again.

Worse yet, the end of any conflict often brings into professional circles the heartfelt belief that "Now that the war is over, we can get back to real soldiering." So we merrily backtrack in that direction. Scary, isn't it? Still trying to fight our kind of war—be it World War Two, Desert Storm, or Operation Iraqi Freedom—we ignore the real war-fighting requirements of today. We want to fight the services' conventional doctrines. We want to find a real adversarial demon—a composite of Hitler, Tojo, and Mussolini—so we can drive on to his capital city and crush him there. Unconditional surrender. Then we'll put in place a Marshall Plan, embrace the long-suffering vanquished, and help them regain entry into the community of nations. Everybody wants to do that. But it ain't gonna happen.

Today, we are stuck with the likes of a wiser Kim Jong Il and a still-elusive Osama bin Laden—just a couple of those charmers out there who will no longer take us on in a symmetric force matchup. And we're going to be doing things like humanitarian operations, consequence management, peacekeeping, and peace enforcement. Somewhere along the line, we'll have to respond to some kind of environmental disaster. And somewhere else along the line we may get stuck with putting a U.S. battalion in place on some demarcation line between two adversaries, embedded in a weird, screwed-up chain of command. And do you know what? We're going to bitch and moan about it. We're going to dust off the Weinberger Doctrine and the Powell Doctrine and throw them in the face of our civilian leadership.

The truth is that military conflict has changed and we have been reluctant to recognize it. Defeating nation-state forces in conventional battle is not the task for the twenty-first century. Odd missions to defeat transnational threats or rebuild nations are the order of the day, but we haven't as yet adapted. We all know it, but we won't acknowledge it.

THE OBLIGATION
TO SPEAK THE TRUTH

In April of 2003, I was invited by the U.S. Naval Academy to address the midshipmen in a lecture hosted by their Center for the Study of Military Ethics. I chose as my topic "The Obligation to Speak the Truth." I told these future leaders that speaking the truth could be painful and costly, but it was a duty. Often those who need to hear it won't like it and may even punish you for it; but you owed the truth to your country, your leaders, and your troops.

I have been amazed that men who bravely faced death on the battlefield are later, as senior officers, cowed and unwilling to stand up for what is right or to point out what is wrong. There are many reasons for this, from careerism and the hope of personal gain, to political expediency, to a false sense of obedience, to a kind of "Charge of the Light Brigade" mentality: As long as guys are dying out there, it is morally reprehensible to criticize the flawed policies and tactics that put them in that predicament. Bullshit.

I vowed long ago to a wounded young lance corporal in Vietnam that I would never shrink from speaking out. If it required an end to my career, so be it. Later, I was blessed to serve under great leaders who allowed me to speak and welcomed and encouraged my input, even when it was contrary to their views. These men taught me more about courage than I learned on any battlefield—people like Hugh Shelton, who, as chairman of the Joint Chiefs of Staff, required all of us four-star commanders (CINCs and service chiefs) to read a book by H. R. McMaster, then a bright young Army major and a celebrated armor officer in Desert Storm (as a captain he commanded Eagle Troop of the 2nd Armored Cavalry Regiment during the Battle of 73 Easting, the biggest tank clash since 1973 in the Sinai). The book, *Dereliction of Duty*, details the failures of the Joint Chiefs to speak out during the Vietnam War; they knew they were building a military campaign on lies, but they pressed forward anyway into the Valley of Death. At a breakfast meeting on January 29, 1998, which was led by Major McMaster, the chairman's message was clear: He expected us to speak out. I experienced the same sort of encouragement under exceptional commanders like Generals Al Gray, Bob Barrow, Jack Galvin, Mick Trainor, Fred Haynes, Jim McCarthy, Joe Hoar, Binnie Peay, Bob Johnston, and Admiral Snuffy Smith. We need more leaders such as these.

Moral courage is often more difficult than physical courage. There are times when you disagree and you have to suck it in and say, "Yes, sir," and go do what you're told. There are also times when you disagree and you have to speak out, even at the cost of your career. If you're a general, you might have to throw your stars on the table, as they say, and resign for the sake of some principle or truth from which you can't back away.

Careerism is corrosive to the principle of truth telling. So is political expediency. In both cases, the hope of personal gain outweighs personal integrity and honor. "Don't rock the boat" leads to moral blindness about threats to the mission or the lives and welfare of the troops and of their families. The troops are interested in more from their leaders back home than statements such as, "We back them one hundred percent." That's the mentality of the château generals in World War One who sent hundreds of thousands of fine young men to useless deaths. If you make a political mistake, the troops have to pay for it with their blood. Our political and military leaders must be held accountable for their mistakes. Somebody has to tell them that the measures of success they're selling are not what is really happening on the ground.

The troops want leaders who understand them, fight for them, and appreciate what they're going through. Credibility is lost in their eyes if their leaders are silent when things are not right. To them that silence is either incompetence or careerism. It is not a demonstration of support.

I have often been called "outspoken." I am. Too many of our senior commanders have been "Stepford Generals and Stepford Admirals." They fail in their obligation to speak the truth. And when they do, they're vilified. Recently, the Army chief of staff testified that we would need 300,000 troops to pacify Iraq. Everybody in the military knew he was right. But the party line down from the Pentagon decreed that the number was half that, and he was pilloried.

Incidents like that are not lost on our subordinates. Many are disgusted and disillusioned, and leave the service of their country. Others learn that following the party line is the course to high rank.

In the lead-up to the Iraq war and its later conduct, I saw, at a minimum, true dereliction, negligence, and irresponsibility; at worst, lying, incompetence, and corruption. False rationales presented as a justification; a flawed strategy; lack of planning; the unnecessary alienation of our allies; the underestimation of the task; the unnecessary distraction from real threats; and the unbearable strain dumped on our overstretched military, all of these caused me to speak out. I did it before the war as a caution, and as an attempt to voice concern over situations I knew would be dangers, where the outcomes would likely mean real harm to our nation's interests. I was called a traitor and a turncoat by Pentagon officials. The personal attacks are painful, as I told those young midshipmen, but the photos of the casualties I see every day in the papers and on TV convince me not to shrink from the obligation to speak the truth.

OUR OBLIGATION to tell the truth extends even to the media.

Over the past forty years, we have seen strange things happen with regard to the media. To be sure, there are few Ernie Pyles out there—great journalists who make combat come alive the way that the boots on the ground experience it—but there's nothing inherently wrong with the media. It has the same percentages of good guys and bad guys as other fields.

Yet technology has changed things. The media are on the battlefield; the media are in your headquarters; the media are everywhere. And the media report everything—good and bad, warts and all. And everyone knows that the warts tend to make better stories. As a CINC, I was chewed out by seniors maybe five times; four of the five were about statements I'd made to the media. At that stage of my life, it didn't really bother me—because where in hell did I go from there? But if you are a lieutenant or a captain and you see another officer get fried, you have a different reaction. The message is clear: "Avoid the media." And the message hardens into a code: "They are the enemy. Don't be straight with them."

And that is bad. That is bad because we live in the Information Age. Battlefield reports are going to come back in real time, and they are going to be interpreted—with all sorts of subtle shadings and nuances—by the reporters and their news editors. But the relationship between the military and the media, which should be at its strongest right now, has bottomed out. It has begun to heal a little, but a lot more must be done. We need to rebuild a sense of mutual trust. My uncles in World War Two generally experienced a friendly press—with Bill Mauldin's Willie and Joe cartoons and Ernie Pyle's stories. The press then was part of the war effort.

G.I. Joe was lionized and bad news was suppressed—if not by the military then by the media. The relationship generally remained positive through the Korean War, despite its ambiguities. But the relationship soured during and after Vietnam, for a number of reasons—not the least of which was mounting distrust of government by the media and the American people.

The military and the media need to regain the mutual trust that once existed. It will be hard, given the recent past and the speed and sophistication of today's media technology, but it's crucial to protecting one of our most cherished freedoms, while keeping vital operational information secure.

LEADERSHIP AND LIFE

You can't lead unless you love those you lead. That's principle number one. All other leadership principles flow out of it. Too much leadership training focuses on the leader and not enough on the led. Your charges are your family. In professions that are truly callings, you have to have that. In my profession, guys put everything on the line and can die for it. We have to care about these guys. They have to mean something to us. We must know what makes them tick; who they are; what they want and need; what motivates them.

I remember talking to Prime Minister Meles of Ethiopia a few years ago. Before he became leader of his government, he was a fighting general in a twenty-year-long revolution. He *knew* his troops. They'd lived and fought together for two decades. One day during the fighting, his troops had to pass through a minefield, without any of the mechanical devices we use for our protection. He had no choice. He had to send troops ahead of everybody to find lanes. Many of them died, but his forces successfully made the passage.

When he told me the story, tears were in his eyes for the troops he'd lost. If you don't or can't feel that, then you shouldn't lead.

The second principle is to know yourself. Few leaders are as good as they think they are. And commanders develop skills in finding measures of success that make them look good, such as body counts. What's the real measure of success? You get it from truly understanding the conflict and by seeking feedback from the guys with boots on the ground. They're there; they know. An ego can be bruised by feedback, but it's critical truly to know how you stand as a leader. True leaders seek feedback regardless of the news. They learn from it.

All people come in three parts: body, mind, and spirit. No one is complete unless all three are developed and tended to. As a leader, you need to care for these in yourself and in those you lead.

Each leader needs a code to live by. That code can be formed by many factors. Our family, our schooling, our faith, our friends, and our calling in life can all be counted among those factors. My daughter once asked me what I would die for. I thought about that a lot before I answered her. I knew the answer would truly define me. I told her I would die for my faith, my family, my friends, my freedom, and my flag—the five "Fs," a simplified expression of my code. But a code is worthless unless you live it. Words like *integrity, ethics, honor,* etc., need to be lived and not just uttered.

You never stop learning unless you decide to. I have an unquenchable thirst for knowledge. It is an obsession for me. My sources for learning are all around me. When I make a mistake or fail, I have to know why. I need to know what makes things and people tick. I am amazed at how much people miss by not observing the world around them with an open curiosity.

I have learned more from sergeants than I have from generals. The troops relate to a leader by testing him or her to see if they relate to them, to see if they're open to them and listen to them. They want to know if they're fundamentally honest with them. This is not a "buddy" thing. Leaders can't be buddies with the led. But the troops want to be able to say: "I can talk to this captain. He listens." If you don't listen, they will be polite, but you can forget about their respect . . . or about getting the truth where the rubber meets the road. You want them to tell you: "Sir, this is not working." Or: "It is working." Or: "Yeah, it's working okay, but it could be better." When you know such truths, and can do something about them, that's when you have real success.

I love to teach. It is a principal function of leadership.

My teaching philosophy is based on two principles. The first has to do with the mission of the teacher. His role is to provide the students with the facts and with a clear articulation of the varying views, opinions, and options on a given subject. His purpose, after he has provided this framework, is to then teach the students *how* to think and not *what* to think about the subject. You want to teach the student how to ask the questions that really count and not how to give answers that satisfy conventional wisdom and long-fossilized received opinions. If you know how to ask the right questions, the best answers usually follow . . . though it may take time.

The second principle deals with the foundation of thinking. It must have a set of values at its base. This requires teachers to emphasize the importance of a values-based thinking process without imposing personal interpretations of those values. The values will be more powerful in a student's life and in his way of thinking, his decision making, and in how he defines his ethical code if he has discovered and defined them on his own.

The greatest enjoyment for a teacher is to see that moment of discovery or that moment of doubt that wasn't there before, but now presents the student with a spur to reason.

Learning is guided discovery. The guide is the teacher. His scholarship provides the factual basis for the student's journey of discovery; and his leadership, personal example, and mentoring skills provide the moral basis. A teacher's competence, therefore, comes in two inseparable parts. He must be expert in his subject and he must be qualified in his leadership ability. Technical competence alone is not sufficient. Leading and teaching are synonymous. You cannot assume to do one without the other.

As a teacher, I strive to meet the obligations articulated in this philosophy. It requires me to develop in myself the mental, physical, and spiritual qualities I desire to impart and instill in my students.

As a young captain, I began writing down everything I believed about my profession. I expressed my beliefs, asked others to challenge them, and sought more insight into each of them. I continuously changed or altered them as a result.

Over time these dynamic beliefs settled into three categories: those that I was absolutely sure were right; those that I was pretty sure were right;

and those that were up for grabs. It was an even split, with new ideas coming and some old ones going; they were in a constant state of morphing over time. I called these my "Combat Concepts." To me they were a mechanism for continuous learning.

The particular concepts themselves don't matter as much as the process. This process was so important to me that I extended it from war fighting to other areas—leadership, life, other people, team building. I kept asking myself: "What makes people tick? What do they want in life? What makes teams tick? How can I bring them together more strongly and effectively?"

I'd write down my thoughts on these things, but they were always open to challenge and to change. I wanted always to be able to keep examining my core. I learned long ago that when you stop examining your core, you can really be shaken when you take a hard hit.

AMERICA AND THE WORLD

Our country is great. It has become great because it strives to be good. That is, our country is values based . . . values we hold dear in good times and bad. Our country is admired, respected, envied, and hated for its greatness. To some it is the beacon that Jefferson said we should strive to be. It offers hope and promise. As a first-generation American, I know what that means. Everything is possible here.

We have to stay with all that. We might not always succeed, but we must always try. It's important *not* to stop being America when we take bad hits. It's most important for America to be America when it's hardest to be America. When the going gets tough, the temptation is to start compromising on our values. After 9/11, it's been hard to be America. True leadership is not to slip into compromises.

WE ARE now an empire. Not an empire of conquest in the traditional sense. We are an empire of influence. Our power, our values, our promise affect the world. We are more than Jefferson's beacon. We are an expectation of better things. The world demands of us the delivery of the promise we project. We are seen to have an obligation to share our light. Other peoples want help, leadership, and guidance in getting to where we are. They want our help in reaching their potential. But they don't want or expect us to put them on the dole. Go back to what I said about teaching. They want us to show them how to move up to what we are. They don't want handouts.

We are, however, reluctant to deliver. We have never comfortably settled on our role in the world or on our obligations to the other citizens of this planet. The Wilsonian dream of using our blessings to better the world has always clashed with the opposing isolationist heritage to "avoid foreign entanglements." In my view, this will be the true issue with which we will have to come to grips in this century. The world at our gates demands it of us.

And it's not a clean, well-ordered world. It's messy. A lot of folks don't like us. Or they envy us. Or they don't like the way we throw our weight around.

In a sense, it's going to be back to the future: Today's international landscape has strong similarities to the Caribbean region of the 1920s and '30s—unstable countries being driven by uncaring dictators to the point of collapse and total failure. We are going to see more crippled states and failed states that look like Somalia and Afghanistan—and are just as dangerous. And more and more U.S. military men and women are going to be involved in vague, confusing military actions—heavily overlaid with political, humanitarian, and economic considerations. And those representing the United States—the Big Guy with the most formidable presence—will have to deal with each messy situation and pull everything together. We're going to see more and more of that.

Certain of these collapsed states will continue to provide sanctuary to extremist groups who will continue to use these bases to plan, train, and organize for strikes against U.S. forces and other targets. Natural and man-made humanitarian catastrophes will continue to be on the rise; along with civil strife that seems out of control in many parts of the world. Regional hegemons and rogue states will learn the lessons of our wars with Iraq and develop what we call "asymmetric" capabilities—threats designed to exploit our evident military vulnerabilities and gaps. These threats range the spectrum from weapons of mass destruction and long-range missiles to low-tech sea mines and terrorist tactics. All are designed to challenge a perceived weakness in our military, political, or psychological ability to use force.

Victory no longer happens when you capture the enemy capital. And we can't just declare victory in a photo op on an aircraft carrier. These events signal that the home team is ahead in the third inning. The game goes nine innings—or longer if necessary; and victory happens when you put in place a lasting, stable environment.

Globalization and the explosion of information technology have meanwhile made the world ever more interdependent and interconnected. Geographic obstacles such as oceans and mountain ranges no longer provide impenetrable boundaries. Economic, political, or social-related instability in remote parts of the world will likewise continue to affect our security interests and well-being on our ever-shrinking planet. Added to that will be the continued rise of non-state entities, such as nongovernmental organizations, transnational criminal groups, extremist organizations, global corporations, and warlord groups, all bringing a confusing new dimension to a world previously dominated by the interactions of nation-states.

In recent years, an arc covering a large part of the earth's surface—from North Africa to the Philippines, and from Central Asia to Central Africa—is chaotic and in turmoil. We are going to be dealing with this turmoil for decades. Remote places such as Somalia, Haiti, Bosnia, Serbia, Kosovo, Rwanda, East Timor, Aceh, Colombia, and others have become flash points that required our intervention at some level. At the same time, the need to contain regional threats such as Iran, Iraq, and North Korea still remained a major military requirement. These became more threatening as they developed greater military capabilities aimed at denying us access to their regions and to our allies within those regions. More and more, our security interests have drawn us into remote, unstable parts of the world.

As a result of these commitments, our shrinking and adjusting armed forces were hit by an onslaught of strange, nontraditional missions that pressured their dwindling ranks and resources with an operational and personnel tempo that was not sustainable. With some exceptions, the U.S. military resisted these missions and the adjustments it should have made in doctrine, organization, training, and equipment needed to meet this growing new mix of commitments. Traditionalists in the military leadership insisted on holding the line; they wanted to fight only our nation's wars, and hoped to go back to "real soldiering" as they were mending a transitioning force suffering from all the pressures on it. One of our most senior military leaders was quoted as saying, "Real men don't do OOTW"—a term that became the title for all of those messy little low-end commitments (we now call these missions "Stability Operations").

THE TWENTY-FIRST-CENTURY MILITARY

Several serious questions and challenges face our military. The first has to do with the growing number of these nontraditional threats. Will these continue to increase, with new types added to the confusing mix, and will we rely on the military as our principal instrument to deal with them? Second, can we afford the kind of military that can meet all the potential challenges ahead? The third question relates to the much-needed military reform. Can the military change, reform, or transform to meet the challenges of the new century and adapt to the rapid development of new technologies that could radically alter the military as we know it today? The fourth issue deals with the interagency reform necessary for other agencies to move in parallel with military reforms. Can we meet the demand for better decision making and the integration of all the instruments of power (political, economic, informational, etc.) to solve the multidimensional challenges ahead?

No one can predict the future, but we can make judgments on the growing number of threats that now face us. Some of these will not be what we have grown used to preparing for.

Our security interests will require that we have a military capable and prepared to respond to:

★ A global power with significant military capabilities.

★ Regional hegemons with asymmetric capabilities, such as weapons of mass destruction and missiles, designed to deny us access to vital areas and regional allies.

★ Transnational threats that include terrorist groups, international criminal and drug organizations, warlords, environmental security issues, issues of health and disease, and illegal migrations.

★ Problems of failed or incapable states that require peacekeeping, humanitarian assistance and disaster relief, or national reconstruction.

★ Overseas crises that threaten U.S. citizens and property.

★ Domestic emergencies that exceed the capacity of other federal and local government agencies to handle.

★ Threats to our key repositories of information and to our systems of moving information.

This demanding list of requirements does not include many of the clean, clear war-fighting missions our military would prefer. We have sworn to defend against "all enemies foreign and domestic." But today the "enemies" that threaten our well-being may include some strange, nontraditional ones.

At this moment in Iraq, we are dealing with the Jihadis, who are coming in from outside to raise hell; crime on the streets is rampant; ex-Ba'athists and Fedayeen are still running around making trouble; American soldiers are getting blown up; suicide bombings have driven out the UN and many NGOs; and there is a potential now for the country to fragment—Shia on Shia, Shia on Sunni, Kurds on Turkomans; you name it. It is a powder keg. If there is a center that can hold this mess together, I don't know what it is. Civil war could break out at any time. Resources are needed; a strategy is needed; and a plan is needed.

This is not the kind of conflict for which we have traditionally planned. War fighting is only one element of it. Some people on the battlefield don't play according to our rules. They do not come in military formations and with standard-issue equipment. They come in many different forms; and all of their agendas are different.

The destabilizing environment in which we may commit forces to confront many of these threats may be further degraded by the effects of urbanization, economic depression, overpopulation, and the depletion of basic resources. The world has become reliant on natural resources and raw materials that come from increasingly unstable regions, with the compounding problems of a poor infrastructure and environment. Access to energy resources, water sources, timber, rare gems and metals, etc., is becoming a growing rationale for intervention and conflict in many parts of the world.

We will also require that our forces continue to meet the peacetime demands of engagement and shaping. The importance of maintaining stable regions by building viable, interoperable coalitions with the forces of regional allies will remain necessary to ensure our security in key areas of the world. Military engagement produces dividends in deterrence, confidence building, and burden sharing, and also demonstrates our commitment and resolve. Yet these tasks will continue to tax our already thinly stretched forces.

Some proposals have been put forward to achieve—and afford—a military transformation by drastically cutting our force structure, removing forward-based and -deployed forces from overseas, and stopping modernization. Advocates of such a "strategic pause" think we can withdraw from the world and opt out of interventions that threaten our interests. They are wrong. They are blind to the world as it is. We cannot gamble on a self-ordering world. The risk to us could be great—even fatal—if we are not capable of dealing with an unforeseen threat that emerges from this disordered global environment.

The need right now is critical to transform our military in a deliberate and thoughtful, yet significant, way. Americans must acknowledge this need and support investment in this transformation for it to succeed. This will require a stronger and closer relationship between Americans and their military. This relationship has drifted apart, and has even been strained at times, since the end of the Vietnam War and the institution of the all-volunteer force.

What should be the shape of that transformation?

The military traditionally goes out there and kills people and breaks things. From that, we determine how we are going to straighten out the mess or resolve the conflict. Once upon a time, we looked at the other elements of national power—political, economic, information, whatever— to figure out how we could bring them to bear. That's what George Marshall did at the end of World War Two. It has not happened in recent times.

The military does a damned good job of killing people and breaking things. We can design a better rifle squad than anybody in the world. We can build a better fighter, a better ship, a better tank, a smarter bomb. We are so far ahead of any potential enemy right now in those kinds of technological areas, in the areas of expertise, of quality of leadership, and of all the other elements that make military units great on the battlefield, that you wonder why we keep busting brain cells working to make it better, or to transform it into something else.

Transformation has to include finding better and more remarkable ways to tap into technology, our own brainpower, our training and education, and creative ways of redesigning our organization to make our military even more efficient and more powerful on the battlefield.

But transformation has to go beyond that.

What is the role of the military beyond killing people and breaking things?

Right now, the military in Iraq has been stuck with that baby. In Somalia, we were stuck with that baby. In Vietnam, we were stuck with that baby. It is not a *new* role, and it is going to continue. We have to ask ourselves *how* the military needs to change in order to actually deal with these political, economic, social, security, and information management challenges that we've already been facing for a long time. If those wearing suits can't come in and solve the problem—can't bring the resources, the expertise, the organization to bear—and the military is going to continue to get stuck with it, you have two choices: Either the civilian officials must develop the capabilities demanded of them and learn how to partner with other agencies to get the job done, or the military finally needs to change into something else beyond the breaking and the killing.

What could this mean?

It could mean that we return to a military that's a calling and not just a job. For more than a quarter-century, we have been operating with an All-Volunteer Force—and the American people tend to forget that, until the volunteers stop showing up and reenlisting. The troops will start getting out because they're deployed too long and too often. We need sufficient forces to meet our commitments, have the time for our forces to be properly trained, and provide for the quality of life that supports a first-rate military.

We were building an All-Volunteer Force with professionals, not mercenaries. The troops certainly don't mind a better paycheck, but first and foremost they truly want to be the best military in the world. We owe them that and we owe them the care they deserve after serving our nation.

It could mean military civil affairs will change from being just a tactical organization doing basic humanitarian care and interaction with the civilian population to actually being capable of reconstructing nations. That will require people in uniform, and maybe civilian suits as well, who are educated in the disciplines of economics and political structures and who will actually go in and work these issues. Either we get the civilian officials on the scene who can do it—get them there when they need to be there, give them the resources and the training, and create the interoperability that is necessary—or validate the military mission to do it.

It could mean we would at last go into each of these messy new situations with a strategic plan, a real understanding of regional and global security, and a knowledge of what it takes to wield the power to shape security and move it forward. Where are today's Marshalls, Eisenhowers, and Trumans, who had the vision to see the world in a different way, and who understood America's role and what had to be done in order to play that role?

Our military men and women should never be put on a battlefield without a strategic plan, not only for the fighting—our generals will take care of that—but for the aftermath and for winning the war. Where are we, the American people, if we accept less; if we accept any level of sacrifice without an adequate level of planning?

It kills me when I hear of the continuing casualties in Iraq and Afghanistan and the sacrifices being made. It also kills me to hear someone say that each one of those is a personal tragedy, but in the overall scheme of things, the numbers are statistically insignificant. Bullshit. We should challenge any military or political leader who utters such words. The greatest treasure the United States has is our enlisted men and women. When we put them in harm's way, it had better count for something. Their loss is a national tragedy.

As I reflect on my own forty years of military service, and my later years of diplomacy and peacemaking, I have to ask: "What is our legacy?" My son is now a Marine captain. What have we left for him to look forward to?

We all know that burgeoning technology will widen his horizons beyond anything we can imagine. It will also present new questions of ethics and morality that we have barely begun to fathom. Yet he must also live with the organization I have had to live with for forty years. Napoleon could reappear today and recognize the Central Command staff organization: J-1, administration stovepipe; J-2, intelligence stovepipe—you get the idea. This antiquated organization is oblivious to what everyone else in the world is doing: flattening organization structure, with decentralized operations and more direct communications. This must be fixed.

My son will have to deal with the inevitable military-civilian rift and drift—which will become more severe in the future. He will also have to deal with the social issues we have not been able to fix. And they will get tougher, within a national debate over why we still need a strong military. My son's generation must ultimately face the question of how much the military should be a reflection of U.S. society. The people of America will get the military they want, in due course, but it is up to the military to advise them about the risks and consequences of their decisions.

My son will face nontraditional missions in messy places that will make Somalia, Afghanistan, and Iraq look like a picnic. He will see a changed battlefield, with an accelerated tempo and greatly expanded knowledge base. He will witness a great drop in the sense of calling. People entering the military will not be imprinted with his code. On his watch, my son is likely to see a weapons of mass destruction event. Another and worse 9/11 will occur in some city, somewhere in the world where Americans are gathered. When that nasty bug or gas or nuke is released, it will forever change him and his institutions. At that point, all the lip service paid to dealing with such an eventuality will be revealed for what it is—lip service. And he will have to deal with it for real. In its wake, I hope he gets to deal with yet another—and better—Goldwater-Nichols arrangement.

What will we expect of him as a battlefield commander? Brains, guts, and determination—nothing new here. But we would ask for more than battlefield skill from our future commanders. We want character, sense of moral responsibility, and an ethical standard that rises above those of all other professions. We want him to be a model who accepts the profession of arms as a calling. We want him to take care of our sons and daughters and treat their lives as precious—putting them in harm's way only if it truly counts. We'll expect him to stand up to civilian leadership before thinking of his own career.

And I hope that we would think enough of him and his compatriots to show some respect for them along the way.

I have been all over this globe and exposed to most of the cultures on it. I am fascinated by them. I love the diversity. I want to understand them and embrace them. I could never understand prejudice or rejection or the sense of superiority that drive the hatemongers of the world. I lived through a tumultuous period of our history when our own minorities broke from second-class citizenship into full participation in this wonderful dream we call America. I have been proud of their accomplishments and contributions. They have proven the bigots wrong and made our nation greater. I hope the dream we have struggled to realize can be extended to the rest of the planet.

INDEX

ACKNOWLEDGMENTS

Working on this book has been a long, hard process. Thanks to the friendship, encouragement, patience, prodding, creativity, and skillful contributions of Tom Clancy, Tony Koltz, Neil Nyren, Marty Greenberg, and Fred Williams, this project was made possible.

—Tony Zinni